SCHUMANN

The Inner Voices

of a Musical Genius

SCHUMANN

The Inner Voices

of a Musical Genius

Peter Ostwald

Northeastern University Press
Boston

Northeastern University Press

Library of Congress Cataloging in Publication Data

Ostwald, Peter F.
Schumann: the inner voices of a musical genius.
Bibliography: p.
Includes index.
1. Schumann, Robert, 1810–1856. 2. Composers—
Germany—Biography. 3. Manic-depressive psychoses—
case studies. I. Title.
ML410.S4087   1985   780'.92'4 [B]   84-1690
ISBN 0-930350-57-x
ISBN 1-55553-014-1 (pbk.)

Designed by Janice Wheeler. Calligraphy by Jean Evans.

Composed in Garamond #3 by Graphic Composition, Athens, Georgia. Printed and bound
by Murray Printing Company, Westford, Massachusetts. The paper is Glatfelter Offset, an
acid-free sheet.

MANUFACTURED IN THE UNITED STATES OF AMERICA
90 89 88   5 4 3

For Lise

Contents

List of Illustrations

Preface

enius and madness have often been thought to be related in some way. In the life of Robert Schumann it is particularly difficult to draw a line between the two. The problem of distinguishing between his creative and his psychotic behavior has confounded many biographers, musicologists, and psychiatrists. Thus far no single diagnosis has done justice to the facts.

The popular view, that Schumann had a deteriorating, essentially organic disease of the brain, stems from Josef von Wasielewski's famous biography of the composer, first published in 1857. Still widely read and quoted today, it reflects the prevailing views of nineteenth-century psychiatry. Schumann's widow, Clara (an outstanding musician herself), was deeply offended by the book and, in hopes of giving the world a more complete picture of her husband, turned over to her daughters a collection of his diaries and letters. Ironically, these documents formed the basis of a biography of Clara herself, written by Berthold Litzmann. It was Litzmann's impressive work, however, that enabled the psychiatrist Paul Möbius to construct (in 1906) the first longitudinal, developmental study of Robert Schumann's madness.

Möbius proposed the diagnosis *dementia praecox*, then considered to be a progressive mental disorder with a very poor prognosis. The diagnosis was changed to schizophrenia when in 1911 Eugen Bleuler included Schumann in his famous textbook about these illnesses. Bleuler's was the first modern (that is, twentieth-century) effort at explaining schizophrenia in both psychological and physiological terms, and he felt that there were patients who did recover or who, like Schumann, staved off some of the more disabling symptoms through their creative activity. But this diagnosis had already been challenged (in 1906) by Hans Gruhle, a psychiatrist who reasoned that Schumann's madness had been a manic-depressive psychosis, complicated by terminal brain changes.

Thus the debate has continued for more than a hundred years, with no real solution. None of the diagnostic methods needed to refute the presence of organic disease—X rays, brain-scans, laboratory tests, and the like—was available to those doctors who had actually examined and treated Schumann. And without additional facts about his daily behavior, neither could a psychological understanding of his madness be obtained. When, in 1959, the psychiatrists Eliot Slater and Alfred Meyer tried to draw up a "calendar" of the composer's emotional life, they were forced to conclude that his "variations of mood cannot be adequately accounted for by circumstances."

Today it is often asserted that Schumann had syphilis, an incurable infection in his day. The evidence for this disease is open to question, however. Schumann began to manifest his mental disorder long before he could have contracted syphilis. He continued to be aware of severe mood swings as he grew older, and to note with amazing precision his anxieties, conflicts, and helpless indecisiveness, as well as his momentary joys and brief ecstasies. Until he was forty-three, when he made a nearly fatal suicide attempt, Schumann's diaries, correspondence, literary work, and musical compositions reflect an orderly and methodical intellectual capacity. Even while he was hospitalized, he wrote letters to his wife, his friends, and his publishers that were not disorganized in either form or content. (He could no longer compose, however—a problem that he had observed during every major depressive episode beginning in adolescence.) The only positive information we have of any physical or mental deterioration stems from Schumann's last few months in the mental hospital where, deeply dejected, socially isolated, and physically ill, he died after prolonged self-starvation.

To tell his story, I have gone to Germany, where a great deal of new information about Schumann has become available during the last ten years, including diaries and household books for nearly every day in his life beginning at the age of seventeen. I have also reviewed his letters, autobiographical essays, and unfinished novels, as well as medical records and legal documents, many as yet unpublished. A fresh look at Schumann's life, and particularly his recurring mental disorder, seems called for.

Many people have been very helpful to me. Gerd Nauhaus was my main source of information because he was editing Schumann's household books while I did my research, and he was willing to give me access to all his findings, as well as all the other documents available in Zwickau, Schumann's birthplace. To Dr. Nauhaus I owe the greatest debt, not only for help in interpreting these materials but also for technical and critical advice in writing the present book. (All translations, except where noted, are my own.)

In Dresden, Dr. Willi Reich gave me access to valuable unpublished material in the Sächsische Landesbibliothek and allowed me to remove hair samples of Schumann, Clara, Brahms, Joachim, and other important figures for toxicological study. In Leipzig I was greatly helped by Kurt Masur, director of the Gewandhaus, who introduced me to many musicians and scholars and allowed me to participate in the 1981 International Schumann Symposium there. Brigitte Berenbruch was of enormous assistance in tracking down documents at the city archives and the Robert Schumann Museum in Bonn. Professor Hans Schadewaldt of the University of Düsseldorf was a warm host and helped me to find informative documents in that city, where Dr. Joseph Kruse let me work in the archives of the Heinrich Heine Institute.

Closer to home I want to thank Dr. Nancy Reich, who is working on a biography of Clara Schumann and has been willing to share her findings with me. Professor Joseph Kerman of the University of California in Berkeley gave me important advice on how to focus and publish my research. Dean William Reinhardt of the University of California in San Francisco provided a grant to defray some of the initial expenses. I have also benefited greatly from discussing my work with medical historians, including Dr. Erwin Ackerknecht of Zürich, Dr. Francis Schiller of San Francisco, and Dr. Ruth Friedlander of Berkeley (who helped me find documents pertaining to the Carus family, two members of which had treated Schumann).

Numerous friends and colleagues were willing to read portions of the manuscript and give me helpful advice and criticism. These include composers R. Murray Schafer and Kirke Mechem (as well as Kirke's wife, Doe), psychiatrists Joseph Stephens, Wolfgang Lederer (and his wife, Dr. Alexandra Botwin), and the late Klaus Berblinger, and music critics Joseph Horowitz and Arthur Bloomfield (and his wife, Anne). I am especially grateful to Professor Nathan Malamud of the Department of Neuropathology at the University of California in San Francisco for his painstaking analysis and critique of Schumann's autopsy report, and to Dr. Anna Burton of New York for her psychoanalytic insights regarding Schumann.

David Pitchford, Kay Welch, Wayne Shifler, and Renee Renouf Hall helped with the laborious job of typing. To Livia Gollancz in London I am deeply endebted for her early encouragement in regard to publication of this book, which took its final shape under the skillful guidance of Deborah Kops, Ann Twombly, and Penelope Stratton in Boston.

Finally I want to express sincere appreciation to my wife Lise Deschamps Ostwald and to Paul Hersh, both concert pianists with whom I have collaborated in lecture-recitals about Schumann that served to deepen my respect and admiration for his compositions, and to Walter Rex, Robert Kadarauch, Jonathan Khuner, and Stephen Levintow, with whom I have played all of Schumann's chamber music. It was through these many wonderful hours of music making that the composer's inner voices came truly to life.

I.
Crisis, 1854

ust past noon on Monday, 27 February 1854, a hulking figure suddenly emerged from a house on Bilkerstrasse and turned left on the cobbled street. Although it was a cold, rainy day in Düsseldorf, the man wore only a thin robe and slippers. His face was pasty, his eyes were downcast, and he was sobbing. Walking unsteadily, as if on tiptoe, he headed for the Rhine River, only four blocks away. There, on the Rathaus Ufer overlooking the west bank, he stopped. A narrow pontoon bridge led to the other side, and to get across it one had to pass a tollgate. Absentmindedly he searched in his pocket for money. Finding none, he smiled apologetically and offered his silk handkerchief as a token fee. Then, before anyone could stop him, he rushed down the incline leading to the bridge, ran part way across, paused briefly, and threw himself headlong into the icy torrent.[1]

Some fishermen on a nearby boat went immediately to the man's rescue and managed to pull him out of the water, only to see him try to jump in again. They finally used force to bring him ashore. There a bystander recognized the man as Dr. Robert Schumann, a distinguished composer and music critic, who until recently had served as the conductor of Düsseldorf's symphony orchestra and choral society. At forty-three years of age, he was suffering from severe mental illness.

This was not the first time Schumann had become suicidally depressed. Extreme sadness and preoccupations with death had troubled him since his adolescence, when within one year his sister committed suicide and his father died. Medical doctors had tried to help him on several occasions, most recently by telling him to bathe in the Rhine, and in the summer of 1853 he had been sent to the North Sea for plunge-baths. These reduced his melancholia temporarily, but they also increased his dread of disease and dissolution.

Schumann had had a long-standing fear of madness; for years he had read widely about mental disease. He pondered what it would be like to lose his mind and even incorporated some of his disturbing fantasies into musical compositions. An intensely emotional person, in childhood he had learned to control his tempestuous feelings by forcing himself to be extremely orderly and to follow an almost compulsive work schedule. But bouts of internal rage, and guilty fears about not always being able to live up to his own extremely high ideals and expectations, occasionally derailed him. Then he would become morose and agitated, withdraw socially, and begin to worry excessively about his health.

Schumann's recent psychosis was precipitated by a visit late in January 1854 to the city of Hanover, 259 kilometers northeast of Düsseldorf. Even though traveling had always upset him, and he was just back from an arduous concert tour in Holland with his wife, Clara—a concert pianist—he had wanted to take this trip. The ostensible reason was to conduct his well-known oratorio *Paradise and the Peri* (op. 50) in Hanover and his newly rewritten D minor Symphony (op. 120) in Frankfurt. (Although Schumann was still under contract to the Music Society in Düsseldorf, he had stopped conducting there because of a great deal of criticism and was hoping to continue his career elsewhere.) Even after both performances were canceled at the last moment, he insisted on going. And though Clara was in the fifth month of pregnancy (her tenth) and finding it more difficult to travel and play the piano, she agreed to accompany him.

There was a strong and rather more private motivation behind the Schumanns' desire to go to Hanover: they wanted to visit two young friends who were living there. These men—Schumann called them "two young demons"[2]—were supremely gifted musicians whose vitality and charisma had made an impact on him during the past year. One was the violinist Joseph Joachim, then twenty-two, who had recently performed under Schumann's direction. The composer regarded Joachim as a wise and steady influence, a kind of "physician [who] always put me in a good humor."[3] The other young man was Johannes Brahms, then twenty years old. Schumann had met Brahms at the end of September 1853, found him enchanting, and soon started to promote him as the most important new composer of Europe. His remarks about Brahms had a messianic ring: "a young eagle suddenly and unexpectedly flown from the Alps. . . . One could compare him to a gorgeous stream. . . . I believe that Johannes is the true Apostle."[4] Schumann had obviously become greatly excited.

Passionate feelings about attractive young men were not new to him, however. Several of Schumann's adolescent infatuations with men had blossomed into romantic attachments, and during his early twenties he had lived with a handsome young musician, Ludwig Schunke, until Schunke died. Then, in his late twenties, Schumann became romantically involved with the beautiful Clara Wieck, a remarkable pianist, whom he married. He wrote some of his early piano pieces for her and she inspired many of his later songs, chamber-music works, and symphonic compositions. In their thirteen years of marriage, the Schumanns had produced seven children—there were two miscarriages—which meant that Clara's concertizing, which helped earn income for the family, had to be curtailed.

During that January visit to Hanover Clara played twice at the court, ruled over by a blind king, George V, the grandson of England's George III and an enthusiastic music lover. She was pleased with herself, although disappointed that one of her concerts had to be canceled. Schumann was having less success professionally. A performance of his *Fantasy for Violin and Orchestra* (op. 131) was harshly criticized in the press, and he abruptly asked Joseph Joachim not to play a string quartet which had been scheduled. A rehearsal of Schumann's newly written Violin Concerto also went badly. It had been composed expressly for Joachim, who was expected to edit the solo part but had had no time to comply. The composer seemed in a strangely expansive mood, much more talkative and animated than usual, as if he were trying to deny his annoyance. Brahms, who admired him, remained "very quiet,"[5] a reaction most likely to Schumann's peculiar behavior. He felt a mixture of pity and attraction, not only toward the older man, but also toward his younger wife.

The foursome tried out much new music, including an impressive piano sonata by Brahms. Soon there were more signs of Schumann's emotional disturbance, a noticeably "angry mood," and, on 27 January, "much drinking,"—"too much," according to his diary.[6] Before returning to Düsseldorf Schumann spent a "restless night,"[7] indicative of sleep problems that would quickly become much worse.

On 4 February, back at home, Schumann noted in his diary that he worked "diligently" on various projects, including an anthology (which he hoped to publish) of quotations about music by the Greek philosophers, by Shakespeare, from the Bible, and from various other sources.* Clara thought he might have been working "too strenuously" on it,[8] but in fact Schumann was only superficially involved. His mind had returned to the "young demons." A letter written to Joachim on 6 February alludes to telepathic communication with his "companions" in Hanover: "I have often written to you with sympathetic ink, and now between the lines of my letter there is a secret message that will break through later." He also revealed an unconscious fantasy: "I dreamt of you, dear Joachim, that for three days we were together. In your hands you were holding heron feathers, from which flowed champagne—how prosaic! but how true!" He then remarked, cryptically, "Music is now silent—at least outwardly."[9] Two other letters Schumann wrote that day show that he was struggling to suppress anger, an emotion that made him uncomfortable. The first was a caustic letter to Julius Stern, a conductor whose job in Berlin he wanted in exchange for his own in Düsseldorf.[10] The other was a blunt note directed to Richard Pohl, a writer who had worked with Schumann on texts for vocal compositions and was now complaining about the composer's recent silence.[11]

The following day, Schumann was able to control himself fairly well. He wrote a calm, factual letter to the poet Hermann Rollet.[12] With Clara, he also briefly attended a ball at the governor's residence. But a letter written to his publisher Georg Wigand on 8 February has a querulous, sarcastic tone, provoked perhaps by Wigand's annoyance with Schumann's all-too-many proof corrections.[13]

After another day spent on his anthology of quotations, he dashed off an unusually agitated letter to the composer Robert Franz: "Dear Franz, isn't it good that we have music, which enables us to escape in a moment from the meanness of this world."[14] He still was able to control his emotions during the day, but at night he was starting to have a "very strong and tormenting auditory disturbance."[15] Clara, with whom he had sexual intercourse that night, had to stay up with him because he couldn't sleep. "He always heard one and the same tone, and from time to time another interval as well," she recorded in her diary. "During the day this stopped."[16] But twenty-four hours later he was again hearing sounds: "a sad night (ear and head complaints)."[17] On Sunday, 12 February, he hallucinated constantly, according to Clara, hearing "music that is so glorious, and with instruments sounding more wonderful than one ever hears on earth."[18] Schumann's own diary specifically mentions "Eine Feste Burg," a Bach cantata.

Many times since his first nervous breakdown at age twenty-three, Schumann had successfully transformed his wildest flights of fancy into mu-

---

*Schumann called his anthology *Dichtergarten* ("Poet's Garden"). It was never published.

sical compositions. Some of his best works, including *Kreisleriana* (op. 16), his early songs, his *Spring* Symphony (op. 38), and the *Manfred Overture* (op. 115), were written at the urging of inner voices. This time, however, it seemed impossible for him to organize his mind creatively, and after several days of sporadic and exhausting effort he felt ready to give up. He threatened to "destroy his mind," wrote Clara, "if this doesn't stop. . . . His auditory disturbance had escalated to such a degree that he heard entire pieces from beginning to end, as if played by a full orchestra, and the sound would remain on the final chord until Robert directed his thoughts to another composition."[19] "Exquisite suffering," reports Schumann's own diary entry dated 13 February.

The next day, on a walk with Ruppert Becker, concertmaster of the Düsseldorf orchestra, Schumann "unburdened himself about a strange phenomenon," as Becker recalled: "It is the inner hearing of wondrously beautiful pieces of music, fully formed and complete! The sound is like distant brasses, underscored by the most magnificent harmonies." While they were having a drink at a restaurant, Becker noticed that Schumann's "inner concert started and forced him to stop reading his newspaper." He told the young violinist, "This must be how it is in another life, after we've cast off our mortal coil."[20] Later Schumann jotted in his diary that in the evening he had been "severely carried away [*mitgenommen*] (wondrously beautiful music)."[21]

Another witness to Schumann's psychosis was Dr. Richard Hasenclever, a physician, amateur poet, would-be conductor, and frequent visitor to the Schumann home on Bilkerstrasse. Although medically trained, he had never assumed any responsibility for the composer's treatment. Hasenclever was not a psychiatrist, and his relationship with the Schumanns was somewhat ambiguous. A family friend and artistic collaborator, Hasenclever had recently provided the text for *Das Glück von Edenhall* (op. 143), a choral ballade composed by Schumann. But he was also a spokesman for the Music Society of Düsseldorf, which after many disagreeable conferences had decided to relieve Schumann of his responsibilities as conductor. Observing his friend's rapid psychological disintegration, he decided to seek the advice of Dr. Böger, another local physician.

About Böger's qualifications we know only that, like Hasenclever, he had worked mainly in military hospitals.[22] (Clara called him a *Regimentsarzt*.) It isn't clear exactly what treatment he recommended, but soon after Böger intervened the composer seems to have become quieter. For the first time in three months he was able to transform some of his inner voices into music by writing them down. During the night of 17 February he composed a melody for the piano (which bears a certain resemblance to the slow movement of the violin concerto he had recently written for Joseph Joachim).

But Schumann's psychotic delirium evidently did not allow him to distinguish this "theme" from his disturbing auditory hallucinations. With delusional certainty he told Clara that angels were singing the melody. "After completing it he lay down and fantasized all night long, always with his eyes open and raised to heaven," she recorded. "It was his fixed belief that angels were hovering around him offering the most glorious revelations, all this in wonderful music; they called out to welcome us, and before the end of the year we would both be united with them."[23]

The next day Schumann's exaltation changed to terror. He composed nothing more, and for the first time in many years did not make a single note in his daily diary. Clara observed "a frightful change! The angels' voices transformed themselves into the voices of demons, with horrible music. They told him he was a sinner, and that they wanted to throw him to hell. In short, his condition grew into a veritable nervous paroxysm; he screamed in pain, because the embodiments of tigers and hyenas were rushing forward to seize him."

She called Dr. Hasenclever and Dr. Böger, who barely managed to calm Schumann down. "Never will I forget this sight," she wrote. "I suffered the most agonizing torture along with him. Half an hour later he said the voices had become friendly again and were trying to give him courage." After going to bed for a few hours, he got up again, this time to make corrections in his Violoncello Concerto (op. 129), composed in 1850. He said this work relieved him somewhat from the "eternal sound of the voices."

Sunday, 19 February, he spent in bed "under the great agony of evil spirits!" Schumann "would not let himself be talked out of believing that supernatural and otherworldly creatures are soaring about him, but he accepted the idea that he was very sick." Clara told him that his "cranial nerves were terribly overstimulated." Nevertheless it seemed impossible to divert him even momentarily from his delusions about ghosts. On the contrary, in a melancholy voice he told his wife, "Surely you don't think, dear Clara, that I would tell you lies." She wrote, "I had no choice but to give in quietly, because with arguments I would only get him more excited. At 11 o'clock that night he suddenly became quieter, the angels promised him sleep."

On Monday Schumann sat at his desk most of the day, "paper, pen, and ink in front of him, listening to the angels' voices, writing some words occasionally, but only a few, and then always listening." His face had an "unnaturally blissful" expression, and Clara worried "how will all this end?" Schumann was writing in his diary again, mostly about financial matters, and noted that he had given Clara her weekly allowance. Ruppert Becker visited that day, and in his presence Schumann was able to hide his disturbance. "It would never have occurred to me to believe there's an illness," wrote Becker. "I found him just as he usually is; for half an hour we spoke

together, then I left. I've never seen Frau Schumann look so distressed! . . .
She sits at his bed throughout the night and listens to every movement."[24]

Clara's diary mentions that her husband "spoke constantly about being
a criminal and that he ought to be reading the Bible."[25] For several more
days he spoke about the alternately good and bad spirits around him. But
then the quality of his hallucinations suddenly changed. Instead of hearing
music, the voices now spoke to him in words. That seemed to calm him.
He wrote a few letters, intermittently composed variations on the theme he
had heard a few days earlier, and on 24 February he went walking again
with Becker, who observed him "conversing quite rationally, except that he
told me the figure of Franz Schubert had appeared and sent him a magnificent melody, which he had written down and composed variations on."[26]

As Schumann's psychosis worsened, he began talking about his fear of
harming Clara and urged her to leave him alone. As she recorded in her
diary,

> I would then leave him for brief moments to quiet him down; then I would
> go back to him and he would be better. Often he complained that his brain
> was going around in circles, and he would then maintain that shortly it was
> all going to be over for him, saying farewell to me, giving all sorts of instruc-
> tions about his money and compositions, etc.[27]

On Sunday, 26 February, the day before his suicide attempt, Schumann
complained much less, suggesting that he had made a decision. In the evening he played the piano for Albert Dietrich, a student composer who had
followed him to Düsseldorf, choosing a sonata written by another young
musician, Martin Cohn. Schumann was in a "state of such joyous exultation
that sweat poured profusely from his brow, after which he ate a huge dinner
in terrible haste." Later, he "suddenly got up from the sofa and asked for his
clothes, saying he had to go to the insane asylum because he could no longer
control his mind and did not know what he would do at night." Alarmed,
Clara called the landlord to calm her husband down. She also summoned
Dr. Böger, and while waiting for him to arrive, Schumann made unmistakable plans to leave the house, which upset Clara even more. He "put everything together that he wished to take along, watch, money, music paper,
pens, cigars, everything most clearly thought out." To forestall a separation,
she played on his sense of duty and family obligation, asking, "Robert, is it
your wish to abandon your wife and children?" "Yes," he said, "it won't be
for long, I'll come back recovered!"

When Dr. Böger finally arrived, he demanded that a male attendant,
Herr Bremer, come to the house to stay with Schumann in his room, instead
of Clara. Schumann apparently liked the new arrangement, chatted with
Herr Bremer, read some newspapers, and finally fell asleep. For a while his

wife hovered anxiously next door, but she finally accepted the separation and invited her friend Elise Junge to spend the night with her. In the morning, Clara again wanted to be close to her husband. She held onto him, and talked with him about his delusions. "He was so deeply melancholic that one cannot describe it! When I only touched him he said 'Oh Clara, I'm not worth your love.'" She tried to tell him it was not true, reasoning that she had always "looked up to him with the greatest, deepest veneration."

Later that morning Clara conferred with Dr. Hasenclever and Albert Dietrich about what to do next. Schumann had been psychotic for over two weeks, had threatened suicide, and was asking to be taken to a hospital. Clara was at her wits' end, and during this discussion she asked their twelve-year-old daughter, Marie, to keep an eye on him. Having no real awareness of the seriousness of her father's illness, Marie allowed him to go, sobbing, into the bedroom. From there he walked into the hall and then out of the house through the front gate. "I can't describe what I felt," wrote Clara after discovering that he had disappeared. "I only know that it was as if my heart had stopped beating." Everyone rushed frantically around the neighborhood to find him. But Schumann was on his way to the bridge.

Following the suicide attempt, two men dragged the disheveled, water-soaked composer through the town filled with costumed revelers (it was the pre-Lent carnival season) and back to his house. The doctors decided it would be best to separate him completely from his wife. Clara left the house immediately to stay with Rosalie Leser, a blind woman who throughout this period had become her closest friend. Two male attendants moved in to guard Schumann day and night, while Clara's mother, Frau Bargiel, was sent for from Berlin to supervise the household and help care for the children. "What terrible days," wrote the unhappy Clara. "I was not allowed to go to him, but received reports about him every hour." Schumann, on the other hand, did not complain about missing his wife. "He seldom asked about me. . . . He liked having the two attendants around, and in general was mild and friendly toward others."

For twenty-four hours this arrangement seemed to work. Schumann got out of bed and spent the whole day at his desk. He wrote several letters and copied his *Theme and Variations*, which he then sent to Clara with the request that she perform them for Fräulein Leser.* But she noted that he suddenly became violently excited once more. Wanting to please him, Clara had intruded with a small gift of violets and a few oranges. "Now the doctors no longer tolerated his being up and around," she wrote, "nor did they let anyone from his familiar circle come close to him." Schumann kept insisting

---

* The *Theme and Variations* was not published until 1941. Johannes Brahms also composed a set of variations—op. 23, for four hands—on Schumann's quasi-hallucinatory theme.

that he wanted to be hospitalized: "Whenever he saw the doctors he always pressed them to bring him to an asylum, because only there would he regain his health."

Thus the fateful decision was reached—it struck Clara as "the most horrible news"—to seek hospital care for Schumann. But where? Certainly not in the local asylum, which Schumann regarded with dread. Although it had "pleasant surroundings and was well-managed," according to Pliny Earle, an American psychiatrist who had just completed an inspection of all the German mental hospitals,[28] with its 110 "inmates," the Düsseldorf asylum would not be able to provide the privacy and isolation that Hasenclever and Böger were seeking for their patient.

Thus it was decided to send him to Endenich, a suburb of Bonn, where Dr. Franz Richarz, an experienced psychiatrist, ran a small, exclusive, private asylum. Dr. Hasenclever had already referred several distinguished patients to Endenich, including the painter Alfred Rethels, one of Schumann's friends, who happened to be hospitalized there at the time.

Clara, however, resisted the plan. "Him, the magnificent Robert, in an institution!—how could I possibly tolerate this!" She was nearly swayed by some of the townspeople, who, as gossip began to circulate, wanted Schumann placed not in the hands of a psychiatrist, but in those of a "stern preacher." We have this information from Johannes Brahms, who arrived in Düsseldorf on 3 March. "Brahms said he only came to cheer me up with music, if that were my wish" wrote Clara. "Now he wants to stay here and later to dedicate himself properly to Robert, when he is again sufficiently recovered to be allowed to have visitors. It is really touching, this friendship."[29] Brahms later noted with evident pride that Clara "would have gone crazy without me, her little man, who among all the female busybodies was the only male able to talk sense to her."[30]

The next day, Saturday, 4 March, the carriage for Endenich stood waiting at the gate. Clara's diary reports that "Robert dressed himself in great haste, got in with Hasenclever and his two attendants, didn't ask for me or for his children." She wanted him to take along a bouquet of flowers from her. Schumann "held it in his hands for a long time without thinking about it, then suddenly smelled it and smiled, while holding Dr. Hasenclever's hand. Later he gave each one in the carriage a flower."

The ride to Bonn took eight hours, during which time Schumann became "restless, always asking whether they wouldn't be arriving soon."[31] He accepted hospitalization willingly, and not until the day before his death, two and a half years later, did Clara see him again.

II.

A Vulnerable Personality, 1809–1828

Johanne Christiane Schumann (née Schnabel) had already borne five children before her last child, Robert, was conceived, when she was close to menopause.* The preceding infant, a girl named Laura, had died in March 1809—either at birth or shortly thereafter, leaving Frau Schumann depressed. Her three previous children having been boys, Robert Schumann's birth, on 8 June 1810, probably evoked a mixed emotional reaction, happiness at having a healthy child and sadness that he was not a girl. "I squeezed you to my breast and heart with tears of joy," his mother wrote twenty-five years later, on his birthday. "It was prophesied that there would be a hard struggle with your birth—your good father was equally speechless and happy, because he too had silently worried about the child-birth." [1]

The ancestry of Schumann's father, August Schumann, can be traced back to small farming villages in Thuringia for five generations, beginning

---

*Owing to the absence of church records, her age cannot be determined precisely, but it has been estimated that Schumann's mother was born in 1767, which would make her six years older than her husband. We know from her son's letters that her birthday was November 28.

with Johann Schumann, born in 1650. Robert's grandfather, Johann Friedrich Schumann, was the first to break away from the agrarian life, serving as pastor in Endschütz's tiny Lutheran church (which still stands today). Pastor Schumann's first wife—Robert Schumann's grandmother—Christiane Magdalena Böhme, was the daughter of a textile merchant. She is described as having been "incessantly sick," with the apparent result that the family was subject to considerable poverty. The first of their six children, Robert's father, August, was born on 2 March 1773.[2]

August grew up during Germany's era of *Sturm und Drang* (storm and stress), an era that aimed at reducing the impact of French classicism and the enlightenment upon European culture. Shakespeare's plays, recently translated, had led German poets and writers to emphasize sensory awareness, heightened passion, freedom of expression, and creative originality. Johann Wolfgang von Goethe (1749–1832), whose early novels and plays were closely associated with *Sturm und Drang*, called this an "epoch of forced talent" because so many gifted young men exhausted themselves struggling to display their "genius."[3]

A shy, bookish youth with considerable talent for writing, August Schumann was unable to obtain a higher education, and after his family left Endschütz for Weida, only ten kilometers away, poverty plus religious orthodoxy nearly throttled his literary ambitions. According to his friend and biographer, C. E. Richter, a deep conflict between August's restrictive upbringing and the liberating power of *Sturm und Drang* drove him "close to insanity."[4] At eighteen, he capitulated to his family's wishes, based on economic necessity, and attempted to become a businessman.

August Schumann's checkered career eventually took him to the small town of Zeitz. There he found employment as a clerk in a bookshop and met Johanne Christiane Schnabel, daughter of the town surgeon. Dr. Schnabel insisted that if the poor clerk had serious intentions about his daughter, he should establish a business of his own. August therefore returned to his parents in Weida, and for the next year and a half devoted himself assiduously to writing books, with the hope of making a profit.

Here we see the beginnings of a pattern that August Schumann's much more famous son Robert would repeat: creative activity motivated by the desire for marriage, for approval from one's prospective father-in-law, and for money. August Schumann "quickly wrote eight books and earned the goodly sum of 1,000 thalers,"[5] an impressive sum for so young an author, but hardly enough to support a family for very long (a thaler was worth approximately one dollar). The money he earned did allow August Schumann to invest in a small grocery and general store located in Ronneburg, where he moved after marrying Johanne Schnabel, in October 1795. Their first child, a daughter named Emilie, was born nine months later.

Illness seems to have complicated this marriage from the very beginning. The tremendous effort of writing so many books in so short a time evidently exhausted August. In the first year of his marriage he had "a severe exacerbation of dysentery treated by Dr. Sulzer," which led to "almost incessant illness."[6] Frau Schumann also spoke of her husband's many years of suffering from lower abdominal complaints and gout. Schumann's invalidism forced his wife to take over the store, thus enabling him to write at least five more books undisturbed. A creative malady perhaps? Sir George Pickering's biographical studies of illness-prone writers, scientists, and other creative people show how enforced abundant leisure can enhance productivity.[7]

August Schumann's books span a wide range of subjects, from the fanciful to the practical.[8] For example, *Solomon the Wise and His Fool Markolph* (published in 1797) is the reworking of an old German folk tale about a pharoah's desire for Solomon's wife. It converts the Old Testament theme into a gothic horror story, filled with magic, intrigue, and violence. (Hundreds of similar books emerged during the German romantic era.) At the other end of the gamut was his *Addressbook* (1800), which systematically listed businesses, factories, shops, apartments, and so on, throughout Upper Saxony.

The house in Zwickau where Robert Schumann was born (now the Robert Schumann Haus, containing exhibition rooms, a library, and a concert hall). (Photograph by the author.)

When the birth of a son, Eduard, in 1799 forced his wife to stop managing their store, August established a publishing business. At first he produced mostly his own books (fourteen new titles by 1803), but he later added translations (and other materials) from his substantial private library. These ventures were not very successful, however, so the arrival of two more sons, Carl in 1801 and Julius in 1805, served to further increase the family's economic problems.

Finally, lack of sufficient funds compelled him to enter into a publishing partnership with his younger half-brother Friedrich in 1808, and to move to the small town of Zwickau. A year later, August experienced the death of both his father and his daughter Laura. It was therefore a stressful time during which his son Robert was conceived.

By the time Robert was old enough to go to school, his family had become relatively affluent. Schumann Brothers Publishing Company could boast that its pocket editions of the classics (akin to our paperbacks today) not only produced a good income but were also "the first to call attention of the German people to the best European writers," including Goethe, Schiller, Scott, Byron, and Cervantes.[9] But in spite of outward success, August Schumann continued to be a troubled person, and an invalid of sorts. He would often leave home to receive treatment in Carlsbad or other health spas, as was the custom in those days. The example he presented—of an ailing person dejected over his disabilities—undoubtedly imprinted itself on the mind of his sensitive youngest son.

It did not seem possible for Robert's mother to offset this negative impact of parental sickliness. On the contrary, her own suffering, a chronic depressive disorder, contributed significantly to the boy's personality development. Johanne Christiane Schnabel came from a medically oriented family. Her father had been a military surgeon, and her brother also was a doctor, who practiced most of his life in Russia. The family seems to have been well respected and rather conventional.[10]

Robert Schumann's first biographer, J. W. von Wasielewski, described the composer's mother as "gifted with a natural understanding, but raised under the influence of restrictive, small-town circumstances. She showed no cultural or educational development that went beyond the average, although her outward appearance was charming and she had a certain talent for presenting herself well."[11] In the early years of her marriage to August she had a great deal of energy and used it very effectively to supervise their store while he, as the writer Marcel Brion puts it, "burying himself in his own den, smoking pipe after pipe, wrote medieval stories of monks and cavaliers."[12] In Zwickau, as their older sons grew up and gradually took over the family business, Frau Schumann invested this energy more in herself, her depressive symptoms, and her relationship with their youngest and very exceptional child, Robert.

The year of Schumann's birth, 1810, saw the beginning of Napoleon's conquest of eastern Europe. His hometown, Zwickau, is located on a strategic trade route between Saxony and its neighbors to the east, Silesia (now Poland) and Bohemia (now Czechoslovakia). Once a thriving community of ten thousand, this town had already been reduced to a population of less than five thousand as a result of the Thirty Years' War, and in 1812, when Schumann was only two years old, Napoleon's invasion produced further devastation.[13] About 150,000 foreign troops marched in and out of Zwickau, and his birthday that year was eclipsed by the spectacle of Napoleon and Empress Josephine passing through on their way east. The next year witnessed the return of thousands of soldiers, this time defeated and bringing with them disease and famine. Saxony was in utter chaos; troops seized the mills; the townspeople began to starve; noises of cannons, and especially the awful bombardment of Leipzig, further terrified them. Nine percent of Zwickau's already decimated population was wiped out. Frederick Niecks, an early Schumann biographer, luridly writes that "severed arms and legs lay heaped up in front of hospitals, and in the wretchedness of these places a murderous epidemic typhus soon developed and spread devastation through the whole town."[14] It goes without saying, then, that the first years of Schumann's childhood were tumultuous.

Schumann's mother apparently fell victim to the typhus epidemic, and while she was ill Robert had to leave home and live with another family, named Ruppius. He made a fairly good adjustment to the new environment, as seems clear from a self-conscious autobiography written when he was fifteen: "Three weeks flowed by easily for me, because in her [Frau Ruppius's] honor one must say that she accomplished a great deal in the education of children. I loved her. She was my second mother, and, to make a long story short, I stayed under her truly maternal supervision for two and a half years."[15]

But in looking back on this separation from his biological mother, his temporary attachment to a second mother, and his subsequent reattachment to the first, the adolescent Schumann also commented poignantly:

> Once every day I went over to my parents, but otherwise I didn't concern myself about them any longer. Still very clear in my memory is that I couldn't sleep the night before moving out of this house, and that I cried throughout

the entire night. Also once before, when Frau Ruppius was away on a trip, I got up alone during the night when she was to return and sat at the window, crying bitterly, so that early in the morning they found me, asleep, with tears rolling down my cheeks.[16]

It seems that music played an important role in reducing the boy's loneliness, and in helping him organize the powerful emotions evoked when he had to adjust himself first to one woman and then to the other. His real mother, Johanne Christiane, loved to sing. She prided herself on being called "the living book of arias," and in being able to get her son to sing back "with beautiful intonation and in the right rhythm."[17] Psychologists now know that this mirroring of sounds and gestures is essential for the development of an empathic relationship between children and their parents; it normally leads to trust and forms the basis for agreement on the meaning of messages exchanged.[18] Schumann's innate musical talent probably heightened the importance of sounds in communication with his mother. And not only did she communicate her love, but she also passed on other thoughts and feelings—including, probably, her helpless feeling of being easily overwhelmed. "I just couldn't handle things on my own," Johanne Christiane wrote in a letter explaining why, under the stress of war and economic hardship, she felt that "to have four sons is really too much for a mother."[19]

Johanne Christiane Schumann (née Schnabel), Robert's mother. (Painting by L. Glaeser, 1810, the year of Schumann's birth.)

Music runs deep in the soul of Thuringia, the land of Luther and Bach, and of the Schumann ancestry. But what did Zwickau, in Saxony, have to offer by way of models for musical excellence? Unfortunately, it had more of a "peasant orientation" than an artistic milieu and did not offer Schumann much musical stimulation. Local craftsmen were employed mainly as nail-smiths, tanners, clothmakers, and linen weavers, and there was little indigenous musical activity. (Until 1846 Zwickau remained a center mostly for itinerant musicians.) Nevertheless, the organists of St. Mary's Church (consecrated in 1118) had achieved something in the way of distinction. Ludwig Krebs, one of Bach's most promising students, had played there from 1737 to 1743. And it was a church organist, Johann Gottfried Kuntsch (1775–1855), who became Schumann's first music teacher.[20]

Schumann started lessons at age seven and continued them sporadically until he was an adolescent. He remembered Kuntsch as "a good teacher who was fond of me," and in later years dedicated some pieces for the pedal-piano to him (opp. 56 and 58). But Schumann soon felt he knew as much as his teacher about keyboard technique and the rudiments of harmony. He believed Kuntsch's playing "was only mediocre." "Models I could not have in the little town," he wrote, "where I myself may have been regarded as one."[21] Thus as a child he had already begun to pursue the independent path that was to characterize his lifelong musical trajectory. In his autobiography he mentioned "starting at an early age to compose. . . . First efforts probably already 1817–1818. Dances." He evidently could absorb and quickly assimilate the musical ideas of the few composers whose work was available from scores, manuscripts, and the occasional municipal concerts that Kuntsch organized in Zwickau. He participated in some of these concerts, at age eleven, for example, playing the piano in Friedrich Schneider's *Das Weltgericht*, then a popular oratorio.

Above all, Schumann had a remarkable talent for improvisation, and he used this gift not only for his own satisfaction but also to entertain and amuse his friends. Almost every biography of the composer mentions his uncanny ability to produce musical portraits that captured people's mannerisms, movements, speech patterns, and physical appearance in sound.[22] Surely this childhood play was the precursor of later creativity. As the musicologist Vladimir Stassow points out, Schumann was "a portraitist who painted people, their likeness, their physiognomy, mentality and passions. That was what constituted the greatest fortune of his life and his most sublime enjoyment through art."[23]

The boy was obviously proud of his accomplishments. "I was dutiful, childish, and attractive," he wrote. "I studied assiduously, and at 6 years was sent to a private school. In my seventh year I learned Latin, in the eighth French and Greek, at nine and one-half I entered the fourth grade of our Lyceum."[24] His intelligence, precocity, and exhibitionism helped Schumann form friendships. One of his first affectionate ties to someone outside the family circle was with an older boy, August Vollert, who was a regular visitor at the Schumann house for two years. The two boys played the piano together, an important interaction, and one that foreshadowed Schumann's many future relationships based on a mutual love of music.[25] None of his older brothers were inclined toward the arts. Thus his piano-playing friend became a kind of soul-mate with whom Schumann's most intimate feelings could be shared.

Another childhood event that he treasured for many years was a five-week trip with his mother to Carlsbad, a vacation resort and health spa. Frau Schumann took Robert there when he was eight years old, and what seems to have made the greatest impression on him was seeing, and possibly hearing, the famous pianist Ignaz Moscheles (1794–1870). "How everyone honored him and stepped out of his way and how he walked through the crowd so modestly," Schumann later reminded his mother. "In all these things I want to use him as my model."[26] (He also expressed a desire to study with Moscheles, but never did.*)

Schumann's father insisted that all of his sons be very well educated, and their schoolwork was regularly supplemented with books from the family's private library, which was rumored to contain 4000 volumes. That may explain why Robert was far more erudite than many other musicians of his time. Indeed, bookishness and literary pursuits were so strongly encouraged in his home that literature soon became his second love. When he was seven years old, his publisher father moved to a house in the Amtsgasse, where home and business were combined. There the youngster was pressed vigorously to develop his verbal abilities.

In his autobiography, Schumann recalled that he was only nine and a half years old when "my life now already started to be more restless. Overburdened with schoolwork, I wasn't zealous enough, although I wasn't lacking talent in any way. The anxiety when one hasn't prepared himself—this all made a bad impression, and the only pleasant years of childhood really became a burden." An unconscious conflict between loyalty to his father's expectation for verbal excellence and devotion to his mother's need for musical communication may have contributed to Schumann's anxiety, which he tried to reduce by withdrawing from social stimuli. "I much preferred going for walks all by myself, and I would pour my heart out to nature,"[28] reports his autobiography.

---

*Schumann never completely lost his reverential attitude for Moscheles. "Over 30 years ago in Carlsbad I saved as a relic one of the concert programs you had touched," he wrote the older man in 1851.[27]

A brief acting career also is mentioned.

> I, my brother [Julius], and some other school friends had a really nice theater which made us well known all around Zwickau, and even famous (sometimes we collected 2–3 thalers). We performed completely extemporaneously, cracking horrible jokes and making outrageously silly puns.[29]

Schumann's father encouraged this behavior, lavishing extraordinary praise on his exhibitionistic youngest son, buying him scores, music stands, and most important, the gift of an excellent Viennese grand piano. The boy responded in kind, giving "daily performances after dinner for my father" and noting "free improvisation at the piano . . . carried away by the fire of my playing." After hearing his first opera at age nine, he tried to compose— "several numbers for an opera, many vocal pieces, many things for the piano"—but all without proper instruction. At eleven he completed a "Psalm 150" for singers, piano, and orchestra. "I lacked all knowledge, I wrote precisely like a child," he admitted. "The total lack of any leadership is perceivable in my hearing, technique, and especially theory."[30]

Along with his brothers, Schumann also became briefly involved in the family publishing business. He helped his father collect and translate essays for an illustrated biography titled *Picture-Gallery of the Most Famous Men of All Countries*.[31] This early exposure to languages, foreign affairs, and historical figures no doubt further excited his ambitions and stimulated his verbal abilities. (The three older brothers followed their father's footsteps and became publishers: Eduard and Julius in Zwickau, and Carl later in Schneeberg, where he established his own company.)

Schumann described an early interest in girls. His first crush was on Emilie Lorenz (who eventually married his brother Julius). "Would you believe it? Already in my eighth year I came to know the art of Amor," wrote Schumann. "I loved [Emilie], really quite innocently. . . . I will never forget that once when we were leaving French class I gave her a totally disconnected, despairing love-letter wrapped around a penny (probably so she could buy herself a dress). Oh what sweet foolishness."[32]

He also fell in love with a girl named Ida Stölzel:

> Although she was only nine and a half years old, I wrote her several poems. My brother Carl (who incidentally was in love with her sister Ernestine) snitched a copy once, so I had to listen to that poem many times. But nothing bothered me. We loved each other for two years, quite intimately and childishly, and didn't abuse this love in any bad way. We constantly kissed each other, and every Sunday I bought her a quarter's worth of candy—in short I was happy.[33]

Thus, it seems that Schumann approached puberty with a personality structured around two clear lines of identification. One was with his mother, his primary love-object, whose singing had alerted him to the pleasures of musical communication. The other was his father, whose emphasis on verbal interaction promised social success. And yet weaknesses were also associated with each parent: self-pity and depression with his mother (traits that worsened as she grew older), and physical disability and chronic invalidism with his father.

Even given how disparate and contradictory these dimensions of his parents' personalities were, Schumann was able to integrate them well enough to develop an ambitious, productive, and surprisingly stable sense of self. In addition, his partial identification with three older and capable brothers seems to have augured well for the healthy consolidation of masculine strivings.

Yet danger lay ahead. Schumann's early separation from his mother and temporary adoption by another woman had flooded him for a considerable amount of time during sensitive years of childhood development with emotions of mourning, and may have engendered a pathological fear of being unloved. But the only disharmonies he had mentioned up until this point involved his anxieties at school—which were nothing very unusual, and which he reduced by withdrawing from friends and dwelling more in an inner world of music and fantasies.

From a defensive pattern of that sort can arise intellectual superiority— but also psychopathology. Schumann's parents and social environment had encouraged creative activity—literature, drama, and music. These activities undoubtedly helped him to express his libidinal and aggressive energies in safe and acceptable ways. However, Schumann was already beginning to experience some anxieties that led to social withdrawal, loss of contact with peers, and autistic reverie. But his imagination seems not to have been pulled too far as yet in unfathomable directions.

Curiously absent from accounts of his developing psyche is any information about how he coped with violent, hateful, or destructive impulses. The play-acting with his brothers suggests that experience with such impulses was not foreign to him, and it seems unlikely that he could have been deaf to stories about the horrors of the war, or blind to scenes of butchery described in some of his father's library books. His achievement-oriented parents probably punished their children in some way, and we can also surmise that the siblings fought with each other. And yet suffering, and thoughts of retribution or revenge, seem to have been unmentionable to Schumann at this point. Why that was so is difficult to say with certainty. The psychoanalyst William Niederland has noted that there seems to be an association between auditory sensitivity and the fear of being beaten. According to Niederland, people who are sensitive to sounds sometimes store memories of harsh sounds—such as crying and screaming—in unconscious regions of the mind, whence they may emerge in fantasies but not as articulated words.[34] (The inhibition of rage came to be, as we shall see, Schumann's lifelong problem.)

When Schumann was fifteen, two deaths in his immediate family, separated by only ten months, disrupted what had been a fairly smooth personal development. The first and most traumatic loss was that of his sister, by suicide. The other was that of his father, who died unexpectedly while his mother was away.

We know little about Emilie Schumann, who was fourteen years older than Robert and undoubtedly had been an important female influence during his childhood. Because she was the oldest child, and by all known accounts very sensitive and intelligent, her parents seem to have favored her until their last, and most gifted, son came along. (Perhaps Robert's taking the spotlight from his sister had something to do with her decline, which progressed rapidly when he entered adolescence.) Although we don't know what specific behavioral problems Emilie may have exhibited, apparently they were serious enough to cause concern to her parents. "Was her conduct while entertaining really so bad?" her father asked in a letter from Carlsbad dated 18 July 1824, which praises Robert for being "so alert to Emilie's moral conduct. . . . Your mother has recommended stricter supervision."[35]

A contributing factor in her derangement seems to have been a chronic skin disease, which, in C. E. Richter's words, "threw its poisons onto the most precious parts of her body"—meaning, presumably, her genitalia. Perhaps she suffered from neurodermatitis (a nervous skin disease) with intense itching of the vulva, or psoriasis. We also know that she became mentally ill—"a relentlessly progressive emotional illness [revealed] occasional traces of quiet madness."[36] "Quiet" madness suggests a depressive stupor or catatonic schizophrenia. But of course Emilie might have had a toxic-organic psychosis, even syphilis, given the skin disease. According to an earlier biography of Schumann, Robert played "Ländler and waltzes for Emilie to dance to,"[37] suggesting a kind of music therapy—which probably did little to stave off the ultimate catastrophe.

Exactly how Emilie died is somewhat mysterious. Gustav Jansen, a devoted Schumann scholar, claims that she "threw herself into the water during a fever-paroxysm."[38] The medical historian Sutermeister asserts that she jumped from a window.[39] A book written by Schumann's daughter Eugenie suggests that Emilie may have died in bed; but that does not rule out suicide, either by jumping or by immersion.[40] In Zwickau, where the suicide took place, it is generally believed that she drowned herself.*

The loss of a sibling can be devastating. It not only leaves a gap in the family structure, but also upsets the internal equilibrium of the surviving family members. A prolonged period of mourning is often needed to repair the damage, and grief may be renewed by anniversaries or other reminders of the death. When a suicide is involved, grief is usually compounded by other disturbing emotions, such as self-blame for having failed to prevent the disaster, or anger directed at the victim. These connections between mourning and pathological depression were brilliantly described by Sigmund Freud, and subsequent studies have shown that there may also be relationships between sibling-loss in childhood and creative behavior. (Many writers, artists, and composers have incorporated images of their dead relatives into their work.)[42]

Schumann responded to the suicide of his sister with a great deal of agitation and rumination. He also tried to describe his emotions: "I was a foaming wave, screaming as it rises, why must I be tossed around by the storms like this?" A few years later he noted a "longing to throw myself into the Rhine," a suicidal preoccupation undoubtedly related to his sister's death.[43] In his early twenties, Schumann tried to leap out of a fifth-story window, and after that he repeatedly complained about a fear of heights, which was probably a safeguard against jumping. How this defense finally gave way in Düsseldorf we already know.

Ten months after Emilie's death, and before Schumann had fully adjusted to that loss, their father, who had been sick for years, died suddenly at the age of fifty-three on 10 August 1826, a date Schumann often noted in his diaries and associated with mourning. His mother, herself unwell, was out of town, at a distant health spa, and unable to comfort her children. "I railed against fate," wrote Schumann. "Isn't it terrible to be robbed of such a man, such an affectionate father, a loving poet, a keen observer of human nature and a capable businessman?"[44]

It is reported in many biographies—although it cannot be documented—that Schumann's father, before his untimely death, had made arrangements with Carl Maria von Weber, one of Germany's most distinguished composers, and then director of the Royal Opera in Dresden, to take Robert on as a student. Such training might have made a significant difference in Schumann's personal development and musical career. An ex-

---

*Emilie's suicide was actually not the first such occurrence among Schumann's relatives. A cousin of his grandfather, Georg Ferdinand Schumann, killed himself in 1817. It is not known whether his death was ever discussed with Emilie or with Robert, who was only seven years old at the time.[41]

cellent pianist, Weber (1786–1826) had been an arch-romantic and led a rather wild life before marrying and settling into respectability. He might have provided a fitting role model for Schumann, but he died in 1826, the same year as Schumann's father.

It is important to note that Schumann's determination to become a writer, and his incessant keeping of diaries to record daily experiences and fluctuations in mood, began at this time of mourning for his father. It would help to write "a dull, insipid diary" thought Schumann, whenever he felt "painful hours eating up the memories of happier times."[45]

Schumann's first biographer, Wasielewski, says that "his demeanor reversed itself into almost the opposite [of the] predominantly cheerful disposition he had shown before. . . . The maturing youth became more meditative and taciturn and generally showed such a proclivity for daydreaming that this hampered communication, not only spiritually but socially as well."[46] Mourning for his father was coupled with a renewed tendency to eschew social situations and engage in lengthy inner dialogues—some of which are recorded in his diaries. This narcissistic inclination probably helped him maintain inner balance. Schumann did not give up human relationships completely, however; in fact, he began to show signs of another tendency: to seek new attachments with a few carefully selected people, who he hoped would be loyal friends (and thus protect his battered psyche against further damage). One of the first was with an older boy, Emil Flechsig, the first of a series of transitional friendships with males.

The choice of Flechsig as an object of devotion had several determinants. In the first place he had been selected by Robert's mother "to be a fitting companion for her precious darling," as the older boy later put it.[47] In the second place, Schumann, like many sensitive, artistically inclined teenagers, was beginning to experience a passion akin to homoerotic love, and Flechsig, having recently moved to Leipzig to attend college, quickly became the target for all sorts of mixed emotions. "On your chest, on your sympathetic bosom I must pour out my heart," reads a letter dated July 1827. Finally, Schumann yearned for friendship. "I have no friend, I have no beloved, I have nothing," he wrote Flechsig.[48] Although he tried to disguise his erotic fantasies—"I am writing in hieroglyphics," he confessed[49]— the emphasis on love is unmistakable. One of his poems written at this time calls Flechsig "an Adonis, smiling gracefully" (*ein holdlächelnder Adon*).[50]

Soon Schumann's letters to Flechsig became more urging, more demanding. He proposed that they be roommates, and that they write plays together, "like Beaumont and Fletcher." He envisioned it as a working relationship, and idealized not only the pleasure but also the pain. Schumann "would heave sighs" while his friend "would smile," and "it will be exquisitely disagreeable for us to write tragedies together."[51]

Emil Flechsig, Schumann's boyhood friend and his college roommate in Leipzig. (Water color sketch by A. Bach.)

Flechsig was more hard-boiled than Schumann. He called him "a reasonable fellow, rather dreamy and inattentive . . . and ruled by the absolute certainty that in the future he would be a famous man. Famous in what was very undecided as yet, but famous under any circumstances."[52] Commenting on Schumann's adolescent indecision, Flechsig recalled:

> First he let loose on philology for a while, just about his weakest side. . . . Soon he changed to heraldry, pursuing that just as eagerly. Later he wandered into Germanic poetry and got stuck there. . . . He would write love poems to former and nonexistent favorites, then began working on tragedies. He was so fond of reciting poetic works that he almost killed me and Roller [another student] with his great zeal.[53]

Schumann's involvement with poetry, while it may have had a self-therapeutic function and in its excess antagonized a few friends, did not produce much immediate satisfaction in his search for a vocation. Even his brothers would not publish it—not surprisingly, for many of the poems seem naïve and maudlin. (Besides, Schumann's basic talent was for music even though he believed that both music and poetry "spring from the same source and have the same function";[54] the primary appeal of his poetry is the rhythm, not the content.) The following example is from a collection he called *All Sorts of Things from the Pen of Robert on the Mulde* (the Mulde

River is where his sister Emilie is thought to have drowned herself).[55] Titled "Longing" (*Sehnsucht*) the poem is dedicated to a girlfriend, and it may have been the text for a song:

Sterne der blauen	*You stars in the blue*
Himmlischen Auen	*Heaven's pastoral view*
Grüsst sie mir freundlich,	*Bring friendly greeting,*
Die ich geliebt.	*To her whom I love.*
Weit in die Ferne	*Off in the distance,*
Möcht' ich so gerne,	*Where I would go,*
Wo das geliebte	*This loving maiden*
Mädchen mir weilt.	*Is waiting for me.*
Schweigende Sterne	*You stars that are silent*
Grüsst mir die Ferne,	*Greet in the distance,*
Grüsst mir das Mädchen,	*And also the maiden,*
Das ich geliebt!	*The one whom I love!*

While giving a speech on poetry, the young Schumann began to blush, stammer, and stop talking. He had forgotten his lines and lost his way in his thinking, an early manifestation of the social anxiety that later became a personality trait (and still later interfered with his success as a conductor). He was painfully aware of the inner confusion, which was part of his identity conflict. "I really don't know as yet what I am. I believe I have imagination, and nobody can talk me out of that. But I'm not a deep thinker. I can never pursue a logical argument once I've got it started. Whether I'm truly a poet—one cannot be made into one—will have to be decided by posterity."[56]

Posterity did not have to wait very long. The adolescent Schumann was eager to consolidate his energies in literary work, as befit the son of a writer and publisher. Grieving for his father, he soon found a temporary symbolic replacement, a man whom he could idealize: Jean Paul Richter.*

Jean Paul (1763–1825) was an almost exact contemporary of August Schumann, but he was a far better educated and much more successful writer; his novels, an embodiment of German romanticism, were popular at the time. Thinly disguised autobiographies, they dwell on subjects that range all the way from morbid preoccupations with death to light-hearted portrayals of family life. Jean Paul had an uncanny ability to combine the rebellious mood of *Sturm und Drang* with more traditional, conventional attitudes. In an almost free-associative way, he would quickly spin out his ideas, which produced a confusing and contradictory text but yet allowed seemingly incompatible ideas to coexist. He often portrayed the main char-

---

*Johannes Paul Friedrich Richter was his real name; he had changed it to Jean Paul, in keeping with what was then considered fashionable.

acter of his novels as two people, a literary device of the "double-personality" then much in vogue. (Robert Louis Stevenson's famous thriller *Dr. Jekyll and Mr. Hyde*, Fyodor Dostoyevsky's *The Double*, and Sigmund Freud's early theories about unconscious mental processes are some examples of this nineteenth-century interest in double personalities.)[57]

Schumann's diary is filled with observations about Jean Paul, whom he considered "superhuman";[58] he devoured many of his novels, including *Titan*, *Siebenkäs*, and *Hesperus*. One book in particular, *Adolescent Years* (*Die Flegeljahre*), "enraptured" him. It concerns a pair of twins, Vult and Walt, who symbolize contrasting sides of a man's character. Vult is more aggressive and independent. He runs away from home, while his shy and more retiring brother Walt attends law school, preparing to manage their father's estate. When Walt has difficulty with his final examinations, Vult reappears miraculously to help him. They agree to stay together for life, traveling and writing books. (Walt is to do the poetry and Vult the satire). On one of their adventures they meet a beautiful heiress, Wina. Walt falls in love with her but is afraid to make any advances, so he asks his brother to do it for him. They exchange clothes and attend a masked ball, where Vult, disguised as Walt, wins the girl. But Vult feels he cannot love Wina without betraying his brother, so he runs away.[59]

Clearly inspired by Jean Paul's book, Schumann later imagined a double personality for himself: his audacious, more manly self he called "Florestan" and his shy, passive self he called "Eusebius." But for the time being he mostly hero-worshipped Jean Paul and organized a reading circle, a sort of fan club, among his friends. It helped reduce his social anxiety and pull him out of his depression.

Under the spell of Jean Paul, Schumann began writing novels. One of these, *June Nights and July Days* deals centrally with the loneliness, sadness, and sexual frustration that were part of his own adolescent experience:

> In the holy temple of Nature, man trembles and gently casts off his mortal coil, allowing his loving psyche shyly to emerge. Oh, no man can be alone at heart when he wanders through the flowers of nature, and when he is without a boyfriend, without a girlfriend, without his beloved, he has to be unhappy."[60]

This novel, along with many other literary efforts of Schumann's adolescence, remained unfinished, a sign not only of the internal difficulties he was having but also that he was continuing to gravitate in another direction, toward the realm of music. Never did Schumann completely lose sight of his first love, which was bound up so closely with his attachment to his mother. Even the verbosity of Jean Paul's writing seemed to have a distinctly musical quality for him (he thought it was similar to Beethoven's music[61]), and he felt that it taught him to appreciate counterpoint much better.

Along with his poetry and unfinished novels, Schumann continued to write autobiographically, and he often revealed that sexual frustration was a problem for him. In Zwickau, for example, he found at least three females tantalizing, but they gave him little satisfaction. His "first fiery love" was Nanni Petsch.[62] A letter to Emil Flechsig suggests a worshipful attitude— "I want to sink to my knees and pray to her like a Madonna."[63] But his diary reveals a more carnal interest: dancing, squeezing of hands, sexual excitement, and ruminations about "whether it might damage a young man to love his ideal, especially a young man who is a student." Schumann's contact with Nanni was not without anxiety: "My hands shook, my voice trembled, I grew dizzy."[64]

Soon he transferred his affection, but not totally, to another girl, Liddy Hempel. "Nanni appears angrily in my eyes when I think of Liddy."[65] Her parents were friends of the Schumanns, and her father encouraged the romance by lending Robert money and inviting him to their house. Once when Liddy failed to meet him at an appointed place, Schumann headed for the nearest tavern and proceeded to get drunk. "I began to feel well again: the Tokay made me happy," he told Flechsig. "The passions rising within me are still too powerful and I want to drink champagne."[66]

For several years Schumann felt pursued by the girl—"Liddy often hungers for love from me," says his diary[67]—a projection, perhaps, of his own need for love. He even seems to have had rescue fantasies in which a girl would save him from some sort of catastrophe. For example, in January 1827, with "the image of Liddy hovering before my eyes all day," he went to inspect the ruins of a burnt-down church in Mosel, a nearby village. The sight of it put him into "a gruesome state," and he became panicky. "I had to get out, I wanted to see Liddy, my guardian angel, who's already directed me so often. Have you abandoned me?"[68]

Schumann shared his worries, and one assumes his sexual frustration as well, with boys from school. For instance, after his upsetting visit to the ruined church, Schumann sought out a friend called Staeger, with whom he talked about "a whole lot of hellish things" and "raged to high heaven and cried." One of the topics they discussed was suicide, which was not an uncommon preoccupation among adolescents in those days. (Goethe's novel *The Sufferings of Young Werther* (1774) had stimulated waves of suicidal thinking and behavior in Germany and elsewhere.) "We talked about our innermost dreams," wrote Schumann, "and [Staeger] answered me with unending compassion. 'Maybe I still have enough strength to control myself.' I wouldn't be able to control myself—no, I could never surmount that—a self-murderer!! Ugh, how I shudder through and through as I grasp these two thoughts. I tremble. I lose myself in the labyrinth of hellish dreams."[69]

Schumann's adolescent diary, written in the kaleidoscopic style popularized by Jean Paul, suggests that his "bad dreams" contained themes of being unacceptable to—or, worse yet, rejected by—his girlfriend. For example: "Does she love me? This I ask all day long and can't come up with an answer. A cold 'Maybe,' perhaps—that horrifies me—a strong 'No' could smash me to pieces."[70]

Why was Schumann's fear of rejection so all-pervasive, not only during adolescence but also throughout the rest of his life? Could he answer this question, or at least correct attempts to answer it for him, we might feel more confident in finding the truth (insofar as truth can ever be established through a psychological inquiry). Suffice it to say that his fear probably stemmed from some loss of basic trust in his mother, whose exhausted condition during his infancy may have necessitated the pretense that she was loving while in fact she couldn't take care of him. This ambiguity in their relationship—to be discussed in more depth shortly—may have maimed not only his capacity for trusting other women but also his ability to exist without having a woman close by. On top of that, Emilie's suicide engendered a loss of faith in human relationships.

Another example of an ambiguous, albeit important, early love relationship was Schumann's infatuation with Agnes Carus, a singer. She lived in Colditz, sixty kilometers to the north, but went to Zwickau occasionally to visit her brother-in-law, who regularly held soirées to which he invited Schumann. The singer, eight years older, already married and a mother, was looking for a piano accompanist. In his lonely turmoil, Schumann yearned for someone who might encourage his musical development. They worked on vocal music, especially the songs of Franz Schubert, who then was practically unknown outside Vienna. Soon Schumann's feelings for Agnes, probably stimulated by her appealing looks and pleasing voice, were unmistakably erotic. "Sitting alone at the piano with her for two hours, it was as if all dormant depths woke up mightily; she must have seen it in my eyes," says his diary.[71] Her name was often his last entry for the day. "I will go to bed and dream of her, of her. Good night Agnes . . . Agnes, good night." He often dreamed "beautiful, beautiful dreams of Agnes."[72]

Did his inamorata symbolize, on an unconscious level, a sister, a mother, or some other person around whom he could organize his thinking? We can only speculate, but the diary provides important clues. For example, at midnight on 13 July 1828, he recorded an almost stream-of-consciousness reverie: "She's probably asleep right now; I've been having good fantasies, because she was alive in my fantasies and with her the entire firmament of sounds." This idea evidently helped him cope with the death fantasy that followed: "All is so quiet; there's only the wailing of an abominable cat, like a lament of death, this caterwaul signifies dying, and I'm not far from that; only one kiss from her and I would do it gladly." Perhaps the thought of Agnes and of (her?) "holy sounds" enabled him to fall asleep.[73]

Schumann's attachment to this woman, which lasted five years, was complicated by the presence of her husband, a physician who became not only an oedipal rival but also his first psychiatrist. Ernst August Carus was the medical director of a large hospital in Colditz, located in a huge, forbidding, old castle.* The castle was then being converted into an insane asylum and, according to the Colditz historian Dr. Peter Bräuer, Ernst and Agnes Carus lived there.[74] Doctor Carus was an amateur musician who had studied organ and horn and who occasionally did some composing and conducting.[75] He was known as a kindly administrator, who allowed his patients to attend, and even participate in, concerts held in the castle.

It was during his vacations, while visiting Dr. Carus and his wife in Colditz, that Schumann established a highly charged, ambivalent relationship with the couple.[76] Both the excitement and the fear of closer involvement with them probably was a function of his exposure to the milieu of madness that Colditz provided. Conditions at the asylum must have been frightening for someone as young and impressionable as Schumann, troubled as he was by the recent psychosis of his sister. (Even the experienced American psychiatrist Pliny Earle, on his inspection tour of German asylums in the nineteenth century, was amazed to find that more than four hundred "inmates" of Colditz existed in deplorable hygienic conditions—"each patient can be bathed only once in five weeks.")[77]

While psychotherapy as practiced today was almost unheard of in Schumann's time, many physicians did use a kind of "moral treatment" to influence their patients.[78] Presumed causes of mental disease were explained, undesirable behavior was criticized, healthy attitudes were encouraged, and support and reassurance were given. It is likely that Dr. Carus spoke this way to Schumann, but probably more as a friend, and not in any formal clinical relationship. For that they were too close. Dr. Carus liked the young pianist, nicknamed him "Fridolin" (the hero of a ballad by Friedrich Schiller), and seems to have tolerated his flirtations with Agnes, for a while at least.

Their relationship changed after they moved to Leipzig. Dr. Carus had become professor of medicine at the university there and Schumann, as will

---

*The castle has dominated the village of Colditz since the fifteenth century. At various times it has been used as a fortress, prison, poorhouse, and concentration camp.

be seen shortly, had enrolled as an unwilling law student. Agnes continued to play the role of a flirtatious, adored, but unavailable love-object for him. That forced her husband to encourage Schumann to socialize elsewhere, to bring him, as he put it, "into countless families—they think it would be good for my career."[79] In fact it was partly as a result of Carus's effort to reduce the tension that had built up between Agnes and "Fridolin" that Schumann met the piano teacher Friedrich Wieck and his daughter, Clara, the two people who were to have the most lasting influence on him. Clara Wieck, not yet nine years old, was invited to perform at a party at the Carus home on 31 March 1828.[80]

The influence of Agnes Carus and her husband might be seen as a kind of therapy for Schumann. They encouraged him to be more self-expressive and to try to behave in more adult ways, perhaps even in the realm of sexuality. His erotic attraction for Agnes Carus could of course not be expressed directly, but in the course of their long relationship it became possible for him to sublimate some of these yearnings, which he often did through music. Schumann's diaries also suggest that Dr. Carus, whom he teasingly referred to as "boorish," "bungling," and "sleepy,"[81] was a safe target for mildly rivalrous, aggressive feelings.

It was generally not in Schumann's nature to display anger openly, or to behave defiantly, particularly towards an older man. His outward submissiveness, as well as his anxious inhibition of sexuality, seems to suggest unresolved oedipal conflicts. Schumann had been deprived in early adolescence of opportunities for genuine competitive struggles with his father, so that men like Carus, and later Wieck, became partial substitutes. (We will soon observe how Wieck reactivated Schumann's latent conflicts between obsequious and rebellious behavior.)

As for his libidinal yearnings, those that were not successfully sublimated through symbolic activity fed his increasingly troubled relationship with his mother. Giving pain and pleasure to each other had been a keynote to their relationship for some time, and Schumann's first letter to his "good, treasured mother" when he was seven years old exemplifies the tone: "You won't take it badly that I haven't written you yet, it gave me much pain that I didn't write you." Another, written a year later, pleads, "Don't take it unkindly that I have offended you, for surely I will exert myself day in and day out to get rid of my faults."[82]

Thus at a critical phase of adolescence, when Schumann was beginning to look outside his family for emotional attachments, he turned back to his mother as the primary source of womanly affection. This cost him dearly and resulted in a serious dilemma: along with the love his mother held in reserve for him, her youngest child, came disapproval of his pursuit of music. Despite her pleasure in his precocious musical ability, Johanne Christiane objected strongly to the idea of ever having a musician in the family. He may have won an oedipal victory of sorts by continuing to be a mama's boy, but at the price of having to curb his aggression and make it appear that he was *not* seriously interested in music. (That Schumann had feared his mother's disapproval already at an earlier age is suggested by his confession to her "that to be allowed to compose [he] had to be secretive.")[83] How Schumann tried later through appeasement to curry favor with his mother is seen in a letter he wrote at the age of seventeen.

> Good mother, I've often offended you. I've often misjudged your best intentions. Forgive this stormy, hot-tempered youth who will now make up for it with good and honorable deeds, and a virtuous lifestyle. Parents must make demands on the life of their child! My father is already dead; thus I now owe much more to you, my dear mother. To you alone I am obligated to prepare myself for a happy life, for a cheerful, cloudless future.[84]

III.

Challenges and Opportunities, 1828–1829

Schumann experienced a range of emotions during his first extended stay away from his family. Some of these feelings, such as loneliness that drove him to tears, he tried to put into words, using poetic imagery and metaphor. Others, like anger toward his family for not giving him the support he felt he deserved, he either tried to deny or transformed into querulous complaining. He tried to behave chivalrously by engaging in rivalry with boys and expressing his eroticism with girls, but he often seemed just maladroit. Finally, his intense and at times pathological anxiety was converted into a number of symptoms—both physical and psychological. (Musical composition, which later brought Schumann some relief from anxiety, was something he mastered only very gradually, and hesitantly. He was no child prodigy like Mozart or Mendelssohn, nor did he, like Bach or Beethoven, have a family tradition of musical accomplishment that could direct his energies.)

Schumann was not yet eighteen years old when he wrote to his friend Flechsig that he was planning to join him at the university in Leipzig, where he hoped to find "that Greek lightheartedness which always views life from the happy midpoint between joy and tears." Separation from his mother posed some threats to be sure, and Schumann confessed that he felt "hurled out into the night of the world, without a leader, a teacher, or a father." He besought Flechsig to "be my friend even if I should turn out to be unworthy of your friendship. . . . Guide me into the active life and pick the mad youth up again when he falls down."[1]

But before going to Leipzig, Schumann, restless and yearning for an intimate friendship, took off on a vacation trip with another student, Gisbert Rosen. They went to Bayreuth to pay homage to Jean Paul, then headed south for Nuremberg. Schumann compulsively crammed his diary with details of their meals, lodgings, sightseeing, expenses, social activities—and sexual exploits: "wild excitement"; "pretty girls"; "finger games under skirts"; "smiling whores."[2]

While stopping in Augsburg Schumann engaged in a brief flirtation with Clara Kurrer, whose father, a prosperous chemist and friend of the family, gave him a letter of introduction to Heinrich Heine, then living in Munich, the capital of Bavaria. The week spent there, attending concerts and visiting famous art galleries, seems to have been a high point of the vacation. When he met Heine, whom he expected to be "an ill-tempered, misanthropic man," Schumann found instead "a human Greek Anacreon who shook my hand in a most friendly way. . . . Only around his mouth is there a bitter, ironic smile; he laughs about the trivialities of life and is scornful about the pettiness of little people."[3] This unforgettable experience encouraged Schumann, years later, to set Heine's poems to music.

After Munich, Schumann seems to have felt a distinct letdown. He commented on the "pain" he had when separating from Rosen, who was scheduled to go on to Heidelberg, and during the return trip a peculiar "melancholy and deep yearning for something grand" settled over him.[4] Before returning to Leipzig he stopped in Zwickau, where he evidently provoked some consternation by remaining for only a few hours. "Nobody there has ever heard anything, much less seen anything, of Nuremberg, Augsburg, Munich," wrote the suddenly sophisticated traveler.[5]

Schumann seemed upset and was probably homesick. "I long with all my heart to return to my quiet home where I was born and have spent happy days in nature," he wrote to his mother after only a few days in Leipzig. "Nature, where can I find it here? Everything is so artificial: there are no hills, no valleys, no woods where I can really give free rein to my thoughts; no place where I can be alone. Only in my locked room. Downstairs there is interminable noise and commotion. That is what keeps me from having any peace of mind."[6] He complained about an "unending inner mental struggle" over choosing a course of study: "Frigid jurisprudence smashes you down with its ice-cold definitions from the very beginning and can't please me at all. Medicine I don't want, and theology I'm not able to study."

Although he was not fundamentally interested in law, Schumann felt compelled to "go ahead with jurisprudence, no matter how cold and dry it may be."[7] There were several reasons for this decision, all of them related to pressure from home. The first was financial. His father's will had provided a very substantial inheritance of 10,323 reichsthalers, plus 200 thalers per year if Robert chose to go to a university, in which case another 100 thalers were allotted for the cost of final examinations.[8] (The will also stipulated that until he was twenty-one, all decisions about his education, place of residence, and finances had to be made by a legal guardian, Johann Gottlob Rudel.) The second reason had to do with prestige. Leipzig, like other universities of that day, offered three courses of study, theology, law, and medicine. It was customary for boys from poorer families, if they wanted an education, to enroll in the theology curriculum. For Schumann, who came from an upwardly mobile, relatively affluent family, to do this would have been unseemly. Medicine, his grandfather's and uncle's profession, might have been acceptable, but young Schumann either was uninterested or was unwilling to make that kind of personal commitment.

There is some doubt about how seriously Schumann worked on his law studies at the university. Emil Flechsig claimed that although Schumann registered as a law student and signed up for several courses, "this was, and continued to be, his only participation in the Academy. Otherwise he never set foot in a lecture hall."[9] Nevertheless, years later he asked for, and obtained, a certificate stating that he attended classes, and his behavior in business and other matters requiring a knowledge of the law showed considerable sophistication.

It was Schumann's wish, which he obliquely communicated to his mother, to study music in Leipzig. "I really want to have my old, dear, beloved piano here," he wrote her. "It brings back the best memories of my boyhood and adolescence; it has shared everything that I have ever felt, all my tears and moaning, but all the joys as well."[10] He rented a piano instead, and he spent much of his time improvising—"fantasizing," as he called it—which inevitably increased his social isolation and solitude. He avoided the boisterous aspects of student life, especially the "Burschenschaften" that many German students flocked to at the time. These were the militant, highly nationalistic fraternities, given over to dueling, the martial arts, and other aggressive pursuits, which the sensitive Schumann abhorred. Instead, he joined a smaller, more liberal group, the "Marcomannia," to which his friend Rosen also belonged. There is no evidence that he participated in sports, but he did take long walks in a park at Zweinaundorf, a suburb east of Leipzig. A letter to his mother talks of going there "all alone for entire days to work, write poetry, etc."[11]

It was in this park where he experienced his first mental disorder. The symptoms began just before his eighteenth birthday. "I was agitated, but I don't know by what. It seems to me that I'll go mad one day," says the diary. There follows the description of a severe anxiety attack—"My heart pounds sickeningly and I turn pale. . . . I didn't know whether I'm still alive; often I feel as if I were dead." Two days later (29 May 1828), he was in the park reading *Siebenkäs*, one of Jean Paul's most chilling novels, in which a man pretends to be dead and goes through a mock burial in order to terminate his unhappy marriage. "*Siebenkäs* is horrible, but I want to read it again a thousand times," wrote Schumann, hoping apparently to subdue his terror through compulsive reading. Suddenly something else captured his attention. "I sat among the trees altogether enraptured and heard a nightingale. I didn't cry—and I thrashed around with my hands and feet: because I felt so happy. But on the way back to Leipzig I seemed to be losing my mind: I did have my mind, yet I thought I had lost it. I had actually gone mad (*wahnsinnig*)." [12]

What Schumann described sounds like a dissociative disorder, a momentary disorganization caused by overwhelming stress. [13] He was probably experiencing violent fantasies stimulated by reading *Siebenkäs*. (In a long letter written the following week, he reported that Jean Paul "often brought me close to madness." [14]) The fantasy of being buried alive as a means of escaping an unhappy marriage must have evoked intense anxiety, as well as sadness and anger, probably related on an unconscious level to unacceptable death wishes against his father and coupled with guilt because his father did actually die (despite the boy's valiant efforts to entertain him, soothe him with music, and help in his publishing business). It is important to note that what Schumann described as his first episode of "madness" included not only a sensory component (his inability to focus attention on his reading) but also a motor element: he could no longer control his limbs but "thrashed around" as a result of the overpowering feelings.

His acute mental disorder was also related to some important changes then taking place in the relationship with Dr. Carus, the therapeutic father-figure who was stimulating both negative and positive transference feelings, as well as his friendship with Emil Flechsig, who had become his roommate.* Dr. Carus was just recovering from a lengthy illness, and his wife seemed more alluring than ever, "a holy image sleeping ever chastely in my soul," as Schumann's diary describes her. [16] The imagery in *Siebenkäs*—the termination of a marriage—may thus have applied to Schumann's unconscious wish to take Dr. Carus's place. In that case, pseudo-death might have

---

*They moved into an unusually spacious apartment on the Brühl, which must have caused other, less affluent students to be curious and perhaps envious. [15]

symbolized both the attainment of his wish, and punishment for having wished it.

Homicide and suicide are equated on some level, and Schumann, toying with the idea of being buried alive, may have been contemplating his own death as well as that of Siebenkäs. Several comments in his diary right after the "madness" episode point in this direction. "When I went to Carus, I trembled terribly and seemed to be going into a tomb, into a tomb. . . . Alas! I seem to be going under, nobody loves me, nobody hates me, nobody cries for me!" [17]

It was a distinct advantage for Schumann to translate these disturbing fantasies into words, for it allowed him to reflect on himself and to neutralize some of his intolerable emotions.

As for the friendship with his roommate, there seems to have been some trouble from the start. "Flechsig told me I'm a little pest," reports Schumann's diary. "Flechsig is nothing but a fussy little pedant, but that in the highest degree, and there's nothing I loathe more. Therefore I just can't love him any longer." [18]

As Schumann fell out of "love" with Flechsig he began to dote on a new friend, Wilhelm Götte, whom Schumann likened to "Napoleon in his 24th year." It must have been breathtaking for the lonely freshman to have a friend who seemed "so noble, so lean, so dignified, so superhuman." [19] They were inseparable, for at least eight weeks, frequenting the Leipzig taverns, engaging in endless bull-sessions, and communing over heady questions about life and death. Schumann had difficulty putting his love for Götte into words. "A nameless and endless something which cannot cross one's lips," he called it in a long letter, "a great, overwhelming desire [that] arises in those of a lyrical nature (I am one of them) when the gentle world of sounds breaks open, or at night, or during a thunderstorm, or when the sun rises." [20]

While with Götte, Schumann seems to have felt emotions that reminded him of elemental forces, of nature, and even of music. This time he experienced no mental dissociation. On the contrary, he appears to have enjoyed his euphoria so much that he often helped it along by drinking alcoholic beverages. Soon he discovered that a mild state of intoxication— "getting high" (*knill*), as he called it—would encourage fantasies to flow uninhibitedly, which was a great boon for someone who wanted to do creative writing (or so he thought). Schumann, just eighteen, wrote a long essay (which was never finished or published) trying to describe his feelings for

Götte. It seems to be a link in Schumann's search for a creative synthesis. In addition, his fanciful and sometimes enigmatic phrases foreshadow a literary style that he would one day, as a music critic, make famous. The opening is translated here as faithfully as possible to preserve Schumann's style.

On Geniality, Getting High, Originality,
and Other Items
"Fantaisie Scherzando"

by Robert Schumann
1828/Dedicated to his friend Götte

Motto:
It's a remarkable thing that most people would like to be genial and don't even know what it really is—it sounds so nice!

Second Motto à la Jean Paul:
Youths! Drink as much champagne as you want; but above all be genial and remain so.

(June 1828)

Geniality, getting high, and originality are very closely related concepts, generally speaking, at least all three are volcanoes, spewing lava, from which one or the other boldly goes forward. Geniality likes to erect its temples in wine cellars, and getting high is like a handyman, or finally even the left hand itself. Originality is the foot. Besides, a youth wants to understand geniality differently than a man; genial men even hate genial youths for the most part, because both look at each other through reducing lenses. The logical, calcified blockhead would very much like to be genial, but he wheezes away like a fox with sour grapes. One usually thinks of genial youths as having beautiful faces, often sadly pale or glowing with Italian heat. In other words, beauty may be (in mimicry of the sisters Grace and Charity) a most essential covering that entices us to geniality. Available for everything but fit for nothing—now like butterflies, flimsy, flitting, fluttering, flying, and fondling—now like elephants, sullen, slow, trampling and crushing—now soft and gentle like virgins—now strong and wild like a lion woken from its slumber. Female delicacy and frailty, male brutality and destructiveness—like a chameleon that assumes every color and shading—.[21]

"Geniality," as used by the German romantics, denotes a blend of creative genius and amiability. To that definition Schumann added other desirable traits, such as strength, warmth, attractiveness, and what he called "sentimentality." His model for geniality clearly was Götte.

Schumann tried to be angry in this essay, with curious results. For example, he mentioned "genial youths [who] do so damned little . . . they get up on their hobbyhorse and ride through mud and slime to the source of inspiration." Especially scathing is his criticism of the college fraternities, and their patriotism: they were "a murky, muddy, stagnant pond. . . . Being a man, and humane, is much more than being a German and Germanic."[22]

While Schumann's essay extols the virtue of "getting high"—parts of it were obviously written under the influence of alcohol—he wanted to distinguish this pleasant, productive state from true intoxication:

> I'm talking about getting high [*Knillität*], gentlemen, certainly not about drunkenness [*Besoffenheit*]. As much as the one is elevating, the other is degrading. That's why an intoxicated student can be distinguished from a drunken peasant. Some say that all people are mildly intoxicated and that sobriety is the lowest degree of this. That's almost like saying all men are naturally rich and that poverty is the lowest degree of wealth. Gentlemen, that sounds funny but it ain't true. *Love* is the real sensorium of chaste sobriety, and we only *will be* intoxicated.

These comments refer to experiences reported in the diary, for example: "When I'm drunk or I vomit, then on other days my imagination was more suspended and elevated. I can't do a thing while I'm drunk, only afterward."[23] Schumann got "high" not only from alcohol but also from nicotine and caffeine. "Heavy cigars turn me high and poetic; the more my body runs down, the more my mind gets excited. . . . Black coffee also makes me drunk, but not as black."[24]

Later in the essay, Schumann also tried to articulate his conflicts about intimacy with women. He was still yearning for his distant beloved, the idealized mother-sister-figure Agnes Carus, but at the same time he was looking around at other attractive figures. Some of them evidently were "ordinary" girls (perhaps prostitutes).

> The first thing about genial girls that strikes us is their free, lovable carelessness [*Nachlässigkeit*]. This marks a happy medium between complete sensuousness and virginal modesty and chastity; it hides the most beautiful shapes so as to make them even more revealing. Everywhere is charm, which the soulful Graces often seem to dispute, with heavenly strokes. Youthful lightness, the swinging gait, a flowing gown, a careless-comely hairdo, feathery locks—all this flows together in the charming image of a sprightly, human Grace. Now her lips sound forth, the eyes smile roguishly, dimples form playfully in her cheeks, merrily she pulls her captivated hearts behind her—but there is only one that she loves passionately (and this distinguishes her from ordinary girls who usually can love two at a time) and with all the fire and all the flames of their young soaring hearts they give themselves totally to that one.

So far there has been no mention of sexual intercourse in Schumann's writings. Perhaps he was still a virgin. The "genial" woman was his ideal, but he nevertheless engaged in much teasing and probably exciting flirtation with available women. For example, his diary mentions visiting the Hotel de Pologne, one of Leipzig's better-known dens of iniquity: "The whores—embraces—voluptuous pleasure—my innocence rescued by a most clever move."[25]

Schumann was plagued by sleep disturbances. We have seen evidence of this symptom in childhood, as he anxiously awaited the return of his mother. The problem became more serious in Leipzig, where, according to his diary, he not only had trouble falling asleep but often deliberately kept himself awake, by late-night reading, writing, or "fantasizing." Sometimes he was up at four or five in the morning, writing letters or going on walks. Many of these activities seemed designed to combat the passivity needed for falling asleep. When Schumann did allow his mind to drift, he would see and experience a profusion of images and emotions, which taxed his ability to keep his mind organized. Floating in and out of consciousness, he would have vivid, phantasmagorical dreams about "beloved people as distorted, elongated faces and in ghostly, pale outlines."[26] He also had "waking dreams" of an almost hallucinatory intensity. For example, he reported in his diary that one night Therese Schumann, his favorite sister-in-law, "stood before me and softly sang 'sweet home.'" He had just seen her while visiting Zwickau, and now, back in his lonely isolation at college, he yearned to see her again. "In the evening as I was falling asleep, every minute of the day and of the past drifted by darkly once more, and like a soft echo of the soul I heard how the sounds melted and faded away, and how the last one quivered 'sweet home' just feebly. Then I fell blissfully asleep."[27]

He also had nightmares in which he observed himself dreaming—"strange dream within the dream."[28] In a twilight state, sometimes while drinking or smoking, he would hear musical hallucinations.* For example, one diary entry reports "No falling asleep—and a cigar in bed around 12 o'clock—continuous music throughout the night and loathsome sleep."[31]

The stimulation of books Schumann was reading may also have contributed to his sleep disturbance. Diary entries from the early months of 1829

---

* After the death of Franz Schubert, which he learned about in December 1828, Schumann reported an "exalted night and the Schubert Trio continuously in my ears—frightful dreams.[29] Flechsig said that he "went into such an excitement over the first news of Schubert's death that I heard him sobbing the entire night."[30]

give examples: "J. Paul's *Gianozzo* and his life and death—bad sleep"; "Bed-lecture: *Manfred* by Byron—terrible night"; "*Childe Harold* in bed—terrible night with death dreams."[32] Reading had to be done in the dim and flickering light of candles or oil lamps, which may have spurred disturbing fantasies. Many creative people of the early nineteenth century were interested in moods evoked by darkness. The painter Caspar David Friedrich, for example, gave shape to the dark melancholy of the night in scenes of ghostly forests and crumbling ruins, and it has even been said that electric lights, with their steady brightness, brought the romantic era to an end.[33] Schumann, being nearsighted, was probably frightened by some of the fluttering, indistinct outlines he perceived late at night.

Hoping to gain understanding and better control over his nocturnal symptoms, he consulted several medical textbooks, such as *Lenhossek on the Emotions*, a contemporary psychiatric text,[34] as well as some of the older professional literature, for example, *Philosophical Remarks About Human Suffering*, by Karl H. Heydenreich, published in 1797–1799. Whether these books reassured Schumann or alarmed him further is open to conjecture.

It seems fairly clear, however, that sexual arousal—perhaps masturbation—contributed to his insomnia and dreams. For example, his diary contains such entries as "Only one kiss from her [Frau Carus] and I would be happy to die. . . . She at the window—terrible sweaty night. . . . Excited night and beautiful, magnificent dreams of her, of her."[35] Medical textbooks of that time almost universally denounced so-called self-abuse as a potential cause of madness, a view that would have added to any conflict Schumann might have had about masturbating.

Moralistic concerns also found expression in some of the novels Schumann was trying to write. In a letter to Götte, he complained of "the danger that I might yet smear another few pages full of these endlessly stimulating things."[36] One unfinished story is about Gustav,

> a painter, poet, and actually a composer, who . . . must learn to hate and to love. He grows up in isolation among graves. Flowers and his harmonica are the only things that keep him occupied. The only person he knows is his sister, Selene, who is a feminine Gustav [a self-portrait à la Jean Paul?]. . . . Gustav does not believe in God—he is gloomy and shut up within himself, but well-rounded and made more devout by his femininity.[37]

The tale becomes morbidly erotic. (What Schumann wrote about Selene may have been a fantasy about his sister's madness.)

> She rushed through the cemetery, bare-breasted and with a long white night-gown carelessly dangling from her body, to read an inscription on the grave-stone. "Here lies a broken heart." Smiling, she sat down on the grave. Now a

skeleton . . . sat next to her and threw its arm around her. "You want a kiss," she said shyly. The skeleton laughed, gave her an icy kiss, and left. "I must have sinned," she cried out, and went into the church, where the skeleton was sitting at the organ, playing a waltz.[38]

Sometimes Schumann's writing suggests that he may have wanted to be both male and female, a desire that the psychoanalyst Lawrence Kubie thought was fundamental to much of human creativity.[39] For example, a poem written at the end of 1828, when Schumann was eighteen years old, has the flavor of a bisexual fantasy:

Und wie den Jüngling wild der Jüngling liebt,	*And how wildly one youth loves the other youth,*
Und wie er ihn umarmt, und wie er mit ihm weint,	*And how he embraces him, and how they weep together,*
So bist Du jetzt; einst warst du mir Geliebte,	*That's how you are right now; once you were my feminine beloved,*
Jetzt bist Du mir Geliebter.	*Now you are my masculine beloved.*
Und aus den Blüthen deiner Liebe	*And from the blossoms of your love*
Wand sich die Freundschaft sanft hervor.[40]	*Arises friendship, softly.*

Several entries in Schumann's diary mention homosexuality more explicitly (it was not a topic one could be very open about; male homosexuality was illegal and was punishable in many countries). For example, after a trip to a tavern in Leipzig with his friend Johann Renz in March 1829, he noted "pederasty" in his diary. After returning to the tavern the next day, he recorded a "voluptuous night with Greek dreams."[41]

Shortly after the pederasty episode, Schumann had recurring "bad dreams about broken cups."[42] Flechsig—with whom he was not getting along at all (he called him a "drunk son-of-a-bitch good-for-nothing . . . an unmusical, mindless ass . . . a dead mummy"[43])—wrote an account of how the dream came true:

Schumann had been given a beautiful cup by Therese, his sister-in-law. He drank from it daily. One morning he told me that he dreamed I had broken the cup, and he warned me to be careful. The dream repeated itself. I was very careful not to touch this cup, and yet I did manage to break it, in an almost unbelievable way. While hastily reaching for another object—I hadn't grasped it firmly—the cup hurtled through the open door with a violent thrust of my hand. It flew into the kitchen, and fell directly into the cupboard. Nothing else was damaged, only this particular cup had broken into two pieces.[44]

Dreams can be interpreted in many different ways. This one deals directly with an actual event in Schumann's life, and the fact that it recurred and troubled his sleep for nearly two weeks invites further analysis.* The cup was a gift from his sister-in-law, and his unrelieved terror that it might be broken could relate to separation anxiety experienced as a result of the recent move away from his home and family. (Cups are often interpreted as unconscious symbols of gratification, as well as danger. Many myths and fairy tales tell of cups containing poisons or magic potions.) In addition, his fear of Flechsig's clumsiness—Schumann had recently observed him coming home late at night, intoxicated, and breaking the bed[45]—suggests castration anxiety. The "pederasty" Schumann had just witnessed, pondered, or perhaps even participated in undoubtedly increased his fear of sexual behavior and possible punishment. On an even deeper level, Schumann's nightmare about broken cups also hints at his fear of mental disintegration and suicide.

Leipzig's rich cultural environment served as a stabilizing factor in young Schumann's distraught life at the university. Within walking distance was the Gewandhaus, formerly a cloth merchants' hall, now used for concerts by an orchestra founded in 1781. At the State Theater he could hear operas, directed by the popular composer Heinrich Marschner, whom he came to know personally. Liturgical music was performed in the two churches, Thomas and Nicholas, where Johann Sebastian Bach had once been choir director. And thanks to the Carus family, Schumann was invited to private soirées, where he could meet and hear visiting or local performers. Thus he was able to make contact with people whom he could admire and who had similar interests, and through them he began to take more pride in his own lyrical talents.

Just before leaving Zwickau, he had completed two songs for Agnes Carus, one based on a text of his own ("Light as Fluttering Sylphs"), the other on a poem of Ernst Schultze ("Transformation").[46] In Leipzig he set to music several poems by Justinus Kerner (1786–1862), a medical doctor much involved with the supernatural who had just published a book about

---

*It might be worth emphasizing at this point that there is a clear distinction between psychoanalysis and psychobiography. Both lines of investigation rely on the study of dreams, fantasies, symptoms, and other forms of behavior, including creativity, which have unconscious determinants. But psychoanalysis can be done only in privacy, with a living subject who supplies hunches, associations, confirmations, or denials in the interpretative dialogue with the analyst. Psychobiography is a totally different undertaking, done in a public forum and usually focused on subjects who are dead. For further discussion of this distinction, see Runyan (1982), pp. 192–222.

his own parapsychological studies. These were Schumann's first truly original compositions,[47] and he felt sufficiently pleased with them to send copies to Gottlob Wiedebein, a well-known musician in Braunschweig. Wiedebein replied promptly. "Your songs have many defects, a great many, and I would like to call them the sins of youth." He urged the young composer to discipline himself and above all, to look for "truth in melody, in harmony, and in expression—in short, poetic truth," advice that Schumann promised Wiedebein he would take. "The knife of the intellect will ruthlessly scrape away everything that unruly fantasy tries to smuggle in," he wrote.[48]

To his mother, however, Schumann wrote differently. He knew that, were he to declare openly his interests in studying music, she would be disappointed and probably stop sending him money. He felt it necessary to reply to what he called his mother's "dreary conclusions about [her] mental and physical condition" by promising to be a good boy, never behave "like a bully," attend college "regularly like a machine," and treasure as "a talisman against every sin" a ring she had sent him.[49] Their interdependence precluded defiance. While Schumann did admit that he was playing the piano a great deal, he breathed not a word to his mother about the charismatic piano teacher, Friedrich Wieck, to whom, like a moth nearing a flame, he was becoming irresistibly and fatally drawn.

Wieck, then forty-two years old, had grown up in a tiny village (Pretsch, near Torgau) under conditions of extreme poverty. As far as is known, he was an entirely self-taught musician (he had a degree in theology), who throughout his career depended on members of his immediate family for fame and success. His wife, Marianne Tromlitz, whom he married in 1816, performed both as a singer and a pianist and also helped her husband with his teaching.[50]

When Schumann arrived in Leipzig, Wieck was promoting what he claimed was an original and foolproof method of keyboard instruction and using his children to demonstrate its efficacy. Wieck hoped to fashion his daughter Clara, born in 1819, into the world's greatest living pianist. In fact, he had conceived the idea even before she was born.

Wieck was a difficult man. He suspected that his wife was having an affair with his friend, the pianist Adolf Bargiel, and his accusations led to divorce. ("You yourself are to blame for your wife's erratic course," Marianne's father wrote to Wieck at the time. "Spend more time with her and avoid every opportunity which could bring her together with Bargiel."[51]) It is not known whether she was indeed having an affair, but she did later marry Bargiel. In 1824, when Clara was only five years old, Wieck demanded and won sole legal custody of his children.

Clara's childhood was not a happy one. Her diary (often written or dictated by Wieck himself) states that "since both my father and my mother gave many lessons, and the latter played one to two hours a day, I was left mostly to the care of a maid."[52] Perhaps because of that, Clara was very slow in learning to speak; she did not begin using words until she was four, a symptom perhaps of emotional neglect. Sadly, her diary notes that she did not enjoy speaking—this probably made the taciturn Schumann attractive to her—and that her parents complained—wrongly—that she was hard of hearing.

We can imagine the tongue-tied but very pretty Clara's first encounter with handsome, homesick Robert Schumann. A mutual acquaintance, violinist Johann Täglichsbeck, described him as "a powerfully built but slender young man, with a blooming, not exactly red-cheeked but colorful face, very well framed by his rather long, brunette hair, combed in a heavy curl from one ear to the temple. His eyes were deep set, dark, and glowing with passionate enthusiasm. His whole appearance was thoroughly noble, his bearing elegant, and, above all [he exhibited] a great kindheartedness."[53]

His relationship with Wieck was problematic from the beginning. Schumann's attendance at lessons seems to have been erratic. He refused to practice finger exercises like a beginner, and his performance at the piano struck Wieck as uneven and undisciplined. Flechsig said that Wieck nicknamed Schumann "the hot-head" (*Tollkopf*).[54] Part of this behavior may have been a reaction to the proximity of Clara Wieck. She was only a child, yet Wieck favored her over all the other students. Schumann seems to have been simultaneously repelled and attracted. His first memory of Clara went back to the summer of 1828, and in recalling it a decade later he said nothing about her musical talent. ("You were painting letters, trying to write while I studied the A minor Concerto [by Hummel], and you kept turning to look at me.")[55]

In his diary Schumann emphasized that he was attracted at this time by another pupil of Wieck, Emilie Reichold. Statements such as "she unfolds much grace at the piano," and "passionate movements while playing the piano inflame the listener" suggest that a womanly figure at the keyboard could stir him erotically.[56] With Emilie he also went to parties, danced, made "pleasant conversation and enamoured eyes," and played piano duets, including the earliest piano pieces known to have been composed by Schumann, his *Polonaises for Four Hands*. But his main interest obviously was in Wieck, not only as a teacher but also as a source of contact with other musicians. Through Wieck he also met the opera director Heinrich Marschner. Schumann made many observations in his diary about this composer's unpleasant personality, his songs, and the evenings they spent together.[57] Marschner's successful opera *The Vampire*, based on a drama by Lord

Byron, was then being produced in Leipzig. One of Schumann's reasons for attaching himself so closely to this composer, and for immersing himself so deeply in Byron's poetry, was that he too wanted to write an opera one day.

Indeed, in the privacy of his rooms with Flechsig, Schumann, in what his roommate called "a foolish posture," was trying to compose. "He always puffed on cigars, and the smoke irritated his eyes," Flechsig recalled. "Therefore he forced his mouth forward and pushed his cigar up as high as possible. He would squint his eyes, and make peculiar grimaces. The cigar also bothered him because he liked to whistle the melodies of the songs, or rather hum them through his lips, and whistling with cigar in mouth was just about impossible."[58]

In addition to the Kerner songs and the polonaises for Emilie Reichold, that year (1828–29) he wrote a set of variations on a theme by Prince Louis Ferdinand of Prussia. These were musical experiments, improvised at the keyboard and written down in trial-and-error fashion. Schumann's earliest compositions are often mere fragments and, like his prose works, incomplete. Later he would reuse some of these ideas for more successful compositions. At the moment he had a great deal of enthusiasm, very little training, and a growing tendency to take charge of his emotions. These often presented themselves to his conscious awareness in the form of inner voices, auditory representations of feelings that were partly erotic. Thus, for example, he referred to tones as "veiled Venus shapes," and he observed that "music does not still the conflict of emotions but excites it, leaving something confusing and unmentionable behind."[59]

Schumann's most ambitious early composition by far was a quartet for piano and strings, which has only recently been reconstructed and published. A richly melodious work, it is full of daring harmonic progressions, and already punctuated by the inexorable dotted rhythms that were to become his trademark. His use of form elements, simple chords, scales, and arpeggios was still rather crude, especially in the first movement. The wildly rolicking, syncopated second movement seems mislabeled as a Menuetto. His diary records how he sweated over this work and how passionately he rehearsed it. A year later, in January 1830, Schumann was ready to "recobble the quartet into a symphony."[60] For the time being, however, it served a social function. He invited cellist Christian Glock (a medical student and later his doctor), the violinist Täglichsbeck, and a viola-playing theology student, Christoph Sorgel, to join him in playing the quartet for his friends. They began to play together every week, performing not only Schumann's work but also difficult trios by Beethoven, Schubert, and other established musical figures. These animated evenings were sometimes attended by Dr. Carus and Friedrich Wieck, one reason perhaps for the stage fright the young composer often had. Lively discussion followed the chamber music, but

Schumann preferred to listen, and his uncommunicativeness in speech puzzled many of his acquaintances. "He was not sufficiently clear and open to disclose himself, or to make himself understood," reported a fellow student.[61]

Thus it appears that Schumann depended on music more than conversation to reconstitute a social network he had lost when he left home. His father was replaced by a series of mentors—Dr. Carus, Herr Wieck, and Kapellmeister Wiedebein—who provided direction and nourished his musical talents. As with his brothers, with his chamber music partners he could enjoy exhibitionistic play. But because Schumann had no reliable womanly figure in his life as yet, his mother remained the main object of his yearning for acceptance, and the fact that she did not fundamentally approve of his desire for an identity as a musician was a source of recurring distress for him.

IV.
Metamorphosis, 1829–1830

Not long into his university career in Leipzig, Schumann became restless and discontented. "I'm often completely martyred by this petty life with its wretched people," he wrote to his mother. He complained of "such sadness that when my heart fills up it wants to overflow and to cry and to smile and cry some more."[1] These were symptoms of recurring depression, an emotional disturbance that would interfere with his enjoyment of life for years to come. In correspondence with his friend Gisbert Rosen he disclosed many of his depressive fantasies, using words that he sometimes borrowed from Jean Paul.

> Oh, what would a world without people be?—an endless cemetery—a dreamless sleep of death—nature without spring or flowers—a dead, uninhabited peep-show.[2]

Hoping that a change of environment might reduce his depression, Schumann decided to move to Heidelberg, where Rosen was studying law, and to "swarm around" with his friend in what he fantasized would be a "blooming paradise."[3] Schumann also had a new authority-figure in mind, Anton Justus Thibaut, an eminent jurist who was professor of law in Heidelberg. He reasoned, correctly, that his mother would approve of such a move. Schumann wrote her that this would allow him to pass the difficult Saxon bar examination the next year. What he did not disclose to her was his much greater interest in Thibaut as a musician. The professor had recently published a book titled *About Purity in the Art of Music*.[4] Thibaut was a well-known scholar of early church music, especially that of the Netherlands and of Palestrina. He had also founded a choral society, which Goethe, Spohr, and Weber had joined when they were students in Heidelberg.

Eight months would elapse before Schumann could implement this plan to move, however, and he had some misgivings. "It's recently become terribly difficult to leave Leipzig," he wrote Rosen. "A beautiful, happy, devoted feminine soul has ensnared mine; it has cost me a battle, but now all that is over and I stand here, firmly, with suppressed tears, looking hopefully and courageously into my Heidelberg blossoms and Mayflowers. The first thing I will look for in Heidelberg is—a beloved."[5] Whose "feminine soul" this was is impossible to determine. But we do know that his mother tried to delay his departure because of the "life-threatening" illness, tuberculosis, of his brother Julius. "My mother made me swear not to leave her in case he might die; otherwise she would be all alone, etc., etc."[6] This illness would have a profound effect on him over the next few years—but for the moment his brother was not the source of anxiety.

That same week he reported on a "very brilliant concert in Zwickau, attended by 800–1000 people; naturally I also let them hear my fingers! I can't get away from the joyous festivities."[7] At the Zwickau concert he performed a popular showpiece, Moscheles' *Alexander Variations*, and another virtuoso work, the first movement of Hummel's A minor Piano Concerto. Here perhaps was a more fundamental reason for his reluctance to leave Leipzig. He may have realized that future success as a musician would be difficult unless he had more—and more consistent—training. After his last music lesson with Wieck (on 9 April 1829), Schumann seems to have been so disoriented that for six days he misdated the entries in his diary back to February.[8] But finally, on 11 May 1829, he left Leipzig for Heidelberg.

After a ten-day trip—during which he did some drinking, sightseeing, and ogling of young women with a young poet, Willibald Alexis, he had met on the way—Schumann arrived in Heidelberg, the citadel of German romanticism and site of one of Europe's oldest universities. He soon met Gisbert Rosen (who received him "with open arms") and took his first lesson with Thibaut.[9] Heidelberg days were to prove busy, and full of much drunkenness. Schumann made a witty and prophetic observation. "My lodgings," he wrote his mother, "face the insane asylum on the right and the Catholic church on the left, so that I'm really in doubt whether one is supposed to go crazy or become Catholic."[10]

His long letters to his mother embroider the daily events of his life with colorful and often amusing detail. But biographers who rely on these documents without carefully checking the diaries may easily conclude, as does Wörner, for example, that Schumann's stay in Heidelberg was "nearly devoid of the self-destructive self-tortures" that characterized his later years.[11] "I am cheerful, yes sometimes really happy," he wrote to his mother several months after his arrival. "I am diligent and orderly. The law, with Thibaut and Mittermayer, tastes excellent, and now for the first time I feel the true dignity of jurisprudence." He claimed that his fellow students were "very quiet and refined . . . the most prominent and esteemed persons in and around Heidelberg." In addition, "he who studies here [meaning himself] is greatly diverted by his great, lyrical nature from sensual and spiritual indulgence in wine-drinking. That is why the local students are ten times more sober than those in Leipzig."[12]

All this was blatant deception: Schumann's diary shows that hardly a day went by without some bingeing, and that in Heidelberg he was regularly afflicted with "dull hangovers." The evidence certainly indicates that he often relied on alcohol to alleviate anxiety and depression. But usually his drinking had the opposite effect: after a binge, Schumann often felt more restless and depressed than before. For example, at the end of June 1829, he wrote, "Saturday, the 27th, a dog's day—very dissatisfied with myself—with everything else too . . . I'm pretty high on beer. . . . Sunday, the 28th, a dog's Sunday— no cigars, piano out of tune, weather out of tune, no money, no friends, no fun."[13]

These fragments, often penned while Schumann was inebriated, suggest much loneliness, yearning for intimacy, and a repetition of the frustrations that, in Leipzig, had troubled his relationship with Flechsig. This time there was "great tension" between him and Rosen. Before moving to Heidelberg, Schumann had written him that "the more physically separated we are, the closer and more related we become spiritually, and that's how it should and must be between us."[14] Now their proximity may have stimulated an excitement that Schumann found nearly intolerable.

During a four-day vacation with Rosen and two other students, Schumann reported "cruising around in Karlsruhe . . . I very high. . . . We bathe ourselves in baths at Baden-Baden. . . . Losses [at the gambling Casino], etc." On returning to Heidelberg he did more imbibing: (7 July

1829) "Much drinking in the museum"; (9 July) "Drank much beer—wandering around at night and the fear of myself"; (17 July) "Champagne—enormous scandal . . . I unconscious"; (18 July) "Endless hangover and shit."[15] "Madness in my breast," he wrote, during a week of nearly uninterrupted bingeing after his nineteenth birthday.[16] Two evenings in a row he fell asleep with a burning cigar in his hand, setting his bed on fire. Schumann seems to have been almost delirious at times.

These symptoms are ominous, suggesting that the change of environment had not helped his depression. In Heidelberg Schumann no longer had the steadying influence of Dr. Carus or the musical guidance of Wieck. Rosen did not offer the companionship and friendliness that he had expected. Thus he drank to excess, in a misguided effort at self-medication. Some people, of course, can quaff large amounts without any immediate side-effects; they develop a tolerance and may become addicted, like true alcoholics. Schumann's drinking was of a different pattern, however. He easily became physically ill and mentally confused after drinking too much. It was precisely this behavior that Wieck later made the focus of accusations against him.

Students in Heidelberg were given two months off late in the summer so that they might enrich their education through travel. Italy was a favorite destination for these grand tours. Having no funds of his own, Schumann needed an advance from his inheritance. On 3 August 1829 he sent a melodious and charmingly seductive letter to his mother, hoping to cajole her into approving his plans for such a trip. "I'm sure you will be pleased to give me a friendly hand again," he wrote, "and say, 'Good Robert, a young man like you must travel and trim and round off his bodily wings a bit so that he can soar better with his mental ones, even if it costs money.'" Schumann played blatantly on his mother's heartstrings: "Italy, Italy, has been humming in my heart since childhood, when you told me, 'You will see it, Robert!'"[17]

His mother could not resist these blandishments and gave her permission. But Rosen, whom Schumann had begged to accompany him, refused to go. Thus on 20 August 1829, he set forth alone on one of the few journeys he would ever take beyond the borders of Germany. Along the way he tried to make contact with friends or strangers. In Basel he visited coffeehouses, enjoyed "the merry life in the baths" with an acquaintance, and on his way to Zürich, wined, dined, and danced with a widow who had "tantalizing fiery looks." But when he made sexual advances, the woman "suddenly fled as if her husband were still alive."[18]

Schumann's travel diary indicates that he was generally elated and full of energy. Of a walking tour to Zug, for example, he wrote: "Excited, in a cheerful mood . . . laughing as I ascended the Albis . . . charming walk through meadow-flowers and leafy woods . . . skipping down the mountain like a gazelle . . . excited by wine." [19] He seemed intent on capturing every nuance of emotion and every fleeting sensation. He hastily noted each fragment of experience, then incorporated his observations into letters that became longer as his distance from home increased.

There is a driven, almost frenetic quality to Schumann's incessant observing, storing up, and transforming of daily events. "I do not take things objectively, the way things really are," he told his mother, "but rather the way I perceive them subjectively, within myself, and thus can live with greater ease and freedom." Also, there seems to have been a therapeutic dimension to his symbolic activity, which he saw as genuinely creative: "The more confining the world is from the outside, the larger it grows from within, through one's fantasies. Thus I've been painting all the dark Alps more beautiful, and higher, perhaps." [20]

Schumann's letters from Switzerland show how much he still yearned for his mother. In fact, he treated her like an imaginary companion. "Travel with me now across the dozen laughing lakes, and climb with me to the top of the mountains," he wrote. "Sit next to me now, and let me squeeze your hand. . . . Take a map so that somehow you could come along." [21] His letters to other members of his family indicate that he missed them as well. For instance, he wrote the following to his brother Eduard's wife:

> Just now I saw a most beautiful Italian girl who reminded me of you, my dear Therese. If I could only paint everything for you, the dark blue Italian sky, the gushing, bubbling green of the earth, the apricots, lemons, hemp and tobacco . . . and finally the big, beautiful fiery-seductive eyes of the Italian girls, almost like yours. [22]

Schumann's unmistakable preference for music becomes increasingly apparent, for even while traveling he eschewed interpersonal relationships to accommodate this cherished activity. Wherever he found a piano he "rushed for it" to practice and improvise, sometimes with hotel guests listening and applauding. At the Hotel Reichmann (in Milan), "a beautiful Englishwoman seemed to fall less in love with me than with my piano playing." He went to Bellini's early opera *Bianca e Fernando* not once but twice, with different friends, and found the ballet "enchanting." Leonardo da Vinci's visual masterpiece *The Last Supper* left him feeling, by contrast, "very inartistically cold." [23]

Schumann mentioned some of his adventures only in his diaries and not—understandably—in his letters; for example: "Voluptuous scandal during the night with the naked tour guide and the naked waitress"; "The inaccessible barmaid and my decision—unsatisfied—forced gaiety"; "The homosexual who thrust himself on me, and my sudden departure"; "Coffeehouse and the girl constantly looking around, certainly a whore"; "Real fear of ladies."[24]

These and many similar observations suggest that while he may still have been sexually inhibited, Schumann was now experimenting with different kinds of behavior. Perhaps the foreign environment, the distance from home, and the fact that he was traveling alone contributed to his greater sense of freedom. That he had one and possibly several homosexual encounters seems clear, but whether he actually slept with prostitutes is not. As will be discussed later, some biographers have questioned whether Schumann might have had syphilis. If he in fact did, it would not be too far-fetched to assume that he contracted the disease during this vacation.

By the time he reached Venice, Schumann was sick, but nothing in his diary suggests that it was a venereal disease. He was short of money, despondent, drinking too much, having anxiety attacks, and probably coming down with dysentery. His diary entries report the details:

[23 September] Anxiety for days about how to go on—terrible dizziness and nausea following the trip—rum—nothing helps—terrible state—vomiting—vomiting—the most horrible night—coffee—the round, fat, rank stewardess—noise in the alleys—screaming—fiddling—bitten by fleas—mosquitoes—tossing around in bed—cursing—nothing—no sleep.

[24 September] Terrible diarrhea and stomach ache . . . loss of appetite . . . solitary, joyless mourning . . . resting on the grass and sorrowful glances into the sea and the unending distance . . . fears about not making ends meet . . . nobody as empty of joy as I am—the funeral barge . . . intolerable pain.[25]

The combination of physical and mental disease made him feel "like dead," and that brought back tormenting memories of his father's death, made explicit on 9 October, when he heard a young man speak about a similar bereavement. "The specter of dead people seems to be pursuing me," wrote Schumann.[26] Medical attention was in order, but Schumann's lifelong pattern of hide-and-seek with doctors already manifested itself in Italy, where he avoided treatment as long as possible, then finally "out of fear" consulted someone.[27]

He recovered quickly, but the improvement did not last long. In Cremona he had another episode of "frightful vomiting," apparently associated with increasing financial distress. Schumann considered selling his watch. From Mantua he wrote a friend about his "indescribable depression." When he returned to Milan he was able to borrow some money, and an inspiring performance of Rossini's *La Gazza Ladra* also seems to have elevated his spirits considerably. Yet three and a half weeks remained of his vacation, and the diary's lighthearted descriptions of his daily escapades are punctuated by mention of disturbing symptoms, such as "loathsome dreams," "deathly fear," and "nosebleeding during the night."[28]

As will become increasingly apparent, Schumann was not a good traveler. Many of his reactions during this trip foreshadowed behavior he would exhibit while accompanying his wife on concert tours. Environmental stressors undoubtedly played an important role, for example, the fleas and mosquitoes that he mentioned in Italy, oysters he had been eating, noise, and rum. But always there was homesickness, his lonely terror of bad memories, and the generalized anxiety that expressed itself as "dizziness and nausea." It was thus with great relief and joy that Schumann found himself in mid-October, "back on German soil" seeing "German faces" again.[29] He stopped briefly in Augsburg, where Clara Kurrer's family welcomed him, replenished his purse, and helped him return to Heidelberg.

In a letter written shortly after his return, Schumann mentioned how good it felt to be out of his "old, formal apartment and snuggled into a warm little poet's den that bears an uncanny resemblance to my old green one in Zwickau."[30] The same letter discloses a new twist in his relationship with Gisbert Rosen. An old friend (and relative by marriage), Carl Semmel, had come to Heidelberg and managed to "splinter" Schumann's "faith" in Rosen. "A pitiful, childish youthful pride has come between us," he told his mother, "which one often finds among youths who love each other so warmly. I love Semmel differently than Rosen. With the first my love has been more masculine, firm, well-behaved; with Rosen it is more talkative, girlish, full of feeling."[31]

Such frankness between Schumann and his mother in regard to his love for men may seem surprising, but one must understand it in the context of their relationship. He regularly told her many details about the way he lived, and on several occasions he even invited her to visit his rooms. (She never did.) Perhaps he meant to reassure her that he was not seriously involved with any other woman. To love men (in the Platonic sense) was also part of the romantic ideal of "geniality," and Schumann always looked for male friends who would be able to reciprocate, as we see, for example, in letters he received from Gisbert Rosen.[32] Finally, it seems possible that by telling his mother so much about his love for men he was being provocative, in an unconscious expression of hostility he may have harbored toward her.

Now that the college semester had begun, Schumann was forced once again to contend with the realities of his education. Mournfully but not altogether candidly, he wrote home about music, specifically about his piano playing. "O Mother!" says the letter, "these things are almost finished for me, and I play rarely and very badly. The torch of music's beautiful genius is being gently extinguished, and my entire musical ambition seems like a magnificent dream that once existed but now can only be dimly remembered." Since he needed his mother's emotional and financial support, however, Schumann pretended to be seriously committed to his bread-and-butter studies—"The law continues to chill and disfigure me, so that no flowers of fantasy will grow this spring."[33]

Whatever motivation Schumann may have had for a university education seems by now to have completely disappeared. According to Theodor Töpken, a law student and amateur pianist with whom Schumann often played duets, "The whole time that he lived in Heidelberg, piano playing was Schumann's main occupation. It really constituted his entire course of studies. One often saw him already at the instrument in the earliest hours of the morning." Especially impressive was Schumann's ability to improvise. "Ideas would pour out of him with an inexhaustible abundance," wrote Töpken. "From only a single thought, which he allowed to take shape in every possible way, there welled up and gushed forth everything, as if all by itself."[34]

The self-critical pianist, however, was "not satisfied with his technical progress," and Heidelberg, with its predominantly academic environment, was hardly a place for him to improve. The sympathetic Töpken said that Schumann "would have liked to reach this goal more quickly than was naturally possible. We thought about ways and means to shorten the process."[35] That would explain the ingratiating letter Schumann wrote to Friedrich Wieck (five days before the one telling his mother of his supposed resignation from music): "Alas! Why did I ever leave your Leipzig, where the whole Olympus of musical art was so magnificently unlocked for me, and where you were like a priest, gently but patiently removing the veil from this blinking apprentice's eyes!" Perhaps to flatter Wieck, he expressed dissatisfaction with Professor Thibaut: "It pains me greatly to observe that this lovely, inspiring and integrative [law professor] has so one-sided and truly pedantic an approach to music." Schumann's fantasy was "suddenly in a flash to stand at your [Wieck's] street corner, music under my arm, to come for a piano lesson."[36]

In his frothy style, Schumann discussed a Rossini opera, a Schubert rondo, and a variety of performers he had recently heard. About his own playing, he told Wieck:

> I believe that I've not regressed nor advanced very much, which honestly amounts to a standstill. Yet I feel that my touch has become much richer when I play

loudly, and it is much more liberated and energetic when I play softly. I am very well and modestly aware of my superiority over all Heidelberg pianists— you have no idea of their slovenly and rough performance, and the poking, whimpering and rumbling of their playing.

At the end of the letter Schumann made an elaborate request, asking Wieck to send him

> all of Schubert's waltzes (I think it's ten to twelve folders), Moscheles' G minor Concerto, Hummel's B minor Concerto . . . all of Schubert's compositions that have appeared since opus 100 . . . everything of interest in the way of piano compositions that has appeared in Leipzig since my absence and that you think I would like. You know my taste. Something new by Herz and Czerny can also be included.

Schumann seems to have been embarking on a collector's course. He was less interested in practicing all this music than in studying it. He wanted to compose but felt "so overflowing with nothing but sounds that it was impossible to write anything down."[37] An analysis of the work of other composers would, he hoped, provide ideas about how to proceed. "If you only knew how pressured I am, and driven from within," he wrote to Wieck. "If I had written them down, I would by now already have gotten to opus 100 in my symphonies."

With Schubert as his model, he did attempt to compose a symphony. Fragments of the manuscript have survived as clear proof that at the beginning of his career Schumann did not compose exclusively for the piano. He had, however, only a very limited exposure to orchestral instruments—the weekly meetings of amateurs he attended at Thibaut's home were devoted almost exclusively to choral music—and his self-expression was still restricted to the keyboard. Thus today we know the young Schumann best as a composer of bright, short piano pieces, which he called "butterflies" (*Papillons*).

The butterfly—symbol of the eternal soul yet evocative of the frivolous pleasure seeker, the social butterfly, enchanting for the moment, insubstantial but magnificent—was an appropriate image for Schumann's first original compositions in Heidelberg. Many of them were waltzes. Those that have survived in his early sketchbooks either are unfinished or were modified to become parts of later compositions.[38] Five of them can be heard in Schumann's *Papillons* (op. 2), a suite that celebrates scenes from Jean Paul's *Adolescent Years*. (In his own copy of this book, Schumann wrote comments that indicate his attempt to make literal connections between his musical ideas and Jean Paul's description of a masked ball.[39]) Elegant waltzes and a polonaise are rudely interrupted by a giant boot, which jumps onto the dance floor "as if propelled by itself." Not only does it sound as though Schumann had a delightful time with these pieces, but a characteristic musical style of nervous rhythms and languid harmonies emerges. The final piece incorporates a historical note—an old seventeenth-century "Grandfather's Dance." *Papillons* comes to a quiet end as six bells ring out to announce the approach of dawn. (It should be mentioned that the bells were an afterthought; Schumann's early drafts show no such device.) Sounds of the masked ball fade away slowly as the pianist releases one note at a time from a sustained dominant seventh chord.

Another of Schumann's early compositions was *Theme and Variations on the Name Abegg* (op. 1). The variations are written in a style of virtuoso piano playing that was fashionable at the time and that may resemble the way Schumann was trying to perform in public. The name Abegg, mentioned several times in his Heidelberg diary,[40] probably had several associations. Two brothers, Otto and August Abegg, were fellow students. In addition, he knew a family by the name of Abegg in Mannheim. Schumann dedicated his variations to a fictitious "Mademoiselle Pauline Comtesse d'Abegg," an example of the type of word game he was fond of playing. (Rhymes, alphabetized lists of names, and puns appear throughout his college diaries.)

The musicologist Eric Sams has suggested that Schumann may have hunted deliberately in a cipher book for the "tonal analogues" between words and music that so frequently appear in his early compositions.[41] No such computational practice is mentioned, however, in his diary, nor did his students, friends, or wife ever notice it. More likely these associations between words and musical themes were generated quite spontaneously (perhaps even unconsciously) in Schumann's mind, part of his creative process at this youthful period, when it was not yet clear whether his career was heading in a literary or a musical direction. (Tonal analogues are, of course, not unique to Schumann. The most famous example is Johann Sebastian Bach's fugues based on the letters in his own name, BACH.*)

An early portrait of Schumann shows him to have been slender, poised, and elegant. He seems almost dandified, if not effeminate. While it is hazardous to judge these things from a stylized painting (and a miniature at that), it is impossible not to notice the slightly tilted head, the puckered lips, and the drooping wrist.

This was probably a pose. Despite his flirtation with the aristocratic life in Mannheim, Schumann could not, and never did, feel at ease among the

---

*In German musical notation, H stands for B, and B for B flat.

Miniature portrait of
Schumann at age twenty.
(Artist unknown.)

nobility. To his mother he wrote, "Court air for me is stuffy air, yet I can't turn the invitations down. . . . Quite elegantly and like a cavalier I stuttered 'Your Serene and Royal Highness,' and when she graciously dismissed me I received a few envious glances."[42]

On the other hand, Schumann sought and enjoyed flattery. He sulked when people did not appreciate him, and he would become despondent when other musicians (especially, later, his wife) upstaged him. His Heidelberg diary contains a long list of "Speeches about My Piano Playing," laudatory for the most part, which he assembled the way a young concert artist today would collect favorable press reviews.

> Music teacher Faulhaber: "in you I recognize an extraordinary master"
> Professor Morstadt: "superb"
> Music Director Hofmann: "such beautiful, quiet passion"
> Mayor Mays: "Oh!—Herr Schumann plays rapturously"
> Bookseller Groos: "Well I've heard Hummel—but—I must say. . . ."[43]

Having come as they did from some of Heidelberg's most prominent citizens, these comments indicate that Schumann was able to pass himself off as an exciting, if not exceptional, pianist. His pleasure over this success was marred, though, by the realization that he had hardly any serious competition. "Musicianship here is of course at a low level," he wrote to his mother. "One just can't imagine a capable piano player; I'm already very well known as one."[44] Except for his occasional forays into Mannheim, where the competition was much greater, he was totally unknown outside Heidelberg.

This discrepancy between what Schumann expected of himself and what he was able to deliver may account for the peculiar approach-avoidance behavior he was beginning to manifest, a symptom probably of increasingly disabling stage fright. At one point he accepted an invitation to a soirée given by an English family in Heidelberg. (He was trying to learn English at this time and even practiced the language in some of his notebooks.) But as the evening approached, according to Wasielewski, he "lost interest in following through. His friend Töpken . . . urged him to keep his promise, but he stayed home. His absence was of course very much resented, and all relationships with this family came permanently to an end."[45]

That was unfortunate, because it reduced Schumann's opportunities for social experience. The persistent fear of women may have added to his social anxiety, as can be surmised from jottings such as the following: "Christmas party . . . my piano playing—praise heaped on praise; and successful improvisation—the girls pursue me—danger of social games and my lucky escape with Rosen by telling lies."[46]

At the beginning of 1830, Schumann's life again seemed to vacillate between extremes of revelry and drudgery. His January diary entries are instructive, mentioning "mad improvising," "fatigue," "cutting off all invitations," "the girls," "'O Mr. Schumann, when you play you can take me wherever you want,'" "indiscreet thoughts," "tears," "to the tavern with fellow students," "stumbled at the beginning of my Abegg variations, but able to play them to the end," "interminable applause and congratulations," and so on.[47]

When not with people, he would work almost maniacally at the keyboard: "Two hours of finger exercises—ten times the Toccata—six times finger exercises—twenty times the variations alone—and in the evening it just wouldn't work . . . angry about it—really deeply."[48] The Toccata Schumann mentioned was probably that formidable finger-stretcher in C major (originally in D major), which he later revised (op. 7) and dedicated to his friend Ludwig Schunke. A milestone in Schumann's development as a composer, it forces piano technique to the limit while preserving something of its Baroque traditions. Schumann was also attempting, without success, to compose a symphony and a piano concerto at this time.

Schumann's diary shows, unmistakably, a recurrence of disturbing symptoms: His January entries, for example, report "Bad sleep with bad dreams about ghosts and my good, honest mother"; "Constant dreams of home and Julius with stupid music"; "To bed sober and difficulty falling asleep"; and "Falling asleep on Rosen's lap until 4:30 in the afternoon."[49] He also mentions, for the first time, the psychophysiological disorder of his right hand, which within a few years would completely terminate his career as a pianist. "My numb finger" (*mein betäubter finger*), says the diary on 26 January 1830.[50] (*Betäubt* could also be translated as "anesthetized," "stupe-fied," "stunned," or "deafened.")

Soon after making this entry, Schumann stopped practicing and plunged headlong into one of the wildest sprees recorded in the diary. Four times he called it "the most debauched week of my life."[51] On 9 February he wrote of "madness" (*Wahnsinn*) and "loss of consciousness." He reeled from one tavern to the next, and went to innumerable parties, including a masked ball, where, according to Niecks, he dressed as a woman.[52] (Such behavior was not unusual among college students at the time, but it seems to have disturbed Schumann profoundly.) On several occasions he lost consciousness and had to be carried home. "Found in front of the door, with holes burned into my leg," says his diary. As in Leipzig, the light had to be on all night in his room, to forestall a delirium. On the first of March he "woke up at 5:00 A.M. terrified, bathed in sweat, on fire; I'm suddenly sober and luckily able to put it out."[53] These experiences were so frightening that for the following week he tried to remain completely sober.

He also noted once again the terrifying auditory disturbance, which had bothered him so much in Leipzig when he was "getting high," and which would be a recurring problem during his lifetime battle with mad-ness. "Terrible, half the night with eternal sounds" says the diary entry dated 10 March. "Buzzing and poetry in my ears."[54] Probably related to alcohol toxicity, these unbidden noises and voices made Schumann realize that he must exert more self-control. The next day he tried playing the piano—"good" and "bad"—gossiped with numerous people, and learned, to his dismay, of "the careless publicity about my champagne drinking." Then the cycle started again: "sadness . . . wine . . . high . . . solid sleep . . . terrible hangover."[55] On 18 March 1830 he came for the first time to the brink of suicide. "I'm terrified and disgusting—drunk because of bore-dom—very high—my longing to throw myself into the Rhine."[56]

A number of defenses against suicide seem to have been operating dur-ing that existential crisis in Heidelberg, and Schumann alluded to these in an essay appended to his diary around the time of his twentieth birthday that year. It is a self-analysis of "Schumann, the youth I have long loved and observed," written in the third person.[57]

His first reason for wanting to stay alive was an egocentric conviction that he was a very special person: "I would not wish to count Schumann among the ordinary people. He is distinguished from the masses by his talent for many things, and his unique individuality. . . . He is born 'to be the first.'"

Another reason was Schumann's intense craving for emotional experience, even for painful feelings: "His melancholic temperament expresses itself more in a capacity to feel than to observe. . . . His emotions are stronger than his ability to strive toward a goal. His intelligence is based less on reflection than on giving in to his feelings." Because death would have put an end to this, it had to be avoided.

Finally, Schumann's emotional attachment to his mother was probably life-saving. (We know that suicides occur more often after such love-bonds are broken.) But it was difficult for him to admit this, and he would rationalize his dependence on her by suggesting that she was dependent on him. For example, he wrote her, "Hey mother! Can you again not get out of your easy chair? You've been sitting there for two interminable hours without saying a word, just singing an apathetic old song, and running your hand up and down the window."[58] This letter also suggests that Schumann was genuinely concerned about his mother's pathological depressiveness, and that he may have felt helpless in his inability to do anything to cheer her up.

The essence of Schumann's conflict in Heidelberg was that he felt irresistibly drawn in a direction he knew his mother could never approve, toward musical virtuosity. By excelling at the keyboard he endangered the love that had given birth to his musical instincts in the first place. Thus the stage fright that was hampering his performance, and even the disability of his right hand, may have been unconsciously directed to achieve a compromise. Being "sick" could make him feel more in harmony with his mother. A letter to Dr. Carus written in September 1830 describes some of the early manifestations of Schumann's hand problem, which would recur every time he tried to give a concert:

> I can't think of finger exercises and scales any more at all; yes! it came to such a point that whenever I had to move my fourth finger, my whole body would twist convulsively, and after six minutes of finger exercises I felt the most interminable pain in my arm, in short a complete breakdown.[59]

Muscular tension, practicing incorrectly without proper supervision, alcohol abuse, and emotional distress undoubtedly contributed to Schumann's hand disorder. But as far as we know he consulted no physician other than Dr. Carus, who probably recognized that Schumann's exaggerated, histrionic description of his physical problems indicated a more fundamental disturbance of his personality.

V.

A New Beginning, 1830–1831

chumann had hoped to spend the Easter holidays (1830) with his family in Zwickau. Instead he received a stern rebuff, which undoubtedly contributed to his agony that spring. "Under no circumstances will you come home for Easter," his brother Julius wrote. "It would hardly have been worth the effort of making the long trip to Heidelberg for you to attend college for only a few months. Think it over carefully before you decide to leave, because once you quit Heidelberg you probably won't go back so soon."[1] In response Schumann wrote an angry letter to his mother about "this eternal, nauseating—money," asking "why on account of 200 florins [the amount it would cost him to go home] should I destroy any happy hopes and a present adjustment?"[2]

Schumann has often been portrayed as a spendthrift, and his hyperbolic letters from Heidelberg asking for money easily give this impression. "In money matters generally," says Alan Walker, "Schumann must be considered as irresponsible."[3] And yet his diaries suggest just the opposite. They contain an impressive amount of financial data, and Schumann's almost obsessional accounting of every penny spent and received would seem to indicate that he was not only very anxious about money but also conscientious and eager to conserve it. Of course he had debts, which he was never reluctant to reveal to his mother.

Painfully aware that his family would not pay for a trip back to Zwickau, he briefly considered accepting "a pressing invitation"[4] from Rosen's brother to go to London for the holidays but soon abandoned the idea. (In fact, never in his life did Schumann cross the English Channel.) Instead, he decided to go back to Frankfurt, where he had been with his poet friend Willibald Alexis the year before. This decision was an important one. Niccolo Paganini, one of the most charismatic musicians of the romantic era, was to give four concerts in Frankfurt and Schumann, after years of expectant waiting, would finally witness one of the Italian's performances.*[5]

Paganini, then forty-eight years old, had a fabulous reputation. Musicians marveled at his virtuosity, which was enhanced by a physical deformity that allowed his hands and arms to twist in awesome ways. Paganini was also a very clever showman who did nothing to discourage rumors that he was in league with the devil and capable of raising the dead. An aura of wizardry surrounded him, leaving audiences spellbound.

All of this appealed greatly to Schumann, who had a propensity to be dazzled by superhuman feats and a willingness to believe in magic. He heard the great man on Easter Sunday, and in his diary exclaimed about "Paganini, a man who despises the public, like Götte."[6] This observation suggests that the violinist's gaunt appearance and Napoleonic self-confidence may have evoked memories of Schumann's genial friend in Leipzig. "Ecstasy in bed and gentle dreaming" were noted that night. But Schumann also had reservations about Paganini: "doubts about the ideal in art and his lack of grand, noble, priestly artistic repose."[7]

For years Schumann could not resist the Italian's music, which has a unique glitter and provides innumerable technical challenges to the performer. He transcribed many of his virtuoso *Caprices* for the piano (opp. 3 and 10), gave him a cameo role in the *Carnaval* (op. 9), and fashioned an ultra-violinistic variation in the style of Paganini in his *Symphonic Etudes* (op. 13). (Even at the end of his life, while he was hospitalized in Endenich, Schumann wrote piano accompaniments for some of Paganini's solo pieces.)

For three months after the concert in Frankfurt, Schumann debated his future with himself and with his mother. "If only you were with me, then I wouldn't have to say a thing but could just look into your eyes," he wrote her in early July. The letter focuses on his disenchantment with jurisprudence and describes a spartan daily routine. "I get up early. I work from four to seven, then from seven to nine I'm at the piano." After classes with

---

*Schumann's diary mentions Paganini long before he ever heard him play.

Thibaut he took language lessons. Evenings he went out, "to be among people and in nature."[8]

Schumann nagged his mother persistently with complaints about wanting "to be a great lawyer" but not having it in his "heart to go further";[9] as a result, she urged him to seek counsel from Professor Thibaut and asked if law didn't please him, "why did you choose it?"[10]

Presumably he did consult the professor, but not with the results Frau Schumann would have preferred. The letter she received several weeks later reveals the extraordinary intensity of her son's identity crisis. In it, he declared that his "entire life" had been "a twenty-year battle between poetry and prose, or call it music and law." Now he was "standing at the crossroads, terrified by the question: Where next?" He believed that music was "the right way," yet he felt that "the way was barred" by his mother's "good maternal warnings [against] an uncertain future and an insecure income."[11] (While this accusation was somewhat justified, it overlooked Schumann's own reservations and hesitations about following his "genius." Indeed, he sometimes felt that he had none. Moreover, the ghostly hand of his father still exerted an influence over him, pushing him toward reading, writing, and poetry and distracting him from the piano.)

Whatever the origins of Schumann's conflict may have been, he was agonizingly obsessed with doubts. "Nothing can torture a man more than the thought that he has prepared himself for an unhappy, dead and insipid future," he wrote. It would seem that the plan he now proposed to his mother was designed to counter his fear of the future. "I have reached the certainty," he told her, "that by working diligently and patiently for six years with a good teacher I will be able to compete with any pianist."[12]

This was a combination of naiveté and megalomania. Schumann seems to have been unaware of his "competitors." Franz Liszt, a year his junior, was already making a name for himself, having played in Vienna, visited England three times, toured the French provinces and Switzerland, and performed an opera in Paris. Felix Mendelssohn, only a year older than Schumann, had been training with the best teachers since childhood, was known throughout Germany (where in 1821 he played for Goethe) and in Paris and London, and had recently revived and conducted J. S. Bach's *St. Matthew Passion*. Frédéric Chopin, the same age as Schumann, had been in the public eye since childhood and was on the brink of an illustrious career.

In preparing himself to compete with Europe's leading pianists, Schumann envisioned first returning to Wieck in Leipzig, "later to Vienna and, were it at all possible, to study with Moscheles," his boyhood ideal. Technical training at the keyboard would be the main objective, for wasn't "all of piano playing just mechanics and dexterity?"[13] (Schumann's letter to Dr.

Carus later that year suggests that he may have emphasized mechanical dexterity to impress his mother, since "lay people don't understand these things." Yet dexterity was clearly important for more than its impact on Frau Schumann. In responding to Dr. Carus's criticism of his narrowmindedness, Schumann claimed that "greater mechanical power would give me greater control over the [musical] substance."[14]) The comment is interesting, for it was a denial of the physical limitations of his right hand and the pain he knew would develop after hard practicing.

The final decision he left to Wieck and to his mother. Having blamed her for "barring" his way to music, he now begged her to be his agent. "*You yourself please write Wieck and ask him directly what he thinks of me and the plans for my life.* Please give me an *early* answer and a decision. . . . There is no time to lose."[15]

The request disturbed Schumann's mother. "All this has upset me so much that I feel emotionally ill," she wrote Wieck (whom she had never met). But in her helplessness she complied with her son's wish and "with trembling and inner anxiety" asked Wieck to be the arbiter of his fate. She praised her son as "a good person [whom] nature has given . . . talents that others can only obtain with effort." In addition, she referred to him as "a young, inexperienced person who only lives in the higher spheres and does not want to go into a practical life." Her concern for his financial security clearly was uppermost: "When the time comes for him to show what he can do, he will have spent his entire modest fortune and [will] still be dependent on other people."[16]

Wieck, an entrepreneur who was not indifferent to Schumann's "modest fortune" and knew the young man's limitations only too well, responded with his own brand of hyperbole: "I give my pledge to make your son Robert, with his talent and his fantasy, into one of the greatest living pianists within three years," he wrote to Frau Schumann, promising that one day Robert would "play with more imagination and warmth than Moscheles, and with more grandeur than Hummel." After warning the uneasy mother that "Robert's greatest difficulty lies in the quiet, cool, thoughtful, and restrained mastery of the mechanical basis of piano-playing," Wieck offered his "eleven-year-old daughter [Clara] whom I'm just beginning to show to the world" as proof of his excellence as a teacher.[17]

One could speculate whether Wieck might not have been thinking about a potential son-in-law. After all, Schumann came from a good family, and was affluent, handsome, and extremely talented. Wieck may have been looking for a younger man sufficiently like himself to teach, promote the "method" of which he was so proud, and follow in his footsteps. He emphasized to Schumann's mother that Robert ought to think about becoming a piano teacher, since that would "earn a very good and very plentiful income."

Friedrich Wieck, Schumann's piano teacher in Leipzig and later his father-in-law. (Artist unknown.)

Wieck also seemed determined to improve Schumann's character, specifically his "manliness." He wanted to give him daily lessons and "to completely silence" his fantastic imagination. "Like my Clara, he will work at the blackboard every day on three- and four-voice exercises." Six months might be required, Wieck thought, to see whether Schumann could conform to this regimen. Should he fail, he wrote to Frau Schumann, "then let him go peacefully and give him your blessings."

Frau Schumann relented, but not without a struggle. "Your last letter has shattered me so completely that since receiving it I've relapsed into my totally depressed state," she wrote her son.

> I do not reproach you, since that would lead to nothing; but I cannot *approve* your views or your ways of dealing with things at all. Look at your life since your good father's death, and you must admit that you have lived only for *yourself*. Where will it end?

These anxieties show little confidence in Schumann's abilities: "When you do everything that Wieck demands, you still will not have attained a secure future. Think of your age." But she added,

Don't take this to mean that I want to hold you back, or, as you put it, stand in your way. No, Robert, I only give you my opinions in order to stand by without blame when and if your new career doesn't please you. Your brothers and other people here do not approve of your ways of thinking. So now you are left *completely alone* in handling this matter, and may God give you his blessing!!![18]

This message, plus Wieck's letter, which Schumann's mother enclosed, put the young composer into a terrible dilemma. "Don't ask how everything raged within me after the letters arrived," he wrote Wieck. "It took a long time before my thoughts . . . settled down."[19]

There are no diary entries to provide insight into Schumann's thoughts at this moment. We have only his letters, and the one to Wieck (dated 21 August 1830) suggests a penitent, a humble child ready to submit to authority:

I trust you completely, I give myself to you completely, take me as I am, and above all be patient with me about everything. No criticism will depress me and no praise will make me lazy. A few buckets of really, really cold theory can't do me any harm, and I'll hold still without saying a word. . . . I will follow wherever you want and will never take the blindfold from my eyes. . . . Trust me, then, because I want to earn the right to be called your pupil.[20]

A letter to his mother, written the next day, also suggests submission, and counters her bitterness gently, caringly, and possibly in the fear of losing her.

Believe me, I know how to appreciate that your whole heart is filled with love for me. . . . I wish you were standing here in front of me and could look into my heart—You would say: Follow the new path with courage, hard work, and confidence and you cannot go under.[21]

Schumann did not entirely dismiss the idea of a legal career. A letter to Johann Gottlob Rudel is evidence of his indecision. "If Wieck hesitates with the smallest doubt after six months," he wrote, "then nothing would be lost in jurisprudence, and I could still study for a year and take my examinations, after only four years of studies."[22] Whether this was a ruse, to guarantee financial support from his family, or an "escape clause" designed to provide an alternative in case of failure with Wieck, it was characteristic for Schumann to behave enigmatically and to keep his options open.

Schumann planned a circuitous trip back to Saxony and took the Rhine River steamer north in September. He was feeling excited and flirtatious, enjoyed chatting with the English tourists and teasingly wrote to his mother that "if I ever marry it will be to an Englishwoman."[23] But pleasure soon gave way to dissatisfaction. "Anxiety about the steamboat," says the travel diary (24 September 1830). "I am gloomy and dead . . . restless and dreams about 'fire.'" (There was in fact a fire on board, which damaged the boat.) The next day, he reported "wild life on the steamboat . . . dead and high . . . memories of Willibald Alexis—everything as if in a dream . . . terrible fatigue."[24]

The overland part of the trip was unpleasant—"damned stink in the carriage"—and northern Germany depressing with its "solitary wasteland . . . everything desolate and uncultivated."[25] Whenever possible Schumann practiced the piano, and if there was no instrument to play he would simulate from his bed, on a spring-operated silent keyboard he carried with him to keep his fingers nimble. During the journey he also tried to compose, and there are fragments of music in the diary, including an "Allegretto al Paganini."[26] Schumann decided, on the spur of the moment, to spend a few days in Detmold with Gisbert Rosen. However, his old friend received him "very coldly." They quarreled, apparently after Schumann revealed his future plans, as Rosen did not think he should study music.[27] When, in mid-October, Schumann arrived in Leipzig, he was very depressed.

Details about his first two weeks in Leipzig are unavailable, but a letter to his mother dated 25 October 1830 indicates that he felt "so discouraged, restless, and sluggish that [he] couldn't collect [his] thoughts."[28] Money was still a problem, and he was unable to find suitable lodgings. Finally Wieck, who owned a large house at Grimmaische Gasse 36 and customarily made space available for his students, agreed to rent Schumann two sparsely furnished rooms. This necessitated a "discussion" with his mother about "the fatal business of household matters" including an "urgent" request for the bed he had in Leipzig, some cups his sister-in-law Therese had given him, and even a can of coffee and some sugar. In addition, he asked Julius for a supply of writing utensils.[29]

Schumann clearly was still dependent on his family. "Don't abandon me my good mother and give me friendly words. I crave your gentle protection," he wrote.[30] (In a postscript to this letter, Schumann asked that his mother return to him all the letters he had sent her. "I would like to have them for my literary work, and incidentally to find out whether the year and a half has changed me very much."[31] This request indicates not only his persistent interest in autobiography, but also that he was still thinking of becoming a writer.) His fears of abandonment suggest that he was aware that by choosing to go into music he had in effect alienated virtually every member of his family. His brother Carl, for example, never could reconcile himself to Schumann's career as a musician and, according to his daughter, did not even tolerate having a musical instrument in his home, so strong was his "antipathy to music."[32]

Schumann's six-month probationary period with Wieck is a problematic chapter in his life, for very little first-hand information is available from his diaries. Apparently he devoted most of his time and energy to the piano, practicing "more than six to seven hours a day."[33]

He also often played with Clara Wieck and her younger brother, Alwin. Schumann's fund of ghost stories and his readiness to improvise probably made him a desirable companion, a sort of older brother to the children. Schumann, however, felt "cloistered" in Wieck's house, as he had little access to his own friends and was deprived of the social adulation to which he had become accustomed in Heidelberg. The new living arrangements may also have restricted Schumann's sexual exploits.

A letter to his mother written less than a month after the trial period had begun describes a "disgusting mood."[34] The Caruses were trying, without success it seems, to "bring [Schumann] into countless [other] families"—"I don't go there, and in general don't get out of the house much." He reported that he had "not broken [himself] of the habit of leaving two lights on at night." He added that "barely a few ashes remain of my old warmth and enthusiasm," and that at times "a misanthropic indifference" made him feel like "sacrificing everything." The letter also contains a remark about suicide—"I don't have the money or a pistol to shoot myself"—as well as a threat to "go where there is an epidemic of deadly cholera and chase my unhappy career out of this world."[35]

The reference to cholera is important, because it suggests the tendency toward hypochondriasis that plagued Schumann so much as he grew older. In the same vein, he told his mother of a fear of blindness,[36] but the only basis seems to have been his nearsightedness, which had become more of a problem since he had begun spending so much time reading music at the piano.

An even more urgent "fear" lay behind Schumann's complaints: he had found out that his next birthday, in 1831, would make him eligible for military service. (In 1830, after an outbreak of revolutionary activity in France, the Leipzig police had organized a "Communal Guard" to prevent similar uprisings. Every unmarried man between twenty-one and fifty had to serve if he were in good health and able to carry arms. Many men, Schumann included, sought a deferment on medical grounds.) Anticipating this, he "very urgently" asked his mother for his birth certificate, and, because "in the end they will draft me in spite of my eyes," even threatened to run off "to America or to Twer [Russia]," where his uncle lived.[37]

Here we see evidence of Schumann's willingness to take advantage of certain social benefits that result from sickness. He was probably experiencing another depression. His letter full of complaints was written a week after Clara Wieck made her spectacular debut at the Leipzig Gewandhaus (8

November 1830). It must have already been obvious to him in October, when he moved into the Wieck household, that the teacher who had "pledged" to make him Europe's greatest pianist was in fact grooming an eleven-year-old girl for that role.

Clara's program featured virtuoso pieces by Kalkbrenner, Herz, and Czerny, all of which she performed brilliantly. Schumann, meanwhile, was still having to practice basic scales and arpeggios. Moreover, Clara had been taking composition lessons, and at her Gewandhaus concert she played an original theme with variations. "This young artist's extraordinary accomplishment, in her playing as well as her composing, led to general astonishment and the greatest applause," reported the *Leipziger Zeitung*.[38] Thus Schumann's disturbance was undoubtedly related to the highly competitive situation in Wieck's house, where an attractive, energetic, and female rival was getting far more attention and winning honors that he himself craved. To remain in Wieck's good graces, he would have had to cover up any jealousy and keep his anger under control—which would have the effect of accentuating depressive feelings.

Toward the end of the month, though, Schumann's mood began to swing away from depression toward elation. On 28 November (his mother's birthday), he wrote that "a thunderstorm was hovering over my life, but today is tranquil as a rainbow and only the clouds are weeping." He had commissioned a new portrait of himself, a "painted double" to send his mother "as a way of giving myself wholly to you again."[39] Schumann's spirits rose in response to a warm, encouraging letter he had received at a critical moment, when Wieck was making plans to take Clara to Dresden for concerts. His first music teacher in Zwickau, the venerable organist Johann Gottfried Kuntsch, wrote to say, "I am most pleasantly surprised by the news that you have abandoned the law and now want to dedicate yourself to art, especially to music. . . . The world will count you among its foremost artists, and your art will most certainly give you immortality and much honor."[40] Schumann could "hardly believe it"[41] and was soon filling up with music, a sure sign of impending creativity. "I'm fired up and in flames," he told his mother, "raging along in sweet and fabulous sounds all day." He wanted to compose "a grand opera called Hamlet, and the thought of fame and immortality gives me strength and fantasies."[42]

So ambitious a project was, of course, completely beyond Schumann's reach at the time; without a more realistic channel for his energy, his euphoria became unbearable. Accordingly, he began to experience some mental dissociation: "I feel uncommonly free, light, and in a divine mood, swimming in a pure ether of darkly familiar feelings."[43] Trying to maintain control, Schumann wrote furiously, one letter after another, describing changes in his self-perception. "I've become terribly pale, nasty, mean-looking, and all the Zwickau ladies will be astonished and critical," he wrote his mother. "My portrait should give you a clue to these words . . . and you will ask, 'Is that really Robert???'"[44] He expressed regret that he had not yet achieved Wieck's goal of surpassing Moscheles as a pianist. "Were my talent for poetry and music only concentrated in one focus, then the light would not be so broken up, and I could trust myself more."[45]

A new scheme for self-preservation can now be detected in Schumann's correspondence. "Move immediately out of Zwickau," he commanded his mother, "and stay with me in beautiful Weimar."[46] An ostensibly "crafty reason" for this was to study with Hummel.

Johann Nepomuk Hummel (1778–1837), one of Europe's leading pianists and most prolific composers, had been a child prodigy and a pupil of Mozart, and was an acquaintance of Beethoven and Haydn's successor at the Esterhazy Court. In Weimar, as music director for the Grand Duke, he shared the limelight with Wolfgang Goethe, who was poet-in-residence. Schumann knew, and to a certain extent admired, Hummel's music.* Although he was probably thinking primarily about his own career when he proposed a transfer of allegiance from Wieck to Hummel, this idea now became coupled with Schumann's wish to be reunited with his mother, a fantasy she herself had recently stimulated.

Frau Schumann's letters from this period reveal that she was making a distinct effort to woo her son away from Wieck, whom she did not fully trust.[47] That Robert had "accepted all the demands made by Wieck" gave her "even greater pain" than the "broken heart" he had caused by his career decision in the first place.[48] But now that the decision was made, and Wieck's promise that Schumann would be playing "more beautifully" than Hummel had not been kept, why not go directly to the great man in Weimar?

Thoughts of Hummel stirred Schumann's yearnings for a mentor, as his letters show: "I have four goals, to be a conductor, a music teacher, a virtuoso, and a composer," he wrote his mother. "Hummel unites them all. . . . If only I could for once be Everything in Something, and not, as unfortunately I've always been, Something in Everything."[49]

Hummel was a kind and conscientious teacher. Among his students was a musician who would later be of great importance to Schumann's career: Ferdinand Hiller. Moreover, Hummel's Weimar home, said to have been "regular and peaceful," might have offered a respite from the pandemonium of Wieck's household.[50] But Schumann wavered for over six months before even writing to Hummel to request lessons.

---

*Schumann's earliest efforts to compose a piano concerto (1830–1831) were dedicated to Hummel.

Hummel was not eager to become Schumann's teacher; he regarded his compositions as too unorthodox. And Frau Schumann finally made it clear that she would not leave her home in Zwickau to accompany her son. Thus Schumann never did go to Weimar, and it may have been just as well. The fact was that he could never work with a teacher for any length of time, and he remained an essentially self-taught musician. Moreover, he was not entirely convinced that Hummel—regarded by some as ten years behind his time—was the best teacher.

Schumann also had become hopelessly dependent on Wieck, whose behavior seemed to fluctuate between extremes of contempt and seductiveness. "The other day he told me that nothing could be better for me than to be penniless—then I'd finally amount to something," Robert wrote to his mother.

> When I casually mentioned my plan about Hummel, Wieck took it badly, and asked whether I don't trust him or whether he isn't really the greatest teacher? I was visibly shaken up by his excessive anger, but we are friendly again and he cares for me lovingly, like his own child. You can hardly imagine his passion, his judgment, and his views on art, but whenever it comes to his own or to Clara's interests, he goes wild like a peasant.[51]

Although Schumann did not report this to his mother, he was deeply disturbed by Wieck's cruel behavior toward his children. In exploiting Clara's prodigious talents, for instance, her father would falsify her age, making her appear even younger than she was. Schumann resorted to consulting her diary to discover the truth. He was aghast at what he called Wieck's "Jewish behavior,"* his "squinting at the cash box," his "impure" love for Clara's talent.[53]

One incident in particular made an "indelible impression" on Schumann. It was in August 1831—he had by now long overstayed his six-month probationary period—when he observed Wieck throw his nine-year-old son Alwin to the floor because he disapproved of the way the boy was playing the violin. He "tore at his hair, yelling, 'you wretch, you scoundrel is this the way you try to please your father?'" It was probably no coincidence that this very day Schumann wrote his letter to Hummel.

---

* The possibility of anti-Semitism—this word was actually coined by Wilhelm Marr in 1829, the year Schumann moved to Heidelberg—is implied by this offhand comment Schumann made in his diary. (Wolfgang Boetticher, in a book published during the World War II era, greatly exaggerated this prejudice.[52]) It would have been difficult for anyone in Germany, even a person as sensitive and thoughtful as Schumann, to escape the influence of anti-Semitism. Although he occasionally made nasty remarks about Mendelssohn and at one point accused Wieck of behaving "like a Jew," he never—unlike Richard Wagner—deliberately wove anti-Semitic sentiments into his published writings.

With considerable dismay Schumann noted that Clara seemed totally indifferent to what he called her father's "deplorable villainy."* After Wieck finished battering Alwin, for example, Clara merely "smiled and sat down quietly at the piano with a Weber sonata." Schumann had to ask himself, "Am I among human beings?"[55]

There surely was something odd in Wieck's behavior toward Clara and her abject submissiveness. He sought constantly to travel with his daughter, to control her every move, to censor her mail, to write in her diary, and to keep her away from other men (including, later, Schumann). On their concert tours together, Wieck would share Clara's hotel room and supervise her dressing and undressing, behavior that in a recent film, *Frühlings Sinfonie* (*Spring Symphony*), is made to look luridly incestuous.[56] Indeed, the interest he took in Clara certainly seems to have bordered on incest. Wieck much preferred traveling with her to staying home with his second wife, who didn't seem to complain about this arrangement. As for Schumann, his devotion to his own mother may have blinded him somewhat to what was going on between Clara and her father.

When Schumann turned twenty-one in 1831, he invented two companions, Florestan and Eusebius, who—in his imagination—spoke to him, gave him ideas for literary as well as musical projects, and supported him at times of emotional distress. It is not unusual for children or even adolescents to create imaginary creatures who provide solace and companionship—but when an adult does so, it is a sign of either a very vivid imagination or a psychotic tendency.[57] In Schumann's case it indicated both. The "birth" of his two friends followed a great deal of turmoil and suffering caused by personal and artistic problems.

Schumann had decided in April to visit Zwickau after an absence of over two years. His brother Julius was again gravely ill with tuberculosis and not expected to live much longer. This undoubtedly was a compelling reason for the return home, and it also marked the recurrence of Schumann's very disturbing obsessions with disease and death. He was in a "rather strange mood" in Zwickau.[58] Although his brother did not die, the tuberculosis had advanced considerably, and the chances for long-term survival seemed extremely poor.

---

*In a biographical study of Clara Schumann, Nancy Reich points out that Wieck treated his two sons "with contempt, hostility and cruelty." He wrote his wife (in 1838) that the boys "don't deserve the good fortune to remain in our house. Find an old suitcase and send Gustav [the fifteen-year-old] out."[54]

After getting back to Leipzig in May, Schumann noted with considerable alarm that he himself was ill. "For six days I've guarded myself almost uninterruptedly in my room," he wrote to his mother. "Something hurts in my stomach, my heart, my head, everywhere."[59] The diary gives much more detail.

Schumann had recently embarked on what was to be his first full-fledged sexual relationship with a woman, Christel. (He later referred to her also as Charitas, but he never mentioned her last name in his diary.) Christel seems to have been a member of Wieck's household, perhaps another student or even a servant, but certainly someone known to Clara. She came to Schumann's room nearly every day, often bringing him presents. In his diary there are many references to sexual intercourse with Christel, for example, "Christel in one minute"; "Charitas came completely and was bleeding"; "full of fire and flames."[60]

At the beginning of their relationship, which lasted off and on for several years, Schumann complained of many medical symptoms. For example, the tip of his penis was sore, probably as a result of vigorous sexual activity. (He referred repeatedly to a "wound" (*Wunde*), specifically on the frenulum—Schumann was not circumcised—which may have torn, leading to a "biting and devouring pain."[61] The diary's reports that "only guilt gives birth to Nemesis" and that Christel turned "pale" when she found out about the injury suggest that the couple may have regarded Schumann's "wound" as punishment for their sexual behavior. On separate occasions in May both he and Christel consulted Christian Glock, Schumann's cellist friend who had recently graduated from medical school. Dr. Glock advised that they abstain from sexual intercourse and told Schumann to bathe his sore penis in "Narcissus Water,"[62] a distillate of daffodil bulbs first mentioned by Galen as an herbal remedy for minor skin irritations.

Eric Sams has suggested that Schumann's "wound" (Sams calls it a "sore") may have been a syphilitic chancre.[63] That seems unlikely, however. Such lesions are typically painless, and Narcissus Water would have been a totally inappropriate treatment for so serious a condition. Nevertheless, Schumann may have thought that he did have a venereal disease, and such an idea would have increased his anxiety about further sexual activity. (Several of his remarks in the diary—for example, "Christel in one minute"—suggest premature ejaculation.) Not until 15 June did he try having intercourse with her again, gingerly at first, and "with fear and little enjoyment."[64] He faithfully recorded each attempt in the diary.

Needless to say, the medical complications of what may well have been Schumann's introduction to sexual relations with women had profound effects on his mental state. Right at the onset of his affair with Christel he reported a dream of "one hundred flowering children, all red, dancing around me with their garlands," which suggests fecundity; on a symbolic level the relationship may have stimulated Schumann's confidence in being able to produce something of lasting value. His "beautiful" dreams also made him worry about his "illness." On 13 May, after consulting with Dr. Glock, Schumann had "fantasies full of angel-shapes and seraphs with upward-looking eyes."* That evening, while trying to make his way through a difficult textbook on music theory (Gottfried Weber's three-volume *Attempt at an Orderly Theory of Composition*), he commented angrily, "All this theory! If only I could be a genius, so I could kill all the rotten people with it. I'd like to load them all into a cannon and shoot something to death!"[65]

As the diffuse anxiety generated by his injured penis gradually took hold, Schumann fell victim to all sorts of psychological inhibitions. For example, on 14 May he noted a memory disturbance: "When I was a child I could remember back fourteen days, hour for hour, word for word; today I can barely remember yesterday." (He had met his brother Eduard from Zwickau that day, another reason probably for his ruminations about childhood, as well as his angry tirade about music.) For several days he failed to keep his diary up to date, a lapse he attributed to "laziness."[66]

But that was not the real problem. In fact, during his semi-abstinence from sex, Schumann had been planning yet another ambitious literary project, a play based on the tragic romance *Abélard and Héloise*. Again there was a mental block. "Abélard inspires me, but is too difficult for my philosophical talents," says the diary.[67] That he would choose to focus his attention on this medieval theologian tells us something not only about Schumann's wide-ranging interests—the writings of Peter Abélard (1079–1142) had great appeal among romantics—but also about the nature of his sexual anxiety. Abélard was a brilliant, precocious scholar who had become a priest. But after taking his vows of celibacy, he entered into an illicit relationship with Héloise, the beautiful niece of Canon Fulbert. They had a child and were secretly married. To protect Abélard's position in the church, Héloise left him and retired to a convent. When her uncle found out about the affair, he brutally attacked the young priest and castrated him.

Not surprisingly, Schumann had great difficulty with this play. He finished only one scene, and then quickly turned to something more light-hearted in the style of Jean Paul. It was to be a novel called *Philistines and the Beggar King*.[68] But he could not complete this either. Increasingly frustrated and unhappy, he now began reading one of his favorite authors, E. T. A. Hoffmann, and decided to write "a poetic biography" of him. Hoffmann's talent for music and literature resembled Schumann's own. "One can barely

---

*The similarity of this imagery to the religious delusions reported during the psychotic episode when he was forty-three is very striking.

breathe when reading Hoffman," comments the diary. "Reading Hoffman uninterruptedly. New worlds."[69]

It seems clear, then, that as Schumann was coming of age, his ambitions veered sharply away from music and more toward literature. Poems in the styles of Petrarch and Schiller appear in his diary; he made lists of Shakespeare's plays and compulsively mentioned each female character. Just three days before his twenty-first birthday, Schumann vehemently attacked his first love: "Music, how you disgust me and repel me to death."[70]

His mother's influence becomes apparent. After the *Abegg Variations* (op. 1) appeared in print that year, Frau Schumann congratulated her son "on the birth of your child" but cautioned him not to expect "too much . . .[when] the *big world* takes your child into its arms." As if the strain of producing musical "children" might be too painful for Schumann, she then suggested, "Why don't you make an appearance as a poet?"[71] Schumann's response to all these conflicting influences was to produce "twins": Florestan and Eusebius. Florestan was "born" first, but not without an agonizing labor.

On 8 June 1831, Schumann's twenty-first birthday, he woke up from "a deep sleep as before my birth." He felt "as though objective humanity wants to separate itself completely from the subjective, or as if I'm standing between my existence and my appearance, between form and shadow."[72] Perilously close to the "madness" he had experienced at age eighteen, Schumann pleaded, "my genius, are you going to abandon me?" The prayer was answered by "Florestan the Improvisor." Soon Schumann called him "my bosom friend . . . my own ego."[73] His choice of the name is revealing. In Beethoven's opera *Fidelio*, Florestan is the hero in a dungeon, chained to a rock, starving, and about to be killed by the villain Pizzarro. Florestan is rescued by his wife, Leonora, disguised as a man called Fidelio.* Florestan was a social creature. He symbolized the outgoing, assertive, and masculine side of Schumann's personality and soon was incorporated into his newest literary project. This idea had come to Schumann while he was returning from Zwickau, where he had gone for his "legal declaration of coming of age."†[75] It was to be a Hoffmann-style novel called *Child Prodigies (Wunderkinder)*. All the characters were going to be modeled after Schumann's immediate acquaintances. "From today on I will give more beautiful and fitting names to my friends," says the diary on his birthday. "I shall christen

---

* That Schumann's rescue fantasy may have involved Clara Wieck is suggested by a letter he wrote her in 1837: "Adieu, my Fidelio, and remain as faithful to your Robert as Leonora was to her Florestan."[74]

† In turning twenty-one, Schumann became eligible for military service. He also now had direct access to his inheritance, was no longer forced to beg for periodic allowances from his family, and could make decisions without his mother's approval.

you as follows: Wieck to Master Raro, Clara to Cilia, Christel to Charitas."[76]
Dr. Glock also had a role to play: "the old medical Muse." To give coherence
to the plot and "to connect the threads," Schumann then added "Paganini
[who] must have a wonderful effect on Cilia," as well as "Hummel, the Ideal
Technician."[77]

Meanwhile Schumann was struggling to abstain from sexual activity.
"Gratification of desire brings no satisfaction, but only awakens more desire." Soon he was drinking excessively again. "I grow more miserable every
day," he wrote.[78] He sought relief by playing the piano—"luxuriating in
Chopin"—and by writing letters to himself:

> [19 June] Dear Robert, I beg you, produce something at last and be finished
> with it. . . . A terrible tendency to do things only half-way lies within me,
> to be wasteful and to seek self-destruction, which also shows in boozing.
>
> [20 June] I'm sinking, I'm sinking back into the old slime. Will no hand
> from the clouds come to hold me?

The next nine days he called "evil days for which I hope God and my heart
may forgive me!"[79]

Then, on 1 July, Schumann brought the other twin to light. He called
him "Eusebius." Now Florestan had a partner; Schumann called them "two
of [his] best friends" and claimed that they "cheered [him] up greatly."[80]
Here was a new solution to his creative dilemma. Schumann's novelistic
writing could now proceed in the style of his admired Jean Paul. ("Florestan
and Eusebius" were obviously modeled after "Vult and Walt" from Jean
Paul's *Flegeljahre*.) Giving birth to the twins also seems to have relieved
somewhat Schumann's guilt for whatever sin he wanted God to forgive him.
He never specified what it was: his writing had become vague and confusing
(even illegible), as often happened when he was upset or intoxicated. It is
most likely that his guilt refers to his sexual problem—masturbation or
intercourse would have made his penis sore again. The repeated mention in
his diary of erotic fantasies about Henriette Wieck, another unapproachable
member of Wieck's family, also suggests sexual guilt and frustration.

It is interesting that Schumann came up with the name Eusebius, that
of a Christian saint. He probably found information about him in the eccle-
siastical histories he read while working on his play about Abélard.* Eusebius, a priest living in the fourth century, greatly admired the Christian
martyrs and was himself persecuted for taking an active role in the Arian

---

*I am indebted to Professor Rita Fuszek of California State University in Fullerton for calling
to my attention a treatise on music by the neo-Platonist writer Aristides Quintilianus that
mentions Florestan and Eusebius. It is possible that Schumann had come across this book
during his classical studies in Zwickau, or more recently in Leipzig.

dispute over the relationship between Jesus and God the Father. Eusebius claimed that everything laudable in Greek thinking was ultimately derived from ancient Judaism. He firmly believed that Jesus Christ was the fulfillment of a Hebrew prophecy, and worked tirelessly as a historian, writing books that were partly literal and partly allegorical.

Schumann also noticed the name Eusebius while checking his calendar for August, which has three consecutive name-days, "Clara" on the twelfth, "Aurora" on the thirteenth, and "Eusebius" on the fourteenth. He often mentioned the magic of this proximity. Eusebius' interest in martyrdom, his suffering, and his final execution may also have appealed to masochistic and suicidal elements in Schumann's personality.

The balance between Florestan and Eusebius was perfect. They seemed to hold in check the disruptive fantasies Schumann was having. They provided leadership for his imaginary "Child Prodigies" (later rechristened the *Davidsbündler*). They gave direction to his creative work for years to come. Finally, they probably helped neutralize his sexual conflicts. The "magic" of Clara's name-day's proximity to Eusebius' led Florestan (Schumann) to expect that one day he too might be attached to this girl.

VI.

Cumulative Stresses, 1831–1833

One of the characters in Schumann's intended novel was the "Music Director," modeled after a young conductor and opera composer named Heinrich Dorn (1804–1892), who had recently come to Leipzig to take charge of the Court Theater. Schumann first met Dorn at Wieck's house, and immediately they seem to have rankled each other.

Wieck, who was urging Schumann to become more disciplined, had suggested he study music theory and composition with Christian Weinlich, who was Clara's teacher as well as Richard Wagner's. Schumann, however, preferred Dorn in spite of the antipathy he aroused. The reasons are not too clear. In his rebellious attitude toward Wieck, Schumann may have wanted to study with a younger, more "modern" composer. Also he found Dorn, as well as Dorn's wife, physically attractive. "When can I come to your apartment to begin the lessons you promised me?" asked Schumann in a letter dated the same week he invented Eusebius. "I'm trembling and shivering a bit in anticipation."[1]

The lessons began in mid-July 1831. Schumann reported that Dorn "had prepared himself and seemed anxious, but in other respects was lovable."[2] According to Dorn:

Schumann played his variations on the name Abegg for me. . . . At that time he had never had any theoretical instruction, at least not on a regular basis, because I had to start him with the ABC's of thorough-bass. The first four-voice chorale that he had to show as proof of his knowledge of harmony was an example of the most unruly voice-leading.[3]

Such criticism must have riled Schumann, for he was already complaining after a month of instruction. "I'll never be able to come close to Dorn; he has no feelings and on top of that has the manner of an East Prussian. I prefer to come closer to his wife."[4]

Nevertheless, the two men continued to meet until Easter 1832, with the result that Schumann sketched out an enormously ambitious "plan for the future," which included various orchestral pieces, chamber music, and piano works that he hoped one day to complete.[5] At this time Schumann was obviously thinking of himself as a potentially great composer or writer; he practiced different forms of his own autograph next to his version of "Beethoven," "Mozart," "Haydn," "Napoleon Bonaparte," and other famous signatures. A description of Schumann recorded by Dorn is interesting in its details about the composer's personality and appearance:

[Schumann was] an indefatigable worker throughout this apprenticeship. Whenever I gave him one assignment he would deliver many more. The first lessons in double counterpoint took up so much time that he sent me a letter saying he "couldn't tear himself away" and would I make an exception and go to his house, since he usually came to mine. I went, and found him drinking champagne, with which we then mutually moistened the dry studies. The young man was pretty as a picture, except for the way he squinted his blue eyes. Whenever he smiled, roguish dimples would appear in his cheeks. Schumann was already neglecting his piano playing,* and he lacked the courage to perform in public—he always gave the impression of a shy young man; in private with me he was in better humor, and became more talkative.[6]

It was while he was studying with Dorn that Schumann made his official debut as a music critic, which might have been one of the reasons for the tension between them. He had already written his now-famous accolade of Chopin—"Hats off, gentlemen, a genius!"—in May 1831. Nowhere is the influence of Florestan and Eusebius more apparent than in this article, which was published after considerable delay on 7 December 1831 in the *Allgemeine Musikalische Zeitung*, Leipzig's rather conservative journal of music. (The editor, Gottfried Wilhelm Fink, was reluctant to print such a peculiarly surrealistic article. He probably did so as a concession to the

---

*One reason for this "neglect" of the piano was Schumann's work on *Child Prodigies* and other literary projects.

avant-garde, to which Schumann and Dorn belonged, but not without coupling Schumann's piece with a much more conventional review written by "a reputable and worthy representative of the older school," possibly Wieck.[7]) Even today Schumann's writing about Chopin seems utterly fantastic:

> Eusebius quietly opened the door the other day. You know the ironic smile on his pale face, with which he invites attention. I was sitting at the piano with Florestan. As you know, he is one of those rare musical personalities who seem to anticipate everything that is new, extraordinary, and meant for the future. But today he was in for a surprise. Eusebius showed us a piece of music and exclaimed, "Hats off, gentlemen, a genius." We were not allowed to look at the title.
>
> I turned the pages without thinking—such vicarious enjoyment of soundless music is something magical. Besides, it seems to me that every composer's note-pattern has a distinctive visual appearance.* Beethoven looks different on paper from Mozart, just as Jean Paul's prose looks different from Goethe's. . . .
>
> "So, let's hear it," said Florestan. Eusebius obeyed. Pressed into a niche near the window, we listened. Eusebius played and seemed enraptured. He conjured up countless figures of a most lively animation, and it seemed as if the enthusiasm of the moment made his fingers go far beyond their usual capacity. Florestan's only response, except for his blissful smile, consisted of saying that these variations could have been written by Beethoven or by Franz Schubert if they had been piano virtuosos. But then he looked at the title page and read. *La ci darem la mano, variations* [on a theme by Mozart] *for the pianoforte with orchestral accompaniment*, by Frederic Chopin, Opus 2. "An Opus 2!" we both cried out with astonishment.[8]

Like much of the musical journalism Schumann was to publish over the next decade, this article startles the reader with its frankly personal revelations, which say more about the author than about the music being discussed. He was externalizing his inner dialogues, fancifully disguised as Florestan and Eusebius. The peculiar style is a blend of Jean Paul, Hoffmann, and other Schumann favorites. Not only did he gain considerable attention by writing in this way, but he also gave publicity to composers like Chopin who were then not well known in Germany.

In fact, Schumann's voluminous writings on music and musicians allowed him politely to resolve rivalrous feelings toward Chopin, Liszt, Mendelssohn, and other composers. His age-mates, they were vying for applause in Europe's concert halls. Schumann's so-called criticism was actually a gracious way of giving credit to those he wanted to befriend. Chopin, for example, had already composed two piano concertos and many other published works when Schumann wrote the laudatory review of his Mozart variations. Schumann himself had only just published his second composi-

---

*Schumann was quite right. For a more recent appreciation of Chopin's beautiful musical handwriting, see Hofstadter (1981).

tion, *Papillons* (op. 2), when in a letter to Wieck (11 January 1832) he referred, obliquely, to the possibility of being upstaged by the Polish pianist: "Chopin's first work is in my hands. I believe for sure it must be his tenth. . . . I modestly claim that between it and Opus 2 lie at least two years and twenty compositions."[9]

The appearance of Florestan and Eusebius perhaps softened this blow to Schumann's pride. The day they "stepped into" his life, he had been practicing Chopin "with fire," and Eusebius told him that "Chopin is a jump ahead." Schumann's diary says that Florestan and Eusebius "both encouraged [him] greatly to have the article published."[10]

Lavishly egocentric digressions were probably one reason why the editors of the *Allgemeine Musikalische Zeitung* were unwilling to print any more of Schumann's writing. One cannot read his Chopin article without noticing his anxious preoccupation with his brother's illness: "Of course dear Julius. . . . Do you have enough wine, Julius. . . . Now, Julius, you too can wake up to new dreams and go to sleep!"[11]

We now know that Schumann was deeply troubled at this time by the fear of an infectious disease. The epidemiology of tuberculosis was not well understood in his day, so that patients like Julius often remained at home even when they were in very advanced stages or dying. After his visit to Zwickau in 1831, Schumann worried greatly that he might have been infected.* But the disease he mentioned in a letter to his brother (5 September 1831) was not tuberculosis:

> I have to admit a tormenting, almost childish fear of cholera. . . . The thought of now dying . . . drives me wild. . . . For several days I've been in a kind of feverish state. A thousand plans go through my head, dissolve, and reappear. I even think that a man has the obligation to get out of the way of an epidemic disease, if he can. . . .[12]

Schumann's "tormenting fear" of cholera was actually based on a real danger. As a result of the Polish–Russian war of 1831, a cholera epidemic was spreading into Saxony, and his "thousand plans" included "going away to cheerful Italy for a half-year perhaps, or to Augsburg for the moment . . . or to Weimar and Hummel," in order to escape the epidemic.[13]

The Weimar scheme had already been blocked by Wieck's objections, as well as by Schumann's own ambivalence regarding Hummel, but he now began to pester his mother all over again. "Weimar is just as exposed as Leipzig, since both are on a major highway," he wrote her. "Fourteen days

---

*Considering the high incidence of tuberculosis in his family—two of Schumann's own children died of this disease—it is quite possible that he did at some time contract an infection, which subsequently healed.

ago I firmly convinced myself that I might come down with cholera. I wouldn't have a soul to be with [in Weimar] except Hummel. How sad my life would then be; I might be thrown without pity into a hospital." [14] And Frau Schumann, as she often did, reciprocated in kind, speaking of her own nervous condition: "When I think you [might] come down with cholera, my Robert, my headaches and dizziness return, I tremble." [15]

Like his mother, Schumann had the exasperating habit of frightening people with his worries about disease. The day he announced, in his diary, "Cholera, cholera," Wieck and Clara met Schumann in a restaurant, where he told them "this may be the last time we will be together." Schumann "didn't mean this as a joke," and Wieck "didn't take it as such either." Clara became so concerned that she "clung to [Schumann] ever more firmly," an expression of anxious affection that became an increasingly important part of their relationship. [16]

Thus even when Schumann made progress in his creative work—studying counterpoint, writing publishable material, and improving his social skills—a regressive pull toward states of terror and confusion held him back and contaminated his interactions with other people. It seems that his talent for assembling sounds and words in original ways could also produce morbid, nihilistic fantasies that often interfered with orderly thinking. So often did Schumann feel compelled to reorganize and reshape his ideas that his speech, which required immediacy and spontaneity, was severely constricted. Small wonder, then, that he was driven so incessantly to communicate through written language, and by composing music.

While Schumann's hypochondriacal nervousness was at its height, he was suddenly faced with the prospect of having to live alone. Wieck had decided to take Clara on a prolonged concert tour as far as Paris. This would mean the end of both the tutorial and the housing arrangements with Schumann, who was disheartened and angry to learn of Wieck's plans. "I don't believe that Master Raro [Wieck] really loves art," fumes the diary. "There is something Jewish in his enthusiasm for Cilia [Clara] which already makes him mentally calculate the money her concerts will earn, and I don't doubt there will be plenty of that." [17]

Three weeks before the Wiecks' departure, Schumann began to think of suicide. "I'm in a fatal state of restlessness and indecision and would like to put a bullet through my head," he wrote his brother Julius. [18] Two weeks later he gave instructions on how to dispose of his personal belongings in case of death. This was a real threat. A letter to his mother (21 September

1831) mentions a will, which he was preparing "essentially for your sake, except for a few trifles, such as the piano, which should go to Rosalie."[19] Schumann's description of his cherished grand piano, an heirloom from his father, as a "trifle" indicates the depth of his despair. His diary is filled with angry exasperation: "Piano bad. . . . The morning went miserably, all miserablinsky. . . . Wieck takes sides against me, says I play the Herz variations like a dog. . . . For little Clara these things happen spontaneously."[20]

After leaving Wieck's home, Schumann moved first into a "cold empty room that looks almost formally shabby,"[21] but then found a more attractive location in the suburbs. His mood quickly improved, and by mid-October he was able to feel his "entire nature gradually coming into a healthy balance." The music lessons with Heinrich Dorn seemed to make a difference. "It goes passably with counterpoint," says the diary, "even though all the rules seem to conflict madly with each other and one contradicts the other. The music director [Dorn] is good to me." Schumann was also able to bring Christel to his "new abode."[22]

It was during this period of increasing stress, while Wieck no longer supervised his piano practicing, that Schumann's old hand problem flared up again, leading eventually to the abandonment of his career as a performer. An analysis of this problem shows that it was closely connected to his conflicts with Wieck, his competitive feelings regarding Clara, and his desire to become a creative rather than a performing artist.

The first indication that Schumann again was preoccupied with physical aspects of piano playing was his experiment with a new approach to the keyboard: "I hold the wrist somewhat higher, approximately like de Belleville, except that her graceful undulations are missing." (Anna Caroline de Belleville, a young pianist—then twenty-two—and a rival to Clara Wieck, was then touring Europe.) By elevating his wrists, Schumann probably hoped to increase the lightness and fluency of his fingers. "It's been going magnificently at the piano for the last few days," says the diary. "The notes roll like pearls at times."[23]

The improvement is not surprising, since a high wrist, by causing the hand to droop, reduces tension in the flexor muscles of the forearm. The relaxed fingers are less encumbered as they strike the piano keys, which results in greater fluency. This occurs at the expense of overall control, however, and the sound is often impoverished. De Belleville may have tried to compensate by swaying her body in "graceful undulations," which Schumann, perhaps afraid to appear effeminate, wanted to avoid. He continued to practice erratically, while also pursuing his literary projects as well as trying to compose.

Soon Schumann complained not only of "lameness in my right hand,"[24] but also of feeling overwhelmed by unfinished projects, including a "gigantic composition that demands every bit of my strength."[25] (This was a sonata in B minor that he never completed although a single movement was published in 1835 as *Allegro pour le Pianoforte*, op. 8.) Moreover, the Christmas season was approaching, threatening to engulf him in nostalgic yearnings for his family. By the end of the year he was depressed again, "sinking into the kind of stupor that has been seizing me occasionally for the past few years."[26]

The diary shows 1832 beginning with a resolution: "An artist must always keep himself in equilibrium with life on the outside, otherwise he will go under, like me."[27] Schumann was thinking a great deal about Clara, whose tour had been phenomenally successful; in Weimar, Goethe personally fetched a pillow so that she might sit more comfortably at the piano, and he inscribed a special medallion "for the consummate artist." In Kassel, the famous violinist Louis Spohr introduced Clara to the court and turned her pages. Wieck proudly noted how "everyone listened with astonishment as she played Chopin's Variations, Opus 2." The newspapers in Gotha raved that Clara "surpasses de Belleville."[28] Before the year was over, Clara's *Caprices* (op. 2) would be published.

Schumann's feelings toward his young rival were undergoing a change. After first meeting Clara, he had written in his diary, "It's amazing that there are no female composers. . . . Women could perhaps be regarded as the frozen, firm embodiment of music."[29] Now, after learning of the girl's success as both composer and performer, he adopted a mock reverential attitude: "I often think of you, dear Clara, not the way a brother thinks of his sister or a friend of his girl, but rather like a pilgrim at a distant shrine." But he also teased her ironically, writing "While reading [in the newspaper] how *Fräulein* Clara Wieck played the Herz variations, I couldn't help smiling; oh, but please excuse me honorable Fräulein—one form of address is preferable to all others, and that is not to use a title. Who would ever think of saying *Herr* Paganini or *Herr* Goethe?"[30] Schumann's good-natured teasing may have been a compromise between admiration and envy. He wanted the twelve-year-old pianist to be his friend.

In Paris Clara would meet prominent musicians, including the noted teacher Wilhelm Kalkbrenner, one of whose recommendations was that pianists sit closer to the right side of the keyboard, in order to obtain greater strength and better control over the upper register.* Another of Kalkbrenner's methods was the use of mechanical devices to make the fingers more independent. There were several of these contraptions available, including the "chiroplast," invented by an enterprising bandmaster, Johann Bernard

---

*Before the piano was extended to its modern range, it was recommended—by C. P. E. Bach, for one—that pianists sit at the center or even to the left of the keyboard.

Logier, who required students to place their hands into a machine that regulated the spaces between the fingers. Wieck had actually favored the Logier system of piano teaching at one time, but he later forbade his students to use chiroplasts.

We do not know exactly when Schumann began using a mechanical device while practicing the piano, but it was during Wieck's five-month absence from Leipzig that his diary first mentions a "cigar-mechanism" (*Cigarrenmechanik*).[31] What this was and how Schumann used it to try to strengthen his right hand has been the subject of considerable speculation. Some scholars think it was just an ordinary finger-stretcher of the sort used by many music students.[32] (According to the violinist Sidney Griller, students at the Royal Academy of Music in London called such devices "cigar boxes.") Another theory is that Schumann rigged up a sling-and-pulley arrangement to hold one finger aloft while he was practicing. The sling could have been attached to the piano, to the ceiling, or to his wrist.

Whatever the truth of the matter, practicing with the "cigar-mechanism" proved to be detrimental to Schumann's right hand. As Wieck put it in a book on piano technique published in 1859, the "finger-torturer" used by his "famous pupil" damaged his hand in some way.[33] The details will be discussed shortly. What is important from a psychological point of view is that Schumann's disability coincided with Clara's rise to fame, and before long he would be thinking of her as his invaluable "right hand."[34]

Just before Clara's return from her concert tour, Schumann dismissed Dorn as his teacher because "my entire being rebels against every external influence, and I have to discover things on my own for the first time, in order to assimilate them and put them in their proper place."[35] His diary lists half a dozen new "plans for future hours," including compositions and a "musical novel."[36] Along with the study of Marpurg's treatises on music theory, he wanted to "dismember the fugues from Bach's *Well-Tempered Clavier* one after another into their finest detail." His depression was beginning to lift, and he was diligently composing a new set of piano pieces, the *Intermezzi* (published in September 1833 as op. 4). It was a "beautiful week; clean, pious, sober, and lively."[37]

Wieck returned, full of opinions about some of the musicians he had met—but "as usual Wieck's judgment contained more criticism than praise." Chopin was described as "a pretty fellow, but Paris has made him negligent and indifferent toward himself and art." As for Mendelssohn, "he has enormous success in Paris; his tone and touch don't amount to anything; otherwise he plays furiously, but only Beethoven and Mozart." About the young Ferdinand Hiller, another rising composer and pianist (who twenty years later would have a significant impact on Schumann's career), Wieck commented, "One recognizes a Jew-boy in every measure he plays."[38]

Schumann feared Wieck's "unworthy and mean judgments," but nevertheless he exposed himself to criticism by playing his latest compositions for him. The *Papillons* Wieck called "piquant, new, original, and full of spirit," but he also found many of them to be "American and odd."[39] This response was ambiguous, and Schumann wanted definite approval. Thus he asked to perform his *Papillons* at a homecoming party for Wieck and Clara on 28 May. Dr. and Frau Carus would be there. In order to be ready for this party, he returned to his practicing, and it was during these weeks of anxious preparation that his physical handicap became most worrisome.

Exercise seemed to help at first. "My third finger is improved because of the cigar-mechanism," says the diary on 7 May. But by Tuesday, 22 May—six days before Wieck's party—"the third finger seems really incorrigible." That evening, in the presence of his brother Carl and his sister-in-law Rosalie, he realized that he would not be able to perform: "When I have to play for anyone," he admitted, "I'm overcome by an anxious inhibition of my fantasies that drives me to despair." Schumann felt utterly defeated. "It seems as if I want to abandon my genius, rather than the other way around," he commented in his diary, and mentioned many vague complaints suggestive of a flight into illness: "fatigue and malaise . . . intolerable colds, and headaches." Three days before the party for Wieck Schumann sought out a medical student friend, Robert Herzfeld, who recommended that he rest the third finger and generally take it easy.[40]

In Heidelberg, Schumann had complained mostly about the fourth finger of his right hand, but now he was emphasizing the third. (His handwritten manuscripts indicate that he used standard finger numbering—1 for thumb, 2 for index finger, and so on.) Furthermore, a medical affidavit, which he later used as a means of avoiding military service, implicates his index finger *and* middle finger. This affidavit was supplied by Moritz Emil Reuter, M.D., a close personal friend, who was trying to keep Schumann out of the militia:

> For a long time the continued use of a machine that pulled these fingers strongly toward the back of the hand resulted in a kind of paralytic condition, manifested first in that they possessed only weak feeling, and second in that so far as movement was concerned, they no longer responded willingly. In this way Schumann was forced to give up his virtuoso career; the fingers have remained in the same paralyzed condition . . . in spite of numerous attempts at treatment. When playing the piano [he] cannot use his *middle finger* at all, the index finger only partially, and is in no condition to grasp an object and hold it firmly.[41]

Another Leipzig physician, Raimund Brachman, working on behalf of the city administration, contested Reuter's diagnosis and after re-examining

Schumann, wrote, "As is generally known [the finger-weakness] does not hinder him from playing the piano."[42]

Schumann's ambivalence about performing at Wieck's party came to a head when Wieck suggested that Clara might be a suitable "substitute" for him.[43] She herself had offered to play his new *Papillons*, but he had been criticizing her playing as "lacking in tenderness . . . like a Hussar." There was also something irritating about Clara's personality. On separate occasions he described her as "childishly simple-minded," "silly and anxious," "lame and cold," "capricious and whiny." The night of the party she seemed "mentally and physically tired," and her performance of the *Papillons* disappointed him. "The guests looked at each other in surprise and couldn't grasp the rapid contrasts," says Schumann's diary. "Toward eleven o'clock she played them again, even more slovenly, but with more life."[44]

The following day Schumann reported "tearing into six Bach fugues with Clara, four-handed, at first sight," suggesting that his hand could not have been too disabled. (He had also been working recently on Beethoven's *Hammerclavier* Sonata (op. 106), a work that requires great physical effort.) After returning home, Schumann began improvising at the piano. He was fascinated by a tone sequence, C F G C; Clara had suggested this melody to him. Suddenly "it seemed as if all kinds of flowers and Gods were coming out of my fingers." As Schumann's "thoughts streamed forth" he found it possible to incorporate Clara's melody into his own music.[45] Her C F G C melody can be heard in his *Impromptus* (op. 5).

This process of exchange seems to have delighted them both. From then on Schumann and Clara could engage in endless flirtation and teasing over their musical "offspring." (It should be noted that Clara, close to twelve, was approaching puberty.) She promised to dedicate her *Caprices* (op. 2) to Schumann and then reneged, while he told her his *Intermezzi*, if they were ever finished, would be dedicated to her. (In fact they were not; Schumann dedicated these pieces to the Czech composer Johannes Kalliwoda.) Schumann's playfulness is very apparent in these early compositions, which feature moments of wonderful drollery (the third Intermezzo, for example) mixed with tender yearning. He called them "longer Papillons,"[46] and they betoken a step toward more adult artistic expression and perhaps growing capacity for human relationships. "My whole heart is in you, dear fifth Intermezzo," he wrote. "It was born of unspeakable love."[47]

However, with the approach of his birthday on 8 June 1832, Schumann's anxiety again began to escalate. He had been playing the piano a good deal and was transcribing Paganini's G minor Caprice, when on 4 June a frightening caricature of Paganini, drawn by the deaf painter Johann Peter Lyser, came to his attention. It made a "grisly impression" on Schumann, who commented that the fantasy of "Paganini in a magic circle—the murdered woman—dancing skeletons and pulling, magnetized fog-ghosts" often "hovered over" him as he went on working. The day before his birthday he was feeling better, "playing Szymanowska's* lady-like études" and "on Glock's advice not thinking of the third finger at all."[48] But that evening brought disturbing news of the death of Schumann's nephew Robert, less than a year old. ("Forebodings, dreams, doubles [*Doppelgänger*]," he had written in his diary the day he learned that his brother Carl and his favorite sister-in-law Rosalie had christened their baby "Robert Schumann."[49] Having a "double" was considered a bad omen, and a popular myth of the romantic era was that seeing one's double meant imminent death.)

The unexpected death of his namesake "lay heavily" on Schumann."[50] He went again to the park in Zweinaundorf, where four years earlier he had nearly gone "mad." Nothing frightful happened this time on his birthday, and in a letter home he commented, "How different my thoughts were three years ago in the same place."[51] (It had actually been four years; Schumann's memory slip may have been symptomatic of his anxiety.)

Shortly after his birthday, he got into a heated argument with Wieck over how best to deal with the problem of his right hand. Wieck defended his own system of teaching, pointing to Clara as an example of its success. This probably infuriated Schumann. In the diary he called Wieck a "bad teacher," and two days later he noted that his third finger had become "completely stiff."[52] Nevertheless, he went to Dresden with Wieck the following week and remained there for ten days.†

The diary comments on the bad weather in Dresden and on the "important" people Schumann met there, including the piano teacher Carl Krägen, the composer and music critic Gottfried Weber, and the director of the Royal Opera, Carl Reissiger, who would later become a loyal friend. Schumann seems to have been trying to contact artists and writers who might someday support his career as a critic and publisher. And yet "the whole time" in Dresden he "felt little inclination toward words." Music was constantly in his ears—"the crazy [third] Intermezzo is basically a deep scream from the heart," says the diary. When he returned to Leipzig his major preoccupations were Clara Wieck's concert (on 9 July 1832) and a new composition, "Exercise fantastique," which he wanted to dedicate to "Mr. Charles Krägen" in Dresden.[54]

A letter to his mother in August indicates that Schumann had again

---

*The Polish pianist and composer Marie Szymanowska (1790–1832).

†A letter to Schumann's mother says that he went to Dresden "on the recommendation of my doctor, and also for distraction. It will be necessary for me to work a great deal there."[53]

sought medical advice in regard to his hand ailment and was again debating a change in his career:

> My whole house has become a druggist's shop. It did begin to worry me with the hand and I deliberately put off asking an anatomist [i.e., a surgeon], because I was very fearful of the stroke of his knife, i.e. because I believed he would say that the damage might be incurable. I already started to make all sorts of plans for the future, had almost decided to study theology (not law). . . . Finally I went to Professor Kühl,* and asked him in good conscience whether it would improve—After shaking his head a few times he said, "Yes, but not so quickly—i.e. not in less than half a year." As soon as I had his yes, a stone fell from my heart and with pleasure I did everything that he requested. It was enough, namely to take *animal baths*—let Schurig explain it to you. . . .[55]

Schumann had agreed to a crude and archaic form of treatment, an ancient folk remedy that required afflicted persons to go to a butcher shop, obtain a slaughtered animal (usually a calf, lamb, or pig), and insert their ailing extremities into its moist belly. The warmth of the entrails, blood, and feces was thought to have healing powers.[56] Schumann's letter goes on to describe his treatment as "not exactly the most charming," and jokes that "it is very strengthening. I feel such power and great tension throughout my whole body, that I really would like to beat somebody up."[57]

But manual contact with the internal organs of a dead animal also had a negative effect. Schumann's letter complains of a new hypochondriacal concern—that "something of the cattle-essence might get into my system."[58] The symbolic meaning of an "animal bath" must also be considered. Schumann could not have been unaware of the warm, moist feel of the entrails on his outstretched hand during the treatment—a mingling of sensuality with death. Nor could he have been oblivious to the phallic appearance of his "stiff" middle finger.† Kuhl was in effect asking him to participate in a kind of necrophilia. Considering Schumann's recent anguish over the "wound" on his penis, together with the guilt he had been experiencing over his inability to abstain from sexual activity, we can assume that the animal baths afforded not only punishment for his "sins" but also a substitute form of physical gratification.

Kuhl's treatment obviously focused far too much attention on Schumann's right hand, which at this time was only one of his many problems.

---

* A prominent surgeon, Karl August Kuhl, who was working in Leipzig at the time.
† Then, as now, the "middle-finger jerk" was an obscene insult; in fact, it was well-known among the Romans, who even gave the middle finger a special name, *digitus impudicus*.[59] Many references to this gesture appear in classical literature, with which Schumann was quite familiar.

The letter to his mother mentions "bathing the hand all day in a warm brandy-rinse," which meant that Schumann would be able to "play the piano as little as possible." A letter to his friend Töpken (then an attorney in Bremen) even talks about "a lame and *broken* finger" on the right hand.[60] The myth that Schumann's hand was severely injured gained credence in the 1940s when Robert Haven Schauffler's biography cited a totally unsubstantiated remark by Alfred Meyer, M.D., to the effect that the composer cut into the webs between his fingers to give them more independence.[61] This is unlikely, since such an operation, unless performed by a skilled surgeon, can lead to serious infection and permanent damage to the tendons.

More recently Eric Sams proposed another theory, that it was syphilis, or perhaps the mercury treatment used to combat this disease, which damaged Schumann's right hand.[62] The problem with this explanation is that syphilis does not produce the sort of symptoms Schumann complained of. Two neurologists, Drs. R. A. Henson and H. Urich, who have reviewed various theories of causation of his hand "injury," claim that neurological symptoms of syphilis "would hardly be manifest at the age of twenty or twenty-one." (Actually, Schumann's problems with his hand began when he was only nineteen.) As for the conjecture that mercury poisoning was a pathogenic factor, Henson and Urich point out that "mercurial neuropathy was so rare during anti-syphilitic treatment as to raise doubts on the causal relationship."[63]

Nor does it seem plausible that Schumann had a "trigger-finger," as suggested by L. Carerj.[64] Such a condition results from narrowing of the tunnel through which the tendon controlling a finger must move. The tendon suddenly locks in place and can be released only with considerable effort. This causes a palpable (and often audible) snap—hence the common term "trigger-finger." If Schumann suffered from this condition, he (and his doctors) would almost certainly have described the very characteristic symptoms of this disorder, but they do not.

The most likely explanation is that Schumann had an inflammation of one or more tendons in his hand, associated perhaps with some degree of involvement of the nerve supplying his fingers. This is not an uncommon cause of hand disorders among musicians, especially pianists. Recent clinical research with such patients indicates that their problems usually arise as a result of practicing too strenuously, especially when octave passages, trills, and difficult arpeggios are required.[65] In Schumann's case this physical strain was undoubtedly made worse by excessive stretching of his fingers on the "cigar-mechanism."

Although he bemoaned the fact that he was only a "nine-fingered pianist," Schumann soon discovered certain benefits to be gained by the disability. It kept him out of a contest with Clara, which he probably would have lost.* It provided an excuse for him to avoid military service. It gave him time and energy to devote to creative work, which otherwise would have been consumed by practicing the piano. Finally, it helped him to save face with his family in Zwickau. "I have become fully resigned and consider my hand incurable," he wrote his mother on 6 November 1832. "I want to take up the violoncello again (one needs only the left hand for this) and it will be very useful to me in composing symphonies."[67]

The occasion of a gala concert, scheduled to be held in Zwickau on 18 November 1832, would be the test of Schumann's mettle as a composer. He had been invited to participate. Also on the program would be Clara Wieck, making her local debut. (Schumann's letter telling his mother why he could no longer play the piano says, cryptically, "Clara will give you much to think about."[68]) News of his shattered ambitions as a performer worried his mother and brothers, of course, but there was some reassurance that he would now make good as a composer. Schumann had tantalized them with promises of a symphony.

But which symphony? Schumann's first effort (in 1828) to compose such a work had faltered after only twenty-five pages. Dreading another failure, he was in a heightened state of apprehension two months before the Zwickau concert. He noted that his "mind often disappears"; he berated himself: "You miserable human being, get back to work."[69] In the letter to his mother, he confessed that he was "scared and doubtful" about being able to finish his new G minor Symphony on time, and only two weeks before the concert he humbled himself by approaching Christian Gottlob Müller, a violinist in the Gewandhaus Orchestra, for instruction in orchestration. "I would like to go through one movement of my own symphony. . . . I've become rather mistrustful of my own symphonic talent."[70] (In fact, he had completed only one movement, and even this was barely ready in time.) Two of Schumann's friends hurriedly copied out the orchestral parts just before he left for Zwickau. The concert was a fiasco for him, while for Clara it was a stunning success. "The hall was overfilled," wrote Wieck (who also

---

* As mentioned earlier, Schumann did not stop playing the piano. Gustav Jansen's *Die Davids-bündler* (1883) discusses the changes in his pianistic style that resulted from his disability. Instead of focusing on meticulous passage work, Schumann emphasized the sheer quality of sound. According to a contemporary account, his playing "sounded as if the sustaining pedal were always half way down, so that the shapes flowed into one another. But the melody would softly emerge, a veritable dawning. . . . Schumann must have had exceptional dexterity as a pianist."[66]

participated in the concert, playing on a small organ called the "physharmonica"[71]). "The first movement of Schumann's symphony was played but not understood. It had little, too little, effect on this sort of audience. It is well designed and inventive, but too meager in its instrumentation." But the thirteen-year-old Clara's own recently composed *Scherzo for Orchestra* was enthusiastically applauded, and she dominated the concert with no less than four solo performances. "As she was playing the Herz Bravura Variations," her father continued, "the audience came forward to occupy the entire orchestra so that one could see almost nothing of the musicians."[72] Schumann's mother was very much impressed, and, according to Clara's biographer Berthold Litzmann, she "pulled the childlike figure toward herself with a sudden overwhelming emotion, and softly whispered to her 'one day you must marry my Robert!' . . . It made a deep, inextinguishable impression on Clara"[73]—and, we can surmise, on Schumann as well.

Hurt and humiliated, he decided not to go back to Leipzig, and as Clara and Wieck were leaving he quipped that he would return only in some kind of "disembodied" state,[74] a remark that shocked his mother.

Schumann stayed with his family for the next four months which proved to be a difficult period. In December 1832 he wrote to Ludwig Rellstab, a well-known music critic in Berlin, to thank him for a favorable review of the *Papillons* and to announce that "within a short time I hope to come to Berlin . . . with a symphony under my arm."[75] He worked sporadically on the G minor Symphony, trying to complete a second and a third movement for a performance in Schneeberg, the village near Zwickau where Carl and Rosalie Schumann lived. During the rehearsals he stayed with the bereaved couple. ("Melancholy moods have something very attractive and even a strengthening effect on my fantasies," he wrote Rosalie afterward.[76]) He also saw a practitioner of electrotherapy, Dr. Otto, who applied Galvanic currents to his right hand and arm. "This much too powerfully stimulating treatment deadened the sickly parts even further," Schumann wrote.[77] His diary betrays persistent depressiveness: "Why can't I write, when life flows over me with animation? Why do I grope for you, my diary, when all is quiet and dead?"[78]

Clara Wieck's insensitivity to his traumatic situation is apparent in a teasing letter she wrote "just to make you curious, so you become homesick for Leipzig. . . . Herr Wagner has surpassed you with his symphony, which was performed here. It is supposed to be very much like Beethoven's A major Symphony."[79] Richard Wagner was then twenty years old. To be "surpassed" by him at this point must have been painful for Schumann. "I have withdrawn into a cocoon and sit extremely quietly in the web," he wrote. He did not yet feel "strong enough" to answer Clara directly, and whatever anger he may have felt toward her was quickly displaced onto Chopin. "I don't like his having so many pieces published all at once," he wrote, "because it doesn't seem very smart. After all, fame progresses on midgets' feet and should not be forced. Of course, success can also rush in like a storm, as with Clara."[80]

Finally, in March 1833, Schumann did return to Leipzig. With a new roommate, a law student named Carl Günther, he rented a small apartment in Franz Riedel's house on the outskirts of town. Günther made the following observation about Schumann's lifestyle:

> [He] studied during the day. Evenings he would frequent a certain restaurant-bar, where he spent several hours in the circle of his friends. But he was mostly self-absorbed there, and seemingly passive, so that it might appear to people who did not know him that he was overcome by the beer which flowed in such copious amounts. . . .[81]

Schumann himself noticed that he had become unusually introspective, and in April he subjected himself to a psychological consultation with a local schoolteacher, Karl J. Portius. In a long letter, Schumann tried to reassure his mother that Portius was no "windbag or cheat," but then told her how Portius made use of an electromagnetic device: "One is first brought into magnetic rapport with the machine, then grasps an iron rod that is magnetically attracted or repelled, depending on whether you possess this or that quality, temperament, characteristic, etc." Schumann enjoyed this kind of magical thinking, and he seems to have been reassured when "fast as lightning the magnet shot to 'hypochondria' (but not to depression), to 'quiet,' 'shy,' 'delicate' (remarkably not 'agile'), 'sensitive,' 'kindhearted,' 'stubborn,' 'genial and original,' and 'predominantly emotional.'"[82]

For the next three months Schumann felt somewhat better and became more productive. He completed his *Paganini Etudes*, revised the Toccata he had begun in Heidelberg, and began making sketches for a series of sonatas, all for solo piano. This represents not only a deliberate turning away from the orchestral composing he had recently attempted and failed at, but also a change in compositional style related to his ambivalence about being a pianist. Much of Schumann's early piano music is very taxing and difficult, and, as musicologist Alan Walker has noted, it "exploit[s] the kind of virtuoso technique which [Schumann] could now no longer hope to possess."[83] Nevertheless, in a long letter to his mother—the first in several months—he expressed the surprising belief that he would be cured of his hand ailment after all. Perhaps he was grasping at straws and hoping to reassure her. Or he may again have been trying to deny his physical limitations and planning, with delusional optimism, to perform his own difficult virtuoso compositions in public. A new physician, Dr. Franz Hartmann, was now treating his hand ailment and promising, according to Schumann, that it "will be healed in three months." Dr. Hartmann, prescribed "a tiny, tiny bit of powder" and "a strict diet and little beer, wine, or coffee."[84]

It is not possible to know the exact ingredients of the "tiny bit of powder" the doctor administered; Schumann's diary is silent on the matter. Dr. Hartmann was a reputable Leipzig practitioner who specialized in homeopathy, which was considered a new and controversial approach to treatment. He emphasized the value of general hygiene, sound medical attitudes, and the very sparing use of extremely small amounts of medication (which in homeopathic theory was believed to strengthen the body's natural defense against disease).[85]

It was apparently Dr. Hartmann who also treated Schumann in July 1833 for malaria, which was rampant throughout Saxony and required quarantine.* The patient lost a good deal of weight. "Each day I waste more visibly and grow into a dried-up beanpole without leaves," he wrote Clara. "The doctor has even forbidden me to yearn, namely for you, because it excites me too much." His annoyance was apparent as he added, "I laughed into the doctor's face when he tried to hold me back from writing. Yes, I threatened to attack and infect him with the fever, if he does not quietly give in to me. Now he does."[86]

It was in this socially isolated condition, and while still smarting from the artistic defeats of the preceding year, that Schumann began to feel in some magical way drawn to Clara—"a chain of sparks now attracts us or reminds us of one another," he wrote her on 13 July 1833.

> Tomorrow morning at 11 o'clock on the dot I will play the Adagio from Chopin's variations and at the same time think about you very strongly, yes only you. Now please do the same, so that we can see and meet together spiritually. The point where our Doppelgänger will encounter each other would probably be over the Thomas Gate.[87]

This was the beginning of their fairy-tale romance.

---

* Readers who believe that Schumann contracted syphilis in his youth may want to consider the possible effects of the malaria from which he suffered later. Paroxysmal high fever, such as that produced by malaria, is a well-known treatment for syphilis. Moreover, as was demonstrated in an important epidemiological study of 1,404 *untreated* syphilitics in 1964, 80 to 90 percent of these patients had no sign of the tertiary stage of the disease, but died of other causes (Clark and Danbolt, 1964).

VII.
Breakdown and Aftermath, 1833–1835

hree members of the Schumann family lay ill during the summer of 1833: Schumann in Leipzig with malaria, his sister-in-law Rosalie in Schneeberg with a much more virulent form of the same disease, and his brother Julius in Zwickau, still chronically ill with tuberculosis.

On several occasions over the preceding few years, Frau Schumann had written to say that Julius was dying, and each time Robert dutifully went to see his brother. Now, using his own illness as an excuse, he adamantly refused to go. "You seem to have no understanding of my own tormenting disease," he wrote his mother, "otherwise you would not repeatedly invite me. . . . I haven't gone out because almost every breath of air produces an attack. I'm not even allowed to wash myself." [1]

Without witnessing Julius's actual condition and tormented by his own symptoms, Schumann fantasized about his dying brother: "How is he actually, is he still conscious and able to talk, does he have any hope, did he receive my letter, does he want to see me, does he think of me often?" It is clear from his correspondence that Schumann was empathizing and possibly identifying with his brother's condition. "Were I to take the mail coach [to

Zwickau] I would have to go straight to bed and might never get up again,"
he wrote, and continued: "As I write these lines he [Julius] may be wrestling
with death. O God!" [2]

When Julius finally died on 2 August 1833 at the age of twenty-eight,
Schumann still could not bring himself to go home. His fear of death was
too overwhelming. Even thinking about a funeral would bring back memories of his father's death, his mother's absence at that terrifying moment,
and the ghastliness of his sister's suicide. Much of Schumann's morbid anxiety, his obsessive preoccupation with death, and his ambivalence toward
those he was closest to resulted from trying to defend himself against the
chaotic emotions associated with loss. His only way of dealing with them
now was to crawl into a shell. It was this pattern of social isolation, more
acceptable in the nineteenth century than now, that enabled him to devote
so much time and energy to creative endeavors. It also made him seem very
odd, uncommunicative, and bent on avoiding normal social obligations.

At this time Schumann decided to consolidate all his earlier literary
efforts—poetry, novels, plays, autobiographical writing, and musical essays—into one grand design, a newspaper. Two months beforehand he had
already hinted to his mother about plans for a "new, major musical newspaper." [3] Now, in the throes of reacting to his brother's death, he impulsively
activated this project by sending his brother Carl, in Schneeberg, specific
editorial directions for the newspaper, *Neue Zeitschrift für Musik* (*New Journal
for Music*), in which Florestan and Eusebius would play vital roles. [4]

Although the timing may seem inappropriate, it makes sense in terms
of Schumann's emotional needs, for surely this was a self-therapeutic act.
His family seems to have ignored his ideas. They were far too busy with
Julius's funeral that week to pay much attention to this speculative interest
in publishing a newspaper about music. Furthermore, Carl Schumann had
a more serious problem to cope with: his wife Rosalie's deteriorating health.
Nevertheless, the family did help Schumann later that month with the first
published edition of his *Impromptus sur une Romance de Clara Wieck* (op. 5). *

Further exact details of what happened just before Schumann's nervous
breakdown in 1833 are scarce. He had stopped making daily observations
about himself in the diary, and, in keeping with his plans for a newspaper,
he was now beginning to write for public consumption rather than for private introspection. Henceforth only the most significant personal events would
be summarized in the diary. For example, he recorded frequent "traffic with
Wieck and Clara" and took note of their leaving for Chemnitz (now Karl
Marx Stadt) in August. [5]

---

* He later revised these pieces, and a new edition was published in 1850.

Thus deprived of his most essential musical friends in Leipzig, Schumann seems to have become more restless and dissatisfied. In September he left his roommate and rented a fifth-floor room in an old building, Burgstrasse 21, closer to the center of town. There he enjoyed a "growing circle [of] easy acquaintances," including musicians, writers, and artists. Apparently there were some weeks of debauchery and heavy drinking—"dissolute life," says the diary—and then followed "the night of 17–18 October—most terrible in my life—Rosalie's death."[6]

It was this news that precipitated Schumann's acute breakdown. "I was seized by a fixed idea of going mad [*wahnsinnig*]," he wrote in his diary. She was his favorite sister-in-law; in addition, "We were the same age; she was more than just a sister to me, but there could be no talk of real love. She cared for me, always spoke highly of me, cheered me up, in short, expected the best from me."[7]

Rosalie's death, coming so soon after his brother Julius's, appears to have left Schumann utterly defenseless:

> During the night, from October 17 to 18, 1833, the most terrifying thought that a person can ever have suddenly occurred to me, the most terrible with which heaven can punish you, that of "losing my mind." It overwhelmed me so violently, that all consolation and every prayer became as ineffective as scorn and mockery. The anxiety drove me from place to place—my breathing was disrupted by the idea "what would happen if you could no longer think?" . . . In my endlessly terrible excitement, I ran to a doctor,* told him everything, that I often seemed to lose my senses, that I didn't know where to turn because of the anxiety, yes, that I could not guarantee whether in such a condition of utter helplessness, I might not raise a hand against my own life.[8]

According to Wasielewski, who interviewed many contemporary witnesses, Schumann's "precarious state of violent inner excitement" reached suicidal proportions. Some said that he wanted to "throw himself out of the window during the night," while others denied this.[9] (In view of what is now known about his self-destructive behavior, this was probably true.) In any event, he was quickly persuaded to move down to the ground floor of the house, and to accept Carl Günther as his roommate once again—an arrangement that proved especially beneficial at night, when fear and agitation made it almost impossible for Schumann to sleep.

This acute illness can best be diagnosed as a panic disorder, a state of

---

*Schumann did not record which doctor he "ran to," but we can assume that he consulted Dr. Hartmann, his most recent medical advisor. Hartmann probably prescribed a sedative (perhaps an opiate), as was then common practice in the control of psychiatric illness. Schumann may also have turned to his close friend, Moritz Emil Reuter, for medical advice.

such intense anxiety that he could no longer control his thinking, his breathing, or his motor behavior. He was incessantly preoccupied with suicide and madness.

Panic disorders are usually caused by psychological stress superimposed on a biological predisposition, and what the exact psychophysiological mechanisms are cannot yet be answered with certainty.[10] Suffice it to say that in Schumann's case, a malarial infection (which in those days could not be treated with antibiotics) had probably reduced his resistance. News of Rosalie's death precipitated his breakdown. Not only had she been afflicted with malaria herself, but she also symbolized both a mother and a sister for him. Thus her death would have reawakened much of his anguish over the loss of his sister Emilie. Schumann believed that Rosalie loved him, and that he loved her in return. This feeling had recently been contaminated, however, by disappointment and rage, because Rosalie had replaced him with her own baby, and, worse yet, had given this boy his own name and then not managed to keep him alive. An unconscious desire for revenge may have been gratified by her sudden death and resulted in feelings of both guilt and abandonment. (As far as we know, Schumann did not attend Rosalie's funeral.) Mixed in with all of this was probably his survivor guilt. (Schumann had *not* succumbed to malaria—the same disease that presumably killed Rosalie—and he had also outlived Julius.) Thus secret exultation may have been part of the excitement he felt with his panic, but it was insufficient to drive out of his mind the conviction that he would be the next member of his family to die.

A probable further result of Rosalie's death was that it removed a female object of Schumann's sexual desire, thus weakening his already fragile inhibitions against homosexuality and releasing deep uncertainties about his masculinity. We know that Schumann's propensity for loving unattainable or forbidden women was associated with a desire for intimacy with men, a yearning that we can conjecture had been effectively reduced through the imaginary companionship of Florestan and Eusebius. Recently, however, a group of attractive young men had begun to cluster around Schumann in connection with his newspaper work. Considerable revelry as well as rivalry prevailed in that circle, so that homosexual panic may have contributed to this nearly catastrophic breakdown.

Schumann summed up the period following his breakdown dramatically, as "tortures of the most terrible melancholy from October to December."*[11] He itemized the symptoms in a letter written to his mother in late November:

> I was hardly more than a statue, without coldness, without warmth. Only by forcing myself to work did life return, bit by bit. But I am still so shy and timid that I cannot sleep alone. Also I have taken a basically good-natured man [Carl Günther] to stay with me. I find that I can cultivate something in him, and this stimulates and warms me. Can you believe that I don't have the courage to travel to Zwickau by myself, for fear that something could happen to me? Violent flushing, unspeakable dread, shortness of breath, and momentary lapses of consciousness fluctuate rapidly, although less now than in the days gone by. If you had an inkling how depression has totally shattered my peace of mind, you would surely forgive me for not writing.[13]

His mother had been trying to console him, writing to him about the tears she was shedding for him, and even making an effort to cheer him with "tears of joy" because she had recently seen a favorable review of one of his compositions in a musical journal.[14]

There seems to have been an intense reverberation of feelings between Schumann and his mother during the period of recovery from his nervous breakdown, so intense in fact that Clara, who later published his letters, deleted certain passages, such as the one that follows. (We must remember that Clara had virtually lost her own mother, by divorce, when she was a small child, and that her father probably did not countenance any expressions of longing for or childish dependence on one's mother.)

> My mother, really love me! Because I'm often close to madness when I think of Julius and Rosalie—love me, but really! At night it is so wonderful to know that someone now thinks of me for sure, and maybe prays, and that this person is you![15]

It is also apparent that after his nervous breakdown, Schumann avoided his mistress Christel—the diary does not mention her again until 1836— and that during this interval he may have tried to be celibate or even overtly homosexual. His first partner, if indeed these were homosexual relationships, was probably the roommate Günther. The next would most likely

---

*It is of interest that Schumann seems to have lost or misplaced for five years what he had written about his nervous breakdown and its aftermath, a symptom perhaps of his desire to forget that episode. Not until reaching Vienna in 1838 did he rediscover the unsettling facts (and begin to reveal them for the first time to Clara Wieck). "By accident," says Schumann's diary on 28 November 1838, "this little book came into my hands yesterday. Maybe I'll mark it for the future. Here I've remembered things that I later forgot or confused during the intervening time. Perhaps when I am very old I can work the whole thing out."[12]

have been a well-known pianist named Ludwig Schunke, whom Schumann met in a bar and with whom he lived for almost a year. Their meeting at a local drinking establishment sounds quite fantastic, and it isn't clear whether Schumann, as he implied, was immediately enchanted by Schunke, whether he embroidered the story (he later published it, oddly enough, in the *New Journal for Music*), or whether some of this was a delusional experience.

> A young man approached us in Krause's Cellar. All eyes turned in his direc-
> tion. Some wanted to find in him a resemblance to Johannes [John the Bap-
> tist]. Others thought that if such a statuesque head were dug up in Pompeii
> one would declare him to be a Roman Emperor. Florestan whispered into my
> ear, "There goes Schiller reincarnate. . . ." Before he even whispered his name,
> "Ludwig Schunke from Stuttgart," I heard an inner voice saying: "that's the
> one we are looking for"—and his eyes expressed just about the same thing.[16]

Ludwig Schunke, the same age as Schumann, came from a family of musicians and had been something of a child prodigy, having played in public since age twelve. He had lived in Paris for a while, where he had met Liszt, Berlioz, and other notables. After a brief and unhappy sojourn in Vienna, Schunke went to Prague, then to Dresden, and finally arrived in Leipzig, where he met Schumann.

The rapport between the two men was apparently ignited by a quarrel involving the composer Otto Nicolai, who was also visiting Leipzig. Believing his "name to have been dirtied" by Nicolai, Schunke challenged him to a duel and asked Schumann to be his second.[17] The fight never took place, but Schunke soon moved into Schumann's rooms on the Burgstrasse, where they shared their few belongings, played music, composed, and planned to work together on what was soon to become the newspaper about music and musicians.

It was while he was living with Schunke that Schumann elaborated the idea of the *Davidsbund*, a fraternity headed by Florestan, who, like the bib-lical King David, would rally musical progressives against their reactionary, uncultivated enemies, the so-called Philistines. This was a very romantic idea—Carl Maria von Weber himself had formed such a group*—and much of the material Schumann used in writing about the *Davidsbündler*, as well as many of the names he invented for them, were taken from his earlier, unfinished novel *Child Prodigies*.

---

*In Weber's "Harmonic Association" (*Harmonische Verein*), each "brother" was to adopt a pseu-donym; Weber called himself "Melos."[18] Weber's group was a real association of like-thinking artists, however, unlike Schumann's group of mostly imaginary companions. By 1813 it had fallen apart and no longer functioned successfully.

Schumann's relationship with his "enthusiastically beloved Ludwig Schunke," as Gustav Jansen calls him, undoubtedly helped in the process of recovery from his recent mental illness. Schumann wrote that they were "living out a novel the likes of which may never before have been put into a book,"[19] to which Jansen, editor of Schumann's *Collected Writings*, adds, "They agreed harmoniously on all artistic matters; thus the bond between Schunke and Schumann drew even tighter; in a short time they became indispensable to each other."[20]

Dr. Moritz Emil Reuter, a person genuinely concerned about Schumann's well-being, and himself a member of the *Davidsbund*, seems to have warned him not to become too dependent on Schunke, who had tuberculosis. As Schumann revealed several years later when he described the aftermath of his nervous breakdown to Clara, "The doctor [presumably Reuter] . . . told me 'Medicine would not help here; go find a woman* for yourself, she will cure you immediately.'"[21] It was advice that Schumann ignored for the moment. In the meantime his friend Dr. Reuter "watched like a house-fairy over his little bachelor ailments," and, as Jansen puts it, even "busied himself with inspecting, sorting, and delivering Schumann's dirty laundry to the washer-woman."[22]

Such fraternal devotion was probably essential for Schumann's recovery. "I feel better and fresher," he wrote his mother in early January 1834. "I live very simply, have learned to do without alcoholic drinks, and go walking with my superlative Ludwig Schunke every day." His depression was not altogether relieved, however. "I lack the strength to finish reading your letter," he told her. "Just the thought of someone else's suffering is so destructive that it takes all my working strength away. So beware of letting me know about anything that might make me even the least bit restless."[23]

The first articles about the *Davidsbündler* had just been printed in a local newspaper, *The Comet*, and Schumann was hoping for a favorable reaction from his family. But his mother could not understand what her "beloved child" was saying in his article. (Apparently it reminded her of something by Jean Paul that her husband had once asked her to read. "I recognized the beauty but did not feel the greatness, and your father laughed at me.") She probably sensed Schumann's increasing separation from her, for she reacted with "the only feeling I still have, which is pain," and reminded him of the "deep despair" he once caused her by "going over to art" and thus changing the course she had set for him.[24]

Schumann's mother was now close to seventy, and he must have realized

---

* The word *Frau* that Schumann used means both "woman" and "wife."

that she would not live much longer. In attaching himself so firmly to Ludwig Schunke he seems to have found the security needed finally to achieve the long-delayed emotional separation from his mother and his family in Zwickau. Schunke was also a comrade who, Schumann hoped, would perform his difficult piano music. When his Toccata in C major (op. 7) was published in 1834, he dedicated it to Schunke and not to his brothers, as he had promised earlier. Schunke reciprocated with a piano sonata dedicated to Schumann. "I would give up all other friends for just this one," he wrote his mother in March 1834.[25]

With Schunke at his side, Schumann found the strength to meet regularly with a small group of other musicians who were interested in his plans for a newspaper, including Moritz Rascher, a boyhood friend from Zwickau; Ferdinand Stegmeyer, a Leipzig composer; Julius Knorr, a piano teacher; and his old mentor Friedrich Wieck. The group met each week in a bar-restaurant, the Kaffeebaum (still operating in Leipzig today), at a table especially reserved for the *Davidsbündler*. According to Jansen, "Schumann felt uncommonly well in this animated and cheerful circle":

> Sitting in his usual place at the head of the table, with the indispensable cigar in his mouth, he never had to ask for a fresh glass of beer. It was arranged so that as soon as the barkeeper or waiter noticed he had finished drinking, another glass would be brought to him without a wink. . . . Sometimes it happened that he would leave the place as if on command, very hastily and without saying good night to anyone. This was when he had music in his head and rushed home to write it down.[26]

Schumann's finesse in negotiating the contract for publication of his newspaper indicates that he was making strides toward improved mental control. Dated 26 March 1834, this legal document, undoubtedly drawn up with help from his more experienced brothers, specifies in twenty precise clauses the manner in which the paper was to be printed and sold by the Leipzig publisher C. H. F. Hartmann.[27]

The four editors of what at first was called *Neue Leipziger Zeitschrift für Musik* were Wieck, Schumann, Schunke, and Julius Knorr. (That Wieck allowed himself to be included suggests not only his respect for Schumann's literary abilities but also his interest in making money.) They were to be paid in cash, either when five hundred copies had been sold or on a quarterly basis. Annual subscribers were eligible for a discount. If fewer than five hundred people subscribed, the contract was to become null and void. The editors were required to meet "punctually for a conference once a week" at the Kaffeebaum, and "all letters, correspondence, essays, and musical pieces sent to the paper" were to be forwarded to the publisher by Knorr, who would receive a small additional honorarium for this labor. Implicit in this arrangement was that Schumann, who had conceived of the whole enterprise, had control over the style and content of the newspaper. Yet this was essentially a collaborative venture: "We are artists and friends of young and old," proclaims the first advertisement. "Years of living together, trust, and essential similarity of viewpoint unite us in bringing out this paper."[28]

This was something of an overstatement, but it served to stimulate public interest in the inaugural issue, which appeared on 3 April 1834. Leipzig was certainly ready for a "new journal" since the conservative *Allgemeine Musikalische Zeitschrift*, edited by G. W. Fink, primarily supported the establishment and paid little genuine attention to younger musicians. In publishing a more progressive newspaper of his own, Schumann hoped to show "that German musical taste in the early 1830s was in a lamentable state," as Leon Plantinga puts it, and "lash out at the 'damnable German politeness' and 'shoulder-shrugging' that plagued music criticism of the time."[29]

Schumann's responsibilities as chief editor of the new journal forced him to develop more orderly work habits. His new position also obliged him to articulate in public certain ideas about his *Davidsbündler* that previously had "only existed in the head of its creator."[30] That is, he was compelled, by sifting fact from fantasy, to clarify who these odd creatures were. Many of his contributions to the journal Schumann signed "Florestan" or "Eusebius." He also occasionally used the signature "Raro," which had originally been his *Davidsbündler* name for Wieck. This probably indicates some degree of partial identification with Clara's father during these early days of collaboration on the newspaper. But the editorial name "Raro" had another connotation. It is a condensation of Clara and Robert (Cla*Raro*bert), suggesting the interchange of musical themes and ideas between them.

Schumann sought a new inner synthesis through his music criticism. "Florestan and Eusebius is my double nature, and I want, like Raro, to amalgamate it into one man," he told his former counterpoint teacher, Heinrich Dorn, while trying to explain the curious symbolism.[31] In the *New Journal* he also seems to have discovered a safe outlet for his sometimes violent aggression: "Assembled Davidsbündler, youths and men, you must kill the Philistines, musical and otherwise."[32]

Schumann's published prose is often tongue-in-cheek and deliberately ambiguous. Unfortunately, in translation it loses much of its original potency. A few examples follow. About his friend Ludwig Schunke:

I can see it all still, the dim lights, the quiet walls listening, the almost breathless group of friends, Florestan's pale face . . . while he tells Ludwig, "You are a master of your art, and the G minor Sonata is your best work, especially the way you play it. Indeed, the Davidsbündler would be proud to count such an artist among its members."[33]

About the famous German violinist and composer Louis Spohr:

Since he views everything through tears, all of his ideas run together into formless, ethereal figures. I hardly know what to call this [music]. It's a perpetual droning, pinned and held together, of course, by the hand and mind of an artist.[34]

About another, much younger, Belgian violinist, Henri Vieuxtemps:

His playing has the perfume and shimmer of a flower. When speaking of Vieuxtemps, one thinks of Paganini. . . . From the first to the last note we unexpectedly stand in a magic circle, without beginning or end.[35]

About the controversial French composer Hector Berlioz:

He does us an injustice to publish so few of his compositions and not even attempt a trip to Germany. It is Berlioz's misfortune to be confused with de Beriot, who resembles him as little as lemonade does mock-turtle soup.[36]

It is easy to see why certain musicians were offended by Schumann's polemics, while others were merely amused or flattered by what he had to say. His newspaper definitely influenced the artistic climate of Europe during the middle of the nineteenth century; in fact, in his lifetime he was much better known as a music critic than as a composer. Schumann gained a wide circle of readers throughout Germany and even abroad. His correspondents (whom he paid) in Berlin, Paris, Vienna, and other major cities informed him regularly about musical activities in those places.

His work as a writer and editor had a temporarily rejuvenating effect. "I'm not dead, otherwise you would read about it in our paper," he informed his mother in early July 1834.[37] (She had forgotten to send him a letter for his birthday.) But the *New Journal*—although it provided Schumann with much-needed income—also was an exhausting enterprise that distracted him from composing music. He soon found himself overworked. Julius Knorr had become ill with malaria, leaving "all of the correspondence, corrections, and manuscripts" to Schumann, who complained that Wieck was "always traveling" (he had gone to Dresden with Clara), while Schunke "really doesn't know very much about writing."[38]

Schumann's new "sphere of activity, joy in working, effectiveness in the world, recognition, and praise from the outside," as he put it, seem to have given him a new lease on life. He even grew a mustache. "Don't be shocked," he warned his mother in anticipation of her reaction to this sign of his virility.[39]

Schumann also began to think about getting married at this time. Apparently his fascination with women had been only temporarily sidetracked by the catastrophe of Rosalie's death and his emotional (and possibly physical) intimacy with Ludwig Schunke. In addition, he had an incessant desire for respectability, buttressed by his wish, now that he was achieving some status as a journalist and editor, to follow in the family traditions. Rosalie's husband Carl was planning to marry again, and it seems that Schumann did not want to be left out.

On 2 July 1834 he informed his mother that "two magnificent female beings have come into our circle," and that he was thinking of marrying one of them.[40] Both girls were friends of Clara Wieck, were close to her in age, and like Clara, had influential fathers. Emilie List, age sixteen, was the daughter of the American consul in Leipzig. (Her first name, perhaps reminding Robert of his sister Emilie, may have been both a source of attraction and a deterrent.) The other girl was Ernestine von Fricken, age seventeen, the daughter of a nobleman from Bohemia. Baron von Fricken had heard Clara play in his hometown of Asch and had afterward approached Wieck about piano lessons for his daughter. Wieck, perhaps anticipating Ernestine's affinity for Schumann, accepted her as his pupil and agreed to have her stay at his home in Leipzig.

Schumann's discomfort at being separated from Clara Wieck may have been an additional motivation for marriage. She had recently become quite useful to him as a playmate, providing ideas and inspiration for his musical as well as his journalistic pieces. And Clara, although she was not yet fifteen, was already visibly protective toward the awkward, nearsighted Schumann. "She walks behind me," he had written his mother shortly before his breakdown, "and she gently tugs my coat each time we approach a rock, so that I don't fall."[41]

Wieck was beginning to feel uneasy about Clara's devotion to Schumann and, to separate them, he made arrangements in April 1834 for his daughter to spend six months in Dresden, ostensibly for advanced instruction in composition with Carl Reissiger, Weber's successor at the Royal Opera there. Schumann promised to visit Clara in Dresden, but he did not do so. Ernestine von Fricken apparently had already captivated him. "She is tender and thoughtful," he wrote his mother, and "hangs onto me and everything artistic with the most sentimental affection, is extraordinarily musical—in short, exactly the way I'd wish my wife to be."[42]

Of course Schumann had many reasons *not* to get married. The first was his ambivalence toward women in general and his fear, after the mishap with Christel, of further injury to his penis. Then there was his financial insecurity. Subscriptions to the *New Journal* were few and far between during those early years, and Schumann wanted to reinvest his limited earnings. (The affluence of Ernestine's father undoubtedly was one reason for her immediate appeal.) Finally, the deep loyalty and devotion between Schumann and his roommate was an obstacle to marriage, for both of them. Schunke as well as Schumann had serious health problems, and in living and working together they had come to realize that creative work—writing, composing, and playing the piano—required long stretches of solitude that cannot be easily interrupted by domestic chores and children. (As Schumann put it to Clara several years later, "With so much hustle and bustle around you, I'm not surprised you cannot compose. To create something and be successful at it requires happiness and deep loneliness."[43])

Both Beethoven and Schubert, two composers Schumann greatly admired, had solved this problem by remaining single. Beethoven, although he desired women sexually, always directed his marriage proposals to those who were already married or unavailable for other reasons.[44] Schubert was probably exclusively homosexual.* Whether Schumann and Schunke considered themselves a couple, we do not know. But in view of what Jansen and others more familiar with the spirit of romanticism have written about their relationship, we can well imagine that Schumann and Schunke regarded their love for each other as a kind of artistic "phase."

Two things seem to have disrupted this idyll: Schunke's tuberculosis, for which there was then no treatment, and Schumann's drinking. (The diary notes, succinctly, "living together with Schunke = thereby often a dissolute life."[46]) Dr. Reuter's warnings came none too soon. By midsummer 1834 Schunke's tuberculosis had advanced so rapidly that Schumann felt it

---

*He was actually "the central figure in a coterie of homosexual and bisexual Viennese artists," as Maynard Solomon has recently discovered, and may have contracted syphilis from a male prostitute.[45]

necessary to discuss the matter at length with their mutual friends Carl and Henriette Voigt.

The Voigts were socially prominent Leipzig music lovers who were well known for the protection and shelter they gave to struggling young artists. Schumann was especially fond of Henriette Voigt, whom he described as "a model housewife and mother."[47] Her generosity, tenderness, and modesty may well have increased his yearning for matrimony.

The Voigts instinctively recognized Schumann's extreme separation anxiety regarding Schunke, and they tried in every way possible to be helpful to the two men. They did this first by inviting Schunke to live in their house, where he could get more consistent care than in Schumann's apartment, and second by strongly fostering Schumann's growing attachment to the attractive and energetic Ernestine von Fricken. Clara was devastated when she returned to Leipzig at the end of July for the christening of her father's latest child. The godparents were none other than Robert Schumann and Ernestine von Fricken, looking very enamored. Schumann noted in his diary that "Clara returned to Dresden—very sad."[48]

The affair was no secret in Leipzig. Schumann usually met Ernestine in the Voigt home, whence rumors quickly spread through musical circles. When Baron von Fricken was alerted, he decided to come to Leipzig for a personal meeting with Schumann. There were certain things he did not want a prospective son-in-law to find out too quickly, one of them being that Ernestine was not his legitimate child. He was willing to adopt her, however, on the condition that a future husband would never lay claim to his money or property.

Thus a visit was arranged. The baron presented himself as a humble amateur, ingratiating himself by playing the flute and seeking Schumann's advice about a set of variations he had composed. For his part, Schumann sought to impress von Fricken with his genuine affection for Ernestine:

> I am happy to have your composition as a point of contact. Whether it will spin into a longer thread, holding us together at a distance, I don't know, but that is my wish. . . . You already realize without my having to say it that I am ardently interested in your inestimable Ernestine as an artist. How eagerly I want her to enjoy every step of progress we might make.[49]

The generally euphoric mood of this letter is suddenly interrupted by a lengthy digression in which Schumann reveals his concern with the sad fate of a penniless old composer, Ludwig Böhner, whom he had recently invited to contribute an article to the *New Journal*. "Böhner was as famous as Beethoven in his day . . . but his shabby appearance really depresses me."[50] This may have been intended as an unconscious warning to Baron von Fricken (as well as to Schumann himself) about the risks inherent in a musical career.* Nevertheless, Schumann set to work varying the baron's flute theme, with the result that he composed the *Symphonic Etudes* (op. 13), one of the most astonishing musical accomplishments of the nineteenth century, a gigantic work that propels the piano to the status of a full orchestra and demonstrates its unique expressive potentials.

Symphonic Etudes begins with a rich harmonization of the flute theme. Numerous "études" and "variations" follow. (Schumann thought at first of calling them "pathetic variations" and later removed several that he felt were too sad or sentimental.†) The orchestral tone is apparent immediately, drum beats in Variation 1, horns and trombones in Variation 2. Etude 3 features violin-like arpeggios over a broad, cello-like theme. Flutes and piccolos of a Mendelssohnian delicacy are heard in Etude 9; a languor reminiscent of Chopin in Variation 9.

Schumann's emotional contrasts are immensely powerful and sometimes extremely abrupt, which perhaps accounts for the limited popularity (with audiences, not pianists) of this masterful composition. It was surely his first mature musical work. Schumann had written shorter pieces for the piano, and had attempted a symphony. Now, without an orchestra, he showed what miracles can be achieved at the keyboard. The Finale, which he added later, is a rousing march based on a song from Heinrich Marschner's opera *Der Templer und die Jüdin.*‡

Schumann's relationship to Ernestine von Fricken nearly precipitated another breakdown. The prospect of introducing her to his mother had provoked such anxiety that he was able to travel to Zwickau only in the presence of a physician (his "old medical muse," Dr. Glock). Further complications arose from the hostile behavior of Frau Schumann, who had expressed a distinct preference for Clara. ("The silly girl [Ernestine] is convinced you can't stand her," Schumann wrote his mother afterward.[51])

---

*Ludwig Böhner, a chronic alcoholic, had been the model for E. T. A. Hoffmann's famous "Kapellmeister Johannes Kreisler," the caricature of a mad musician, which later inspired Schumann to compose his *Kreisleriana* (op. 16).

†Five have been published as "posthumous" variations and are now included in many performances and recordings of this work.

‡The tune comes from the patriotic song "Proud England Rejoice." Its personal associations are significant. Schumann, still unmarried in 1837 when he published his *Symphonic Etudes,* had become infatuated with another attractive young man, the British composer William Sterndale Bennett (1816–1875). By ending his first major composition with a march based on "Proud England Rejoice," he may have been trying both to drum out the humiliation of his broken engagement to Ernestine and to celebrate this new friendship. He dedicated the *Symphonic Etudes* to Bennett.

Nevertheless, he tried once again to defy her by giving an engagement ring to Ernestine. The von Frickens then returned to Asch, while Schumann went back to Leipzig with his doctor.

There he fell prey to agonizing fantasies associated with Schunke's terminal illness and Ernestine's absence. "I still cannot forget the unhappy days of Rosalie's death," he wrote his mother on the anniversary of his breakdown in October. "I anticipate further attacks of depression made worse by separation from Ernestine."[52] Abruptly he abandoned the dying Schunke in Leipzig, traveled to Asch for a visit with Ernestine, and then escaped to Zwickau, where he hoped to complete his *Symphonic Etudes*.

But in Zwickau Schumann found it impossible to do any work on either his newspaper or his musical compositions. "Increasing melancholia," he commented in the diary.[53] His thinking, as revealed in letters to Henriette Voigt, showed increasing depression and confusion. Schumann described competing fantasies about Ernestine "with her Madonna's face" and about Schunke "with pain in his face." He hoped to "put a veil over this"—to repress these disturbing images—and begged Frau Voigt, "For heaven's sake not to write when Schunke dies."[54]

This wish, plus Schumann's ambivalence about Ernestine, seems to have engendered the most tormenting guilt—or, as he called it, mental "pain."[55] He was probably experiencing a deep conflict in his conscience for having "abandoned" Schunke, whom he had unconsciously equated with other dying people—his sister Emilie, his father, his brother Julius—for whom he felt somehow, irrationally, responsible. "I am a virtuoso at hanging on to unfortunate ideas," he wrote Frau Voigt on 7 November 1834. "My evil spirit opposes external success and jeers at it. I often drive self-torture to the point of sinning against my entire existence. Then I can never feel satisfied with myself, and I want to turn into another body, or to run away forever."[56]

It was consistent with Schumann's personality that he would repeatedly try to reduce his inner anguish by projecting his self-reproaches onto various external figures, mainly women. This mechanism of defense would then make it seem that these figures—his mother, Frau Voigt, Ernestine, and later Clara Wieck—were rebuking him. Hence Schumann's violent anger toward the women he loved, and his attempt to repudiate them. When news came that Ernestine's father had approved her marriage plans, Schumann bluntly rejected the girl. "In my tormented condition," he wrote Frau Voigt, "I am afraid to accept the precious jewel into my accursed hand."[57]

Schumann's hostility was often subconscious, and to protect himself and others from becoming aware of it he would adopt a facade of gentle amiability. Thus, for some time, he continued to vacillate in his affections for the "precious jewel" by visiting Ernestine's family in Asch and talking of marriage, but without setting a definite date. Schumann in fact renounced the girl long before he ever found out (in August 1835) that she was an illegitimate, adopted daughter and might be disinherited.

Ernestine's illegitimacy is the reason usually cited for Schumann's broken engagement, and he may well have wanted to rationalize it in that way. She, as her letters show, was deeply hurt and infuriated.[58] (One letter suggests that he may have deflowered her.) Many biographies claim that she was intellectually inferior to Clara Wieck, which may well have been true. It is also possible that in the long run Ernestine might have been an excellent wife for Schumann, less competitive and demanding perhaps than Clara. Her loyalty to him, even after her own marriage (in 1838, to Count Wilhelm von Zedtwitz) would become a matter of public record during Schumann's difficult lawsuit against Wieck in 1840.

On 7 December 1834 Ludwig Schunke was found dead, and Schumann immediately returned to Leipzig to take care of his editorial responsibilities there. His *New Journal* was in shambles. "Total disintegration of the whole [*Davidsbündler*] circle," says the diary.[59] Wieck had gone on a six-month concert tour with Clara and another musician, Carl Banck, whom he envisioned as a new suitor for his daughter. Julius Knorr was so inefficient and quarrelsome that the publisher, Hartmann, was about to take legal action. Part of his accusation, as formulated by the attorney Dr. Glciwitz, was that "Herr Schumann is in Zwickau and will probably stay there until Easter, 1835. For nearly half a year already he has shown no concern whatsoever for the newspaper."[60]

Schumann was obliged to act quickly. On 18 December he attempted to reorganize the newspaper in such a way that Knorr alone would serve as his coeditor. But it soon became obvious that the two men were incompatible, and, on 24 December, Schumann bought the publication rights from Hartmann for 350 thalers and signed a new contract, which established him as sole owner. Another publisher, W. A. Barth, agreed to continue the *Neue Zeitschrift für Musik*, now without *Leipzig* in its title. Under this new contract, more outside correspondents would assist Schumann, and the paper would appear twice a week instead of once. For the next six months, Julius Knorr continued to argue over technicalities; to avoid a court appearance on 21 July 1835, Schumann settled—at the last minute, on 20 July—with his former coeditor by paying him 25 thalers.

Schumann's sagacity in handling this complicated situation was remarkable, for, as he himself admitted, he "had been the group's musical visionary and was more accustomed to dreaming his life away at the piano than among books."[61] Even more astonishing is that this "dreamer" produced some of his most important musical compositions while in charge of the *New Journal*. The year 1835, for example, saw the creation of Schumann's *Carnaval* (op. 9), a musical picture gallery, as he called it, of "the many different mental states" stimulated by his betrothal to Ernestine von Fricken.[62]

He explained the origins of *Carnaval* in a letter to Henriette Voigt in September 1834: "I have just discovered that the name [of Ernestine's hometown] ASCH is very musical and contains letters that also occur in my name. They were musical symbols."[63] (In German, "As" stands for A flat, "Es" (pronounced S) for E flat, and "H" is B; "C" is, of course, C.) By playing with these ciphers he found he could generate numerous tone sequences, and he used them in melodies and chords throughout the twenty "little scenes" (*scènes mignonnes*) of *Carnaval*.

As with much of his early music, Schumann enjoyed giving a short title to each piece after it was composed. These titles should not be taken too literally; exact equivalences can never be drawn between words and music. Moreover, the names Schumann attached to his *Carnaval* pieces are cryptic. Some of them, for example "Pantalon et Colombine" refer to characters from the *Commedia del l'arte*. Others are autobiographical: "Eusebius" and "Florestan." "Sphinxes" simply notates the ASCH patterns that are basic to the entire work. One scene is called "Chopin." (The Polish pianist never forgave Schumann for including his name and a parody of his musical style in *Carnaval*.[64]) "Paganini" also appears relatively undisguised. The waltz "Estrella," according to an early edition of Wasielewski's biography, is supposed to refer to Ernestine von Fricken, while "Chiarina" is said to be a spoof of Clara Wieck.[65] "Reconnaissance," "Promenade," and other interludes probably allude to interactions between these main characters and may even have sexual implications. The *Carnaval* ends with a vigorous "March of the Davidsbündler against the Philistines."

Performance of this work requires considerable pianistic virtuosity. When Clara returned from her tour in April 1835, Schumann asked her to play the *Carnaval*, thinking that this would help popularize the pieces in Leipzig. She, though, had been deeply offended by his engagement to Ernestine, and for several weeks maintained a cool reserve toward him. (Clara even pretended to be in love with a cellist she had met on her tour.)

Wieck warned Clara about Schumann's cruel behavior to his fiancée. He wrote into her diary that Ernestine was "like a plant . . . who has wilted and died bit by bit without her customary care. She was burned too sharply by the sun, by Herr Schumann that is!"[66] But Clara was a headstrong young woman, going on sixteen, who for reasons of her own wanted to maintain her relationship to Schumann. For his birthday in June she tantalized him with a beautiful watch-chain, which no doubt symbolized her desire to become more attached. Schumann responded. His diary, on adjacent pages, records "disengagement from Ernestine in the summer and fall" and "beautiful hours in [Clara's] arms."[67] Thus one affair ended, while another, a kind of pre-courtship, began.

That Schumann could woo one adolescent in the home of her disapproving father while he was simultaneously jilting his fiancée and disappointing *her* father raises an important question. Was his quickness to change one love-object for another evidence of a high level of adaptability, or does it suggest that Schumann's psychological resources were again in precarious balance? Quickly shifting and highly ambivalent behavior toward love-objects may indicate a potential for inner splitting, which can foster disintegration in a vulnerable personality. However, for someone as talented and hardworking as Schumann, pathological splitting may also call forth a renewed effort to heal oneself through creative activity.

Fortunately, the two most important trends in his creative work, literature and music, had recently been consolidated in the *New Journal*, an administrative accomplishment that stood in marked contrast to the shambles of his personal life. Schumann was also beginning to compose music of impressive originality. That so many of his early compositions were musical portraits of multiple love-objects or, as in *Carnaval* dramatizations of relationships between himself and other people, is another encouraging sign. It suggests that his creativity was nurtured by the hope of one day fusing his artistry and his masculinity. Now that his desire for union with another attractive musician had become more certain, Clara Wieck, the most outstanding woman pianist of the nineteenth century, seemed to hold the key to Schumann's future not only as a composer but also as a man.

VIII.
The Road to Maturity, 1835–1837

On 30 August 1835, a man arrived in Leipzig whose influence on the musical life of that city has never been forgotten—Felix Mendelssohn-Bartholdy. He was the grandson of Moses Mendelssohn, a ghetto Jew whom erudition and wisdom had brought to the pinnacle of Prussian society, and son of Abraham Mendelssohn, a Berlin banker who upon converting to Christianity bestowed the name "Bartholdy" upon his children.[1] An adolescent genius, Mendelssohn had written some of his best compositions—the scintillating *Octet for Strings*, for example—while Schumann, only a year his junior, was still immersed in Jean Paul and debating career choices. At the age of twenty, Felix conquered London; a performance of Beethoven's *Emperor* Concerto made him the "darling of the British public."[2] He was a remarkable conductor, a skillful, energetic administrator, and the man who spearheaded the nineteenth-century revival of interest in Johann Sebastian Bach's nearly forgotten choral music.

Religious bigotry in Berlin had kept this outstanding musician from positions of leadership there. So in 1833 (the year Schumann had his nervous breakdown) Mendelssohn took on the position of music director in Düsseldorf, but he resigned after only a year and a half and continued to compose and to travel. In 1835 he accepted the directorship of Leipzig's prestigious Gewandhaus Orchestra.

No doubt Mendelssohn had great charm; he was wiry, curly-haired, and vivacious. "A hundred hearts flutter to him the moment he mounts the podium," Schumann wrote about Mendelssohn's Leipzig debut.[3] Their first social meeting was at the Voigts' residence, and Schumann reacted typically, spinning poetic fantasies around this attractive sibling-figure. He gave Mendelssohn the *Davidsbündler* name *Felix Meritis* and mentioned him regularly in his letters, diaries, and the *New Journal*. In a collection of "Reminiscences about F. Mendelssohn from 1835 until his Death," which Schumann evidently hoped one day to publish as a book, he compiled more information about this musician than he did about any other of his contemporaries.[4]

Schumann greatly respected Mendelssohn's musical integrity, and sometimes he almost worshipped him, as is evident in a letter to Therese Schumann (his brother Eduard's wife): "Mendelssohn is the one I look up to like a high mountain. He is really a god, and you should know him."[5] These words are reminiscent of what he had said earlier about Götte, Schunke, and other men he idealized, and of what he later wrote about Brahms. As for Mendelssohn's consummate skill as a pianist, Schumann commented, "I think that's how Mozart must have performed."[6]

Perhaps his praise disguised a certain amount of envy. Suppressed rivalry can certainly be sensed whenever Schumann and Mendelssohn were in the presence of Clara Wieck. In terms of virtuosity and pianistic brilliance she had far more in common with Felix than she did with Robert. Their not altogether peaceful triangle relationship began on Clara's sixteenth birthday, 13 September 1835, when she happily played Mendelssohn's *Capriccio* piano duet with him. Before long Mendelssohn was actively helping Clara with her career, arranging concerts for her, engaging her as a soloist with the Gewandhaus Orchestra, or joining her at the keyboard in recitals. Basically a nonperformer, Schumann was left on the sidelines, commenting that "it always gave Mendelssohn pleasure to take very lively tempi with Clara."[7] Perhaps by way of compensation, he was beginning to compose a series of increasingly difficult piano compositions with Clara in mind, and aiming witty and sometimes even barbed criticism at Mendelssohn in the *New Journal for Music*. "For me, Felix Meritis's conductor's baton is disturbing," says Eusebius after attending one of his concerts.[8]

Squeezed between these two powerful older men, Clara often felt intimidated, if not overwhelmed. She regarded Mendelssohn as an exceptional composer. When he was playing his own music for Schumann, she once commented, "Robert's eyes radiate joy, and it is very painful for me to have to feel I can never offer Robert anything like that."[9]

There were other sources of tension. One was Mendelssohn's close friendship with his teacher Ignaz Moscheles, whom Schumann had admired since childhood. After meeting Schumann in October 1835, Moscheles described him merely as "a quiet but interesting young man," whereas he raved about Mendelssohn.[10] Schumann wanted so much to win praise from Moscheles—he even dedicated his magnificent F minor Piano Sonata (op. 14) to him—yet could evoke only equivocal remarks, such as "very labored, heavy, and somewhat confused, but interesting."[11] Again Schumann used the *New Journal* to his advantage; he invited Moscheles to contribute an article, wherein the older man grudgingly acknowledged that Schumann's work was "a genuine sign of the romanticism awakening and spreading in our time."[12]

"Could we ever quarrel?" Schumann asked rhetorically about Mendelssohn.[13] Indeed they could. After listening to a stirring performance of Beethoven's Ninth Symphony, Schumann complained that the conducting was "incomprehensively fast, so insulting to me that I left immediately."[14] Mendelssohn, who was very touchy about criticism, confessed to a "certain shyness" in Schumann's presence, but after an argument the two men usually shook hands and agreed to remain friends.[15] On many occasions Mendelssohn took the initiative in performing Schumann's music, and he had a profound influence in advising him what kind of music to write and how.

Posterity has not always been kind to their friendship, and anti-Semitism was partly responsible. Richard Wagner bitterly resented Mendelssohn's enormous popularity in the nineteenth century; he made scurrilous attacks on musicians of Jewish origin and held it against Schumann that he would allow himself to be guided by this composer.[16] Actually Felix Mendelssohn-Bartholdy, as he is called in Europe, was demonstrably non-Jewish.* "He firmly believes in his Lutheran religion," Hector Berlioz observed in 1831.[17] But some people, including the Schumanns, could never forget Mendelssohn's origins. "Jews remain Jews," Robert wrote about Felix in the privacy of his marriage diary in 1840. This petty outburst was apparently stimulated by Clara, who in Robert's opinion had been excessively respectful toward Mendelssohn. Schumann informed her that "the rocks we gather for their [i.e., the Jews'] Temple of Glory they immediately throw back at us."[18] The Mendelssohn family later suppressed from Felix's published correspondence almost everything he wrote about Schumann.[19]

The two musicians often had meals together at the Hotel de Bavière, and it seems that they discussed fairly private matters, including their dreams,

---

*His parents even wanted him to drop the first part of this name, but thinking it might confuse the public—especially in England, where he was so well known simply as "Mendelssohn"—he refused to do so.

their childhoods, and their feelings about mutual friends and acquaintances.[20] Schumann also spoke with Mendelssohn about marriage. Both men
were bachelors when they first met and were still closely tied to their families, but they were experimenting with sex. Felix had long been involved in
a uniquely affectionate relationship with his sister Fanny and seemed to
prefer older, usually married women for sexual gratification.

We read in Schumann's "Reminiscences" how he gossiped with Mendelssohn about a beautiful young woman from Frankfurt, Cecile Jeanrenaud. "She is only a child,"[21] said Felix, who was rumored to be more
interested in Cecile's mother than in her. (Cecile was actually two years older
than Clara Wieck.) Mendelssohn married her in 1837. His biographer George
Marek says that Cecile Jeanrenaud was a "soothing woman," whereas Clara
Wieck was "anything but soothing."[22] Therein lies an interesting difference.
Mendelssohn, who was consistently self-directed, well organized, energetic,
could afford to be soothed, while Schumann needed someone to stimulate
him, respect him, inspire him, and keep his life in order. Cecile was not
very musical. She never demanded a place in Felix's artistic work, and their
marriage was relatively tranquil. Not so Clara and Robert's. Theirs was an
uneasy romance from beginning to end.

For many years Schumann had harbored what he called "an unnamed
mixed emotion" toward Clara Wieck.[23] He respected and probably envied
her success—"Clara is the first *German* artist," wrote Florestan in 1833.
"This pearl does not swim on the surface; one must look for her in the
depths, even if there is danger. Clara is a diver."[24] Robert's way of handling
this conflict had been to distance himself from the girl. Now that Clara was
becoming more sexually attractive, and with Mendelssohn as a potential
rival for her musical admiration, Schumann began to reconsider. "Clara grows
more charming every day, yes every hour, internally as well as externally,"
he wrote in August 1835.[25]

Clara's physical maturation is quite evident in a portrait made after her
seventeenth birthday. Schumann's desire for her now seems to have become
much more pronounced. In November 1835 he bestowed on Clara what she
evidently felt was an erotic kiss; she nearly fainted. (Perhaps the fact that
Schumann had imprudently chosen Wieck's front steps as the place to demonstrate his ardor was a factor in Clara's reaction.) One month later she was
in Zwickau for a concert, giving Frau Schumann the opportunity to renew
her earlier advocacy of their future marriage. Schumann was there also, and
as it turned out, this was the last time either he or Clara saw his mother:

Clara Wieck, age seventeen.
(Drawing by Elwine von
Leyser.)

she died in February 1836. Her final wish for their betrothal probably made
a deep and lasting impression.

These developments greatly alarmed Clara's father, who for seven years
had been observing Schumann's fleeting passion for one person after another.
Wanting to spare his daughter from predictable disappointment, Wieck took
her to Dresden once more, in January 1836, this time with the intention of
completely isolating Clara from Schumann by intercepting and destroying
any letters that might pass between them. Schumann reacted with a mixture of sadness and anger: "How my heart suffered and doubted."[26] According to Clara's stepmother, Schumann's Christmas present of pearls for Clara
signified his tears.[27]

Schumann quickly consolidated a new living arrangement. He had been
living alone since the time of Schunke's death, on Halleschestrasse 462 near
the Promenade. Now he moved back to the university district, into an
apartment with Wilhelm Ulex, who had been his companion for some time.
During the years they lived together, Ulex occasionally served, as did Dr.
Reuter, as a go-between who would carry messages to Clara or arrange trysts
behind Wieck's back. (Almost nothing is known about this young musician.

After Schumann's marriage, Ulex moved to Hamburg—Brahms's hometown—where he died in 1858.)

Schumann wrote about "dangerous extremes" of behavior while he was living with Ulex.[28] Their landlady, Frau Devrient, wanted at one point to evict them, and Schumann wrote her apologetically about his "wrecked plans . . . and youthful suffering." He described "elevated moods [that] often lead to overexcitement . . . followed by exhaustion," and added, "I know the right way to soothe such dangerous extremes: A loving woman could do it."[29]

Clara seems to have been equally unhappy in her separation from Schumann. Early in 1836 she seized the initiative and with the help of a girlfriend smuggled a letter to him indicating that her father would not be in Dresden for a few days in February. Schumann went with Ulex to see Clara during this interval, and it turned out to be a momentous visit.

On 4 February Schumann's mother had died. This signaled the end of a decade that he had depended on her, for love and for help (including financial) in making plans and decisions. His mother had been the most essential person in his life—not always a positive influence, but a predictable presence in terms of their mutual, anxious interdependence. He suffered exquisitely both when they were separated and when they were together. Now Schumann had to face their permanent separation. Never again would he be able to please his mother, or to make her unhappy. Finally he was free.

He did not want to go to his mother's funeral, so the invitation to visit Clara must have come as a godsend. In her presence he could pour out his grief, which Clara understood (she had been practically motherless since childhood, when her parents divorced). Thus, with Ulex hovering in the background, Schumann apparently came closer to the wish that Clara might one day be his wife. Whether he actually expressed it we do not know. Her biographer, Litzmann, says only that "both lovers renewed the oath of loyalty never to be separated from each other, come what may."[30] Surely Clara sensed that to be another Frau Schumann would be a great responsibility. She and Schumann also knew the legal requirements: marriage was out of the question without her father's consent.

Schumann's first step was to go to Zwickau for the reading of his mother's will. Then he wrote Clara a letter expressing his love for her and asking her to love him in return (in earlier letters to Clara he had used the formal *Sie*, but in this one he switched to the familiar form *Du*):

> In many ways my future seems more secure now . . . but I still have to accomplish a great deal just to achieve what you can see anytime you happen to step in front of a mirror—in the meantime you too will want to remain an artist. . . . You will carry your own weight, work with me, and share my joys and sorrows.[31]

Clara would never forget these words. They were the motto that would echo throughout her marriage and the subsequent forty years of widowhood.

While he was in Zwickau mourning his mother, Schumann wrote to Clara as though she were actually "standing before" him: "Oh, it feels so close, as if I could hold you." As was clear at other points in his life, he sometimes confused reality and fantasy. He also seemed to believe that by simply putting his "external affairs in order," the more crucial affairs of the heart would arrange themselves as if by magic. His imagination began to picture Wieck as a benevolent father who would "not pull back his hand when I ask for his blessing."[32]

Wieck, not unexpectedly, did just the opposite. After discovering what had happened in his absence, he told Clara he would shoot Schumann if he ever approached her again. Wieck also demanded that she return every letter Schumann had ever written to her. A dutiful daughter, Clara submitted for the next year and a half.

Between February 1836 and August 1837, not a word passed between the two lovers. Schumann's name disappeared from Clara's programs, and only rarely, in private gatherings, would she perform his compositions. The pain of separation was indescribable for Schumann except through music, and it was during this enforced separation from Clara that he found himself addressing her with melodic "themes," transforming thoughts into tones. Schumann's composing, as well as his maturation, was obviously being pushed forward for many reasons, one of them, and an important one, being his expectation that Clara would marry him and that Wieck would bless their union. Because these "tone-thoughts" were directed to someone who encouraged his musical activities rather than to his mother, who had discouraged them, Schumann felt he could make progress as a composer. Nevertheless, he continued to pursue his literary career through the newspaper, and even went so far as to ask some of his correspondents to send him information about "everything that concerns Clara, her mood, [and] her life."[33]

Clara's return to Leipzig in 1836 led to a series of awkward incidents. As their friends and acquaintances learned of the separation, those loyal to Schumann tended to flock to the Voigt circle, while Wieck's cronies socialized at his house. Some, such as Mendelssohn and his concertmaster Ferdinand David, attempted to remain neutral and stay in touch with both groups. When Chopin visited Leipzig that summer, he saw Robert and Clara independently. If both of them happened to be at the same concert or social function, tensions immediately became noticeable, and there would be uncomfortable silences and bewildered glances. To avoid a scene, Schumann usually respected Wieck's wishes by staying as far away from Clara as possible. Nevertheless, Wieck believed that she must always be escorted, and when he personally could not do so he would ask the singer Carl Banck to accompany her, posing as her voice teacher. This arrangement irritated

Schumann—Banck had been his friend and an early collaborator on the *New Journal*. One day a satirical "report," obviously written by Schumann, appeared in his paper lampooning a certain Herr de Knapp (Banck's name pronounced phonetically in reverse) who was attempting to woo an aggressive woman pianist named Ambrosia (a caricature of Clara). Schumann gave her the *coup de grâce* in his newspaper with the stinging comment, "Ambrosia of course does not have a husband, since she herself is a man."[34]

His anger reached the boiling point when Banck, on Wieck's instructions no doubt, told him that Clara had said she no longer wanted to marry him. According to Litzmann, Schumann believed for the moment that it was true, in which case Clara could be seen as a "worthless girl" and he could feel "happy" to be rid of her.[35] The deep frustration he experienced during this crisis is expressed in a letter he sent Clara a few years later:

> The darkest time was when I no longer knew anything about you and tried forcefully to forget you. . . . I became resigned. But then the old pain broke out again—then I wrung my hands—then at night I often said to God—"just let this thing pass by patiently, so that I do not go mad." I imagined at one point that I would find news of your engagement in the newspapers—then something pulled me to the floor by my neck, and I screamed loudly—I wanted to cure myself by forcefully loving a woman who already had me half-ensnared.[36]

That woman was undoubtedly his former mistress, Christel, for his diary for 1836 reports that he "searched [her] out."[37]

Doubts about Schumann's moral character apparently arose in Clara's mind, or were planted there by her father, with the result that Wieck asked Ernestine von Fricken to divulge what had happened during her engagement to Schumann.*

Another result of the separation from Clara was that Schumann decided not to comment in his newspaper on her ambitious new Piano Concerto (op. 7), a work he had actually helped to complete by orchestrating one of the movements for her. Instead he asked the organist C. F. Becker to write the review, but instructed Becker to do the job in less than a week, and that "half a page is sufficient."[39]

The rebuff hurt Clara. She was also becoming painfully aware of her lover's devotion to another potential rival, the twenty-one-year-old William Sterndale Bennett, whom Mendelssohn had recently invited to Germany (and who had inspired the march ending of Schumann's *Symphonic Etudes*).

---

* The letters from Schumann's jilted fiancée are not especially flattering, and their authenticity can be debated, since Wieck's scheming was involved. "Heaven is forever banned to me," wrote Ernestine. "I loved Schumann unspeakably and would have given him my life." Elsewhere she referred to his incessant drinking.[38]

Where the *New Journal for Music* (Becker's article) insinuated that Clara's music did not really merit a review "since we are dealing with the work of a woman,"[40] Schumann himself lyricized at length about Bennett's "precocious artisty and quiet disposition, the cohesiveness of it all, his harmonious language, the purity of his ideas."[41]

"Between Schumann and Bennett, a sympathetic and even intimate relationship dates from the first days of their meeting," wrote Bennett's son J. R. Sterndale Bennett. "Schumann quickly attached himself to this young stranger, coming to his rooms, prevailing upon him to play the piano, taking him as the companion of his daily walks." Their closeness did not go unnoticed by other musicians in Leipzig, including Clara. Mendelssohn, now married, went so far as to tell Bennett, "You are *always* with Schumann," a "reproach" that Bennett's son says "would only refer to personal intimacy [since] there was no professional rivalry between Mendelssohn and Schumann."[42]

Four monumental works for solo piano stand as reminders of Schumann's early travail with regard to Clara Wieck. Each of them contains references to her, direct quotations from her own compositions, or note patterns that suggest her name (often descending scales beginning on C and with A as the third note). Thus we could say that these remarkable compositions portray Schumann's growing dependence on the woman he would one day marry. They also demonstrate his artistic independence. While revitalizing a musical form that had declined after Beethoven and Schubert wrote their great sonatas, Schumann created a daringly original "romantic" style of piano sonata.

The Sonata in F-sharp minor (op. 11) is "dedicated to Clara by Florestan and Eusebius."[43] Schumann later told her that it was "a solitary outcry for you from my heart . . . in which your theme appears in every possible shape."[44] The haunting slow introduction—Charles Rosen calls it "a song without words"[45]—is itself an anomaly among compositions of this kind, since these fifty-two measures contain thematic material that returns again in the Sonata's second movement.

Clara's "Witches Dance," a piece Schumann had first heard when he was twenty-two, marks the opening *Allegro vivace* and is immediately pursued by his own "Fandango" written at that time. An intricate interweaving of these two themes characterizes the entire first movement. The second movement, a poignant aria hinted at during the long introduction to the first movement, was taken from one of the Justinus Kerner songs, "To Anna," composed while Schumann was an adolescent. The third, a rollicking Scherzo, begins with restless jumps and offbeat rhythms leading to a more sober Intermezzo, *Alla burla, ma pomposo*, a kind of polonaise or "marriage dance."[46] The Finale, actually the first movement of this work that Schumann completed (and also its longest), is an ambitious sonata-rondo without development but containing, as pianist Yonty Solomon has put it, "a profusion of ideas, alternating with each other in kaleidoscopic fashion."[47]

The G minor Piano Sonata (op. 22), "dedicated to Madame Henriette Voigt," was begun earlier than its predecessor but not completed until 1839, by which time communication between Schumann and Clara had been reestablished. This sonata is shorter and less innovative than the one in F-sharp minor. It shows an almost classical perfection, and Clara, who probably wished for that in her future spouse, was delighted. "I love it, as I love you," she wrote. "It so clearly expresses your essential self and is not too incomprehensible."[48]

The first movement seems to be designed for Clara's virtuosity, as it charges ahead rapidly, as quickly as seems humanly possible, then becomes faster, and even faster. Another of Schumann's early songs, "In the Autumn," is featured in the tranquil second movement, Andantino. The very fast Scherzo is so brusque and barely digestible that the composer wanted it omitted in public performances. Clara did not like the long final movement of the G minor Sonata. "I can play it if necessary, but the masses, the public, and even the connoisseurs for whom one is really writing don't understand it."[49] Accordingly, Schumann wrote an entirely new movement for her, a Beethoven-like rondo, again very fast and ending with a cadenza, "always faster and faster."

His supreme achievement in the piano sonata genre is the Fantasie in C major (op. 17), "composed for and dedicated to Herr Franz Liszt." Schumann had begun to sketch this work immediately after completing his F-sharp minor Sonata in 1836. Funds were being solicited that year for a statue in Bonn to commemorate Beethoven, and Schumann hoped to contribute this Fantasie under the title "Ruins—Trophies—Palms. Grand Sonata for the Piano for Beethoven's Memorial."[50] (Other grandiose titles crossed his mind, including "Ruins—Arch of Triumph and Heavenly Constellation—Poetry" before he settled on just "Fantasie" in 1838.) An elegant edition was intended, with the dedication in gold leaf, but Schumann's idea was not accepted by the committee.

By now his gaze was more firmly fixed on Clara, to whom he wrote, "The first movement may well be the most passionate I have ever composed—a deep lament for you."[51] A year later, after the work was published, he wrote, "You can only understand the Fantasie if you go back to the unhappy summer of 1836 when we were separated."[52]

A "motto" by Friedrich Schlegel appears on the first page, alluding to the musical communication that had to replace physical contact between Schumann and Clara that year:

Durch Alle Töne tönet	*All the tones that sound*
Im bunten Erdentraum	*In earth's multicolored dream*
Ein leiser Ton gezogen	*Contain one soft sound*
Für den der heimlich lauschet.	*For the secret listener.*

"The 'tone' in the motto is you, isn't that so?" Schumann asked Clara,[53] and his first movement is indeed punctuated several times by allusions to Beethoven's "An die Ferne Geliebte," a song for the distant beloved. The entire movement conveys Schumann's passion for the woman he could not possess. After an agitated beginning, Clara's theme is spelled out in descending octaves, propelled forcefully by means of suspensions.[54] The movement reaches feverish heights, then settles into an almost prayerful repose.

His driving, energetic middle movement apparently stimulated Clara erotically. She wrote from Paris:

> It makes me hot and cold all over. . . . Many images are stirred up. . . . The march strikes me as a victory march of warriors following a battle, and the A-flat major theme makes me think of young maidens in a village, all dressed in white, each with a wreath in her hand to crown the warriors kneeling before them.[55]

Some of Clara's more pugnacious imagery may also be attributed to an important new development. She had consulted an attorney in Paris, and the words she wrote were penned only twenty-four hours after signing a complaint against Wieck that Schumann had prepared. It demanded legal permission for their marriage.

The *Fantasie* in C major ends with a sublime slow movement. The sensation of suspended time stems in part from Schumann's improvisatory reflections on various Beethoven themes, including one from the *Emperor* Concerto, a work that Clara is said to have played magnificently.

The *Grand* Sonata in F minor (op. 14) is a tribute to Schumann's own heroism. Also called *Concerto without Orchestra*, it was conceived at the height of his ordeal with Clara and dedicated to Ignaz Moscheles, who did not much care for the work.* Originally in five movements, Schumann tried

---

*Schumann's dedicatory letter to Moscheles comments, "What mad inspirations one can have."[56] He had some reluctance about displaying this very personal music, and the *Grand* Sonata was never publicly performed during his lifetime. Brahms, who admired it greatly and used it as an inspiration for his own F minor Piano Sonata (op. 5), gave the first concert performance six years after Schumann's death.

valiantly to shorten it, setting huge chunks aside for a second F minor Sonata, which he never finished.[57]

A descending five-note theme signifying "Clara" recurs throughout the *Concerto without Orchestra*, sometimes in an angry mood as at the beginning of the first movement, sometimes tenderly, as in the *Andantino de Clara Wieck*, where Schumann duplicated her melody and then varied it, at times chaotically, as in the tempestuous *Prestissimo possibile* that brings this extraordinary composition to an end.

For Clara Wieck to marry into mediocrity would have been unthinkable. She was endowed with her mother's beauty and had been empowered since childhood with her father's burning ambition for success. A number of Clara's peers were gaining fame on the concert stage—Anna Caroline de Belleville (1808–1880), Marie Pleyel (1811–1875), and Marie Blahetka (1811–1887), to mention only three discussed in a new biography of Clara by Nancy Reich. "Many of her widely acclaimed female contemporaries made splashy debuts," according to Reich, "but one after the other gave up careers when they married or found they could not keep up with the stresses of combining family and profession."[58]

Clara Wieck was the only female virtuoso to attain a pinnacle of artistic achievement, where she remained for more than half a century. To accomplish this feat required allies, and she had to avoid entanglements that might stand in her way.

From the very beginning of Clara's complicated relationship with Schumann, and throughout the sixteen years of their turbulent marriage, it was never clear whether he was a help or a hindrance to her career. Her father, of course, believed the latter and did what he could to prevent their union.

Since parental approval was required for marriage, Wieck also had the law on his side. Clara turned eighteen in 1837, the year Schumann's musical campaign for her reached its apex. She knew that the next three years would be critical, and she also knew that there were not many eligible men of genius in the world of music. Chopin loved Clara's playing, but he was far too ill (with tuberculosis), and already involved with George Sand. Liszt found Clara too stiffly Germanic—"to her one did not make advances."[59] Mendelssohn was of the wrong religious background and had married Cecile Jeanrenaud in 1837. Carl Banck came very close to being Clara's suitor. But his creativity did not match Schumann's, and with the latter's piano sonatas ringing in everyone's ears Banck tactfully withdrew from the field of contention in 1837, no doubt at Clara's request.

Wieck, however, feared the vacuum created by Banck's departure and a month later again whisked Clara away from Leipzig. This time he took her to Maxen, a village near Dresden, to stay for several months on a country estate owned by a friend, Major Anton Serre. That proved to be a tactical error on Wieck's part, for Serre and his wife, Friederike, were fond of Schumann and tried everything they could to mollify Clara's stubborn father. Thus to everyone's great surprise Wieck soon announced that at Clara's next Leipzig concert, a month before her eighteenth birthday, she would play three variations from Schumann's *Symphonic Etudes*.

Schumann took this as a favorable sign, although he had had no contact with Clara for over a year and was still suspicious about her flirtations with Carl Banck. "Are you still loyal and steadfast?" he asked in a letter written the day of her concert, 13 August 1837. Using *Sie* throughout the letter, he proposed that their relationship be formalized.

> You are the dearest thing in the world to me. A thousand times I have thought about everything, and everything tells me it has to be, if we want to and can manage it. Just write me a simple "yes" if you are willing to give your father a letter from me on your birthday [13 September]. Right now he is well disposed toward me and he will not reject me as long as you plead for me.

Secrecy was still of the essence: "Do not tell anyone about this letter; otherwise everything could be spoiled." [60]

Clara wrote her reply twenty-four hours later, on "Eusebius Day," also using the formal *Sie*.

> A simple "yes" is all you ask? Such a tiny little word—yet so important! Couldn't a heart as full of inexpressible love as mine say this little word with its entire soul? I'll do it. . . . Perhaps fate wants us soon again to talk together. [61]

This emboldened Schumann to send Clara a preview of the marriage proposal he was planning to give Wieck. She was terrified of what the outcome might be: "Would God turn my eighteenth birthday into a day of mourning?" [62] Having not spoken directly with her suitor for a year and a half, Clara now insisted on a face-to-face meeting with him, despite the risks involved. They met on 9 September 1837, but the reunion turned out to be less than satisfactory. "You were so stiff, so cold" recalled Clara. "I too would have liked to be more sincere, but I was too excited; I could barely control myself." [63]

Four days later, on her birthday, Schumann sent Wieck his long-delayed proposal. It is a humble document, beginning with an apology. "The right words sometimes fail me. A tremulous hand keeps me from guiding the pen calmly." He begged Wieck to "test me once more . . . then, if you find I pass muster and am reliable and manly, bless this union of souls, which only needs parental consecration to bring it the greatest luck." He swore, "On my word of honor I will not speak with Clara as long as this is against your wishes." He closed with a plea for Wieck's friendship: "I implore you, with the deepest expression that a frightened and loving heart can muster, give your blessings. To one of your oldest friends be a friend again, and for the best child be the best father."[64]

As was to be expected, Wieck replied negatively, leaving Clara "in tears" on her birthday.[65] He berated her for "lacking judgment" and sent Schumann a letter that the composer thought was "so confusing and so doubtful . . . that I now don't know what to do."[66] A personal meeting with Wieck, "a terrible conversation," as Schumann called it, did not help the lovers' cause at all.[67] Wieck again demanded that Schumann and Clara have no private meetings. They were to see each other only "in public, where everyone can witness the spectacle." Furthermore, Wieck made it plain that marriage was completely out of the question. Clara "would lose out as an artist by committing herself prematurely to a man, and anyway she was still too young." Also there were economic considerations. Wieck told Schumann that they would need more money than they thought, for Clara was accustomed to a certain standard of living.[68]

Schumann, feeling "angry" about the proposal he had made, now entered a state of mourning. "Today I feel so dead, so humiliated," he wrote Clara on 18 September 1837. His mental "picture" of her was "dissolving. . . . Oh how everything goes around inside my head." In this state of despair and confusion he now formed an image of Clara as a warrior. "Arm yourself," he wrote her. "Your father will throw you to the first man who has enough money and a title. . . . He will bleed you and destroy me." Schumann's imagery was becoming more violent, and before the day ended he had slipped back into the familiar *Du* when demanding that Clara take an "oath, just as I am doing at this instant, by raising the two fingers of my right hand."[69]

In Schumann's symbolism, these two raised fingers stood for both the disabled fingers he could no longer use publicly on the keyboard and the trigger-fingers of his right hand, in the grips of murderous wishes that had to be restrained. Clara might have been willing to serve as his proxy hand at the piano, but she was not yet up to the challenge of defying her father and Wieck clearly won this round. He was already arranging another concert tour to Dresden, Prague, and Vienna, for Clara's long-awaited debut there. "Am I not a weak girl!" she wrote Schumann. "I have promised my father to be happy and for a few years yet to live for art and for the world."[70]

Clara tried to arrange another meeting before leaving on her trip, but it was too late. All they could get was a hurried "glance" and "good evening" at her triumphant Gewandhaus concert on 8 October, where Mendelssohn had personally led her to the piano. An almost incoherent letter from Schumann arrived the next day.

> So this Clara, I thought, this one is yours—is yours, and you cannot even go to her, not even press her hand. Was there anyone in the entire hall who could imagine my state of mind? Hardly you. I was dead and blissful at the same time, to the point of collapse. . . . I'm really sick, really very sick; one blow and I'll fall over.[71]

Unbeknownst to her, Schumann had been working feverishly on a new composition, but the combined effects of rage, alcohol, and separation anxiety were blocking his creativity. "What is it that robs me suddenly of the strength to work?" he asked imploringly. "When I fantasize at the piano, only chorales come forth, and when I write, there are no thoughts—all I want is to paint C L A R A all over the place in big letters and chords."[72] The music was ready in time for her mid-October departure, and he asked her to take the new composition along on her trip.

This work consists of eighteen short pieces for the piano. Schumann published it later that year at his own expense, under the title *Davidsbündler Dances* (op. 6), dedicated to Walther von Goethe, the poet's grandson and one of Schumann's new friends.

Schumann later told Clara that the *Davidsbündler Dances* contain "many wedding thoughts," and that he had composed them under conditions of "the most beautiful arousal that I can ever remember."[73] These pieces contain innumerable personal connotations. For example, Schumann's choice of "opus 6" is meaningful in that the work begins with a quotation from Clara's own opus 6, a *Mazurka* from her *Soirées Musicales*. Furthermore, he signed many of the pieces "E," or "F," or both "E" and "F," suggesting that different fragments of himself, symbolized as Florestan and Eusebius, were being expressed in the music. The entire composition is organized into two sections showing interesting key relationships, and both sections resolve to the key of C, for Clara.

Several of the pieces also have verbal comments that allude to Schumann's heightened mood while he was composing them, and possibly to his troubled relationship with Clara. (Schumann later deleted these personal comments from the revised version of *Davidsbündler Dances*.) The first section closes with:

Hereupon Florestan stopped, and his lips quivered painfully

while the entire composition ends on a poignant note:

Quite superfluously, Eusebius added the following, while great bliss radiated from his eyes.

The very gothically ornamented first edition of *Davidsbündler Dances* has a bittersweet motto on its title page:

In all' und jeder Zeit	*At all times*
Verknüpft sich Lust and Leid:	*Pleasure and grief go together.*
Bleibt fromm in Lust and seyd	*Keep faith in pleasure, and*
Dem Leid mit Muth bereit.	*Meet grief with courage.*

This "old saying," together with the music of the *Davidsbündler*, aptly symbolizes the artistic and psychological maturation Schumann had achieved by the age of twenty-seven. Having lost his mother, he wished to enter into a new and binding relationship—with a woman, he hoped. Clara had given her consent for such a union. But her angry, unyielding father, an oedipal figure, stood in the way of Schumann's marriage, so that his "engagement" to Clara brought with it the threat of intense dissension. The symbolism of the *Davidsbündler Dances* suggests that Schumann may again have resigned himself to the bittersweet realities of bachelorhood. Florestan and Eusebius dance singly or together, with an occasional moment of pain or bliss: "Pleasure and grief go together."

Schumann's friendly rivalry with Mendelssohn and his affection for Bennett probably enhanced the confidence he felt as a result of the progress he was then making on two fronts, in journalism and in composition. And the Davidsbund fraternity in Leipzig was becoming more accepting of his musical interests than his own family in Zwickau had been. No wonder *Davidsbündler Dances* has been called his most autobiographical work.

IX.

Symbolic Union with Clara, 1837–1839

lara's departure in mid-October 1837 gave Schumann freedom to return to work and pursue new friendships. A mountain of music had accumulated on his desk—compositions by Taubert, Nisle, Chwatal, Zimmerman, and other contemporaries, who might now be forgotten had he not written about them in the *New Journal*. He also kept himself occupied going to concerts, an effective antidote to loneliness. In the mornings were string-quartet sessions organized by Ferdinand David and other players from the Gewandhaus.[1] Orchestral and solo concerts took place in the afternoons and evenings. Thus the busy music critic, in his *Review of Leipzig's Musical Life in the Winter of 1837–1838*,[2] referred to no fewer than eighty-one compositions he had heard, a fruitful experience, no doubt, in terms of Schumann's desire to forge an original style for his own music.

He also wrote about some of the more attractive performers who caught his eyes and ears that winter, in particular "the most interesting appearance of a beautiful singer, Miss Clara Novello from London."[3] "For years nothing has pleased me so much as this voice," wrote the enraptured critic. Rumors quickly started to circulate. Gerald Abraham, in the *New Grove Dictionary of Music*, states that Schumann at this time "contemplated marriage to another Clara whose surname remains unknown."[4]

There were repeated misunderstandings and recriminations during Clara Wieck's trip. Only a month after their separation, Schumann tried to tell her about another young woman, Anna Robena Laidlaw, a pianist Clara's age, who in her absence was performing to great acclaim in Leipzig. "The Laidlaw woman holds me in her heart, I believe. At the farewell she gave me a lock of hair, just so you know it. Surely you can't be at all jealous; I want to get to know you better.[5]

This information upset Clara, who was apprehensive about her forthcoming Vienna debut:

How could you make me sick in this way, and draw such bitter tears out of me? . . . I know you have many girls at your disposal who are as beautiful and maybe also as good as I am, and who would make better housewives than could be expected from an artist.[6]

It was a sensitive subject. They both knew that she had been trained since childhood to be a concert artist and not a wife and mother. Schumann had opened the wound recently by articulating a bit of typically nineteenth-century male chauvinism, saying, "Experience tells us that female artists, good and great ones especially, only rarely love the same man for more than a year, three years at the most." Then he added, hopefully, that "there are also some exceptions, including especially women piano players."[7]

As Vienna approached, Clara's conflict between submission to Wieck and affection for Schumann intensified, and she tried to resolve it by begging the two men once more to be friends. "How deeply moved I feel just now," she wrote Schumann from Prague, "looking at my father and seeing how unhappy he is about losing me one day—I feel obligated to him, yet I've got to love you endlessly."[8] From Vienna: "It pains me when you throw stones at my father. . . . He wants to know I'm happy and means to achieve this through wealth, can you begrudge him this? He loves me more than anything . . . so forgive him, out of love for me."[9]

These entreaties enraged Schumann, but in trying to suppress his "anger"[10] at Clara, he feigned an obsequious, almost masochistic pose toward Wieck. "I love and honor your father more than anyone . . . it is a primitive, inborn tendency of mine, an obedience to everyone who is energetic."[11] Typically, he behaved agreeably and kindly when in fact he was boiling inside. Schumann's submissiveness toward Wieck was rebellion in disguise, suppressed rage transformed into suicidal ideas. Occasionally he broadcast these self-destructive thoughts to Clara, probably as a warning of what he might do. For example, once when she questioned the sincerity of his marriage proposal by reminding him of his betrayal of Ernestine,[12] he countered as follows:

> I've also stopped liking your ring, and don't even wear it anymore. I had a dream of walking along some deep water. Then it crossed my mind to throw in the ring—I have an interminable yearning to plunge in after it.[13]

It was just before Clara's debut in Vienna that he disclosed to her "the dark side of my life . . . the deep secret of a severe psychological illness . . . my brooding, often for hours on end, as I look at your picture . . . and think how will all of this end."[14] We can speculate about the effects of these revelations on Clara. She had her own anxieties and melancholic moods and seemed to cope with them better when there was someone else for her to worry about. It helped her to deny and externalize her own distress. Schumann's demands and outbursts also forced her to be more objective and comprehending, finally to express at the keyboard the feelings she shared with him.

Clara's performance of Beethoven's *Appassionata* Sonata in Vienna was electrifying. Writing in the *Wiener Zeitschrift*, the poet Franz Grillparzer exclaimed, "Her white fingers have seized the key to [Beethoven's] magic and unlocked spirits that now rise up to obey this graceful, innocent maiden."[15] Audiences thronged to her concerts (and Wieck pocketed all the earnings, except for charity events). By royal edict Clara Wieck was given the honorary title of "Imperial Concert Pianist," a singular honor for so young an artist, and a woman at that, who was not even a native of the Austro-Hungarian Empire, or a Catholic. (She even had a Viennese pastry named after her.)

Clearly this acclaim produced a major shift in her relationship with Schumann, who for years had been hoping for success in the world of music and musicians. Vienna was then the musical capital of Europe, and his letters as far back as the summer of 1836 show that he was interested in transferring the *New Journal for Music* to that city.[16] Now Clara was writing, flirtatiously, about friendly conversations with the emperor and empress—"but I'd rather be talking to you"[17]—and official doors were opening everywhere. As Clara's self-confidence increased, her programs also became more serious, shedding the virtuoso showpieces in favor of major compositions by Bach, Chopin, and Schumann himself. The more he heard about this—it had been his wish that Clara should play more "serious" programs—the more fervent became his desire for her.

The ecstatic *Fantasy Pieces* (op. 12) Schumann wrote at this time are dedicated to Anna Robena Laidlaw, but musically they were addressed to Clara. The first piece, "In the Evening," opens with her keynote theme, the familiar descending scale heard throughout his piano sonatas, here embedded in a restless triplet rhythm. This is followed by a Florestanian "Upsurge" (*Aufschwung*) in 6/8 time, leading to Eusebius' gentle, questioning "Why," and a darting, chimerical piece called "Whimsy" (*Grillen*). The internal structure of *Fantasy Pieces* is designed so that each of the four opening pieces in the first part is perfectly balanced against four in the second. The titles of the two sections are arranged around contrastive tonalities, the first around D-flat major and F, "indicating the real world, while those in the second have a lapidary tonality of F," as H. J. Köhler points out.[18]

The remarkable symmetry of this composition demonstrates not only Schumann's creative originality but also his desire to influence Clara through his music. "You want everything [in art] to be stormy all the time, with flashes of lightning, as though it's all new and has never happened before," he wrote her. "But there are also old and eternal states that control us."[19] Clara came to love the *Fantasy Pieces*, and she performed them frequently with great success.

After her second Vienna concert, in December, she complained to Schumann, "You can be home at 10 P.M., while I, poorest one, don't get home until 11 to 12, dead tired, drink a glass of water, lie down and wonder whether an artist is worth much more than a beggar."[20] Christmas was fast approaching, and he assumed that Clara's sadness contained a veiled desire for domestic bliss. He wrote as if they were already married:

> [*22 December*] You look around—and it's me. . . . I will never leave your side and I will follow you everywhere.
> [*31 December*] Slip your arm around me, and let us look once more into each other's eyes,—quietly—blissfully—Two people love each other in this world. . . . How happy we are—Clara let us kneel down! Come my Clara, I feel you.[21]

But with the coming of the new year, he realized that this was a self-deception; his letters became less romantic:

> Of course I too have my terrible hours, when even your image wants to abandon me—when I reproach myself about spending my life as I should, and whether I ought to have tied you, my angel, to me.[22]

Wieck's accusations were beginning to affect him:

People see themselves the way they are seen by others, and after the way your father has treated me I must ask of myself "are you really so bad, have you fallen so low as to justify such discourtesies?"[23]

In attempting to escape his guilty self-reproaches—"I am such an impatient, unsatisfied, unbearable person at times"[24]—Schumann conjured up fantasies of an idyllic childhood:

If I could only be as truly devoted as I was in childhood—I was really a happy child then, assembling chords at the piano, or picking flowers outside; I made the prettiest poems and prayers—and was one myself. But one grows older. Now I want to play with you, the way angels do together, from eternity to eternity.[25]

Schumann's proclivity for fantasizing made it easy for him to engage Clara in make-believe. He spun out fairy-tale plans for "a little museum, with three rooms upstairs and as many downstairs," where they would live happily ever after.[26] Then he added:

You will love the Bach in me, I the Bellini in you—we will often play together four-handed—in the evening I shall improvise for you in the twilight, and sometimes you will sing along softly and then fall blissfully onto my chest, saying "I never thought it could be so nice."[27]

Clara found his "depiction of the future so beautiful, oh so stimulating" that by the end of the month she was making her own plans for cohabitation—perhaps in Vienna.[28] At the end of January she revealed explicit reasons:

In Leipzig I had decided never to live under these circumstances. Just think, dear Robert, in Leipzig I can't earn a penny with my art, and you too would have to work yourself to death to earn what we need. Wouldn't that depress you, also on my account? I couldn't tolerate it. No, let's do it the way I tell you.[29]

Clara's proposal was that she "easily" could earn 2000 thalers a year by giving one concert a year plus piano lessons every day, while Schumann ought to be able to bring in 1000 thalers annually. "What more do we need?"[30] In relating this information to him, she was thinking of her father, who had written into her diary:

I would never give my consent for Leipzig. . . . Schumann may manipulate, philosophize, flutter around, and idealize as he wants; it is affirmed that Clara can never live in poverty and seclusion, but must be able to consume 2000 thalers each year.[31]

Clara assumed, incorrectly, that Wieck would sanction the marriage if they were to live abroad. Schumann was more suspicious—"Maybe your father just wants to get me out of Leipzig."[32] Still, her invitation to move to Vienna seemed irresistible. Besides, it was one of Schumann's "oldest and dearest wishes" to go there. His friend Ludwig Schunke had often mentioned its delights, and nothing could be more tempting than Vienna, "where the most magnificent art and so much external beauty would echo in the hearts of two lovers, and where Beethoven and Schubert have lived."[33]

Thus in March 1838 Schumann threw caution to the wind and wrote Clara to "give me your hand, it's been decided . . . my eager wish, our goal—Vienna."[34] Ecstatically he informed his two brothers that "one of the world's most magnificent girls will in time be mine." He asked each of them for 600 thalers a year (they owed him money) to help him move to Vienna. "This concerns the future of the most marvelous girl, whom I just cannot let go, and who in addition is the greatest artist in the world—and a union that will bring the greatest credit to our family."[35]

His excitement could not be contained. "Oh, if only I don't go crazy [verrückt] with joy." Unable to sleep at night, he fantasized about Clara:

> Suddenly you sat next to me, sewing something. You were worried about me until I finally gave you my hand and said loudly "Wife, you're making me too happy." Then you opened your eyes, moved closer to me, and said with gleaming eyes, "Is that really true?"[36]

In the daytime Schumann rhapsodized at the piano. "Music is the feminine friend who can best communicate everything that we feel internally," he wrote Clara.[37] He even performed briefly in public again.*

But most of his excitement went into new compositions. "I've been composing an awful lot for you in the last three weeks," he wrote Clara in early February 1838—"funny things, Egmont stories, family scenes with fathers, a wedding, in short everything worthy of love."[39]

From this labor resulted Schumann's *Novelletten* (op. 21), one of his longest and most demanding compositions for the piano. (Its title might be meant to suggest novelettes, but it also comes from Clara Novello's name—she was planning to go to Vienna—and he sheepishly explained this to Clara Wieck by pointing out that "Wiecketten doesn't sound good enough."[40])

The work is in eight movements, "intimately connected and written with passionate joy, cheerful and flighty . . . but somewhere I also hit rock bottom."[41] The opening, marked "Emphatic and powerful," has an aggres-

---

*Some months earlier Schumann had asked friends in Vienna to send him a new device for "speeding up the fingers" (*einen Fingerschneller*).[38]

sive, hypermasculine character. The second movement, "Extremely fast and with bravura," is gentle and exotic; Schumann was eager to have it performed and even sent a prepublication copy to Franz Liszt. The third, "Light and with humor," is sometimes thought to refer to the witches' scene in *Macbeth*.[42] The fourth is a waltz, and the fifth a polonaise. Toward the end of *Novelletten* a "voice from the distance" sounds softly in the right hand. It is Clara's descending five-note scale.

In his euphoric state, dreaming of union with his distant beloved, Schumann seems to have felt like the passive recipient of his own creative energies. It was the gratification of a cosmic wish, not uncommon to artists, to have the attributes of both sexes. Schumann described "music pouring into [him], which "often made [him] feel like bursting." He wanted to "sing along" with his inner voices. He felt incessantly driven to compose, to nourish, and to "play with the new forms." Thus he hoped both to subdue the terrifying exaltation that was threatening to escalate into manic psychosis, and to make good use of the abundant energy that was being released. One way to do so, he thought, was to get away from the piano and write something for other instruments; specifically, he had in mind three string quartets.[43]

The idea of branching out and writing music *not* for the keyboard came in part from Mendelssohn, whose advice Schumann valued. Mendelssohn had just completed his own beautiful three String Quartets (op. 44), and the notion of doing something to equal or better the illustrious "Felix Meritis" obviously appealed to Schumann. He probably also hoped to control his raging excitement over Clara by drawing a little closer to the *Davidsbündler* circle.

But she wouldn't have things that way. Clara preferred that Robert busy himself by revising and simplifying the piano music he had written for her, and she chided him gently.

> You want to write quartets? One question, but don't laugh at me: do you know enough about the instruments? I'm happy with the idea, but please be very clear. It would give me too much pain if people were to misunderstand you.[44]

Schumann took this as a reproof, and it stung him, but as usual he disguised his anger: "You write that I ought to make string quartets—but 'please be very clear'—That sounds like something from a Dresden old maid."[45]

Incredibly, considering that Schumann wanted to be another Beethoven or Schubert, he set aside for four years his plans to compose string quartets and continued to pour out music for Clara's piano. (Perhaps he really did appreciate the cautiousness of a "Dresden old maid.") But the work he produced shows evidence of strong inner conflict. In fact, his next two compositions, *Scenes from Childhood* and *Kreisleriana* (opp. 15 and 16), suggest that he may have been hovering precariously between resignation and despair. What probably helped Schumann at this time was his fabulous talent for musical mimicry, plus the skills in communicating his ideas, which he had so laboriously taught himself. Piano compositions in particular enabled him to transform inner chaos into artistic products for others to enjoy. Schumann's audiences were minuscule at first. They consisted mainly of Clara and a few intimate friends. But she, a musical genius in her own right, would gradually attract others to his music.

Giddily he told her about his latest compositions:

> I've put on my frilly dress and composed 30 cute little things from which I've selected about twelve and called them "Scenes from Childhood" [*Kindersze-nen*]. . . . They are like an echo to what you once wrote me, that I sometimes "seem like a child" to you.[46]

Fragments of childhood emotion had come into focus, and by depicting them musically Schumann seemed to be anticipating the joys of fatherhood yet to come. Each "scene" is a brief childhood memory: "Foreign Lands and People," "Playing Catch," "Dreaming," "Being Scared," and other personal experience. "Dreaming" (*Träumerei*) is one of his best-known short pieces, a melody of exquisite tenderness.

Schumann's next composition, *Kreisleriana*, is almost exactly the opposite, a musical portrait of violence and madness. Working on these fantasies concurrently with his *Scenes from Childhood*, Schumann seems to have had another dissociative episode, which he described to Clara:

> I woke up and couldn't go back to sleep—and as I thought my way more and more deeply into you, your mind, and your dream-life, I suddenly said, with innermost strength, "Clara, I'm calling you"—and then I heard it, really loud as if right next to me, "Yes Robert, I'm with you." A sort of horror fell over me, like the ghosts that traffic with each other over the flatlands. I won't do it again, this calling; it really wears me out.[47]

We cannot tell from this letter whether he was hallucinating while half-asleep or just idly ruminating. He tried to reassure Clara that he was leading a "sober, industrious life," and that his melancholia was caused only by "sitting around all night."[48] Schumann wanted Clara to think that *Kreisleriana* was a reflection on her:

> Just think, since my last letter I've again finished a whole book of new things. I will call it "Kreisleriana," in which you and one of your ideas play the main

role, and I will dedicate it to you—yes to you and no one else*—then as you recognize yourself, you will smile fondly.[49]

But this tempestuous music had just the opposite effect. "You shock me sometimes," Clara wrote Schumann after playing *Kreisleriana*. "I wonder if it is true that this man will be my husband? Sometimes I have the idea that I will never be able to satisfy you, but in spite of that you could always love me."[50] Clara probably sensed his physical passion, something he was trying to control in her absence, and she may have been afraid of it. (She was probably still a virgin at this time.) He told her, in regard to *Kreisleriana*, that "there is a thoroughly wild love in some of the movements."[51]

The title itself gives Schumann's preoccupations away. He was thinking about a lunatic, the haunted figure of "Kapellmeister Johannes Kreisler" from E. T. A. Hoffmann's famous stories.[52] Kreisler is a reckless musician, scraping his violin or pounding the piano to bits. Drinking heavily, wandering about aimlessly, he harangues strangers and behaves incoherently in public. Hardly a flattering portrait of Clara Wieck! Yet she may unwittingly have given some impetus to these fantasies by writing to Schumann about Franz Liszt. Clara wanted to introduce the two men, and that excited Schumann. One of the most gifted musicians of the time, Liszt was a striking figure who, like Paganini, could spellbind an audience. According to Wieck, his "passions know no bounds. He often damages the sense of beauty by ripping melodies apart, using the pedal too much . . . breaking strings . . . pulling you into him—so that you drown."[53] Still devoted to her father, Clara adhered strongly to this negative imagery of Franz Liszt.

The juxtaposition of rage and mystery in *Kreisleriana* may well have been Schumann's answer to the many conflicts stimulated all at once by Clara's triumph in Vienna, the fantastic virtuoso Liszt, the spiteful Wieck, and Florestan and Eusebius cavorting madly with each other.

With Clara's return to Leipzig in May 1838, Schumann was back in his old predicament. Clara tried to arrange a secret meeting with him—their first in eight months—which presumably did take place, for his diary reports "the most blissful day."†[54] But generally they could not meet, and Schumann complained that "Our best years, the beautiful time of our en-

---

* When published later that year, *Kreisleriana* (op. 16) was dedicated to Frédéric Chopin.
† He was by now keeping detailed records of his activities again, in a daily "household book."

gagement, must be spent living without each other. Oh, I could rage against him who is to blame."[55] Although he wanted to placate Wieck, he hated the injustice of the edict against seeing Clara. Even his letters to her had to be delivered secretly, by Dr. Reuter. Some of these sound very urgent, for example:

> I long so much to see you, to press you to my heart, that I am very sad—and also sick. I don't know what ails me and yet I do know, your absence ails me. I can imagine you everywhere. In my room you walk back and forth with me. You lie in my arms. But nothing, none of this, is real. I'm sick. . . . I can't stand it much longer.[56]

He told her he was suffering from "mental illness" (*Seelenkrankheit*)[57] and issued "a warning" for her "always in the future [to] deal with me very protectively."[58] This put Clara into a predicament. How was she to disbelieve her father when Schumann, by going to pieces so often, seemed to confirm his dire predictions about emotional instability? She too began to manifest depressive symptoms.

> When I saw you walking by, it was as if I would sink into a coma with pain. Everything turned black before my eyes. Then, when I could no longer see you . . . the tears started flowing . . . an indescribable feeling!!![59]

The situation had become intolerable. Schumann, determined to take Clara up on her suggestion that they live together in Vienna, kept pressing for a definite commitment. Would she agree to get married in two years, around Easter 1840? Clara's hesitation infuriated him. She hinted that she would follow him to Vienna, but she objected that "the separation from my father would be difficult for me and I would have to fight hard. . . . Father might reject me, oh my God, how terrible if it should come to that."[60]

It didn't come to that, not yet. Wieck wanted to capitalize on Clara's triumph in Austria and was planning to take her again to France. Schumann would have to go to Vienna alone.

A solitary trip to Vienna was in itself a source of anxiety for him. Since his breakdown in 1833 Schumann had been afraid of traveling, and he was especially terrified about having to stay in rooms higher than the first floor. His roommate Ulex chose not to come along (he was making plans for William Sterndale Bennett to move into their apartment as soon as Schumann would leave). Schumann invited two other friends—the bookseller Robert Friese and the composer Hermann Hirschbach—but both declined.[61]

Thus another transitional figure came to play an important role in Schumann's life: Joseph Fischhof, a medical doctor and prominent musician (professor at the Vienna Conservatory). Correspondence between them had sprung up earlier that year; Fischhof had sent Schumann "diaries" to publish in the *New Journal for Music*, and Schumann had asked Fischhof for help in moving his newspaper to Vienna. On Clara's recommendation, Schumann invited himself to live with Dr. Fischhof.[62]

The journey was uneventful and a brief stopover with Major Serre and his wife in Maxen helped reduce Schumann's separation anxiety. "Everything overflows here with joy and riches; everyone can do what he wants," he wrote his family in Zwickau.[63] On 3 October 1838 he arrived in Vienna, and he was immediately captivated by the city's physical beauty, elegant parks, and magnificent buildings. But after only four days in what he called "our new home," he complained in a letter to Clara about "a sort of despondency, like someone who has been banished."[64] He found that Vienna was "such a big city that one needs half again as much time to do anything. . . . You cannot imagine what petty rivalries, coteries, etc. they have here. To get on a firm footing one needs to have the nature of a snake, and I don't believe there's much of that in me."[65]

Handicapped by what the Viennese regarded as his "great quietness,"[66] Schumann found it difficult to enter the mainstream of society. With Fischhof, who was Jewish, he felt ill at ease and moved out of his apartment, into a single room at Schönlaterngasse 679. In a dejected state he visited the cemetery at Währing where Schubert and Beethoven were interred, and envisaged being buried between these two composers. On Beethoven's tomb he found a steel pen ("a good omen"[67]), which he took home and later used "on festive occasions" such as writing important articles for his newspaper or composing symphonies.[68] (Fetishes of various sorts seem to help certain artists with their creative activity. Wagner, for example, liked to be surrounded by velvet drapes or other sensuous material while composing.)

In Vienna Schumann frequented the opera, went to the ballet, and attended numerous concerts, including no fewer than three performances of Haydn's *Seasons*. These experiences greatly enriched his musical background, but with his journalistic career he made little progress. Although Clara had written to Count Sedlnitzky, head of the Austrian Bureau of Censors, on his behalf, it did not help. The law said that only Austro-Hungarians were allowed to publish newspapers in Vienna, and Schumann did not want to give up his Saxon citizenship. His friend Tobias Haslinger offered to publish the newspaper for him, but their negotiations came to nothing. Hoping to obtain special dispensation because this was a musical and not a political journal, Schumann waited.

He became increasingly frustrated. If only Clara would join him in Vienna, she might be able to pull some strings. "I don't possess any courtly finesse," he wrote her. "It would make me happy if you could accompany me here and there. . . . You can be like a countess if necessary. How they speak of you here, how beloved and honored you are."[69] Repeatedly he tried to wean her away from her father. "You will have to leave one of us," he wrote her on 24 October. He even put 1000 gulden (about 660 thalers) at Clara's disposal, only to be rebuffed when she answered, "I won't let you break into your capital, because once that starts it never stops, and there are always new reasons."[70]

The last straw was Clara's suggestion that they postpone their wedding after the spring of 1840 so that she could earn more money. Schumann fumed:

> I did not expect you suddenly to smash my last hopes. . . . You have demor-alized and weakened me so much in my activities and thoughts that I want to leave here immediately. . . . Between the two of us we have a nice little in-come . . . and the brains and hands to earn twice or three times as much as we need. But you want by all means to be a millionairess, and with that I no longer want you.[71]

Clara was distraught by his letter, and Dr. Reuter was called on to mediate. He tried to explain to Clara that Schumann was probably exagger-ating: "He likes to cling with all his might to dreary as well as joyful ideas, and you do too."[72] But Clara continued to feel miserable, complaining of heart symptoms and headaches, while Schumann, with the winter holidays approaching, wrote his family that "[I] often felt so depressed that I could shoot myself."[73]

As a Christmas present he sent Clara a short composition called "A Wish."* He also wrote a very long, doleful poem for "a certain bride who absolutely does not want a man in his twenties to be her husband."[74] He seems to have formed no attachments to any other women while in Vienna, and Clara's remark that "it might finally happen that the Viennese women would compete with me"[75] probably tells us more about her own anxiety than about Schumann's behavior there.

As for men, those Schumann enjoyed spending time with either lived too far away (the pianist Thalberg, for example) or were too old (such as Wolfgang Mozart, son of the composer) to offer much in the way of com-panionship. He also met the sad, pre-psychotic poet Nikolaus Lenau in Vienna. They exchanged ideas, and Schumann later set some of his poems to music.

Probably the most important connection Schumann made there was with Ferdinand Schubert, the older brother of Franz Schubert and himself a

---

*Not published until 1852, in an assortment of rarely performed pieces for the piano titled *Bunte Blätter* (op. 99).

minor composer and schoolteacher. On several occasions Schumann visited Schubert's modest flat and there discovered a "treasure" of unknown compositions by Franz Schubert, including operas, masses, and the great C major Symphony.[76] Schumann sent the manuscript to Leipzig, where Mendelssohn conducted the first performance of the symphony on 21 March 1839. In his newspaper, Schumann extolled the "heavenly length" of the symphony. It seemed "like a thick novel in four volumes by Jean Paul"[77] and undoubtedly stimulated Schumann's own ambitions to return to symphonic writing.

While rummaging through Ferdinand Schubert's apartment, Schumann also found a story called "My Dream," which Franz Schubert had written when he was Schumann's age: "I was sad [it read] . . . banished . . . in a distant land. For long years I felt torn between the greatest grief and the greatest love."[78] The story speaks poignantly about Schubert's dead mother and about his ambivalent attraction to a "circle of many youths and old men who walk perpetually as if in bliss," a thinly disguised homosexual fantasy that seems to have appealed to Schumann. He published Schubert's "Dream" in the 5 February 1839 issue of the *New Journal*.

Only a month later Schumann received his final rebuff in Vienna. The Bureau of Censors, cronies of the Metternich regime, officially turned down his special request for permission to publish a newspaper there. His only alternative now was to sell the *New Journal* to someone with the right credentials. Fearing that he would then lose control over the whole enterprise, Schumann temporarily abandoned the idea of moving permanently to Vienna. Finally there was nothing for him to do except finish the compositions he had started, try to get them published, and figure out a way to go home.

While the failure of his mission in Vienna engendered considerable depression, Schumann did a substantial amount of creative work there. Much of the music he wrote shows the influence of the distant Clara, and his attempt to cope with the sad mood resulting from their separation. "Since receiving your letters I've been composing," he wrote her in December 1838; "I can't stop myself with all the music."[79] Another important source of stimulation was a theoretical text he was studying at this time, *Ideas about the Aesthetics of Musical Composition* (*Ideen zu einer Ästhetik der Tonkunst*) by Christian Schubart. This book articulated certain well-known psychological connections between moods and tonalities. For example, the key of C major was said to reveal "innocence, the language of children."[80] Schubart identified B-flat major as the key of "happy love, easy conscience, hope, and visions of a better world," and B-flat minor as the key of "terror, raging doubt, [and] darkest melancholy." Schumann seems to have benefited from this instruction. "It is obvious," says Hans-Joachim Köhler in an excellent analysis of his Vienna compositions, "that Schubart's brief but flexible descriptions of the keys for a short while definitely influenced Schumann's conceptions."[81]

The composer himself wrote from Vienna that his style had been "getting lighter and more feminine."[82] He made this observation in the context of a long, informative letter to a Belgian admirer, Simonin de Sire. "Earlier I used to rack my brains a great deal, now I hardly ever cross out a note of music. Everything happens spontaneously." This easy flow and lightness is apparent in his Arabeske in C major (op. 18). Another of his "more feminine" compositions is the *Flower Piece* (op. 19), a set "of little things," as he told Clara, "of which I have so many, assembled in a pretty way."[83]

Not all Schumann's Viennese music is confectionery, however. He wanted to compose in larger, more serious forms and almost completed a *Concertpiece in D minor for Piano and Orchestra* (unpublished), which is "a cross between a symphony, a concerto, and a big sonata."[84] Reluctant to dampen the spontaneity of his composition, Schumann refrained from rewriting his music. Thus there is a tendency for his emotional ups and downs to echo through the Vienna works. He was aware of this: "All week I've been sitting at the piano and composing and writing and laughing and crying, all at the same time," says a letter to Clara dated 11 March 1839. "You will find this beautifully illustrated in my opus 20, the great Humoreske."[85]

The *Humoreske* (op. 20) begins with a naive quality reminiscent of *Scenes from Childhood*. But then it moves to a tune that resembles a musical clock getting stuck and repeating itself. In a section marked "Hastily" (*Hastig*), Schumann wrote an "inner voice" on a third line, an experiment suggested by de Sire. But this voice is only to be imagined, like a hallucination; it is not to be played. The "voice" is Clara's, singing her own composition, a Romance in G minor. Schumann's internal fusion with her had progressed to the point where he would occasionally lose sight of who had thought of a musical theme first, he or Clara. According to Köhler,

Schumann believed he had stumbled onto a goldmine. On 22 June 1839 he planned that "we shall publish a great deal of music under both our names. Posterity shall see us as one heart and one soul, and not be able to tell what is mine and what is yours. How happy I am." On 2 July he received Clara's G minor Romance, of which he wrote "Your Romance once more confirms that we must be man and wife. Each of your ideas comes from my own soul, just as I must thank you for all the music I write. . . . When did you write the G minor piece? In March I had a similar idea; you will find it in the Humoreske. Our mutual sympathy is absolutely remarkable.[86]

Although they would remain physically separated in 1839—Clara embarked for Paris on 8 January, not with her father but with a French woman as travel companion—Schumann felt so close to her that everything she did seemed related to his existence in one way or another. For example, when in Stuttgart she naively turned for advice to an older, married man named Gustav Schilling, Schumann reacted as if he had been personally assaulted. "A hot anxiety falls over me sometimes. . . . Help me, I'm really a little sick in the head."[87] It seems that Clara, eager to trust the first fatherly person she met on her tour, had confided to him the troubles of her engagement. This gave Schilling, a rather disreputable music critic, an opening. He told Clara that for her own good, as well as Schumann's, she ought to persuade him to move to Stuttgart. Schilling would assume editorial responsibilities for the *New Journal*, and of course share the profits. The whole idea made Schumann "boiling mad." "Never trust anyone with matters pertaining to our future, even if he is in sheep's clothing like this wolf," he warned Clara.[88] She, duly alarmed, urged him to get out of Vienna.

> Leave, return to our Leipzig, there I believe we would be happiest. . . . It pleases me without end that you are composing so much. And even a symphony [the unfinished concertpiece]? O, Robert, that is just too beautiful! . . . You won't mind if I call you the second Jean Paul and Beethoven? . . . Wherever I may be, in England, France, America or even in Siberia, I'll always be your loyal bride, loving you from the heart.[89]

Clara's flattery was linked to a wish that he would write music for her to play in Paris:

> Listen Robert, won't you for once compose something brilliant and easy to understand, something that is a complete and coherent piece without special titles, not too long and not too short? I would so much like to have something of yours to play in public, something written for an audience. I know this is degrading for a genius, but once in a while it would be the politic thing to do.[90]

His *Faschingsschwank aus Wien* (op. 26) is a partial attempt at compliance. The opening Allegro in ¾ time contains a cleverly disguised quotation of "La Marseillaise," a musical greeting to Clara in Paris. It was also Schumann's way of thumbing his nose at the Austrian censors who had given him such a hard time, since under Metternich playing the French anthem was strictly forbidden. The second movement, Romanze, begins in G minor and again refers to Clara's piece in the same key. The third, Scherzino, has so catchy a tune—it wants to be whistled—that we might say Schumann was fulfilling Clara's wish. But the fourth movement, Intermezzo, is a gloomy, agitated piece (in E-flat minor, Schubart's "most depressing" key). The Finale, written after Schumann had returned to Leipzig, is an overly long movement in sonata form, with two interrelated themes and a complicated development section.

Schumann conceived another Vienna composition, *Nightpieces* (op. 23), just before he left the city of his shattered hopes. The first movement is a somewhat monotonous funeral march; its tonal range is restricted and several times falls to the bass-line in both hands. The second movement sounds generally wild and chaotic, with a few moments of Viennese lilt thrown in for good measure. The third is a sarcastic attempt to recapture the more joyful mood of *Faschingsschwank*, while the last movement again sounds sad and resigned.

Schumann had written *Nightpieces* under extremely stressful circumstances. Still undecided about when to leave Vienna, he received a letter on 30 March 1839 that made it mandatory for him to do so immediately. His brother Eduard was gravely ill. Schumann reacted fatalistically. "Eduard's death could be an economic disaster for us [the family publishing business]," he wrote Clara. "Wouldn't you leave me if I were now to become a very poor man and told you to leave me because I would bring you nothing but sorrow?"[91] He claimed to have had a "premonition" of his brother's death a week earlier, and therefore wanted to call the new composition he was working on "Corpse Fantasy."* "I always saw funeral possessions, coffins, unhappy and despairing people. . . . Often I was so distraught that tears flowed and I didn't know why—then Therese's letter arrived and I knew why."[92]

Not only did Schumann cry uncontrollably while working on his "Corpse Fantasy," but he always got stuck "at a place where it seemed as if someone was sobbing 'O God' from a heavy heart."[94] The description suggests an auditory hallucination congruent with his mournful mood.

Despite Schumann's premonition of an imminent death in his family, he did not leave Vienna until 5 April 1839. But Eduard died early in the morning of the 6th, so he was too late. Afraid probably of having to look at his brother's corpse, Schumann did not arrive in Zwickau until 10 April, thus missing the funeral, and he left the next day.[95]

To Clara he wrote:

Half past three on Saturday morning, while traveling, I heard a chorale of trombones—it was the moment Eduard died. . . . I still feel stunned by all the exertion. . . . Without you I long ago would have been where he is now.[96]

---

* Clara persuaded against this title. "The public won't understand what you mean and it will bother them. I think you should settle for the general title 'Nightpieces.'"[93] Clara's pragmatism prevailed, but Schumann's *Nightpieces* (op. 23) *are* funereal, and probably were intended to bother people. The original title seems more fitting.

While Schumann's report of hearing a trombone chorale exactly when his brother died may be somewhat exaggerated, it suggests that he was again hallucinating. The musical character of these inner voices is important because of the way he was able to forge them into works of art. An interesting bit of history is connected with this particular hallucination. One of Schumann's early contacts in Vienna had been a trombone player, Franz Glöggl, whose father had known Beethoven personally. A letter from Glöggl mentions several mourning pieces for trombones written by Beethoven, for a funeral in Linz in 1812.[97] These pieces, called "Equales," were later performed at Beethoven's funeral in Vienna in 1827.

So Schumann was bringing back to Germany not only a pen he had found on Beethoven's grave and musical ideas acquired from Beethoven, Schubert, and other great composers who had lived in Vienna, but also a sound with unique symbolic meaning. The mournful tone of the trombone fits well with Schumann's depressive mood and with his fantasies of a brother's funeral and the concomitant premonition of his own inevitable death.

X.

Delays Before Marriage, 1839–1840

An otherwise reassuring letter from Clara on 9 April 1839 warned Schumann of a "secret" correspondence between her father and her close friend Emilie List, with whom she was then staying in Paris. Wieck was threatening to disinherit her, keep the money she had earned from concerts, and initiate, as Clara put it, "a legal process against us both that could take 3–5 years, unless I let go of you."[1] Frightened by this turn of events, she consulted M. Adolphe Delapalm, a French attorney, and signed an affidavit that Schumann had prepared. Schumann gave this document to his own attorney in Leipzig, Herr Wilhelm Einert, with instructions to attempt an out-of-court settlement. Should this fail, his plan was to file a complaint against Wieck with the Saxon Court of Appeals, asking for legal permission to marry Clara.

As the moment of truth approached, Clara became frantic with indecision. She claimed that "the greatest moment in [her] life" had been when she gave Schumann her legal power-of-attorney.[2] But she dreaded the idea of having to confront her father in court. Wieck's authority as her piano teacher complicated her separation problem. "Do you know what I yearn

151

for? It is to have a lesson from my father," she wrote Schumann on 27 June 1839.

> I no longer have anyone around me who can show me my mistakes. . . . Often I don't even hear the sick notes I play. There is so much I ought to thank my father for, but I've almost never done it. . . . Oh, how eager I now am to be chastised![3]

Clara's vacillation at this critical juncture angered Schumann. There was a furious exchange of letters, and at one point Clara even asked him to postpone their marriage "for another half to whole year."

> Father wants to come [to Paris] this summer and then go with me to Belgium, Holland, England, etc. I have to admit that I can accomplish much more with my father than by myself. . . . One is more highly regarded everywhere in the company of a man.[4]

Nevertheless Schumann instructed his attorney to proceed. Einert tried to negotiate with Wieck on 2 July 1839 but was unable to come to an agreement. That meant they would have to go to court. Extremely pessimistic, Schumann made an alarming threat in a letter to Clara:

> Now all hope has disappeared. . . . All of this has affected me so deeply that if you had been with me yesterday, Clara, I would have been ready to put you and me to death.[5]

Finally, on 16 July, Schumann did file his complaint against Wieck. The court quickly ordered him to appear with Clara and her father before Archdeacon Rudolf Fischer for a preliminary attempt at reconciliation. This meant that Clara was forced to drop her plan for further concerts abroad and return immediately to Leipzig.

Schumann's friend Dr. Reuter suggested that since the lovers had not seen each other for nearly a year they ought to spend some time alone together before confronting Wieck in court. Consequently, they met on 18 August in a hotel in Altenburg, and then visited Robert's relatives in Schneeberg and Zwickau before going separately to Leipzig at the end of the month.

Clara's diary talks of "three happy days together," but she was troubled to observe that Schumann could "no longer find any loving persons" in his family environment. She hoped "to replace what he had lost and accompany him faithfully through life," and yet she wondered whether she would "have the power to tie him down."[6]

As far as the legal situation was concerned, their chances of staying together did not look promising. Clara's father, claiming that business obligations made it impossible for him to attend, boycotted the scheduled hearing with Archdeacon Fischer. He stated bluntly that under no circumstances would he ever consent to the marriage anyway. That brought matters to a standstill. Unable to remain any longer with her father in Leipzig, Clara left for Berlin to live with her mother, who had recently met Schumann and seemed to like him. Not surprisingly, Frau Bargiel sided against her ex-husband Wieck and encouraged Clara to marry Schumann.

During Clara's absence, Wieck tried to reach a settlement with the Leipzig court. He stated that she could get married on the condition that everything she had earned in seven years of concertizing be given to her half-brothers. Wieck also wanted Clara to pay 1000 thalers to repossess her piano and personal belongings stored at his house. Furthermore, he demanded that 8000 thalers from Schumann's capital reserves, a very large sum, be set aside exclusively for her so that in case the marriage failed—which Wieck believed to be inevitable—all interest from this money could go to his daughter.

Needless to say, these brutal financial conditions were unacceptable. "What sort of a husband would agree to such a thing?" Clara wrote in her diary. "It is the husband's duty to rule over his wife's money, not the opposite."[7] Having failed with this strategy to defeat the lovers, Wieck now filed a very long petition in which he asked that a reconciliation conference with Archdeacon Fischer be held after all. It was scheduled for 2 October, but again Wieck failed to appear. Another date, 18 December, was set for the final hearing.

But on 14 December Wieck filed another verbose appeal. Unassisted by counsel, his tactic evidently was to stall the proceedings by handing in long written statements just before every hearing, and then not attend in person. This time he formulated two questions for the court: Do Robert and Clara have the financial means for a successful marriage, and do they have the personal capacity for a happy union? For over ten years Wieck had observed Schumann closely, he wrote. The man was unable to support himself, had squandered his inheritance, and had made a mess of his work as editor of the *New Journal for Music*. He was "lazy, unreliable, and conceited," and "a mediocre composer whose music is unclear and almost impossible to perform."[8]

Next Wieck attacked Clara. She was unfit and untrained to be a housewife. She had unrealistic expectations in terms of the level of support Schumann could provide. Her artistic career would come to nothing if she were to travel with this man, who was "incompetent, childish, unmanly, in short totally lost for any social adjustment, and cannot speak coherently or write legibly." He would "always get in her way." Clara wasn't suited to earn money by giving music lessons, yet Schumann would demand that of her.[9]

Finally, Wieck went so far as to aver that Schumann had "paralyzed one of his fingers and made it useless through stupidity, defiance, and senseless conflict." In addition, he was an alcoholic, had been drinking "since his youth and, notably, almost every night . . . in public beer and wine houses . . . either all by himself or with only one other person." He had a "mystical and dreamy personality." He didn't really love Clara but only wanted to exploit her, as proved by his past relationship with Ernestine von Fricken. Clara had an "inexplicable—I don't want to say crazy—idea that she will fundamentally change this man." [10]

Wieck had obtained some of this damaging information about Schumann through personal observation, of course, but not enough to make a good case in court. During Clara's recent absence from Leipzig, he had broken into her locked letter-box. Thus Wieck had read her private correspondence, copied it, and, in the hope of preventing their marriage, was even sending out libelous information about her relationship with Schumann to various concert managers, musicians, and music critics throughout Germany. (Dr. Reuter had warned Clara on several occasions to be extremely cautious and "secretive" lest any of Schumann's self-revelations fall into the wrong hands. [11])

Clara's behavior in the courtroom was strikingly ambivalent. Despite her father's theft of her private letters, she manifested the "deepest sympathy" for him as he presented his accusations against Schumann. This sympathy is evident in her diary:

> He [Wieck] was so emotionally overwrought that the presiding judge had to make him stop talking, which cut through my soul each time. I could barely stand it, that this humiliation had to happen to him. He looked at me with terrible anger, but only once did he say anything against me. How much I would have liked to plead with him . . . but I was afraid he might push me away, and I sat as if nailed to my chair. [12]

The judge apparently was moved by Clara's sympathy for her father, for he ruled that permission for her to marry would be denied if there was any proof of Schumann's financial irresponsibility and alcoholism. Wieck, given until 4 January 1840 to gather the necessary evidence, finally hired an attorney. Schumann meanwhile escalated his defense. He submitted documents from the Leipzig police and town council describing him as a quiet and decent citizen, not under any suspicion for political misdeeds. When the court reconvened, all charges against Schumann were dismissed except that of alcoholism.

Wieck again waited until the last moment (28 January 1840) to hand in another long disputation, arguing that the grounds for considering Schumann unfit for marriage should be widened to include his financial status.

He also circulated printed copies of his legal testimony in every city Clara was preparing to visit for concerts that year.

After that, Schumann nearly gave up the fight. "Can nothing be done to save us from such nastiness?" he asked Clara. "I'm certainly not going to stop you if you want to go back to your father." [13]

But the legal process, once set into motion, was difficult to stop. Witnesses were already lining up—Mendelssohn, Ferdinand David, and other friends of Schumann on his side; Carl Banck and Louis Rakemann, both old beaus of Clara, on Wieck's. Soon Schumann was hard at work on his rebuttal, which he presented to the court on 14 February. He valiantly tried to persuade the court that he would have no difficulty earning the minimum amount of money Wieck was demanding for Clara, 1500 thalers, 500 of which would come from interest on his invested securities—he listed assets of 12,688 thalers—and the rest from sales of his newspaper, musical compositions, and so on. These figures were inflated, however. He was counting on 4000 thalers that Clara had saved, and he was exaggerating when he claimed he would earn 1000 thalers per year from his publications. [14]

What he did *not* include in the rebuttal was evidence of his financial generosity toward Clara and her mother. To help pay for a trip to Berlin in September 1839, during which he visited them, Schumann had to sell some of his state bonds. For Christmas that year he gave both Clara and her mother expensive dresses, and to Clara's brother Alwin he had just given 5 thalers. [15] Perhaps Schumann feared that this information might be used against him to show that he was financially irresponsible.

As for Wieck's accusation of alcoholism (*Trunksucht*), Schumann told the court that he reserved the right to press a claim for defamation of character against his opponent.* But in a statement that seems self-defeating, he claimed that Wieck had actually been one of his drinking companions. He also quoted a letter from Wieck written when they were still friends, which praised Schumann's character and invited him to be godfather of Wieck's daughter Cecilie. (Several weeks later Schumann also submitted a letter from Baron von Fricken, which reads, "Is old Wieck still so stiff-necked? What could have caused him to become so angry with you? Before 1834 he was so excited about you and, so to speak, brought up his daughter for you." [17])

Seemingly as a last resort, Schumann submitted to the court a diploma, an honorary doctor's degree, which he had received at the end of February 1840 from Jena University. Schumann had been trying to obtain such a degree ever since Clara had received her imperial title in Vienna. First he asked his sister-in-law Therese to intercede for him at the university in

---

*A year later he did make such a claim, successfully, and Wieck was sentenced to eighteen days in prison. [16] There is no proof he ever served the sentence.

Leipzig, saying, "I'm aiming for nothing but the title."[18] He finally succeeded at the smaller university in Jena.* From then on, whenever he and Clara traveled together, he could register as "Dr." Schumann, while she called herself an "Imperial" concert pianist.

Several months were yet to elapse before the court made its decision, months of terrible uncertainty for Schumann. His feelings ranged from optimistic expectation that he would win his suit to utter despair in the belief that he had lost Clara forever. It was also a time when his creative energies organized themselves around a new goal, the writing of songs.

What has aptly been called Schumann's "song year" began in the spring of 1840, while he was awaiting the outcome of his lawsuit against Wieck. It was an astonishing change for someone who for ten years had restricted his musical output to the piano. But his master plan was to compose in much larger formats. Combining the piano with the human voice seems to have been an essential maturation for this future composer of symphonies, chamber music, choral works, and an opera.

Schumann's songwriting also attests his capability for a high level of conceptual integration. Here the literary skills acquired from his father could flow comfortably with the sensitivity for vocal sound nurtured by his mother. In 1839, as the legal process (itself an exercise in verbal skill) got under way, Schumann and Clara started to collect poems by their favorite authors, with the plan that they would add to the collection during the years they hoped to spend together.[20] It was a signal for him to begin composing vocal music again, something he had tried a decade earlier but then had abandoned.

Surely there was a biological determinant to Schumann's upsurge of creative energy as he approached the age of thirty.† Even his erotic behavior up to that point had been somewhat immature; it consisted mainly of daydreaming, punctuated by an occasional affair with a woman or an unsatisfying romance with a man. Now the pattern was changing. Schumann was

---

* It cost him an undisclosed sum of money, paid to the university, and necessitated further cashing of securities.[19]

† It turned out to be his mid-life period. A graphic chart of Schumann's musical output was made by the late Eliot Slater, an eminent British psychiatrist. This graph shows prominent peaks at age twenty-two, when Schumann's right hand was giving way, at age thirty, his song year, and at age thirty-nine, before he moved to Düsseldorf. Implicit in this cyclic ebb and flow of creativity is the notion of a constitutional, biologically determined rhythmicity, probably also related to the composer's recurring disturbance of mood.[21]

Schumann at age twenty-nine, in Vienna. (Lithograph by Josef Kriehuber.)

attempting to interweave his aspirations and personal values with Clara's. He envisioned a life of sexual fulfillment, family happiness, and artistic success. A great outburst of vocal music ensued. Clara seems to have recognized the sexual implications of his songwriting on some level and perhaps even suspected a competitor. "About the songs," she wrote, jokingly, "isn't there perhaps a young nightingale inflaming you?"[22] To which Schumann unabashedly replied, "I was completely inside you while composing them. You, romantic girl, follow me everywhere with your eyes, and I often think that without such a bride one cannot make such music."[23]

In addition to the libidinal pressures, there were strong social determinants to the change in Schumann's creativity: the popular appeal and commercial possibilities of singable music. Songs can be published and sold much more easily than sonatas or symphonies. With his head in the clouds, Schumann had always "ranked song compositions lower than instrumental music and never considered them a great art."[24] But now, with Wieck accusing him of financial ineptitude and his own money calculations pointing to an uncertain future, he had to modify this prejudice.

The influence of Felix Mendelssohn, who always tried to help Schumann and Clara in every way possible, was also a factor. In January 1840 Schumann had begun working on a small piano sonata but soon gave up. Mendelssohn advised that he try to write some music for the voice. Schumann's first successful effort, "The Farewell Song of a Fool" (op. 127, no. 5) is dated 1 February 1840. (The fool is Feste from Shakespeare's *Twelfth Night*, singing "our play is done." One of Mendelssohn's greatest successes, by the way, had been to write incidental music for Shakespeare's *Midsummer Night's Dream*.)

Much can be said about Schumann's *lieder*, which express so perfectly both his romantic genius and his emotional disturbance. Many are poignantly autobiographical. The early songs in particular sound restrained and melancholy, with a predominant theme of lonely isolation. "In song after song the central figure is a rejected suitor," says Eric Sams, who has studied them in detail.[25] Indeed, Schumann often seems to reminisce about some unhappy event of the past, or to apprehend some dreaded future experience. Often his *lieder* have the character of "half-told tales."[26] They reveal as much as they obscure.

During the song year, Schumann was able to free himself from the virtuoso keyboard style of composition, which had been a preoccupation as the result of his handicapped hand. He literally gained physical freedom, as he expressed in a letter to Clara:

> I can't tell you how easy it's become for me [to write songs] and how happy this makes me. I do it mostly while standing or walking around, not at the piano. This is an entirely different sort of music, which doesn't first have to be borne through the fingers—much more immediate and melodic.[27]

While pacing, he would allow the rhythm of the text to inspire a melody, or if that did not happen, he would adapt the poetry to tunes already imagined. Reticence probably kept Schumann from setting his own words to music (or perhaps ambition made him tie his musical kite to the tails of other, more famous men).

At the beginning he preferred to use the words of Heinrich Heine, that most enigmatic and ironic of German poets. The first Heine *Song-Cycle* (*Liederkreis*) (op. 24) deals obliquely with the problem of sexual frustration and Schumann's separation from Clara.

> On arising in the morning I ask whether my sweetheart will come today. Evenings I lament that she again has stayed away, and during the night I lie in anguish half-asleep and dreaming.

Schumann, using Heine's words, sings of tormenting nightmares:

> Madness churns in my soul and my heart is sick and sore.
>
> Blood pours from my eyes, runs from my body, hot blood that records my suffering.

A Heine song called "Poor Peter" (op. 53, no. 3) in an uncanny way foreshadows Schumann's suicidal promenade in Düsseldorf.

Poor Peter totters by, so slowly, pale as a corpse, and shy. People see him in the street but barely stop. "He must have stepped out of the grave," whisper the girls. But no, dear maidens, he is going to descend into the grave. He has lost his treasure. That's why the grave is the best place for him to lie down and sleep for the rest of his days.

Myrtles (op. 25) is a collection of twenty-six *lieder*—one for each letter of the alphabet—with many personal meanings. Schumann intended these songs—based on poems by Heine, Goethe, Robert Burns, and others—as a wedding present for Clara. Song no. 3, "The Nut Tree," based on a poem by Mosen, is in C (for Clara). It "whispers about a maiden who thought the nights and days were too long, and about a bridegroom, and next year." The fifth, inspired by Goethe (in E, for Eusebius), is about a man

sitting alone, how could I do better? My wine I drink by myself. No one sets limits for me. That way I can have my own thoughts.

(Schumann's drinking was then being debated in court.) Many of the *Myrtle* songs are about marriage-related topics—flowers, wives, mothers, widows, and the like. Based on a poem by Burns, song no. 22 declares:

I'll share my wife with nobody. I'll take cuckold from nobody and give cuckold to nobody.

Clara expressed her amazement at the songs: "This I did not expect! My reverence for him grows along with my love. No one alive today is as musically gifted as Robert."[28] When they enjoyed a few happy days together with Clara's mother in Berlin, Mendelssohn was also there and sang Schumann's new songs. Clara accompanied at the piano. But the lovers were soon separated again, while Wieck prepared his arguments.

This lengthy separation led to Schumann's supreme achievement as a songwriter, his *Eichendorff Song-Cycle* and *Dichterliebe*. These masterful compositions also seem to indicate that he worked best in solitude, away from the trials and tribulations of everyday life. Thus they are important clues to the dilemma he would shortly face as a married man with a growing family.

The *Liederkreis* (*Song-Cycle*) (op. 39), based entirely on poems by Joseph von Eichendorff, allowed Schumann to experience the bottom of his depression. Words and music combine in excruciating anguish:

Father and mother are long dead. No one in my homeland knows me any more. Soon the time will come when I shall also be at rest.

An "image of the beloved" resides in the singer's heart. But he is lost in the woods and terrified by "the witch Loreley!" In the fantastic moonlight he watches "the sky kissing the earth" (one of the rarely erotic moments in

Schumann's songs). High up, in a castle overlooking the Rhine, sits an old knight who has turned to stone and is oblivious to a wedding procession passing by. "The beautiful bride is crying," and the singer, close to paranoia, feigns happiness while his "heart is breaking." There is terrible danger. "Beware—don't trust your friend." In an oddly cheerful ending, he discovers that a "miracle" has happened—"She is yours, she is yours."*

According to musicologist Rufus Hallmark, Schumann sought in *Dichterliebe* (op. 48) to create a certain picture of the poet and his beloved. Therefore he intentionally chose *not* to set those of Heine's poems that might portray the girl "as a fickle, shallow person, with a beautiful body but little soul." [29] If that is so, it would lend credence to the impression that Schumann had a compulsive tendency to disguise hostility toward women in general and Clara in particular.

One of the *Dichterliebe* songs, "I Cried in My Dream," seems like a perfect replica of Schumann's early memory or fantasy of abandonment (as reported in his adolescent autobiography; see Chapter II). We can only surmise that he unconsciously equated the possible loss of Clara with the loss of his mother, when she turned him over to Frau Ruppius:

> I cried in my dream; I dreamed you were lying in your grave. I dreamed you had abandoned me. I dreamed you were still good to me. I woke up and the tears were streaming from my eyes.

Aided by Heine's poetry, he captured a tragic mood of resignation in death. The symbolism is of submersion:

> The old angry songs, the bad dreams, let us bury them in a huge coffin, bigger than the Heidelberg beer keg and longer than the bridge in Mainz. Twelve giants must sink this coffin in the sea. Do you know why the coffin is so big and heavy? It contains my love and my pain.

At the end of *Dichterliebe* the pianist plays alone; all singing has stopped. This has an uncanny effect, almost as if the composer were telling of his love for the piano, which has so much enriched his life. The listener also senses his nostalgia for an isolated existence, and perhaps the anticipation that

---

*The old knight is obviously Wieck, the crying bride Clara, and the broken-hearted singer Schumann himself. The Eichendorff *Liederkreis* was not published until 1850, and during this interval Schumann changed the order of the songs. The original ending of the cycle was tragic, with the stony old knight (*Barbarossa*) as victor. As it is now performed, with the oddly happy ending, the listener senses the inappropriateness. That was probably not what Schumann originally intended. He saw the possibility of a negative outcome of his court case quite clearly in 1840, but in 1850, after ten years of often-troubled marriage, he may have wanted to deny that. Hence his desire for the happy ending.

sometime in the future his love for Clara would have to end, and that she (or he) might have to continue without the other.

Schumann's songwriting was interrupted by Franz Liszt's visit to Germany. The Hungarian pianist had been trying to dissolve his turbulent liaison with the Countess d'Agoult, mother of his three children, and was traveling widely to keep out of her reach. When in March 1840 Liszt played in Dresden, Schumann rushed there by train.

Liszt was a great showman. Wild enthusiasm sprang up wherever he made an appearance. But along with a flair for the dramatic, he had a warm and sensitive interest in other musicians, especially composers whose work he respected and tried to popularize. He admired Schumann's music and even before meeting him in 1840 sent letters praising it. For example, he wrote that "two or three times a week . . . I play your *Kinderszenen* to [my daughter] in the evening; this enchants her, and me still more as you can imagine."[30]

The impression Liszt made on Schumann was predictably favorable. In the *New Journal for Music*, he reported that "No artist, with the exception of Paganini, has Liszt's power to enslave an audience. . . . Pale, lean, impressive in profile, Liszt resembles Napoleon as a young general."[31]

What's more, Schumann was enchanted by the resemblance he perceived between Liszt and Ludwig Schunke. "It extends even to their artistry; when Liszt plays I believe that I'm listening to something [by Schunke] I have heard before."[32] Soon he and Liszt were on very good terms and spending entire days together. "It seems we have already known each other for twenty years," Schumann wrote Clara.[33]

Judging from his correspondence, he went to great lengths to make Liszt comfortable during his stay in Leipzig. But his engrossment with Liszt disturbed Clara. "I was jealous of him!" she wrote after waiting anxiously for news from Leipzig.[34] This rivalry was both personal and professional. Liszt was at the peak of success in 1840, with multitudes clamoring to get to his concerts, while Clara, then touring North Germany, found the audiences there strangely unresponsive. Prominent musicians were equally cool. Wieck's vicious propaganda against Schumann may have been part of Clara's problem, but even more serious was that her father had started to promote the career of another young woman, the French pianist Marie Pleyel.

Clara felt isolated from the excitement in Leipzig, where Schumann and Liszt were sharing their latest compositions. (She too wanted to compose but feared that she had no talent for it.[35]) To Schumann, she wrote,

Oh, unhappy me! Here I sit and don't enjoy a bit of the many things all of you do together. . . . I've long intended to come to Leipzig with mother, but then I thought I would disturb you in your cohabitation [*Zusammenleben*] with Liszt.[36]

Clara was hurt that Mendelssohn had not invited her, along with Liszt, to perform Bach's D minor Concerto for three pianos with him and the Gewandhaus Orchestra (Ferdinand Hiller played instead). But after joining the men in Leipzig, she complained in her diary. "I can't be around [Liszt] very long; this restlessness, this instability, so much animation, it's all very exhausting."[37]

From the beginning, out of deference for Clara, Schumann exercised caution in regard to Liszt and tempered his enthusiasm:

But my dear little Clara [he wrote] Liszt's world is no longer my world. Art, the way you practice it and the way I often do it while composing at the piano, such beautiful comfort [*Gemüthlichkeit*] I wouldn't exchange for all of his glamour—and there's also something of the showoff in him, too much.[38]

Liszt often performed music at sight, without preparation—spontaneity, or the appearance of it, was essential to him—and after a fragment or two from someone else's composition he would rush into his own dazzling variations. After hearing him play the *Carnaval* Schumann wrote that he was "deeply moved—it's so different from what I had imagined." But he was also disappointed. For one thing, he disagreed with Liszt's keyboard style, which differed drastically from Clara's, and seemed to distract from the music. Also, as he wrote, Liszt "failed to take into consideration that the musical moods change too quickly for an entire audience to follow."*[39]

After Liszt's departure in April, life settled into its customary routine. Unencumbered now by feelings of rivalry, Clara was able to enjoy a coziness she cherished. Schumann's quiet passivity seems to have calmed her: "He doesn't have to say anything—I like him so well when he just meditates, and I want to eavesdrop on every one of his thoughts."[41]

Clara also appreciated his financial assistance. When they were separated again in May, she quickly ran short of money. In conflict about whether to give concerts in Russia (at the invitation of the violinist Alexis Lvoff), or to ask Schumann for help, she decided for sentimental reasons to return to

---

*It is interesting to compare this with a remark Liszt made in a letter written to Wasielewski a year after Schumann's death: "The public had no taste [for Schumann's piano pieces] and most pianists didn't understand them. Even in Leipzig, where I performed the Carnaval in my second concert, it was not possible to evoke the applause that I usually receive."[40]

Leipzig. Several years in a row Clara had not been able to join him for his birthday, but this year they would be together.

A month later they really had something to celebrate: Wieck was beginning to capitulate. After more than a year of legal maneuvering, he now claimed that it was impossible to get any witnesses to testify against Schumann. Two of them had simply "disappeared." (This was a half-truth. One potential witness, Louis Rakemann, had emigrated to the United States in 1839. Carl Banck, however, was no farther away than Dresden.) Wieck flatly—but weakly—asserted that since all his witnesses were musicians, none would speak out against a music critic. Bitterly he told the court that Clara was no longer worth the sacrifice he would have to make to protect her from what was certain to be an unhappy marriage. Yet he was an obstructionist to the end, refusing to endorse her union with Schumann, and demanding that the court make the final decision. "May [Clara] never regret having persistently rejected the earnest admonitions of her genuinely concerned father," Wieck said grudgingly.[42]

Schumann had started composing songs again even before the verdict was in. A cycle called *Woman's Love and Life* (*Frauenliebe und Leben*, op. 42) presents a woman extolling the virtues of her lover. The poems are by Adelbert von Chamisso (creator of Peter Schlemihl, a foolish adolescent who sells his shadow). "Seeing him makes me think I'm blind," goes the opening *lied*, followed by the woman's tribute to "him, the most magnificent of all, so mild, so good, such loving lips, bright eyes, clear mind, and firm courage." This is one of Schumann's most ecstatic outbursts. His next song seems doubtful. The woman cannot believe it: "I must be daydreaming. Oh let me die in my dream, securely cradled on his chest." Reassured by a ring, she comes to realize that there will soon be a baby who "must be nourished; only a mother knows what it means to love and be happy. Oh, how I pity a man who cannot feel maternal happiness." This cycle too ends on a tragic note:

> The harsh, cruel man sleeps the sleep of death. The abandoned woman sees that her world is empty. I've loved and lived; now I live no longer.

Schumann was becoming uncomfortably aware that if the court decided in his favor, he would be faced with pressing family obligations, a conflict that he beautifully expressed in his *Songs to Words by Hans Christian Andersen* (op. 40). "Violets in March" is about a shy youth falling in love—"may God have mercy on the young man." In "A Mother's Dream," her "delight in looking upon the sleeping child" is beclouded by dissonances between the voice and the piano. "The Soldier" is about a condemned man marching to his execution. "Musician" depicts the "horrible death" of a man who goes to pieces while playing his violin at the wedding of his sweetheart to someone else.

Schumann's vocal writing—his choral and operatic music especially—is often faulted for being insufficiently dramatic. He surely wanted to sound dramatic, and a violent, macabre quality does come across in some of the songs. But a pious sentimentality often crept in, especially as the composer grew older, and this is not to everyone's liking. Perhaps he could have benefited, as Wagner surely did, from closer collaboration with Liszt, who had a flair for the dramatic and wanted to be Schumann's friend. But loyalty to Clara, who grew to dislike Liszt more and more, stood in their way. Also Schumann never acquired any experience working in the theater, as Liszt and Wagner did, so that he remained a stranger to the technical aspects of musical drama all his life.

Not that Schumann's life was undramatic. When Wieck finally admitted defeat in court, Schumann exclaimed "Juchhe! Victoria!" and promptly announced his victory in the newspaper.[43] But once the matter was settled, he felt irrevocably committed to a life of monogamy (again unlike Liszt and Wagner, who had a succession of mistresses). Florestan the agitator would have to make more room for Eusebius the pacifier. Their inner struggle continued, however, leading to some of Schumann's greatest music as well as to his continuing despair.

XI.
Harmony and Discord, 1840–1844

Even before the legalities were completely resolved—a final verdict had yet to be received from the higher court in Dresden—Schumann began looking for an apartment. He found one to Clara's liking at Inselstrasse 5, close to the center of town. Then, in a defiant gesture, he set the nuptial date for 12 September 1840, one day before Clara would turn twenty-one.

As an expression of independence, Clara gave concerts until the week before the wedding. But she also wished to reduce her financial indebtedness to Schumann,* and fretted that she was getting married without even having "a dowry like any simple middle-class girl."[2] During the ceremony in the village church of Schönefeld, near Leipzig, she prayed "that God may keep Robert in good condition for many, many years." As she reported in her diary, "The thought that one day I might lose him causes my mind to

---

*The preceding Christmas, Schumann had given Clara, in addition to presents, a 100-thaler bond for her mother, who was in financial straits. He also paid 400 thalers to buy Clara a piano, since Wieck refused to release the one she had played on as a child.[1]

be completely confused—may heaven protect me from such misfortune, I couldn't take it."[3]

It seems unlikely that Clara was a virgin when she got married. In spite of Wieck's tyrannical control, she and Robert had occasionally managed to find ways of being alone, and eight days before the wedding they probably slept together in Weimar.* Sexual intercourse between them was frequent and probably satisfying. Clara became pregnant ten times in the next thirteen years, and they had eight children, born in 1841, 1843, 1845, 1846, 1848, 1849, 1851, and 1854. Such a large family, while impressive, was not exceptional in the nineteenth century. According to population experts, men in those days reached their procreative peak between thirty-one and thirty-three (today they reach it six to seven years earlier).[5] Whether the Schumanns used contraceptives is not known, but seems unlikely.† (In those days the preferred method of birth control, short of abstinence, was *coitus interruptus*.)

We know from Schumann's daily chronicles that he was very much interested in sexual activity, which he recorded in considerable detail. We might speculate that he had some anxiety about his sexual performance, going back perhaps to his earlier problems with Christel and other sexual partners. He also had bouts of anxiety whenever Clara became pregnant. While at the beginning her fecundity seemed to have inspired him to compose, having so many children became an increasingly severe economic burden. Thus Schumann's careful recording of sexual intercourse may also have been motivated by his desire to find a way of keeping Clara from being pregnant so often.

For example, after they had their fourth child and first son, Schumann noted "Clara's new fear." When that turned out to be a false alarm, he recorded "Clara's happy discovery."[6] Thereafter, he kept track of each sexual act by placing an "F" (it resembles a sixteenth note) next to the date in his household diary. The frequency varied from every second to fifth day, except when Clara was unavailable or indisposed. "F" disappeared each time she had a baby, then reappeared a month later, with the comment "slept with Clara for the first time." At times of severe depression, Schumann reported some reduction of coital frequency. But he never became completely abstinent.

At the beginning of his marriage Schumann attempted to share as much

---

*Clara was giving concerts there. Robert showed up in her hotel room unannounced, and they returned to Leipzig together three days later. "I can't describe my joy," says Clara's diary.[4]
†Condoms and pessaries were available at the time, but they were unreliable and quite expensive. Cervical caps had just been invented by a German gynecologist, but they had to be custom-made and were very difficult to obtain.

A page from Schumann's household book, February 1850, showing daily entries and the "F" marks indicating sexual relations.

of himself with Clara as possible. He asked her to participate in writing a diary to "record everything of mutual concern to our household and marriage."[7] He urged her to read novels (by Jean Paul) and plays (by Shakespeare) with him. He prevailed on her to join him in studying scores by Bach, Beethoven, Haydn, and Mozart. He even insisted that she compose, and they produced a set of songs together—*The Springtime of Love* (op. 37)—based on poems by Friedrich Rückert. All of this was in keeping with the concept, daringly new in the romantic era, that men and women should be encouraged to relate to each other as equals. It was advocated, especially among artists, that the man be allowed to develop his feminine qualities, and the woman her masculine ones.[8]

For the Schumanns this came about quite naturally. Twelve premarital years of exchanging ideas and music flowed smoothly into thirteen years of physical proximity in marriage. Theirs was a collaboration of the highest order. Encouraged by his wife, Schumann wrote symphonies, chamber music, and other weighty works, thereby establishing himself as a major European composer. Coached by her husband, Clara became familiar with the great masters, performed more serious programs, and remained the foremost woman pianist of her time.

But there was a difference in temperament between these two musicians, which love and sex could not overcome. Schumann yearned for the privacy and solitude necessary for his creative work, while Clara desired the public exposure, travel, and applause of the performers' life. Arguments about this had occurred before the wedding, and they continued. Three weeks after the ceremony Schumann wrote into the marriage diary (where Clara was sure to read it), "I think with horror about the trip to Russia." He did not want, as he said, "to get out of our little warm nest, now that we've barely put everything together."⁹ A week later Clara complained, "If I could only move Robert to go with me to Holland and Belgium." She felt it her duty to earn money long before there were any serious financial problems. Schumann's income was actually on the rise at this time. (November 1840 marked his first commercial success, when he sold 1500 copies of a patriotic composition for chorus and orchestra, *Song of the Rhine*.)

Thus Clara was overruled for the moment. With obvious relief, Schumann wrote in the marriage diary that the trip to St. Petersburg had been cancelled. Before they took any trips, he wanted to write a piano concerto and a symphony.¹⁰ Exactly one month after his wedding day, he made his first "symphonic attempts," which he continued for a few days and then abandoned amid a flurry of social activities, including a "big soirée" in their apartment, at which Clara played trios by Moscheles and Mendelssohn.¹¹

Schumann's dedication to his art was not always a pleasure for her. He was often moody and inaccessible while working, and Clara would tune into his depressiveness. "I'm wholly dependent on his moods; perhaps that's not good, but I can't help it," she wrote two weeks into the marriage, and four weeks later, "It saddens me greatly that Robert thinks he cannot create anything right now, and that this depresses him." Soon she herself was depressed and complaining (in the marriage diary, where he would see it): "I'm constantly exhausted. . . . It is terrible for a man always to be around a lamenting wife."¹²

In December 1840 Clara discovered she was pregnant, and Schumann commented that he was "look[ing] forward to the first little song and lullaby."¹³ Clara's fertility seems to have activated his musicality in an extraordinary way.* Almost as if to be the first to give birth, he produced, in four days and sleepless nights (23–26 January 1841) the sketches for his first successful symphony, the Symphony in B-flat major (*Spring*), op. 38. By 20 February, the entire score had been orchestrated, an ordeal the composer described as follows: "After many sleepless nights comes prostration [*Er-*

---

*The reader will remember that Schumann's early affair with Christel had inspired reproductive fantasies and spurred him to create not only *Child Prodigies* but also Florestan and Eusebius.

schlaffung]. I feel like a young woman who has just given birth—so relieved and happy, but also sick and sore." [14]

While Schumann expressed profound gratitude for "all the love and the willing heart" his wife had shown him during his own "delivery," she, with her baby yet unborn, complained, "Robert has been very cold to me lately, although the reason is very cheering, and no one can participate more sincerely than I with everything that he undertakes, sometimes I am made sick by this coldness. Of all people I deserve it the least." [15]

What she had observed but did not understand was that after the manic-like excitement of his first symphony, Schumann had become pathologically depressed. His personal diary, the household book, shows consecutive days of feeling "unwell." On 19 February he reported "damned much drinking, Stupid Donkey," then a terrible hangover and "unending sickly inner tension," followed by nearly a week of "always melancholy. Desire for debauchery [*Liederlichkeit*]." [16] It was a pattern that would repeat itself over and over again during the Schumanns' marriage.

A further complication—it demoralizes many musicians who live together—was "the misery of thin walls." Their ground-floor apartment was comfortable and spacious, but insufficiently sound-insulated. "Every time Robert composes," wrote Clara, "my piano playing must be set aside completely. Not a single tiny hour can be found for me all day! If only I don't regress too much!" [17] These anxieties were exacerbated shortly after she became pregnant by the arrival of Clara's piano; Wieck had been compelled by a court order to return it to her. Upon seeing the instrument she was overjoyed, but she felt "an even greater woe. . . . The whole unfortunate past rose up in me so vividly that I could not suppress a certain feeling for my father." [18]

Clara's ambivalence lingered. Wieck was still on trial for having slandered Schumann, and Clara, who sympathized with him, feared that her loyalty to her father would upset her husband. It surely did. But Schumann as usual tried to suppress his anger, sometimes unsuccessfully. For example, in the early days of their marriage, he allowed "a stupid word about Clara to slip out." The outburst "pained him all day [until] in the evening he confessed it to Clara." [19]

Schumann's daughter Eugenie, who wrote a sensitive account of her parents' marriage, believed that his "tragic end could have been avoided completely had he been spared the gruesome experience of his interminable struggle with Wieck." [20] While this view overlooks the destabilizing effect of Schumann's mental disorder, it also has a ring of truth. Wieck always stood in the background, and sometimes in the foreground, of Clara's relationship with Schumann. Midway through her first pregnancy, for example, Wieck came to their apartment and denigrated his new *Spring* Symphony by calling it an "Opposition Symphony."*²¹ Schumann's riposte was to call his next symphony the *Clara* Symphony.

Schumann now was coupling his remarkable inventiveness more and more to the composition of forms that did not require a piano. It was almost as if Clara's physical presence, and her devotion to the piano, freed him to compose for other instruments. But he still lacked experience with larger forms and had much to learn about orchestration. For example, while orchestrating the hurriedly written *Spring* Symphony with which he was hoping to make his debut at the Leipzig Gewandhaus, Schumann began learning how to play the violin.²² His knowledge of wind instruments was still so rudimentary that at the first rehearsal the introductory horn fanfare had to be transposed: he had written it in an unplayable range. But with Mendelssohn's help these errors were quickly corrected. (Mendelssohn even offered to let the composer direct the rehearsal, an invitation he wisely declined. Conducting was not, as we shall see, one of Schumann's talents.)

The symphony was an instant success on 31 March 1841, and it continues to be a favorite with concert audiences to this day. The opening moves along with springlike jubilation. The slow movement is lyrical and transparently textured. The energetic Scherzo is followed by a rolicking Finale. The symphony also shows signs of Schumann's limitations as a composer. Full of original ideas, he tended to string themes together without the complex interweaving of, say, a mature symphony by Mozart or Beethoven. Moreover, he often repeated whole sections verbatim with little development, a tendency he never overcame completely.²³

Clara was then nearly four months pregnant. She appeared on the same program, playing two movements from Chopin's F minor Piano Concerto, a duet with Mendelssohn, and short pieces by Scarlatti, Thalberg, and Schumann. "A concert by the Schumann couple," reported the composer in their marriage diary. "The whole world was enchanted, and also in my life this day is one of the most important. My wife realized it too and was almost more pleased by the success of the symphony than she was about herself."²⁴ In his more private household book, however, he reported feeling "very exhausted" the next day. Schumann also mentioned "a little marital torment [*kleine Ehequälerei*]."²⁵

---

*Eager for approval, Schumann thereupon dedicated the *Spring* Symphony to King Friedrich August II of Saxony. The monarch graciously accepted this honor and in return sent the composer a golden snuffbox.

He pulled himself out of the doldrums quickly, though, and continued to compose orchestral music that year, usually at breakneck speed. An *Overture, Scherzo, and Finale* (op. 52), originally called "Sinfonietta," was finished in April 1841. It is a substantial work, all too seldom performed. Then he thought about writing a "Sinfonia Solemnis" to commemorate the unveiling of a statue honoring Jean Paul,[26] but abandoned the plan. In June Schumann composed his *Clara* Symphony,* which was meant to symbolize happiness in their first year of marriage. "I will portray you with flutes, oboes, and harps," he told Clara.[27] She was delighted but also a little alarmed to observe the "incessant composing," which left her husband no time to devote to her. Nevertheless, their marriage, she mused philosophically, had not turned out badly—"so often they say it deadens the soul, that it could take away his youthful freshness! My Robert surely provides clear proof to the contrary."[28]

In May Schumann conceived what was to become one of his best-loved compositions, the A minor Piano Concerto (op. 54), another work obviously intended for Clara. He thought originally of the first movement as a single, long "Fantasy"; the second and third movements were added four years later. Here the composer was at the height of his creative power, writing superbly for both piano and orchestra. The work begins with a single chord. Fistfuls of dotted rhythms by the pianist then cascade toward the sublime first theme, introduced by an oboe. It is reminiscent of Clara's descending scale, heard in so much of Schumann's earlier piano music. The second theme too is an elaboration of this motif, now played by a clarinet with piano accompaniment.

Although the solo part is very difficult and Clara was advanced in her pregnancy, she wanted to hear what the Fantasy sounded like and insisted on trying it during a dress rehearsal of the Gewandhaus Orchestra on 13 August, barely two weeks before she went into labor. Clara had difficulty hearing herself and the orchestra in the empty hall, but she played the Fantasy twice and found it "marvelous!"[29]

As the day of delivery approached, Schumann felt quite keyed up, and he tried to relieve his anxiety by stocking his cellar with a huge amount of wine and champagne.[30] On 1 September Clara had her first, painful, childbirth. "So much stood in danger," wrote Schumann, that

> I did not know how to control myself. But then I relied on Clara's strong nature, on her love for me. . . . At ten minutes to eleven the little one [a girl] arrived—with thunder and lightning, since we had a storm just then. But her

---

* Ten years later he reorchestrated this work and published it as his Symphony No. 4, in D minor (op. 120).

first sounds—and life again stood before us, brightly and lovingly—we were blissful with joy. How proud I am to have such a wife, who in addition to her love and her art gives me such a present.[31]

They named the child Marie. Schumann immediately notified Wieck, who responded with a "ridiculous letter," another rebuff.[32] But Clara's mother came by train from Berlin so she could attend the christening. Clara thought the girl looked "exactly" like Schumann, who wrote dotingly that "whenever the baby gets restless, Clara plays for her, which soothes the child and immediately puts her to sleep."[33]

Clara did not feel altogether comfortable in her new maternal role, however, and she experienced, as with each subsequent infant, a reluctance to breast-feed. "The first child especially produces worries," she wrote. "Rightly such a child is called an anxiety-child [Angstkind]." The baby was not even a month old, yet Clara thought, "It's high time to find another wet-nurse, before it half starves to death."[34] Before Marie had reached three months of age, Clara was already giving concerts.

Small wonder that with all this commotion, Schumann's symphonic writing came temporarily to a halt. On 23 September he began a new symphony, in C minor, but he never finished it. A piece for chorus and orchestra, set to Heine's "Tragedy," suffered a similar fate in October. That month Schumann noted that he "slept with Clara again for the first time." The household book also reports "a violent fit of temper" against her, after which Schumann called himself a dunce. There were many distractions, and he complained bitterly about all the work he had to do on the *New Journal*.[35]

In December 1841 Liszt came back to Leipzig, and now it was Clara's turn to be unhappy. They shared the spotlight in a concert during which Schumann's *Overture, Scherzo, and Finale* and the new D minor Symphony were also played for the first time. (The reception was lukewarm for these original compositions.) "Pandemonium and fanaticism" greeted Liszt and Clara when they played duets,[36] but she found fault with just about everything—"Robert wasn't happy with my playing, also I was angry because Robert's symphonies weren't performed especially well, and there were many little fatalities, with the carriage, the forgotten notes, the shaky chair while playing, Liszt's fidgetiness, etc., etc."[37]

Sparks were beginning to fly. After arranging a party in Liszt's honor for which he arrived late, as was his custom, Clara called him a "spoiled child" and condemned his music as "abominable—a chaos of the shrillest dissonance."[38] Schumann, though, was sorry to see Liszt go.*

---

*Clara turned down an invitation to tour Russia in 1842 because Liszt was planning to be there at the same time. "With this man one must not compete," she wrote. "He will bewitch with his personality anyone he doesn't charm with his art."[39]

In January 1842 Schumann went into another depression. "I'm very bad with Clara. . . . Much drinking. . . . Always sick and melancholy. . . . Still sick [14 February]." These symptoms were clearly associated with Clara's anxious preparations for a lengthy concert tour to northern Germany. Schumann had reluctantly agreed to go with her, but he really wanted to stay home and compose string quartets, an idea that had occurred to him while his depression was subsiding in February. After returning, alone, from the trip in March—this was their first prolonged separation since getting married—he worked on counterpoint exercises and wrote fugues, something he often did while depressed. It was a form of self-therapy, and it absorbed time during a period when he thought life "miserable."[40]

String quartets had long been on Schumann's mind, and several unfinished efforts lay on his desk, some dating back to his premarital turmoil, when Clara had chided him for this ambition. Writing abstract music for only four instrumental voices is a considerable challenge. Schumann had prepared himself by studying the quartets of other composers, most recently those by Mozart, Beethoven, and Haydn.[41] But in his depressed mood, and because of "drinking too much" in April, he could do no composing.[42] Fugue exercises (with Clara, at the end of May) again seemed to help settle his mind, and just before his thirty-second birthday, in June, the ideas suddenly began to flow. He composed almost daily for the next two weeks, and finished the third quartet on 22 June. To Clara he announced, proudly, "three children, barely born, and already completed and beautiful."[43]

It was a stunning achievement. Schumann had composed *Three String Quartets* (op. 41) in a whirlwind of enthusiasm, sometimes beginning a new movement of one quartet before he had even finished the preceding quartet. Nevertheless, each quartet has the stamp of individuality.

The first, in A minor, opens with an expressive introduction in the "wrong" key of F major, a deliberately tantalizing ambiguity (the diary shows that Schumann was aware of it), which continues through much of the Allegro, with its soaring eight-bar melody. The development section, as so often with Schumann, is short and somewhat quirky. The second movement, a lighthearted Scherzo, is evocative of Mendelssohn's effervescent compositions. (Schumann dedicated all three of his string quartets to Mendelssohn.) The broadly sustained Adagio has a solemn inwardness that is vintage Schumann. It also betrays his lingering dependence on the piano (he was still composing at the keyboard much of the time). For example, an offbeat pizzicato accompaniment in measures 20–27 sounds like arpeggios played on the piano. This poses technical problems when four string players instead of one pianist have to perform the music. (It was customary in those days, when there were no phonographs or tape recordings, for composers to transcribe much of their symphonic and chamber music for the piano, so that it could be played more easily in the home.)

Schumann's second string quartet, in F major, begins with an expansive theme that later was much beloved by Johannes Brahms, who found there the germinal notes F A F for his personal motto *"Frei Aber Froh"* (free but happy). The slow movement, a tender theme with variations, harks back to a similar one in Beethoven's string quartet in E flat (op. 127). Schumann's Scherzo, with tricky arpeggiated runs for the first violin and an offbeat trio section, again shows the influence of his training as a pianist, while the final *Allegro molto vivace* is again reminiscent of Mendelssohn. Paradoxically, this quartet, which on the surface might seem derivative, is one of Schumann's most original works. He combined and integrated ideas from past and present, including his own, with proficiency.

The third quartet, in A major, again begins with a brief slow introduction, imaginatively varied in the following *Allegro molto moderato*. (This movement, with its characteristic falling-fifth interval, is responsible for the nickname "Clara" often given to this quartet.) The second movement consists of variations on a theme that is not explicit until half-way through. The slow movement is passionate, with a dotted rhythm accompaniment by the second violin that prepares for the vigorous finale.

Composing three string quartets in such a brief period was exhilarating, but also left Schumann feeling drained and exhausted—"gloomy melancholy." He had moved into a "quiet little nook" of his apartment, in order to work undisturbed.[44] A brief vacation with Clara in August gave him a chance to recuperate. They went to Bohemia where, thanks to Clara's Viennese connections, they were allowed to visit Metternich in his castle. Schumann was in such awe of the "great man . . . his big, wise eyes, his firm, robust stride, and above all that clear, distinct voice," that when Metternich offered to shake hands with him, he was "too embarrassed to take it."[45]

After this holiday Clara "hopefully" reported herself to be pregnant again; Schumann reported "a bad hangover" on her birthday.[46] Whether these announcements were directly related is unclear, but his feeling of simultaneous elation and depression seems to have generated a composition that has become one of the pivotal chamber music works of the nineteenth century, the *Quintet for Piano and Strings in E-flat major* (op. 44). Written essentially for his wife and dedicated to her when published the next year, this quintet is like a small concerto for the piano. Clara could perform it at home or in various private residences without having to worry about a whole orchestra. The combination of piano with string instruments was not new, but earlier works in this vein, by Boccherini, for example, or Schubert's *Trout* Quintet, had included music for a double bass. Schumann's Piano Quintet became the model for Brahms, Dvořák, and other composers. It begins with the piano and string quartet playing together energetically.

Then the piano plays alone, a variation on the opening subject, soon to be joined by the viola and cello in a sensuous dialogue.

In the second movement of the quintet, the piano and strings take turns, varying a somber theme that is often referred to as a funeral march (but should never be played like one). The following Scherzo is full of acrobatics, and one can almost picture Clara proudly showing off her nimble octave scales and setting the pace for the other players. The final movement ends with a fugue.

While completing his Piano Quintet, Schumann started to feel "melancholic" again, and after a few "dreadful sleepless nights" he tried to focus his attention on yet another piece of chamber music. "With great satisfaction," in less than a week he finished his well-known *Quartet for Piano and Strings* (op. 47), like the quintet, in the key of E-flat major.[47] Its slow movement is heart-rending in places, a hint perhaps of the sadness that was again starting to envelop the composer with the approach of winter. As we shall see, the cyclic fluctuations in Schumann's depressiveness often seemed to coincide with seasonal changes, as well as with other external reminders of passing time, such as birthdays and death-day anniversaries.

The "chamber music year," 1842—called that to contrast with the "song year" of 1840 and the "symphony year" of 1841—drew to a painful close. Schumann's last composition, *Fantasy Pieces* (op. 88) for violin, piano, and cello, consists of short pieces in contrasting moods. They resemble the style of his earlier compositions, those written before his marriage. Each movement is a musical vignette, and no effort is made to develop or elaborate the material extensively, as in his quartets and the quintet. (The opening Romance is reminiscent in both mood and key of Mendelssohn's *Scottish* Symphony, composed earlier that year.) Schumann was exhausted. "Writing on the trio is too much—unwell in the evening."[48] His midwinter depression was under way.

To understand better how Schumann's recurring mood swings led to bodily complaints as well as to changes in his behavior, it is necessary to backtrack a bit and examine his physical and mental health more closely. Clara, of course, had been forewarned by her father that Schumann was emotionally disturbed, and she had personally observed his irascible moodiness throughout their long engagement. Thus her attention was focused on his health from the beginning of their marriage. "He has never felt entirely well, which sometimes makes me sad and worried," she wrote only three months after they had begun to live together.[49] Clara did not specify the symptoms, but a month later she reported that "Robert was very bad and due to pain in the throat had trouble eating. He was very displeased about it because he insists that not being able to eat is the greatest misfortune, and I must agree!"[50]

Connections between his symptoms and his creative activity became apparent early. For example, after Schumann finished the *Spring* Symphony, Clara wrote, "Robert is in a vegetative state—he overtaxed himself too much with the symphony."[51] Even more disconcerting was that his complaining always reached a crescendo whenever she wanted to leave Leipzig. When they traveled, Schumann was often exceedingly nervous. For example, his brief vacation to the mountains in 1841 "was spoiled," he said, "by the unwellness I always feel in very high places, when they descend precipitously and steeply. The gruesome bridge from the bastion down to the ground still frightens me, in my fantasy."[52]

Thus the marriage diary proceeds, year after year, to describe a couple whose emotions and fears constantly overlap and interdigitate. (Clara too suffered from depressiveness and a height phobia.) Not only is it difficult to discern how much of Schumann's habitual lassitude, anxiety, and physical malaise was played up or minimized by Clara in accordance with her own fears, but he himself would dramatize or deny his complaints, depending on the circumstances.

Schumann's "horror" of traveling was assuaged temporarily in 1842 by the cancellation of Clara's Russian tour. But when she decided to concertize in northern Germany instead, he agreed to go along and considered conducting his *Spring* Symphony in Hamburg, as he had in Weimar the year before. And yet Schumann had mixed feelings about sharing the podium with his wife. On the one hand, it pleased him to express opinions about how music, especially his own, should be performed; on the other hand, he lacked charisma, and his leadership abilities were so minimal that Clara could easily outshine him.

It should be interjected here that Schumann was generally nervous around orchestral musicians and hated to perform—or even rehearse. A letter from Ferdinand David (concertmaster of the Gewandhaus Orchestra) to Felix Mendelssohn (its conductor) describes what was typical behavior for Schumann when he was faced with such situations:

> Yesterday Schumann was with me and for an hour communicated something silently [*hat mir eine Stunde was vorgeschwiegen*] from which it finally became clear to me that he would have liked to hear his symphony in public once more. I proposed to do this during the horn rehearsal, whereupon by means of gestures he gave me to understand that he wanted to pay [the musicians] for his rehearsal, so that it could be a really thorough one. After that he smoked two cigars, passed his hand over his mouth twice because a syllable wanted to

come out, took his hat, forgot his gloves, nodded with his head, went to the wrong door, then the right one, and disappeared. . . .[53]

Schumann's behavior in Hamburg is also illustrative: he coped with the difficult situation by excusing himself with physical symptoms, in this instance his "eye ailment," a recurring complaint. "I'm so nearsighted that I cannot see a single note or any of my musicians," he told the directors of the Hamburg Orchestra. "Before I dare to conduct I must find a pair of glasses."[54] Either he could not find a good pair of glasses or would not wear them (he did use spectacles later in his life).

Along with comments about his nearsightedness, other health problems are described in the documents filed with the Communal Guard in Leipzig. (It will be remembered that under the threat of military conscription, Schumann had asked his friend Dr. Reuter to submit a medical report. Indeed, the date for Schumann to show up for active duty was in February 1842, so that his decision to accompany Clara to northern Germany at that time may not have been entirely altruistic.)

Dr. Reuter's detailed report, in addition to the matter of Schumann's persistent hand disability, comments that "Dr. Schumann frequently suffers from dizziness brought about by blood-congestion in the brain, heart, and major vessels." The conclusion Reuter drew was that Schumann was afflicted with an "apoplectic constitution," a term that today would suggest high blood pressure. That does not mean the composer actually was hypertensive, although we have no way of knowing. Blood-pressure gauges were not yet in use, and all Reuter had to go on was a clinical impression. Apparently Schumann's face tended to flush, and he would become dizzy and complain of uncomfortable physical sensations: all are nonspecific symptoms that can be associated with emotional excitement, anxiety, anger, or even drinking. The consequences, in Dr. Reuter's opinion, might have been dangerous. His report emphasizes that Schumann ought to avoid exertion because "vigorous walking or other physical exertion causes or worsens" the symptoms.[55]

We do not know whether Schumann took this recommendation seriously. Surely he was no athlete, and the little conducting he did certainly could not be considered strenuous exercise. Sexual intercourse and long walks seem to have been his most intense physical activities. Neither of them slowed down significantly over the years, nor were they associated, as far as is evident, with any increase in physical symptoms, suggesting that if any cardiovascular pathology was present at all, it could not have been a major source of Schumann's complaints. However, Dr. Raimund Brachman, the city physician whose job it was to look for flaws in the medical reports of men asking for deferment, did not contradict Dr. Reuter on this point (although he refused to recognize Schumann's hand problem as a valid disability). In fact, Dr. Brachman, who knew the composer well enough,* went even further than Dr. Reuter. His report states that Schumann's "general appearance confirms such a high degree of cerebral blood pressure as to suggest the danger of a stroke."[57] Thus the possibility of some form of hypertension cannot be ruled out. Indeed, this tentative diagnosis may be compatible with what we have already learned about Schumann's way of trying to suppress any outward display of anger. Behind his dignified, kindly facade there may have raged a malignant hostility that could express itself only through elevations in blood pressure, fantasies about death, and nagging physical complaints. (It should be added that many men requested and obtained military deferment in Saxony in 1842. Whether certain Leipzig doctors encouraged this is not known, but Schumann was already a public figure of sorts who warranted special consideration. Besides, with Dr. Reuter's report before him, Dr. Brachman may have wanted to protect himself as well as the city administration against any possible blame, were this somewhat eccentric and litigious musician to have a medical mishap.)

Schumann's behavior on the trip to northern Germany exemplifies how closely his health problems were tied to his emotional reactions. Things went well enough at first. He had given himself a five-week vacation from the self-imposed editorial responsibilities of the *New Journal* and there were no new compositions on his mind. In Bremen he enjoyed hearing the *Spring* Symphony performed (by another conductor), and he "applauded vigorously" after Clara played so well that the audience "wouldn't let her leave the piano."[58] In Oldenburg, however, an incident occurred that upset him deeply and made him reluctant to tour with his wife again. Clara had been invited to a reception without him, and she accepted and enjoyed the party. When she returned to their hotel, he was obviously upset, grumbling over the "unworthy" way a man in his "position" was being treated.[59] For a great composer to be overlooked—worse yet, overshadowed—by a mere pianist, even though she was his wife, was unacceptable. Besides, Schumann hated to travel, so he refused to go on with the tour. Clara had already accepted a number of engagements in other countries. Momentarily flustered, she canceled one concert, but quickly recovered. (Clara had been through worse scenes with her father.) She found a woman companion for the trip to Denmark, while her husband packed his bags and went home, stating that the *New Journal* could not manage without him.

For Clara the tour was a huge success. In Copenhagen alone she earned close to 1000 thalers. She also met several distinguished people, including

---

*He had received money from Schumann for doing newspaper translations.[56]

Hans Christian Andersen and Niels Gade, a Danish composer, who soon became a close friend. For Schumann the seven-week separation from his wife brought their dilemma into focus, and he tried to explain it to her in a letter.

> The separation has again made my strange and difficult situation more palpable. Ought I to neglect my talent so that I can serve as your travel escort? Have you or should you let your talent go to waste because I am tied to the newspaper and my piano? Now, when you are young and full of strength? We have found the solution; you've taken a companion, I've returned to our child and my work. But what will the world say? That's how I torture myself mentally. Yes, it is absolutely necessary for us to find a way to use and develop our two talents side by side.[60]

In his "dispirited" state, for which he blamed his wife, Schumann was unable to do any composing. "You [Clara] deprive me of all my ideas right now. I can't even put a simple song together right now. I don't know what's wrong with me."[61] The household book reports "terribly much drinking," guilt, and anger.[62]

Thus Schumann could neither tolerate being with Clara when she pursued her career nor accept living without her; his health problems seem to have been related to this dilemma. He craved an ideal companionship with someone who could constantly adjust to his emotional perturbations and cater to his personal needs (a female counterpart to Leonard Woolf). In Clara's absence, Schumann reverted to many of his premarital ways of socializing. He read books, went to concerts, saw some friends (including Richard Wagner, who was in Leipzig at this time*), drank excessively, worked on his newspaper, and fantasized about composing new music without doing very much—"an unworthy life," as he called it.[63]

It is interesting to note that Schumann at this point also contemplated going to America for two years, "to make us secure for the rest of our lives," as he wrote Clara. He thought it was "a terrible decision," but an alternative to "traveling in Germany where whatever Clara earns I would lose from my income and my time." Wisely, he scrapped the "great plan" after reading a poem about someone who committed suicide because his hopes were betrayed in "a foreign part of the world."[64] We can well imagine what might have befallen the Schumanns had they gone to America, where his travel anxieties probably would have become much worse.

---

* Schumann had been in correspondence with him to obtain reports for the *New Journal* about musical activities in Paris, where Wagner lived.

Clara's return to Leipzig on 26 April 1842 ushered in "better days again."* As a welcoming present Robert gave her a new rug. She started writing songs for his birthday in June. While Clara said that she could never equal her husband as a composer, she continued to write music anyway, and he usually encouraged her, perhaps as a way of keeping their relationship in better balance. It was at this time that Schumann composed his string quartets, a definite sign of improved mental functioning.

As mentioned earlier, Clara became pregnant that August, demonstrating a possible biological compliance with their psychological needs. Now Schumann could await her delivery without having to worry about another concert tour. And yet whenever he finished a new work, his dreadful "melancholy" returned, almost as if by composing the music he had warded off mental disorder. Clara, in turn, was terribly unhappy about her enforced confinement:

> An indescribable gloominess has fallen over me the last few days—I think you don't love me any more. . . . In my grief there came many sad thoughts about the future. . . . My most terrible thought is that you should have to work for money . . . and yet, if you do not also let me work, if you cut off every means of earning something, I can see no other way out. I want to earn money, so that you can dedicate your life entirely to your art.[65]

Her worries about Schumann's shrinking capital reserves were exaggerated, however. There was no financial crisis. The Schumann Brothers publishing firm had been sold after Eduard's death to his widow's new husband. The sale brought in a sizable sum for Robert, who also remained in litigation for some time (financial arrangements between the brothers were extremely complicated) over money from his inheritance that had been invested in Zwickau. Schumann was giving Clara regular monthly payments for domestic expenses, as the household books show, and he often added a generous if not extravagant bonus for her personal use. However, he was in the throes of his midwinter depression at the end of 1842, and himself expressing "concerns for the future."[66]

To help him cope with his melancholia, Schumann consulted "Dr. Müller *senior* and Dr. Müller *junior*," father and son, who were specialists in homeopathy. Their treatment—mostly psychotherapy with a little medication (to be discussed shortly)—seemed to be beneficial. Nevertheless, when Clara

---

*Schumann had rushed north, to Magdeburg, to meet her on the way home. (One wonders, incidentally, whether he had paid much attention to his daughter Marie during Clara's absence. His diaries and letters don't mention the child, who was then eight months old. There was of course a nanny to take care of her, but she probably missed her mother.)

left for a brief visit to her father in February 1843, Schumann suffered from "loneliness" and "hangovers."[67] He had been working on yet another piece of chamber music, the *Andante and Variations* (op. 46) for two cellos, a horn, and two pianos. This composition sounds mournful in places, partly because of the somber texture of horn combined with violoncello.* "I believe I was somewhat depressed while composing it," Schumann wrote to a friend.[68] And the household book tells of "the melancholy of a composer."[69]

With the approach of spring, Schumann's energy increased, and he felt driven to produce what he felt would surely be his "biggest and hopefully also best work," an oratorio called *Paradise and the Peri* (op. 50).[70] This marked another critical stage in his creative development: it was Schumann's first major attempt to combine every musical resource—solo singing, choral writing, and the symphony orchestra—into a single composition.

Opera, of course, was the ultimate goal for an ambitious composer of the nineteenth century, and many of Schumann's friends were going in that direction. Some, like Heinrich Marschner and Richard Wagner, were engaged in theatrical work almost exclusively. Even Mendelssohn had written a small-scale (chamber) opera in his youth. Schumann's wide-ranging reading interests had led him to search for a suitable libretto everywhere. First it was Shakespeare's *Hamlet*, later E. T. A. Hoffmann's *Doge and Dogeressa*, then Calderon's *The Bridge of Mantible*. Most recently he had become interested in *Tristan und Isolde* by Immerman.[71]

But the time did not seem ripe. Mendelssohn had been composing oratorios, such as *Elijah* and *Paul*, which resemble Händel's *Messiah* and are modeled after Johann Sebastian Bach's great "Passions." These dramatic works can be performed in a concert hall or in a church, thereby avoiding many of the complications of the theater.† All this appealed to Schumann. He had also been deeply impressed, while in Vienna, by Franz Joseph Haydn's magnificent oratorio, *The Seasons*.

An exotic poem, "Lalla Rookh," by Thomas Moore (1779–1852), struck Schumann as exactly suited to the sort of oratorio he had in mind. The central figure is the fairy ("Peri"), a fallen angel of ambiguous sex who has been expelled from Paradise and wants to get back in. To do so requires a

---

*On Mendelssohn's recommendation, Schumann later rescored this work for two pianos only.
† Opera is always a full-time effort, and the necessary costumes, scenery, directors, prompters, ballet-masters, and the like can make production very costly. In Schumann's day, it was also necessary to obtain permission from the official censors, which was particularly troublesome because the theaters were supported almost exclusively by the ruling aristocracy.

special penance. First he/she travels to India and gathers up drops of blood spilled by a slain hero, but to no avail. Next he/she goes to Egypt and collects sighing last breaths from a maiden who is dying in the arms of her fatally ill lover, but even this precious commodity does not appease the gods. Finally, he/she visits Syria and finds there a hardened sinner who miraculously begins to weep at the sight of a small child reciting its prayers. Peri catches the sinner's tears, and with this gift is readmitted to Paradise.

Schumann's choice of so magical a text seems consistent with his conscious and unconscious motivations. Quasi-oriental themes along the lines of the Arabian Nights were very popular among the German romantics, and in his *Myrtles* song collection he had already set to music two of Thomas Moore's poems. The ambisexual Peri seeking redemption is a lovely symbol of Schumann's guilty innocence, the passive aggressiveness displayed so often in his social behavior. It was probably no accident that the "friend" who had called his attention to "Lalla Rookh" two years earlier had been none other than Emil Flechsig, his old college roommate, who had come to pay his respects to the newlyweds. Flechsig regarded it as a "psychological miracle" that Schumann would be so taken with Moore's poem: he had already translated "Lalla Rookh" for Schumann.[72] But Schumann did not care much for the translation and thus wrote his own libretto. Many of the words are unabashedly sentimental, yet consistent with a romanticized view of the Middle East: "little heavenly flowers," "drops of life," "blood spurting from many wounds," "lethal plagues," and so on. No doubt the composer was excited by this material. He once confided to a friend that "while writing *Paradise and the Peri* a voice occasionally whispered to me 'what you are doing is not done completely in vain.'"[73] And Clara thought she observed an almost pathological elation: "He works on [the *Peri*] body and soul, with such a glowing heat that I sometimes fear it could do him some harm."[74]

Much of the year 1843 was spent on this work, which gratified Schumann's wish to compose something operatic. The oratorio begins with a gentle descending melody in the first violins, picked up polyphonically by the other strings and gradually embroidered into a sumptuous yet delicate overture. A narrator begins the tale, and then different voices enter to tell their stories. Schumann's way of integrating the recitatives with the arias is quite original. Even Richard Wagner, with whom he had recently discussed the future of German opera, praised him for "finding the right form in which to set this wonderful poem."[75] It presaged the future and anticipated some of Wagner's own operatic ideals.*

---

*But Schumann was also looking to the past, and some of his choruses sound like church music. This forthright piety characterizes much of the choral composing he did in later years, when he was less inventive than at the beginning of his marriage.

Paradise and the Peri has a number of scenes with shouting warriors, clashing cymbals, and other operatic paraphernalia. This would seem to contradict the popular belief that Schumann was incapable of writing in this vein. (The Germans even used the *Peri's* more warlike interludes to stir up patriotic fervor during World War II.) Schumann, however, intended the work to be performed as an oratorio, and not on the stage.

With the completion of *Paradise and the Peri*, Schumann had reached a level of artistic accomplishment that he would have difficulty surpassing. Since getting married, he had achieved a musical output that compares favorably with Beethoven's during the same three-year period in his life. (Beethoven too was cruelly handicapped by a succession of illnesses, so that the comparison seems apt.) But Beethoven of course had the benefits of a much earlier start and more consistent training in music. Nor was he faced, as Schumann was, with the obligations of running a newspaper and caring for a wife and family.

While working on his *Peri*, Schumann had been interrupted by several domestic crises. In early April a thief had broken into his wine cellar, which led to time-consuming and irksome visits to the police.[76] Then, on 24 April, Clara went into labor and delivered (the next morning) their second child, a girl, named Elise.

One of the most important changes, and another reason why Schumann could not always devote himself wholeheartedly to the oratorio, was that he had begun to teach at the new Conservatory of Music, which Mendelssohn had founded in Leipzig. It was a model institution, and Schumann was proud to have been invited. (As soon as Clara gained her strength back, she taught there also.) Schumann's first lesson was actually given the day of Elise's christening. He had to go to the conservatory for seven hours a week, to teach a course listed as "Piano-playing and Private Work in Composition."[77]

Schumann is remembered as a very subdued teacher, who seldom said anything and would offer no advice or criticism. He seemed to be listening dreamily, perhaps more to his inner voices than to the efforts of his students. He also had a tendency, already noted by Flechsig in their college days, to pucker his mouth in a peculiar way, as if whistling to himself. Uncomfortable in his role as a conservatory teacher, Schumann often returned home feeling emotionally drained and physically exhausted. Not surprisingly, his tenure lasted less than a year, and his total earnings came to only 120 thalers.

His thirty-third birthday, in June 1843, is noted in the household book as "a melancholy day"; Clara's mother had arrived from Berlin for a "surprise" visit, another interruption.[78] Finally, on 16 June Schumann finished the *Peri*. (He made revisions on the final chorus as late as 20 September, just two weeks before the first rehearsals.)

He decided to conduct the premiere himself, an important decision since he had never led an orchestra in Leipzig before. (Schumann had warned Clara, before they were married, "Don't be too ambitious for me. . . . Never in all your life will you be a conductor's wife.") On a few occasions, when he and Clara were touring together, he had mounted the platform and discovered that holding the stick made him feel "enthusiastic." But he was much too passive and self-absorbed to take command, and although he would beat time, he rarely gave cues or instructions to the players.[79] Whenever possible, Clara would attend the rehearsals and explain to the musicians what she thought he expected. Sometimes she would even direct them herself, from the piano. Her assistance only added to his dependence on her.

The timing of Schumann's conducting debut in Leipzig was critical. Mendelssohn had recently been appointed General Music Director for Prussia, a taxing assignment, and during his frequent absences guest conductors were engaged to lead the Gewandhaus Orchestra. The search was under way for a permanent replacement, and Schumann, with Clara's encouragement, thought he might be suitable for this position. *Paradise and the Peri* would be the test.

Rehearsals with the solo singers went well enough, but when he faced the orchestra for the first time, on 23 October, he encountered difficulties. Clara was scheduled to go to Dresden for concerts of her own and had to leave. But just before opening night, Schumann sent her an urgent appeal to return, saying, "Without you I can't hold a rehearsal." When she arrived back in Leipzig, one of the singers told her, "If only your dear husband could decide to fight a little bit and demand more attention, then things would certainly go better right away."[80]

It must have been fairly obvious to everyone that Schumann was temperamentally unsuited to succeed Mendelssohn at the Gewandhaus. Yet he and Clara, hoping for more security and a steady income, seemed to believe that the coveted position might actually be offered to him. When it went to Niels Gade instead, they were disappointed.* But because Gade was a personal friend, whom Schumann had praised lavishly in the *New Journal*, the composer could not openly express anger or envy for having been passed over.

Thus the Schumanns approached a grave decision: whether to leave Leipzig. He felt at home there, had his newspaper, and so far had been able to do excellent creative work. In spite of his weak conducting, *Paradise and*

---

* A Danish violinist, composer, and conductor, Niels Gade (1817–1890) was first given the title of assistant conductor. Later, after Mendelssohn's death, he was officially appointed as his successor.

the Peri turned out to be a great success (it remains a fairly popular work in Germany, where the subtleties of the text can be appreciated). Nevertheless, other talented musicians were moving in. Clara, for her sake as well as her husband's, wanted to go elsewhere. One possibility was Dresden, for after years of concertizing she had a coterie of admirers there. In addition, her father was now living in Dresden. Clara had repeatedly begged him to make peace with Schumann.

By 1843 Wieck was beginning to feel that his son-in-law had proved sufficiently manly. There were now two grandchildren, and his new compositions, especially *Paradise and the Peri*, were giving him an aura of distinction. Thus on 16 December 1843 the following invitation arrived in Leipzig:

> For Clara's sake and the world's, we can no longer keep each other at a distance. You too are now a family man—is a longer explanation needed?
>
> Where art is concerned, we have always agreed—I was even your teacher— my judgments determined the course of your present career. I don't need to assure you that I will cooperate with your talent and support your beautiful and genuine efforts.
>
> You are joyfully expected in Dresden by your father Fr. Wieck.[81]

Clara was delighted; Schumann less so. It meant another trip to Dresden, for a sort of family reunion. Their daughters stayed behind. Important things needed to be discussed with Wieck concerning Clara's career and Schumann's possible participation in another concert tour.

During the Christmas holiday in Dresden there was much discussion about a trip to Russia. Traveling such vast distances into so rugged a foreign country was, and still is, an enormous challenge, and Schumann made it clear that he did not want to go. Clara had postponed the trip several times, but this time Mendelssohn, with his many international connections, had helped her organize a tour, and it would have been scandalous to renege. Wieck undoubtedly was instrumental in persuading Schumann to change his mind and go along. Perhaps the prospect of hearing his latest compositions performed in Russia was an inducement.

Fur coats and other necessities had to be purchased; the total cost of preparing for the Russia tour came to 804 thalers.[82] Schumann also had to find someone who could manage his newspaper in his absence, and on 7 January 1844 his friend Oswald Lorenz agreed to do so. The next step was to place the children with relatives. On 21 January Robert and Clara arranged for his brother Carl and his wife Pauline, in Schneeberg, to assume this responsibility. Then came hectic farewells, after which the Schumanns departed for Berlin, whence they headed eastward, for concerts in Königsberg, Mitau, Dorpat, and other cities (which are now part of the Soviet Union and have been renamed). It was a grueling schedule, with grimy hotel rooms, missed railway connections, and rides in crowded carriages and bumpy sleds. Loss of sleep no doubt added to the stress of the trip.

Schumann disliked moving from place to place, and the social obligations annoyed him. Often tired and irritable, he found that he could not concentrate on writing articles for the *New Journal* as he had hoped, much less compose any music. He was constantly in Clara's shadow. Reporting on their Russia trip, D. W. Shitomirski observes that in 1844 the composer was known mainly as Clara Schumann's husband.[83]

Schumann's first breakdown, at age twenty-three, had been fairly acute, precipitated by the loss of two close relatives. The second was more gradual, worsening as the time and distance away from home increased. Schumann's problems began in Dorpat (now Tartu), after less than a month of traveling. Clara, who had just given "three brilliant concerts that ignited wild enthusiasm" there, tried in a letter to her father to minimize the illness by calling it a "bad cold" that forced him to stay in bed for a week.[84]

The truth of the matter is that Schumann was having a problem with hemorrhoids. Before finding out what it was, he described the pain euphemistically as "a violent attack of rheuma" followed by "a feverish condition." The diagnosis was made by a Professor Walther, probably from the university —Dorpat had a first-rate medical school—as well as another, unnamed doctor. "Now we see the light," Schumann wrote, obviously relieved, and he spent the next week in bed resting.[85] He also used the time to map out a new and very ambitious operatic project, one that would take him no less than ten years to complete: a musical setting of Goethe's *Faust*.

The Faust legend appealed strongly to many of the romantics, and it had been on Schumann's mind for a long time. His idea of setting *Faust* to music went back at least to his unmarried days, when he had corresponded about it with Hermann Hirschbach, the composer he had wanted to take along to Vienna. A letter to Clara in 1838 describes young Hirschbach as "very Faustian, black magical," and Schumann thought his compositions, now totally unknown, showed "inventiveness striving toward the most incredible . . . similar to my own state of mind."*[86]

---

*Anything having to do with magic always excited Schumann, and he may well have incorporated certain of Hirschbach's ideas into his own creative work. Hirschbach had written an *Overture to "Hamlet"*; an oratorio, *The Lost Paradise*, and string quartets that Schumann called *Scenes from Faust*.[87]

But before he could get much work done, Schumann had to get out of bed so that he and Clara could proceed with their trip. Their next stop was St. Petersburg (now Leningrad), where they were eagerly awaited. Two wealthy amateurs, the brothers Mathieu and Michael Wielhorski, had heard about Schumann's music, and organized a "soirée with orchestra" in their palatial residence and invited him to conduct the *Spring* Symphony. Clara played, but—although he did conduct—her husband stayed in the background at social events.

Schumann's health seems to have reached a plateau during the month in St. Petersburg. Although he complained of his unhappiness, he consulted no physicians there. His music was well received, especially the Piano Quintet, which Clara performed often in Russia. It pleased Schumann that many listeners detected "a certain Slavic breadth" in his melodies.*

A familiar problem soon arose, however: jealousy. It disturbed Schumann that people would cluster around his attractive wife, flattering and sometimes flirting with her while he, unable to make small talk, was pushed aside. The marriage diary is unclear on these points, but cryptic remarks in Schumann's hand, such as "insults that are barely endurable, and Clara's conduct," suggest serious arguments.[89]

Moscow was their ultimate goal, but the Schumanns interrupted the grueling journey to visit a small town, Twer, where Robert's uncle, Dr. Schnabel lived. Schumann had once, in a fit of suicidal despair during his adolescence, considered leaving home and staying with this uncle, his mother's brother. Seeing him now, for the first and the last time, may have been something of a shock. The seventy-year-old man was dying of heart and kidney disease, and Schumann's fear of death probably surfaced. He became much more anxious and depressed after this visit and suddenly experienced an episode of "dizziness" and blurred vision.[90] (He often complained of tension headaches when he was under stress, felt exhausted, or had slept badly; some of these may have been migraine attacks.)

In Moscow, while Clara was practicing, Schumann would go for long walks, make sketches of the Kremlin, or write poetry to shake off his melancholia; for example:

In Moskau, Russlands Wunderstadt,	*In Moscow, Russia's wondrous town,*
Von einer Glocke ging die Sage,	*There's the saga of a bell,*
So riesengross, dass sie im Sturze	*So huge and heavy when it fell,*

---

*Schumann's influence as a composer has been profound in Russia. Tchaikovsky considered his music "organically connected to Beethoven's creativeness and at the same time sharply distinguished from it," and he thought that Schumann was "the most outstanding representative of our contemporary art."[88]

Die Kuppel, die sie trug, hernieder	*That the cupola holding it*
Gezogen in die Erde, wo	*Was dragged into the ground*
Sie selber nun vergraben, jährlich	*And buried there as well,*
Sich tiefer in die Erde bohrend.	*Boring deeper into the earth each year.*[91]

Later stanzas of the poem refer to a "hangman," the "crush of death in the throat," "corpses," a "grave," and other images reflecting Schumann's morbid preoccupations in Moscow. His use of the imagery of "a huge and heavy bell," pulling into the earth "the cupula holding it," might also have been an unconscious allusion to the way he felt he was dragging Clara down.* In their mutual dependence, they both suffered greatly during the four weeks in Moscow. It was the end of spring, the wrong time of year for piano recitals, so that Clara's concerts were poorly attended. Schumann would go to the opera occasionally, and in a touching letter to the Dutch violinist Johann Verhulst, he mentioned his anguished search for familiar faces. "One evening at the theater we saw a double-bass player who resembled you so closely that I immediately wanted to throw my arms around him."[92]

On their way back to Germany the Schumanns had to stop once more in St. Petersburg and again make public appearances. Their behavior at an elegant party was described as follows by one of the guests:

> Clara Schumann performed her husband's Piano Quintet, Kreisleriana, and other pieces that evening. Although we were already getting used to female piano virtuosos at the time, she made a tremendous impression on us. . . . Schumann was silent and reserved all evening, as usual. He only mumbled, unintelligibly, when [he was] asked questions. Something like a conversation did ensue with the famous violinist Molique, but it was only in a whisper, without life or fire. Schumann mostly sat in a corner next to the piano . . . his head bowed down, hair hanging in his face, and with a very thoughtful expression, as if he was whistling to himself. Clara Schumann was a little more talkative. She answered all the questions for her husband.[93]

Despite Schumann's depression, he was able to make it back to Leipzig without mishap, thanks to Clara's assistance. She without a doubt had been the stronger and more dominant partner in this concert tour, which earned them 4796 thalers, an impressive sum, especially considering that they had been gone for only four months. But by proving once and for all that he could do no work as long as Clara was actively pursuing her own career, this trip had also damaged their marriage. Schumann's complaining, physical

---

*Incredibly, he sent his Russia poems to Wieck. This may have been a cry for help, similar to his earlier reaching for support when Wieck was his teacher.

Clara with the Schumanns'
first child, Marie, in 1844.
(Daguerreotype, courtesy of
the Robert Schumann Haus.)

and mental symptoms, depressiveness, and unsociable behavior had become
a terrible burden for them both, and as a result Clara's future as a performing artist seemed in jeopardy.

Their readjustment to Leipzig was not easy, and a gloomy dissatisfaction nagged Clara. "Although we were back in our old domesticity and had
our children again, everything seemed so bleak, so empty. On top of that
came Robert's ever-present indisposition, which had really lasted the entire
trip, but was often disguised."[94] In trying to discover what troubled him,
we can now no longer rely on the marriage diaries. Upon returning from
Russia (on 30 May 1844), Schumann stopped writing what was supposed
to be the chronicle of a happy marriage.*

Outwardly he pretended to be a happy husband and father. A letter
(dated 3 June) to his brother Carl chats comfortably about money spent on
babysitters and the childrens' reaction to having been separated from their
parents. Other letters, to various musicians, even go so far as to say that he

---

*He did, however, continue to keep the household books, daily records of his moods, social
activities, finances, creative work, and illnesses. Clara too maintained an independent diary.

had returned from Russia feeling "well and healthy" and that he was preparing for yet another trip, "perhaps next January already [to Holland]. . . . And then we'll want to go to England."[95] This denial of reality was a prelude to the next phase of Schumann's mental disorder.

XII.
Engulfing Depression, 1844–1845

The massive depression that nearly drove Schumann into a psychosis when he was in his mid-thirties occurred at a time of profound social change. It was the period of industrialization, culminating in the German revolution of 1848–1849. The population was burgeoning; machines replaced hand labor; railways took the place of horse-drawn carriages; tariff agreements supplanted the old barter systems; and the government became centralized.[1] All these environmental transformations affected the way writers, musicians, and artists worked, as well as their view of themselves and their creativity.

Important for the evolution of Schumann's creative work was that the romantic orientation that had nourished his talents since childhood was beginning to crumble. For example, when he grew up, the viewpoint prevailed that genius and madness are inseparable. Many artists of the romantic era confidently engaged in "mad" behavior—debauchery, drinking, drug use, irrational thinking—hoping thus to stimulate their creativity. When Schumann was younger and unmarried he tried to do some of this too, despite his fear of losing self-control and committing suicide in the process.

But after marrying Clara, who thoroughly disapproved of any artistic liberty and eccentricity, he made a great effort to conform.

It is interesting to note that when he returned from Russia, with his wife, Schumann stopped applying the term "madness" to himself. He now used the term "illness" almost exclusively. This too reflected a changing philosophy, which had recently spread from France to other European countries.[2] In 1836, Louis-François Lelut published a "pathography" in Paris that claimed Socrates was mentally ill and not simply possessed by demons, as had been believed earlier. A similar conclusion about Blaise Pascal appeared in 1846. (Ten years later—the year Schumann died—another French psychiatrist, Jacques-Joseph Moreau, depicted over 180 men of genius as being diseased. Soon signs of "nervous degeneration" were being discovered among most of the world's leading artists, scientists, writers, and musicians.)

With his thirty-fourth birthday approaching, Schumann felt progressively "bad" (1 June 1844), "poorly" (2 June), and "terrible" (4 June). He was building to a depression the likes of which he had never experienced. He tried to stave it off on his birthday by presenting himself with a newly published edition of Goethe's *Faust*. Although it was Schumann's wish to proceed with this long-delayed composition, something seemed to be distracting him constantly. First it was the story of *Till Eulenspiegel*, which Schumann thought might be a more desirable text for an opera. The next day he was brooding, but did not say why. Finally, in mid-June he started working on *Faust* in earnest. This didn't get very far. By the end of the month he was thinking of Byron's *Corsair* as an opera. Then all work came to a complete standstill.

In July his obsessive focusing on his poor state of health became especially noticeable. He complained of "sad melancholia" on 4 July, and said he was "half-sick" the next day. He tried to keep busy, working "diligently but under strain" to complete the orchestration for a scene from *Faust*. But there were still further interruptions. In early August he had to start teaching at the conservatory again, and the household book tells of more sickness, and of drinking "a great deal." Schumann tried to contain himself; he allowed an artist from Vienna, Joseph Aigner, to paint his and Clara's portrait. But by 14 August he was "sick with colic" and had to stay home. Although after two days of "improvement" he was working "diligently on Faust," by the end of the month he was in an "accursed melancholic state."[3]

He was now beginning to accept some treatment for his increasing depression. First came an attempt at hydrotherapy—"baths" and a "river-bath."[4] Immersion was a popular treatment for emotional disorders in the nineteenth century; it continues to be used in many European spas. Hydrotherapy may produce some temporary relaxation, and Schumann did seem to feel "somewhat better" after bathing. This improvement continued until the beginning of September, enabling him to take a much-needed vacation with Clara in Halle and the Harz Mountains. But then the depression became much worse again; Clara recorded that "he could barely cross the room without the greatest effort."[5] According to the household book, on 21 September "treatment was started with Carlsbad [cathartic] salts," another nonspecific remedy for depression popular during the nineteenth century.*

Schumann continued to complain of "great malaise after working."[6] He did manage to go to the theater on 24 September, but not before writing to Mendelssohn about his conflicted state of mind: "The Scene from Faust remains on my desk; I'm terribly afraid to look at it again. . . . I don't know whether I will ever publish it."[7]

A week later, he mentioned a medical consultation with "Dr. Müller." This doctor would have been either Moritz Müller, M.D., or his son Clothar Müller, M.D., mentioned earlier. Both were respected and conservative members of the homeopathic school established in Leipzig by Samuel Hahnemann. It was the elder Dr. Müller who had spearheaded a movement among homeopaths to align themselves closely with traditional medical practice and to adopt a critical, scientific attitude toward their new profession. One of his major contributions had been the finding that many patients in those days were victims of drug-induced toxicity.† His son Clothar Müller was the author of several textbooks, one of which is a frequently republished compendium on therapeutics; in it we find that mercury was liberally used by the Leipzig homeopaths for treating "neuralgia, colds, toothache, gastritis, diarrhea, sciatic pain, itching of the skin," and many other nonspecific complaints.[9]

To discover whether Schumann was ever given, or was ever exposed to, this highly toxic metal, the author tested samples of hair from Robert, Clara, and August Schumann, obtained from a collection of Schumann family artifacts at the Saxon State Library in Dresden. Robert Schumann's hair does show traces of mercury, as does his father's, but Clara's does not.‡ This

---

* Emotional disorders of the type that afflicted Schumann are often associated with a slowing of physiological as well as psychological functions. Thus digestive disturbances may result, such as constipation, which would have made Schumann's hemorrhoids worse. Some doctors even believed that depression was caused by the retention of bowel products, a process of so-called auto-intoxication. Hence the popularity of cathartics.

† "Müller opened the eyes of medical science," writes the historian Tischner, "to the fact that new symptomatic manifestations frequently do not belong to a patient's illness, but represent the effects of the treatment instead."[8]

‡ The chemical tests were performed with the kind assistance of Selig Gellert, M.D., with an X-ray analytic spectrometer at Kevex Laboratory in Foster City, California. They disclosed not only traces of mercury, but also lead, zinc, and manganese, a contamination that can be

does not prove, however, that Schumann and his father were exposed to mercury as a result of medical treatment: First, the Schumann collection is not dated, so it is impossible to tell at what age each sample was taken. Second, mercury was also used for blocking hats, and we know from the household book that Schumann did wear a hat.

Around the time when Drs. Moritz and Clothar Müller were advising Schumann and possibly treating some of his symptoms, he decided to travel to Dresden again. Later he said that the doctors had told him to go, but this seems unlikely. (The household book shows that he made his decision for Dresden *before* consulting Dr. Müller on 1 October; that evening he also spoke with his old friend Dr. Reuter. [10]) It is doubtful that *any* doctor would have advised Schumann to travel in the depressed state he was in. But he and Clara, surely with Wieck's approval, were beginning to look to Dresden as a place for them to resettle. Clara hoped that "another environment and other people might have a wholesome effect." [11] Thus Schumann took it upon himself to reconnoiter ways of moving to Dresden permanently. On 3 October 1844 he departed, alone and by train, for the Saxon capital.

It is easy to imagine the dilemmas facing the sick composer as he stepped off the train. Dresden, with a population of 100,000, had 40,000 more inhabitants than Leipzig. It was a city of great beauty, the seat of one of Europe's wealthiest courts, with a treasure trove of baroque art to which painters, sculptors, and architects flocked. Its Royal Opera House was flourishing in the wake of Carl Maria von Weber's leadership. It would have been a heavenly place for a Florestanian youth, but by 1844 Schumann was more the low-key Eusebius.

His initial reaction was strongly negative, and he immediately sent distress signals back to Clara in Leipzig. "The trip was frightful and Robert thought he could not survive it," she wrote. A week later she arrived at his hotel and discovered that "Robert hadn't slept a single night, his fantasies painted the most dreadful pictures, in the morning he was generally swimming in tears, he gave up completely." [12]

Unfortunately, Schumann's daily records deal mostly with financial matters and give little indication of what had happened. But an observation of Clara's, that her father "wanted to tear [Robert] forcefully" out of his depressed state, may be pertinent. [13] To get to Wieck's house, the acrophobic Schumann would have had to cross one of the high bridges spanning the Elbe River. And although he was now on speaking and visiting terms with Wieck, perhaps their relationship had never recovered from the bitter lawsuit. In addition, Wieck's earlier attempts to "normalize" Schumann and make him

---

attributed to the fact that these hair samples had been immersed in water that flooded the Dresden Library during the bombing raids of World War II.

more "manly" had usually provoked intense anger, which the younger man tried either to suppress or to neutralize with good-humored remarks. Now, however, he was at a new low, and Wieck's ill-timed bullying probably flooded Schumann with inexpressible rage. There were "dreadful pictures" in his mind[14]—but Clara's diary does not tell us what they were. Perhaps he was again thinking about suicide.

What caused Schumann to slide into so severe a depression in his mid-thirties? A combination of stresses seems to have been involved. Most immediate was the depleted state he had been in since returning from Russia. Drained of energy, he felt increasingly discouraged over the slow progress of his *Faust* music, and he found that literary work was becoming a source of constant frustration.[15] ("A musician would rather write notes than letters of the alphabet," he had told his friend Verhulst the year before, in a letter apologizing for not having written to him sooner.[16]) Schumann even wondered whether he ought to give up his responsibilities as critic and editor in order to have more time for composing music. His chances to be appointed director of the Gewandhaus in Leipzig had by now vanished completely. Clara's career, by contrast, was on the upswing, and her intrusive father was again playing a leading role.

With Clara supporting him during this crisis, Schumann gradually regained his composure. They decided to rent a temporary apartment in Dresden, and spoke at length with Wieck about staying there at least during the winter.

Two months were required for Schumann to settle his affairs in Leipzig, which he did with great effort. In the meantime Clara, six months pregnant, gave farewell concerts, including one at the Gewandhaus that featured "the most difficult concerto [she] knew," Beethoven's *Emperor*.[17] Friends wanted to entertain them for the last time, and at an unforgettable party, they heard a thirteen-year-old violinist play in Mendelssohn's *Octet for Strings:* Joseph Joachim, who, with Johannes Brahms, would become one of Schumann's "demons."*

The most urgent decision Schumann had to make in 1844 was in regard to the *New Journal for Music*. The year before, he had been invited to merge his newspaper with another musical journal, a step that would have led to greater involvement in publishing. But Schumann said no. He was growing tired of the business. Now, in the midst of his depression, he decided to

---

*Joachim had arrived in Leipzig the previous year, when Schumann was so preoccupied with *Paradise and the Peri* that he hardly took notice. But Mendelssohn did, and recommended composition lessons for the child prodigy. After hearing him play at his debut, Schumann is said to have "gently touched Joachim's knee, and with the other pointed to the starry sky, saying in his inimitably kind way, 'Do any creatures up there realize how beautifully a little boy here on earth has been playing the Kreutzer Sonata with Mendelssohn?'"[18]

abandon the *New Journal* completely. On 20 November he sold it to Franz Brendel for the paltry sum of 500 thalers. [19]

That was a fateful decision, and probably an unwise one. The newspaper had been Schumann's main source of contact with the outside world and a vehicle for him to publicize his ideas. Most of his personal acquaintances were coworkers or correspondents for the *New Journal*. It also represented a symbolic as well as financial connection to his family's publishing enterprise. With the decision to sell the *New Journal*, Schumann put himself into a position of not only increased economic uncertainty but also enforced idleness. Although he hoped to fill the extra time with composing, it would prove difficult to do so.

Musical composition had never been a full-time occupation for Schumann. He would do it sporadically and very quickly, usually in the wake of a sudden inspiration. The long stretches of time between composing were often filled with other activities—reading, correcting proofs, worrying about his symptoms, and writing articles for and editing the *New Journal*. Now the balance had shifted to interminable moping over his illness. The loss of a verbal outlet through the newspaper may also have contributed to Schumann's despair. (Any real or symbolic loss usually makes a depressive disorder worse.)

Schumann's abandonment of his newspaper work could also explain in part why he found it necessary to write so much choral music as he grew older; he always needed to express himself with words. Although there is great merit in the music Schumann set to texts, it often sounds more pedantic and less inspired than the abstract, nonverbal music he composed for the piano, other instruments, and the orchestra during the last ten years of his life.

On 13 December 1844 the Schumanns moved into a first-floor apartment to the rear of Waisenhausstrasse 6. Books and clothing were unpacked, furniture rearranged, pianos brought in, and children acclimatized to their new habitat. One can imagine the chaos. Nevertheless, within eight days the composer "began working a little again," [20] and by 23 December he had completed one major piece of *Faust*, the Finale, a stirring ensemble of solo voices, chorus, and orchestra. Already he was thinking about a first performance of this work.

But Christmas, with its many anniversary associations, again proved to be insuperably stressful. Almost every day "the old man" (Wieck) came to the house, and reciprocal visits were expected over the holidays. On four consecutive days Schumann felt so exhausted that he did "nothing" in the daytime. But on the evening of 27 December he took a "solitary walk to Weber's grave," which seems to have rekindled old feelings of mourning and regret. The next day he had such a "violent nervous attack" that he decided to seek medical help.[21]

The first physician to be consulted in Dresden was Carl Gustav Carus (1779–1868), a relative of the Leipzig doctor who played a significant role in Schumann's adolescence, and probably the most prestigious physician who would ever treat him. Dr. Carus was one of Germany's famous "natural philosophers," men who combined scientific curiosity about specific subjects with a deep humanistic interest in the world at large. Not only had he studied the epidemiology of mental diseases and distinguished himself as an anatomist, a surgeon, and an obstetrician, but he had also written books about language and symbolism. In 1827, the Saxon Royal Family appointed him their court physician in Dresden. This is where Dr. Carus first heard and came to admire Clara's piano playing. Even before the Schumanns moved to Dresden, he invited them to his home and asked them to participate in musical functions. Obviously, the Schumanns' contact with "Hofrat Carus," as the household book calls him, was more than just a professional one, and he soon became their trusted friend, introduced them to other socialites in Dresden, and served as godfather to their next child, Julie (born 11 March 1845).

On 3 January 1845 Schumann spent the evening with Carus and told him about his eyes. (Nearsightedness, blurring of vision, and other ocular complaints recur throughout his medical history.) The doctor must have noticed how depressed Schumann was, or perhaps the composer himself asked for help, for Dr. Carus referred him to another physician, Dr. Carl Helbig, who practiced hypnosis. (Most likely Dr. Helbig was a follower of Franz Anton Mesmer (1734–1815), a charismatic Viennese physician who had popularized hypnotherapy throughout the continent.) The treatment, "magnetizing by Dr. Helbig," started in early January.[22] This does not mean that Dr. Carus stopped giving psychiatric advice to Schumann, and probably also obstetrical advice to Clara. A letter to Mendelssohn later in 1845 says, "Hofrat Carus recommends that I take early-morning walks, and these do me a lot of good."[23] He also mentioned the "bad effects of Carus' pills,"[24] but did not specify what they were.

Dr. Helbig's "magnetizing" seems to have helped Schumann at first. A great believer in magic, he bought himself an "amulet" against evil spirits, which he began wearing on 20 January.[25] All this in the context of trying to compose *Faust* music may have temporarily strengthened Schumann's unconscious identification with certain elements in Faust's character. But as might be expected with a treatment that emphasizes regression, Schumann seems to have become somewhat confused and disorganized.

We do not know how often or for how long Dr. Helbig put the composer into a trance, but one of the first things Schumann commented on after seeing this doctor was his daughter Marie's "dangerous illness." In his depressed, entranced, and probably somewhat bewildered state, he may have briefly confused the child's condition with his own ("Marie's improvement—my severe unwellness" he reported on 8 January).[26]

Another effect of Helbig's hypnotherapy may have been that it dissuaded Schumann from doing any further work on his music for the *Faust* scenes. Whether that was helpful is debatable. Schumann was repeatedly looking at other opera texts and discarding them, including the *Lohengrin* story (which Wagner would shortly use). When he did return to *Faust* a few years later, he composed music that is often thought to be inferior to what he had written prior to consulting Dr. Helbig. As we know from a letter Dr. Helbig later sent to Wasielewski, he held the opinion that "composing the epilogue for Goethe's Faust made such great demands on Robert Schumann that he fell into a diseased state while completing the end of this piece of music." Moreover, he seemed to believe that Schumann's entire involvement with musical composition may have been psychopathological. He compared it to an addiction, much like "a similar group of illnesses frequently observed among men such as accountants who are unduly occupied with one and the same thing (always calculating, etc.)." Helbig's advice was that Schumann should involve himself "at least occasionally with another sort of mental effort than music." His goal was to stop Schumann from "clinging to the musical ideas coursing through him."[27]

Not surprisingly, the composer rebelled vigorously against this notion and began presenting Helbig with a host of new complaints, new anyway to this particular doctor, who may not have realized that many of these symptoms—fear of death, heights, and medicines and poisons—had plagued Schumann during his earlier depressive episodes. Schumann also expressed a "fear of all metal objects, even keys."[28] This particular phobia may have been a reaction against Dr. Helbig: hypnotists in those days often used magnets, keys, and other metallic objects to transmit so-called animal magnetism to their patients, and Schumann probably viewed this intervention as a danger to his identity as a composer.

As he became more negativistic toward hypnotherapy, the doctor tried using medication, which his patient also refused. Finally he ordered "cold plunge-baths." According to Helbig, this treatment restored Schumann "to the point where he could again cling to his usual, one and only! occupation, composition."[29] That was certainly a favorable outcome, and the Schumanns retained the doctor as their family physician throughout their stay in Dresden.*

Schumann recovered gradually, but never completely, from the massive illness that coincided with (and may in part have been worsened by) his uprooting from Leipzig and resettlement in Dresden. His household books and travel diaries reveal emotional perturbations that continued after 1845. He had good weeks and bad weeks, productive months and unproductive ones, as he had for years. He remained always the keen observer of every symptom; he himself admitted to being a hypochondriac.

Schumann commented regularly on the weather in Dresden and how it affected him. A flood of the Elbe River in March was "frightful—the crucifix falls down," he wrote, as if he were trying to link a cosmic event to his personal experience. He continued to be profoundly impressed by birth and death anniversaries, especially those of important people. For example, on the anniversary of Beethoven's death in March, his diary reads, "sick in the evening—sleepless night," and the next day, "sick, half imaginary, half real." In addition, he was still prone to jealousy-induced anxiety. He complained of "nervous disease" on the day he received "news that Mendelssohn has written organ sonatas."[32] (Schumann himself was then studying counterpoint again and trying to compose for the organ.)

Clara's health, especially her annual pregnancies, was another source of disquietude. On 11 March 1845 their third daughter, Julie, was born, and only three months later Clara made a "strangely exciting announcement" of another possible pregnancy. Then she had a "worrisome fall," and Schumann had to have a mineral bath to calm down. Clara's "certainty" several weeks later that she was pregnant seemed to dissipate his anxiety, which may have been worsened by a guilty wish that this time she would miscarry.[33]

In the background of their relationship always loomed the conflict between Schumann's unwillingness to travel and his wife's desire to do so. The Beethoven Festival in Bonn in August 1845 brought all this to the surface again. Clara was planning to go there to perform. Schumann agreed to go,

---

*After Schumann's death in 1856, Dr. Helbig recommended that a plaster cast be made of his skull to compare it with those of Beethoven, Mozart, Haydn, and other composers, and also for "psychological considerations."[30] Accordingly, Professor Hermann Schaafhausen in 1885 actually removed Schumann's head from his body, which is buried in Bonn. His research showed the skull to be normal.[31] This line of investigation must be understood in the context of nineteenth-century science. The collection and study of various parts of the human body were deemed necessary to disprove erroneous conceptions about anatomy and physiology that had crept into clinical medicine as a result of edicts against human dissection. Many earlier textbooks contained information that was based on animal studies, since human cadavers were often unobtainable. The skulls of people of "genius" were of course considered prize specimens, just as today we regard their brains as of great value (in fact, Albert Einstein's brain was removed for scientific study). Incidentally, Schumann's skull is now nowhere to be found.

but the prospect of traveling produced many anxieties, as reported in the household book: "exhausted condition" (22 July), "bad anxiety at noon" (24 July), "crisis of decisions" (26 July), and for three days, "sick," "sick," and "very sick—preparing for the trip" (28, 29, and 30 July).[34]

They departed on schedule, but Schumann complained of such "anxiety and dizziness" that they decided not to go as far as Bonn, but to do some sightseeing in Weimar instead and then spend a few days in Zwickau. There Schumann felt "at home" immediately. A "cozy" visit with his brother made him feel "somewhat better." He noted 10 August as "the day my father died," suggesting another anniversary reaction. After reading his father's old publications, he felt "much better" and returned to Dresden, having been gone for less than a fortnight.[35] About a week later he started taking plunge-baths, and after two treatments Schumann felt well enough not only to celebrate Wieck's birthday but also to attend a performance of his *Spring Symphony*.[36]

Despite his physical and psychological complaints, Schumann was beginning to do some composing again, but it was mainly the sort of counterpoint exercises he had relied on, as a way of settling his mind, during earlier depressive episodes. He rented a special musical instrument, called a pedalpiano, that has an extra set of strings and hammers, making it easier to play fugues, and worked on Bach for a while. Schumann even proposed to the publisher Härtel in Leipzig "a really beautiful edition of J. S. Bach's Well-Tempered Clavier," but the project never materialized.[37] Instead, he wrote his own fugues. Julie's birth in March had given rise to a veritable "passion" for them.[38]

Before the trip with Clara, in August 1845, Schumann had composed several fugues based on the name BACH, and he published an impressive amount of contrapuntal work later that year and the next.* The six BACH *Fugues* in particular must have required enormous concentration, since not only are they based on a musical relationship between Bach's name and the notes of each fugue subject, but they also incorporate an intricate mathematical system, the so-called Bach numbers, which Bach himself had used to provide cohesion in his contrapuntal work.[39]

The psychiatrist Miriam Linder emphasized that Schumann concentrated on fugue writing in order to dispel his malaise and reorganize his thinking in 1845. If we consider that contrapuntal rules are often quite logical, and would, like a game of chess, strengthen one's belief in a rational system, this emphasis is correct. However, Dr. Linder went on to say that "Schumann's dependence on classical and polyphonic rules is an equivalent of the eccentricity of the schizophrenic who . . . tries to defend himself

---

Studies (op. 56), *Sketches* (op. 58), and the BACH *Fugues* (op. 60.)

against the danger of disintegration in his personality."[40] Schizophrenia is not a diagnosis one can apply to Schumann with a great deal of confidence. His illness in 1844 and 1845 resembles more closely a major depressive disorder, with some paranoid thinking (not unusual in illnesses of this sort) plus alternating agitation and apathy.*

An important point raised by Dr. Linder concerns the changes in Schumann's style of composing after 1845. She thought that she could detect "a disturbance of affective rapport in the music," as well as discontinuity in his compositions: "a new period, with another Schumann, has broken out."[41] These observations are debatable. In evaluating the quality of musical compositions, "affective rapport" depends as much on one's aesthetic taste as it does on clinical judgment. Surely many listeners would agree that some of Schumann's later music—for example, his *Manfred Overture* (op. 115) or his *Concerto for 'Cello and Orchestra* (op. 129)—communicates as much passion and excitement as anything he wrote earlier.

As for the question of discontinuity, we have observed sudden shifts in Schumann's work many times before, such as when he started to write only *lieder*, or focused almost exclusively on chamber music for a year. Schumann's creative style after his massive depression does not represent a distinctly "new period." In fact, no better example of *continuity* in his music can be adduced than the *Concerto for Piano and Orchestra* (op. 54). The first movement, we will remember, was written at age thirty-one, while the composer lived in Leipzig. Now in Dresden, four years later, he added an Intermezzo, *Andante grazioso*, and a Finale, *Allegro vivace*. The seam is flawless. There is no reduction of inventiveness, rhythmic vigor, thematic variability, or emotional expressiveness. It is one of Schumann's supreme achievements.

---

*Dr. Linder's impression of schizophrenia has been shared by a number of psychiatrists and will be discussed at greater length in Chapter XVII, along with the theory that Schumann may have had a slowly progressive organic brain disorder due possibly to an infectious process like syphilis or a circulatory disturbance.

XIII.
Plateau, 1845–1849

The five years Schumann spent in Dresden, 1845 to 1850, were by far his most musically productive. Not only did he complete a greater number and variety of projects there than at any other time, but he also realized at long last his desire to compose a German grand opera. At the same time he did some conducting—which never became his strong point—and helped organize musical events. Nevertheless, these were difficult years for him, with repeated bouts of illness. He often described himself as "melancholy," "exhausted," and "weak."[1] In his social behavior Schumann seems to have become more formal and more ritualized—Eusebian almost to a fault. Gone was the impetuous Florestan. Some people thought he was overly pedantic, even eccentric in his compulsive work habits and withdrawn demeanor.

Gone too was the critical Schumann. Although he continued to comment about music in his letters, he stopped his newspaper work completely. In April 1846 he was invited to take over the editorship of Leipzig's *Allgemeine Musikalische Zeitung*, but he declined. He wanted to conserve his limited energies for composing. The only thing of literary value that he published in Dresden, besides his vocal and choral music, was a five-page *Theaterbooklet* (1847–50) and his *Musical Rules for the Home and for Life*.[2]

As for Schumann's composing, it had come almost to a standstill in 1845. Counterpoint studies and the completion of his piano concerto were about the only things he had been able to do. In September he wrote Mendelssohn that "there is a great drum-beating inside of me, and trumpeting for several days (trumpet in C); I don't know what to make of it."[3] Whether this had anything to do with the C major symphony he was thinking of writing is hard to say. Schumann's household book reports "pounding in my head and anxiety state" on 8 September 1845, a sign perhaps that he was responding to the pulsations of his blood vessels, which might have been increased if he did have hypertension (as Dr. Brachmann had suspected in Leipzig). For the time being, the composer decided to take things easy. He enjoyed several visits with Richard Wagner in the fall, both at his and Clara's apartment and at Wagner's home. In addition, the Schumanns attended the premiere of Tannhäuser (Robert liked it more than Clara did) and, on 17 December, Wagner's first reading of his Lohengrin text, which must have reminded Schumann how quickly he was falling behind Wagner in terms of operatic work.

It was becoming more difficult for Schumann to be spontaneous with his composing. In what seems to have been a desire to wipe away traces of his wild youth, he even went so far as to revise some of the best music he had written before marrying Clara—the *Davidsbündler Dances* (op. 6), for example.

Suddenly before Christmas, however, he entered into a state of feverish excitement, a telltale sign that a new idea was emerging—this time it was a symphony. "Symphoniaca," he wrote in the household book on 14 December. Proceeding with the same alacrity that had characterized much of his earlier work, he completed the first movement in three days. On Christmas Day he reported "musical excitement in the last movement," and by 28 December his sketches for this symphony in C major were almost finished.[4] (The orchestration, as we will see shortly, took much longer.) Published in 1847 as Schumann's Second Symphony (op. 61), it was really the fifth symphony he had composed, if we count the early one in G minor and his 1841 "Sinfonietta."

Schumann's C major is not an easy symphony to play or to listen to, and he himself (in a letter written to a conductor in 1849) connected the work with his lingering melancholia:

> The symphony was written in December 1845 while I was still half sick; I feel as though one must hear that in it. Not until the last movement did I begin to feel well again; really, after the whole work was completed, I became better

again. But otherwise, as said before, it reminds me of a dark time. . . . That my melancholy bassoon in the Adagio, written into that place with special affection, did not escape you gave me the greatest pleasure.[5]

This wonderful Adagio, which Schumann mentioned so self-effacingly, is actually one of his finest achievements in symphonic writing. He created an arching, eight-measure theme of great beauty that resembles, in its melodic structure, the aria "Erbarme Dich" from J. S. Bach's *St. Matthew Passion*. It is played first by the strings, then repeated in counterpoint by the oboe and bassoon. (When Brahms later analyzed this movement, he discovered a reference to Bach's *Musical Offering*.[6])

Schumann's progress as a symphonist, and some of the trouble he would have in his future career, stemmed in part from an important new relationship that had sprung up in Dresden. Ferdinand Hiller (1811–1885), a gifted composer and expert conductor (who in 1843 substituted for Mendelssohn at the Gewandhaus) had also moved to Dresden. He was in the process of organizing a series of concerts that were advertised to "include symphonies, overtures, and other large ensemble pieces of the classical masters, as well as significant compositions from the newer and newest era."[7] Hiller seems to have had an affinity for the introverted Schumann.* Soon there was talk about how Robert and Clara might participate in the orchestral concerts.

Hiller respected Schumann as a composer. He also must have realized that there would be little competition with him as co-conductor of the orchestra. Hiller was by far the better leader and administrator, and both Schumanns saw in him a potential ally in their effort to upgrade musical performances in Dresden, a city that catered much more to the visual arts and the theater. (Generally rather intolerant of the Dresden musicians outside her father's circle, Clara had found that Hiller was "the only one with whom one can have a decent talk about music"[9]) Thus Hiller soon came to play a role somewhat analogous to Mendelssohn's in Leipzig. He was able to coax Schumann out of his shell by encouraging his participation in concerts, some of which featured Clara as a pianist. On 4 December 1845, for example, Hiller and Clara appeared together for the world premiere of Schumann's new A minor Piano Concerto.

After his feverish work at the end of 1845, 1846 stands out as Schumann's most fallow year. It began with a trip to Leipzig, where Clara performed his piano concerto at the Gewandhaus, with Niels Gade conducting. After returning to Dresden, Schumann so "tortured" himself making changes in the score of the concerto that he had to see Dr. Carus. A few days later

---

*He is said to have welcomed Schumann to Dresden with the remark "It's good to have you here; now we can be silent together."[8]

he got into an "argument" with the sculptor Ernst Rietschel, who was engaged to do a double portrait of him and Clara on a bas-relief medallion (now located at the Robert Schumann House in Zwickau). Hiller thought that Clara's profile should be in front of her husband's, but Schumann wanted it the other way. It took a week of sitting for the sculptor before the job was finished to everyone's satisfaction. [10]

Then, in February, Schumann interrupted the work on his new symphony to read Dante's *Divine Comedy* and the second part of Goethe's *Faust*. This caused a great deal of "head-excitement" (*Kopfaufregung*), as Schumann called it, [11] complicated by his anxiety over the beginning of Clara's labor pains. Their fourth child and first son, Emil, was born two days later. *

Four days after the baby's birth, Schumann started to orchestrate his symphony, but he made only "small progressive steps" because of innumerable distractions. [12] (The first movement did not get finished until May, and the entire symphony was completely orchestrated only by the end of the year.) In the household book Schumann mentioned the "melancholic weather" and his own "melancholia." Sometimes he felt "very nervously exhausted" (*angegriffen*). In March, when reporting that he felt "very unwell," he used the untranslatable term *Kopfangegriffenheit*, which means something like "head weariness" or "head affliction." Apparently his head was spinning, a problem reminiscent of his post-drinking ailments in earlier years. Also in March he mentioned a new and puzzling symptom: "the organ of hearing peculiarly out-of-tune" (*merkwürdige Verstimmung des Gehörorgans*). [13]

Schumann mentioned the ear problem only once that entire year, but it recurred in Düsseldorf, close to the approach of his psychosis. It seems to have been a transient symptom, but a very frightening one, which Clara later described as "constant singing and rushing [*Brausen*] in his ears, every noise would turn into a tone." [14] That would certainly be a distressing experience for a musician, especially an overwrought composer attempting to orchestrate a symphony. (Dr. Helbig's letter to Wasielewski mixes the auditory complaint with all of Schumann's other symptoms in a confusing way.)

There are several possible causes of this type of hearing disorder, the most common one being a middle-ear infection. Another possibility is acute labyrinthitis ("Meniere's Disease"), an extremely unpleasant condition produced by swelling of the soft tissues within the bony ear canals. Patients afflicted with this disease typically complain of severe dizziness, headaches, and physical malaise. Schumann had all of these symptoms. Moreover, his

---

*Emil Schumann was a sickly child whose failure to thrive and sudden death at sixteen months was a source of great distress to his parents. There is no record of what his illness was, but the high incidence of tuberculosis among Schumann's offspring must be kept in mind.

auditory complaint of "peculiarly out-of-tune" hearing resembles closely the characteristic auditory *distortions* of Meniere's Disease. (Unlike Beethoven, who had a far more serious hearing problem, Schumann did not go deaf.)

Two days after his acute ear attack, Schumann felt a little better. He decided to stop smoking and "lazed about for a while."[15] Then, on 10 March, the day before Julie's birthday, he again complained of nervous exhaustion (*"Sehr angegriffen"*). After that, he felt "brighter" (12 March) and "better" (13–15 March). "Putting my mind completely to rest is helpful for once."[16] To accomplish this, he took another therapeutic water bath. The improvement persisted until the end of the month, when he reported "in the evening, stupid melancholia."[17]

Not until May did Schumann have another spell of "severe dizziness," and then without any auditory disturbance.[18] Clara had gone to Leipzig over the Easter holiday (12–13 April) for a performance with Jenny Lind, the famous Swedish soprano, and Mendelssohn. It was after this brief separation that Schumann began for the first time to use "F" to denote sexual intercourse, suggesting that part of the stress he was experiencing may have come from his marital relationship.

As Schumann grew more accustomed to his sick role, one that was modeled to a certain extent after his invalid father, he described his disease as "hypochondria." Clara too complained a good deal about her health in 1846,* so the term "hypochondria of a married couple," mentioned in the household book, certainly may have been an appropriate one.[20] They took several brief vacations with the hope of recuperating, but often these trips involved as many disruptions as life in Dresden.

After a few days in Maxen, for example, the rural suburb where their friends the Serres lived, Schumann began working "assiduously" on his C major Symphony, only to be interrupted by a visit that evening from Wieck. Although the next day he complained of "always severe dizziness," he was able to receive other visitors, including the Dresden poet and painter Robert Reinick, with whom he discussed opera texts. More visitors arrived shortly: "old Kuntsch from Zwickau" and Clara's mother. There was much partying; Schumann "didn't feel well" and spent an "agitated night." He summed it up as "living in the country with some hypochondria."[21]

There being no physician available in Maxen, Schumann turned for

---

*She had "breast pain" in May,[19] and in November she was so sick that she actually canceled a concert, which was highly unusual for her.

advice to a Captain Noël (evidently a friend of Major Serre), who practiced phrenology, the art of making a psychological diagnosis by palpating the skull. The results of the phrenological examination, which Schumann recorded in his travel diary, included "organs of foresight well developed, fearfulness which even stands in the way of my good fortune . . . ambition . . . love of truth, great candor . . . thoroughly kind-hearted, modesty, determination."[22]

Noël's examination, which was probably as confusing as the one Schumann had requested years earlier from Herr Portius (see p. 96), may have baffled him. "In the afternoon played chess with myself and fainted," he wrote.[23] This sounds somewhat like the dissociated states he experienced as a youth while wandering through the park in Leipzig. Soon he was so upset that he couldn't keep his eyes off an old castle along the Elbe River, which was used as an insane asylum.*

What had been intended as a working vacation obviously was not helping Schumann. Clara too was unhappy. She had become pregnant again. Thus they decided to go to Norderney, the largest of the Frisian Islands off Germany's northern coast. Norderney has a warm climate during the summer, healthful drinking water, and excellent facilities for hot and cold bathing.

The Schumanns stayed there a little over one month, from 15 July to 21 August, in a guest house overlooking the beach. Here Clara had a miscarriage. Schumann's diary doesn't tell us whether they anticipated (or perhaps even desired) this to happen. He mentions that Clara preceded him to the baths because he had a cold. Although he first reported that bathing had a "good effect" on her, she suddenly became "very unwell" and in the middle of the night had to be seen by Norderney's resident physician, John Paul Bluhm.[25] We do not know what he prescribed for her, but we do know that she was no longer pregnant after his "treatment." (Her next baby did not arrive until 20 January 1848.)

Schumann seems to have benefited from the medically supervised bathing. He immersed himself over two dozen times and meticulously recorded both the air and the water temperature for each bath. He felt bored, however: "boredom," "ghastly boredom," and "unbearable boredom" were recurring daily complaints from 13 to 17 August.[26] He undoubtedly wanted to

---

*This asylum, called Sonnenstein, was considered a model institution and training center. (The American psychiatrist Pliny Earle called it "the morning sun of a new day in the sphere of insanity in Germany."[24]) One reason for its favorable statistics was that incurable "inmates," as they were called, were customarily transferred out, to prisons until 1829, and thereafter to the much larger asylum in Colditz, where Schumann as a teenager got his first taste of such places.

return to Dresden and get back to work. (On 8 July 1846 Mendelssohn had given Schumann a new copy of Immerman's *Tristan und Isolde*, a story that had interested Schumann for years. His eagerness to compose an opera in Dresden was thus intensified.)

Clara, however, wanted first to give a concert. She had attracted attention to herself by registering at the fashionable resort as "the honorable chamber music virtuoso of His Majesty, the Emperor of Austria." (Robert signed simply "Dr. Schumann.") Jenny Lind also visited Norderney that summer, and soon these prominent women were invited to appear in public. We know from a letter Schumann mailed on 2 August that Clara was planning a concert even before she had fully recovered from her miscarriage.[27] Because of the heat (or perhaps the program), her concert was poorly attended. Clara performed some short pieces by Schumann, sandwiched between selections from the music of Mendelssohn, Scarlatti, and other composers who were better known than her husband. A week later they returned to Dresden.

Schumann continued his bathing, in the Elbe River. Soon he felt so much improved that he began working on the C major Symphony again. Clara too was in the mood for composing, and wrote a Piano Trio (op. 17). Both of them were cheered when the influential Viennese music critic Eduard Hanslick came to see them at the end of August.* For a while Schumann even toyed with the idea of becoming involved in music criticism again.[28]

In the middle of September the Schumanns moved into a new and more spacious apartment, at Reitbahnstrasse 20. Only once did he mention any symptoms of "nervous excitement" while living there, just before Richard Wagner visited in late September. Schumann made steady progress in orchestrating the symphony, but he complained that his "joy was dampened somewhat" when Ferdinand Hiller suggested some corrections. These evidently gave Schumann a headache.[29]

Clara too was beginning to feel much better, and she went briefly to Leipzig to perform Beethoven's G major Concerto at the Gewandhaus. (For the first time she added two of her own cadenzas.) Schumann himself traveled to Leipzig twice for performances of his new symphony. (The premiere, on 5 November, led to an unflattering review and criticism of Mendelssohn's

---

* Hanslick had written a glowing review of *Paradise and the Peri* earlier that year, and Schumann had invited him to Dresden. They became friends and Hanslick continued to be one of Schumann's staunchest supporters. (Later he became an advocate of Brahms's music as well.) Wagner thoroughly disliked Hanslick and caricatured him as "Beckmesser" (first called "Hans Lick") in his opera *Die Meistersinger*.

conducting.) But there was no recurrence of psychiatric symptoms. The "hypochondria of a married couple" seems to have temporarily abated.

Not until the end of 1846 did Schumann register any significant distress. He had been dislodged once more, this time to accompany his wife to Vienna, and his creative work as usual came to a grinding halt.

Their motivation for renewed travel was mixed. Both he and Clara had friends in Vienna, but Schumann recalled being miserable there during his earlier stay and did not want to risk another trip. For her part, Clara felt it was important to seek career opportunities abroad. Dresden had disappointed her. Wieck, on whose support she had always counted, was in the process of promoting a competing but far less talented daughter, Marie, and there may have been a touch of sibling rivalry when Clara described Marie's playing as "always mechanical, always joyless . . . very deficient in strength and endurance."*[30]

On 24 November the Schumanns, with their two older children in tow, embarked on their tour, which was to last nearly five months. At first they complained very little. He seems to have tolerated his second visit to Vienna much better than the first. But for Clara it was a disappointment. She was having pain in her arm. In addition, her recitals were poorly attended and not well reviewed. Even when joined on stage by the Russian pianist Anton Rubinstein, she barely produced sufficient income to cover her expenses. "I found none of the enthusiasm of 9 years ago," wrote Clara, who soon decided that she and Vienna were not a good match and that her husband would not like it there "in the long run."[31] At her third concert, planned for 19 December, Schumann was to conduct his Piano Concerto and the *Spring* Symphony. But Clara asked that it be postponed. She was sick, and so was he, with what he called a "diplomatic indisposition" (he probably wanted to get out of his obligation to perform).[32]

Christmas was an ordeal. "Robert and I could give each other nothing," Clara wrote, "since we hadn't earned a thing as yet! I felt truly sad in my inmost heart. It was the first Christmas that I not only gave my dear Robert no joy, but had to depress him." The New Year's holiday was worse. Clara, feeling totally defeated, wrote that she was "in such a mood as to swear never to give another concert in my life. . . . I pity poor Robert, who is now also involved in this disagreeable pursuit of concerts."[33]

---

*Wieck chose to come to Vienna while the Schumanns were there, to promote yet another new protégé, the singer Minna Schulz, whom he considered his adopted daughter.

Their rescheduled performance took place on 1 January 1847, and it was a fiasco. "The applause was cool and obviously intended only for Clara," reported their friend Hanslick.[34] After the concert Schumann was speechless. A further debt of nearly 100 gulden had been incurred, and when he finally managed to speak, it was to utter a tragic prophecy—"Calm yourself, Clara, ten years from now all this will be different."[35]

The final concert was rescued by Jenny Lind. "She herself asked to sing in our concert on the 10th," recorded Schumann, who observed how "Clara glows and adores" the singer.[36] And well she might have, for thanks to Jenny Lind's participation, this one concert alone earned enough money to pay for the Schumanns' entire trip. But the proud Clara felt guilty about it. "I couldn't defend myself against the most bitter feeling that one song by Lind accomplished what I, with all my playing, did not."[37] A "farewell matinee" in their private quarters was reassuring. Schumann's A major String Quartet was performed by the famed Hellmesberger Quartet, and Clara played her own newly composed Piano Trio.

On the return to Saxony, there was one concert in Brno (Brünn) and two in Prague. It gave Clara "much pleasure" when after a successful performance of his piano concerto Schumann was asked to take a bow. "He behaved so very comically on stage, I almost had to shove him out because the audience wouldn't stop calling for him."[38]

Their next stop, after resting for only a week in Dresden, was Berlin. Schumann had been invited to conduct his *Paradise and the Peri*, and he displayed his usual ineptness on the podium. From Clara's description of the first rehearsal, we learn that after he was introduced by the regular conductor he "mutely took a bow without speaking to the assembled musicians and singers." After the three-hour rehearsal Schumann seemed "very tired," and Clara tried to help by directing from the piano, to the astonishment of the regular conductor. Within twenty-four hours the musicians were so dissatisfied and hostile that some of the soloists tried to back out. Schumann was "most out of sorts" and wanted to postpone the performance or not conduct at all. The rehearsal continued to go badly, and, to Clara's horror, one of the regular conductors tried unsuccessfully to instruct her husband "how and where to conduct . . . how he ought to stand while conducting."[39]

The following day Schumann diplomatically went to bed and let his wife coach the singers. But for the performance, on 17 February, "he lost all his fear and courageously stepped to the podium." All went well until the third part of his oratorio, when "three of the soloists became totally lost." Clara felt like "sinking into the ground."[40]

Schumann's debacle in Berlin suggests that neither he nor Clara had sufficiently good judgment to realize that he had profound limitations as a performing musician. This had been amply demonstrated years earlier, when he had defaulted as a pianist. Yet a certain pretense needed to be maintained. How much this denial of reality reflected a worsening of his mental illness is difficult to say. Schumann's peculiar shyness, his inhibited speech, his performance anxiety, and his social awkwardness were longstanding character traits, tolerated by those who knew him well but not by those who were critical of him or demanded more than he was capable of giving. Thus under stress he was at his worst.*

Berlin was Mendelssohn's territory, and both Schumann and his wife were probably overly anxious to make a good impression there. Clara in particular hoped to use the Prussian capital as a base of future operations. She made friends with Fanny Mendelssohn, the composer's sister, and thought seriously of moving there. (Clara's mother also lived in Berlin.) It was difficult for her, though, with Schumann accompanying her, to make a good impression in Berlin's courtly circles.† Clara's diary contains a specific example. She once was asked to play in Count Redern's mansion for what she described as "the most formal world including the King, the Prince of Prussia, the Duke of Mecklenburg, and others." It was customary those days for the nobility to treat musicians condescendingly, like servants. Clara said that she "did not feel at all comfortable among these many royal personages." At the same time, she could not bring herself to "associate with the artists awaiting their turn in an antechamber; it stirs my indignation." So she simply played and then rejoined the remaining guests, including her husband, who apparently felt so ill at ease that he didn't say a word.[41]

At the end of March 1847 they returned to Dresden, disillusioned about living elsewhere but prepared to console each other and cope as best they could with the vicissitudes of family life. Clara began making a piano transcription of her husband's C major Symphony, but she soon became pregnant again, and Schumann had to complete the work. Then he finally turned in earnest to a long-delayed project, composing an opera.

When it came to opera, Schumann was handicapped in several ways. First, he was in conflict over the suitability of the text. He had been searching for a perfect subject for years. A very long list of stories, ranging from

---

*It may be worth noting that later that same year he was observed to conduct with quite sufficient energy in Zwickau. It was during a music festival held in his honor; the orchestra was not nearly as capable, or as demanding, as the one in Berlin; and the music they played was familiar.

†The Schumanns' Saxon dialect, often a subject for ridicule, may have been an additional handicap.

Hamlet to *Tristan und Isolde*, can be culled from his diaries and project books. He would flirt with each new text, sometimes even start setting one to music, only to change his mind, convert the project into something else, or drop it entirely. Basic to this conflict seems to have been his aspiration as a writer, reflecting no doubt the primary identification he had made with his father. As a newspaper editor, Schumann had capitalized on this identification. Now he felt called on to perfect it by writing a libretto. Also, it is possible that deeper in his psyche there was lingering the inhibitory influence of his aria-singing mother, the woman who had first stimulated and then thwarted his earliest musical development. That Schumann finally chose to glorify womanhood when he composed his opera may be important in this respect.

Another source of conflict probably was the political climate in prerevolutionary Germany. Richard Wagner and a number of other German composers were striving to achieve a nationalistic opera style at this time, one that could easily be distinguished from the Italian influence prevailing in most European theaters. The idea of a Germanic opera certainly appealed to Schumann, and we know that he discussed it with Wagner. But deep down Schumann was no nationalist, as we can surmise from his early diatribe against German patriotism (see p. 39). He often received visitors from abroad, including the United States, and he expressed delight when he heard that *Paradise and the Peri* had been performed in New York.[42] Moreover, both he and Clara thought seriously about visiting, and perhaps even settling one day, in London.

Schumann was often drawn to potential opera subjects that were *not* truly Germanic. For example, before returning to Dresden in 1847, he had decided to compose an opera based on the story of Mazeppa, a seventeenth-century Cossack hero who fought for Russia. It would have been a dramatic work (Liszt and Tchaikovsky both later composed music on the subject), filled with violent and erotic scenes.[*] Schumann even went so far as to ask his friend Robert Reinick to write a libretto for the story. But then he changed his mind in favor of a much tamer and more feminine theme, that of Genoveva (St. Genevieve).

His motives for finally deciding on *Genoveva* are not entirely clear. He made the decision when Clara became pregnant again in 1847, which may be significant. We know from a letter Schumann sent Reinick that Clara was fond of the story and approved of her husband's rendering of the text.[43]

---

[*]Mazeppa is seduced by a woman whose jealous husband strips him, ties him onto the back of a wild horse, and sends him into the Polish wilderness to die. There he is rescued by cossacks, who ask him to be their leader in fighting on the side of Russia in a war against Sweden. Mazeppa accepts. In victory he is honored and personally befriended by the czar, whom he then betrays in favor of the enemy.

As will become apparent, his Genoveva text—an adventure-seeking husband leaving his castle while his demure wife remains obediently at home—is almost an exact reversal of Schumann's marriage. Thus we might speculate that it was his conscious desire to honor Clara (and perhaps his unconscious desire to punish her, for in the story the husband condemns his wife to death) that led him to turn his one and only grand opera into a paean to womanly virtue.

But Schumann's feelings about his wife were obviously not his only motivation. He knew perfectly well that *Genoveva* was a popular subject in Germany at the time, and that by switching to it he might be able to spare himself some of the political repercussions that could ensue from an opera about the Slavic Mazeppa. From a theatrical point of view, however, the switch was unfortunate.* Operas about women tend to do badly at the box-office. Even Beethoven had to admit this when he recast *Leonora* as *Fidelio*. (There are exceptions, of course—*Aida*, *Carmen*, *Tosca*, and *Manon*, for example—but they are hardly saintly women.)

Two different versions of the St. Genevieve legend were available in Germany, one by the venerable Shakespeare scholar Ludwig Tieck (1773–1853), the other by a younger poet, Friedrich Hebbel (1813–1863), whom Schumann greatly admired. His first step was to ask Reinick again to do the libretto, but after a few false starts they disagreed and he invited Hebbel to Dresden, hoping they could work together on the opera. When Hebbel arrived in July 1847, he found Schumann so inarticulate and nondirective† that a true collaboration proved to be impossible. Finally Schumann wrote his own libretto, a task that occupied him for most of the rest of the year. In essence, the story is as follows:

> Siegfried, a crusader, leaves his castle to go to war. He asks Golo, his trusted friend, to watch over his wife, Genoveva. Fearful and lonely, she invites Golo to comfort her by singing of her absent husband. The song excites both of them, and Golo takes advantage of Genoveva by trying to force himself on her. She repulses him with insults, calling him a bastard. Humiliated and vengeful, Golo searches out Siegfried, who has been wounded in battle, and tells him that his wife has been unfaithful. Siegfried believes him and condemns her to death. After returning to his castle, however, he finds that Genoveva is innocent after all, and that his friend has betrayed him. Golo is banished and dies. The opera ends happily, with the lovers reunited and the populace rejoicing.

---

* Schumann's *Genoveva* has never been considered a great success. But we must remember that it was his first opera. Even acknowledged masters of the theater—Donizetti, Rossini, Verdi, Wagner, Puccini—were unlucky with their initial efforts.
† He was depressed. Emil, his only son, had just died.

In the popular folk legend, Genoveva is spared the executioner's ax but must roam the forests in solitude, isolated from all human contact and befriended only by animals. Perhaps that unhappy outcome frightened Schumann. He weakened the plot by prettifying the ending of his opera. In addition, he also sentimentalized it by framing many scenes in a sort of religious tableau, in accordance with the earlier, more romantic, Tieck version.* (We must not forget that Schumann was trying to make a name for himself in Dresden, which was the Catholic capital of a predominantly Lutheran province.)

The overture to *Genoveva* is superb, one of Schumann's best orchestral compositions, and it is still performed today. He sketched it in just five days (1–5 April 1847) while in the heat of inspiration, having not as yet begun to grapple with the difficult libretto. But the rest of the opera seems anticlimactic. Schumann had delayed composing the music until after Christmas—the intervening distractions will be mentioned shortly—and much of the excitement he expressed in the overture seems to have been dissipated.

To be sure, *Genoveva* has glorious moments. The opening chorale, a prayer in the style of Bach, is very moving. Siegfried's interactions with his wife are more stately than erotic, and Golo never sounds as villainous as one would expect. Even his attempted rape in the second act seems rather tepid. The most dramatic musical parts are the choruses involving a rebellion by the serfs in Siegfried's castle, and one of the great moments is Genoveva's aria in Act 4, "My last hope is fading."

The effectiveness of *Genoveva* depends, of course, on its interpretation and staging, which is difficult because so much of the action is internal: Schumann's characters tend to talk about what they feel, rather than dramatize their behavior. He used leitmotifs to interconnect the various scenes, but unlike Wagner's they are quite subtle and not always easy to identify. Nor did he differentiate the main characters very well by assigning to them distinctive ways of singing.

While Schumann was still working on the libretto for *Genoveva*, he became very "enthusiastic" about Weber's opera *Euryanthe*, which he heard in Dresden.[45] It has been suggested that he used *Euryanthe* as a model, especially in writing the orchestral interludes, and by including a magic mirror scene (in Act 3).[46] *Genoveva* also contains references to some of Schu-

---

*Schumann once invited Richard Wagner to hear him read the libretto he had written for *Genoveva*. This acerbic critic, who would flare up violently if anyone dared to comment negatively on his own opera texts, had the following to say: "I called [Schumann's] attention to the big mistakes and suggested necessary changes, and thus I discovered how things go with this peculiar man. He would only allow me to be carried away by his work; any interference with his enthusiasm would be warded off with touchy obstinacy."[44]

mann's other favorite operas, *Don Giovanni*, for example. (In addition, with its languid, almost motionless music, it seems to anticipate Debussy's opera *Pelléas et Mélisande*.)

Schumann approached the composition of *Genoveva* in a very orderly and well-organized fashion, something one would not expect had his mental capacity been declining. He counted the bar numbers and calculated the timing exactly. He wanted the opera to last no more than three hours, including the pauses. He also wrote out the ranges of the soloists, planning these rather conservatively to avoid extremes. His autograph score has numerous markings and corrections in brown crayon and red ink, showing that he was a careful proofreader. He undoubtedly made many passes through the score before he was satisfied with it.[47]

He also worked with great celerity, finishing the first act (both sketches and orchestration) in less than a month, by which time he had already started to sketch the second act. Act 3 was sketched in one week, and the final act took only twelve days to sketch. By 4 August—only nine months after he started *Genoveva*—the orchestration of the final act was complete.

Even more astonishing is that during much of the time while Schumann was planning his opera, he and Clara had to face personal bereavements that left them in a state of mourning. (This accounts for some of the delays between the composition of the text and that of the music.) First came the unexpected death, on 14 May 1847, of Fanny Mendelssohn, who collapsed suddenly while playing the piano and died within four hours, apparently of a brain hemorrhage, at age forty-two. Fanny's death was not only frightening but also very painful for Clara, who had felt the beginning of a close friendship with her during the recent visit in Berlin. Next came the death of Emil, who was barely sixteen months old. Clara was again pregnant when Emil died, on 22 June 1847, and for a long time she felt "unwell and terribly weak."[48] Although their son's death was difficult for the Schumanns, it did not come as a shock, for he had been sickly from birth.

They were not prepared, though, for the death of Felix Mendelssohn. This was the worst blow of all. When news of his sudden collapse reached Dresden on 1 November, Clara reported "great terror."[49] He had been bleeding intracranially, probably from a ruptured aneurysm, and died after a few days of agonizing pain and mental confusion.[50] Schumann rushed off (without Clara) to Leipzig, first of all to consult his friend Dr. Reuter and then to attend the funeral. (In view of Reuter's earlier verdict of an "apoplectic constitution," not to mention Schumann's old fear of following in his sister Emilie's footsteps, the news about Mendelssohn must have been shattering.) He tried to calm himself by viewing and describing his friend's body:

The noble corpse—his forehead—the mouth—surrounded by a smile—he resembles a glorious warrior, like a victor—about 20 years older than when he was alive—two heavily engorged blood-vessels stand out on his brow.[51]

After returning from the funeral, Schumann spoke "incessantly" about Mendelssohn.[52] He was flooded with memories of their past friendship and for some time worried fearfully that he would die in just the same way.

Schumann also stopped his work on *Genoveva* several times to compose other things. He wrote two Piano Trios (opp. 63 and 80) in 1847 and made considerable progress on his *Scenes from Faust*. A more personal interruption occurred on 20 January 1848: the birth of another son, whom they named Ludwig in memory of another great friend of Schumann's, Ludwig Schunke.

Schumann reported that he often felt "very joyful" while composing his opera, a feeling that seems to have persisted even once he completed it.[53] A new cycle of creative abundance was beginning, one that would produce a torrent of new compositions. The reasons for this upswing are complex. Internally there seems to have been another shift in Schumann's mood. Having been depressed and underproductive for so long, he was now moving into a phase of happy overwork that would last several years. Some very important external events were also affecting his behavior. One of these was the death of his only remaining brother, Carl Schumann, in 1849.* This left Robert as the sole survivor of his generation and may have convinced him that time was running out. He probably felt that unless he continued to work "diligently" (*fleissig*) his reputation as a serious composer, which had only recently consolidated, might again be challenged.

The other external event that deeply influenced Schumann's work pattern was the revolution of 1848–1849, which swept over Germany and forced him to flee from Dresden. The uprisings began in France and spread quickly to other states, where disenfranchised citizens, displaced laborers, and frustrated students were joining together to confront the entrenched aristocracies and demanding more freedom. Because Prussia and Austria were at that time competing for control over all the other German-speaking

---

* Carl knew he was dying and had sent a farewell letter to Schumann in March 1849.[54] Taken to Carlsbad for bloodletting, Carl expired there. His wife, who took the corpse back to Germany, wrote about "attacks which raised the fear of paralysis." Carl's "face showed how he was fighting, but he couldn't speak and fell over on his right side," apparently having suffered a stroke.[55]

states, a situation of dangerous instability had arisen. Fierce fighting broke out in Vienna in 1848, and Metternich was forced to resign. There was chaos in Berlin. "Enormous political excitement," says Schumann's household book.[56] Thousands of people had been killed. Finally the king of Prussia capitulated to the liberal elements and announced that he would allow his country to enter a confederation with the other German states. An elected National Assembly began meeting in May but got nowhere because of the absence of democratic traditions. There was not even a shared religion that could serve to unite the different states. Thus a governmental structure had to be designed along economic and political lines, and this led to endless debates about general principles. The frustrated Assembly finally appointed a regent, who, it was hoped, might be able to rule autocratically. But this appointee had no power, and the confederation collapsed. Rioting flared up anew, troops re-entered the cities, and Germany continued to be polarized.

Schumann's sympathies lay generally with those who wished to see Germany united under a federal government. But unlike Wagner, he feared violence too much to take any active part in the revolution. Schumann did write a few patriotic songs. In 1847 he composed "Nightwatch of the Confederacy," "Freedom Song," and "Battle Song," all for unaccompanied male chorus. These were followed in 1848 by "To the Weapons," "Black-Red-Gold," and another "Freedom Song." Schumann sensed, correctly, that "in the long run this politically rather inactive Dresden will be unable to withstand the raging surf."[57] Wanting to get away before the shooting started, he and Clara explored possibilities for moving to another city, but no offers for him to conduct or teach elsewhere seemed to be forthcoming. "Vienna and Berlin are not cities for a musician right now," Schumann wrote to the music historian Gustav Nottebohm.[58] Leipzig too had nothing to offer.*

Thus, somewhat reluctantly it seems, Schumann began a new career in Dresden as conductor and teacher. First he organized a choral society, the *Verein für Chorgesang*, which met on an irregular basis.[59] Then he accepted two private students for music lessons. Finally he agreed to take over a job that Ferdinand Hiller had recently vacated, as leader of a male chorus called *Liedertafel*. (Hiller was now living in Düsseldorf, where he was director of the orchestra and chorus, another position he later passed on to Schumann.) The *Liedertafel* provided no salary, but it gave Schumann the opportunity to perform his own choral compositions, which could then be published for profit. For example, his patriotic *Three Songs for Male Chorus* (op. 62) brought Schumann 56 thalers.

---

*When Niels Gade resigned the Gewandhaus directorship in 1848, Julius Rietz, a capable administrator and conductor but hardly a notable composer, was appointed to this position, which Schumann still hoped to hold.

All these activities conflicted with his creative work. He complained very little in 1848, but his friends often observed that he seemed tired and distracted.[60] Serious economic problems were pressing him. To pay his taxes that year, Schumann had had to ask his brother Carl to return part of the money he had invested in the family publishing business. (After Carl's death his wife took the business over.) Clara became pregnant yet again in 1848, which was an additional strain. She did no teaching that year, and the few concerts she could give during the revolution were mainly charity events, for the relief of victims of this upheaval.

In 1849 fighting actually broke out in Dresden. Alarmed by the sound of shooting and of bells ringing in all the towers, the Schumanns hid in the house. The next day they tried to go downtown, only to find that the pavements and sewers had been torn up to make barricades which blocked all traffic. Revolutionaries, armed with scythes, were everywhere—"the greatest anarchy," wrote Clara.[61]

In trying to maintain order, the royalists called in trigger-happy Prussian troops. The result was carnage. "In walking through the town," Clara said, "we had to view the frightful spectacle of 14 corpses lying in the hospital courtyard. They had been killed the day before and prepared for public exhibition in the most gruesome manner. . . . The tension was dreadful."[62]

Schumann's behavior under these stressful conditions, as well as Clara's, again demonstrates a role reversal: he became passive and meekly submissive and she performed heroically. When volunteers came to their neighborhood looking for men who could serve in the militia, Schumann ran into the house to hide. Clara, convinced that they "wanted to take him," made some excuses. After the coast was clear, the two of them, with their oldest daughter Marie, ran to the train station and escaped. (Clara had quickly made arrangements for the housekeeper to stay with the other children.)

Their flight took them by train to Mügeln (twelve kilometers) and then on foot (two kilometers) to another village, where they stopped to eat and to wait for news. "The next train did not bring anything reassuring," wrote Clara. "One constantly heard cannons thundering, and with the children still in the city my anxiety that entire day was horrendous." She wanted to go back, but "since word had spread that the insurgents were searching for men able to bear arms and forcing them to participate in the fighting," they stayed overnight in Maxen, with their friends Major and Frau Serre.[63]

Two days later at 3 A.M., Clara, who was nearly seven months pregnant, returned to Dresden, accompanied by two other women. They walked about four kilometers "across the fields, under continuous cannonading," encountering scythe-armed rebels along the way. She made it to their house, where, as she wrote, "I found the children still asleep, tore them out of their beds immediately, had them dressed, packed a few important items, and in one hour we were together again, outside in the fields."[64]

Modestly, Clara added that "my poor Robert had also spent some anxiety-filled hours, thus was doubly happy now."[65] In fact, as we shall see, Schumann had managed his anxieties by jotting down the main events of each day in his diary and withdrawing into a strange dissociative rapture that allowed him to go right ahead with his creative work.

When there was a lull in the fighting Schumann did venture into Dresden with Clara, but only briefly, to see how her father was doing. "It's barely possible to give a picture of such devastation," she wrote, "thousands of holes in the houses from cannon-fire, entire slabs of wall collapsed, the old opera house completely burned down, as well as three beautiful homes in the Zwingerstrasse. . . . It's terrible to look at this. . . . How many innocent victims have been killed, hit by shells inside their rooms, etc., etc." The city, "swarming with Prussians, who lie around on straw in the old market-place," was declared to be in a state of siege. Proclamations had been posted to round up agitators. Richard Wagner, an active participant in the revolution, had escaped to Liszt's house in Weimar.[66]

The Schumanns elected to remain close to home, but not on the Serre estate, which had become overcrowded with refugees. On 11 May they moved to a tiny pastoral village, Kreischa, where Robert maintained his hermetic concealment for the rest of the month. Clara, with her amazing ability to endure these many environmental upheavals, shielded him constantly from further interruptions so that he could continue composing. Schumann was working on his beautiful *Song Album for the Young* (op. 79). Then he embarked on *Five Hunting Songs* (op. 137) for double male chorus and four horns and wrote the Motet (op. 93) with words (by F. Rückert)— "Don't Despair in the Valley of Pain." As Clara perceptively noted, he was able to "cast an air of supreme peacefulness over all these songs, they all remind me of spring, joyful as the blossoms."[67]

Remarkably, Schumann's Kreischa compositions exude much more of a bucolic, peaceful feeling than might have been expected from the "imagery of a ghastly [*schauerliche*] revolution" that he mentioned in his diary.[68] Clara herself seems to have been surprised to observe how "the external terror awakens his inner poetic feelings in such an entirely opposite way."[69] Schumann's peculiar detachment and withdrawal during the revolution seems consistent with a personality that was always striving to maintain solitude and avoid external discomfort.

He explained to Ferdinand Hiller the odd way his creativity was inspired by the revolution and fighting in 1849: "[This has been my] most fruitful year—as if the outer storms have driven me more into myself. Thus I've found a counterweight against the terrible things which broke in from the outside."[70] Schumann was clearly not oblivious to his environment. One of the songs he wrote immediately after returning to Dresden exudes a tragic mood, consistent with the destruction he found there. It is the "Harper's First Song" (op. 98a, no. 4), with the following accusatory words by Goethe:

Ihr führt ins Leben hinein,	*You bring this poor man into the world,*
Ihr lasst den Armen schuldig werden,	*You let him feel guilty.*
Dann überlasst ihr ihn der Pein;	*Then you abandon him to pain;*
Denn alle Schuld rächt sich auf Erden.	*Since here on earth all guilt must be avenged.*

An amusing story about Franz Liszt's visit to Dresden in 1848 reveals something of the way Schumann and his wife behaved in the presence of other leading musicians during the revolutionary era. Liszt was then at the end of his most glamorous phase, the so-called Glanzperiode.[71] He had just separated from his mistress, Marie d'Agoult, was more or less abandoning their three children, and had given a spectacular series of concerts in Vienna. His flamboyant lifestyle was a pointed contrast to that of Schumann, who seemed to be turning into a detached, unapproachable, stuffy homebody.

This was a very difficult time for composers who had new works that they wanted to have performed. Liszt, with his extraordinary virtuosity, had hit on one solution—he would make piano transcriptions of orchestral and vocal compositions and play them in public. (His keyboard replica of Berlioz's *Fantastic Symphony*, for example, created as much if not more enthusiasm than the original orchestral version.) Clara, still jealous of Liszt, continually criticized him, and even Schumann thought some of his song transcriptions were "really abominable."*[72] Nevertheless, they invited him to dinner, along with Richard Wagner, Professor Bendemann from the Art Institute, and other important Dresdeners. They also invited string players who could join Clara for chamber music.

True to form, their guest of honor failed to arrive on time. Finally, two hours late, "Herr Liszt stormed through the door," Clara wrote, just in time to hear Schumann's new piano trio.[73] He liked it, but he thought the piano quintet, which followed, was too "Leipzig-like." Schumann took this to be

---

* His complaining was not so harsh when Liszt made transcriptions of Schumann's own songs, such as "Dedication" (*Widmung*) from the opus 25 song-cycle, the transcription of which is bound with Schumann's personal copy of the first edition.

an indirect attack on the recently deceased Mendelssohn, whose memory he worshipped. He withdrew, silently, into reverie.

After dinner, Liszt sat down at the piano and indulged in what Clara called "such disgracefully bad playing that I really felt ashamed to have to stand there and not be able to leave the room as Bendemann did." The discussion turned to opera, and Liszt spoke highly of Giacomo Meyerbeer (1791–1864), a fashionable Berlin-born opera composer. (Schumann and Wagner, with their interest in distinctly Germanic opera, were in direct opposition to the Meyerbeer tradition.) Suddenly Schumann lost his temper—he called it his "rage"[74]—when Liszt made another unflattering reference to Mendelssohn. Grabbing his guest by the shoulder, Schumann told him to keep his mouth shut, and blurted out that Meyerbeer was "a midget compared to the great artist Mendelssohn—who are you to talk that way about him?" Then he stalked out of the room. There were embarrassed apologies, and Liszt supposedly said to Clara, "Tell your husband that there is only one person in this world from whom I would calmly accept words like those he has just uttered."[75]

In his memoirs, Wagner recalled this episode and others unflattering to Schumann. He was then an assistant conductor at the Royal Opera, where Schumann was hoping to have *Genoveva* produced. But Schumann detested Wagner's conducting and the way he organized musical events in Dresden. Communication between these two men of genius was extremely difficult. Wagner could talk people's heads off—"He has an enormous gift of gab and is stuck full of suffocating ideas," wrote Schumann—while Schumann's in-articulate behavior was just as frustrating. "[He] remained mute for almost an hour. Well, one can't just talk all the time! What an impossible man," wrote Wagner.[76]

The flurry of composing that capped Schumann's stay in Dresden had begun with the writing of *Genoveva* and continued throughout the revolutionary upheavals of 1848 and 1849. In August 1848 Schumann composed his famous *Album for the Young* (op. 68), in time for his daughter Marie's birthday. It was probably an enjoyable way to get his mind off the burden of *Genoveva*. "I don't know that I've ever been in such a good mood as when writing these pieces," he told his friends. "I felt as if learning to compose all over again, and here and there you'll also find traces of my old humor."[77] Correctly predicting that this would be the most popular of his compositions, Schumann insisted that the album be published in a highly attractive format, and he received 226 thalers for it.[78]

Almost anyone learning to play the piano is exposed to these delightful tunes, so perfectly designed to fit the hands and mind of a child. Even their titles are appealing: "Soldier's March," "Humming Tune," "The Poor Orphan," "Rough Rider," "The Happy Farmer," and so on. A second album for more grown-up pianists soon followed, containing personal vignettes such as "Echoes of the Theatre," "In Memory of Mendelssohn," and "Nordic Song" (a "greeting to Niels Gade," based on the notes in his name, G A D E).

Schumann was thinking of the musical education of his own children, as well as others, when he composed this music. (Again this is an indication of good reality contact.) He even made a list of *Musical Rules for the Home and for Life*, which he later published.[79] There are no fewer than sixty-eight of these maxims for children, some of which follow:

- Don't just tinkle the keys!
- Dragging and rushing are equally bad mistakes.
- Try to play easy pieces well and beautifully; it's better than giving a mediocre performance of something difficult.
- Play rhythmically! Many virtuosos sound the way a drunkard walks. Don't emulate them.

Schumann emphasized ear training as "the most essential" feature of a musical education, and he also took aspects of health into consideration:

- After you have finished your musical labor for the day and feel tired, don't strain to do any more work. It's better to rest than to work without freshness or pleasure.

Unfortunately, Schumann often ignored this good advice. For example, within twenty-four hours after completing *Genoveva* he embarked "enthusiastically" on another huge project, *Manfred* (op. 115).[80] Again his choice of this subject was motivated by personal considerations: his father had translated and published Byron's writings, which appealed greatly to the German romantics. After slaving for months over an opera about a tragic woman, Schumann probably wanted to immortalize a heroic man, Manfred, in whom he may have seen aspects of his own fate:

Look on me! there is an order
Of mortals on the earth, who do become
Old in their youth, and die ere middle-age,
Without the violence of warlike death;
Some perishing of pleasure, some of study,
Some worn with toil, some of mere weariness,
Some of disease and some insanity,
And some of wither'd or of broken hearts.[81]

Schumann had just turned thirty-eight. He was probably contemplating certain parallels between himself and Manfred, a daredevil perched on an Alpine cliff brooding about an "impulse to jump" into the void. Manfred is distracted by "a lovely sound, a living voice, a breathing harmony," and he allows a chamois hunter to rescue him. Yet filled with guilt for "destroying" a woman whose "faults are mine," Manfred finally asks for the "blessing of madness."

In perfect sympathy with this tragedy, Schumann produced one of his most successful works, the *Manfred Overture*. Here his command of the musical forces is impeccable and his sense of form undeniably masterful. Less well known today are the fifteen scenes that follow the overture, which include sung or spoken dialogue from Byron's poem. Some of the music is spine-tingling, some of it rather sedative.

Clara's pregnancy that year produced its usual emotional turbulence in her husband, who complained of "the melancholy bats still swarming around me sometimes; they scare the music away."[82] Hoping to fight off a depression, he quickly composed the *Forest Scenes* (*Waldszenen*) (op. 82), a haunted, surrealistic set of fantasy pieces that Clara didn't much care for (although she performed them occasionally, cutting out the episodes that upset her).

The first piece, "Entrance," is calm enough, suggesting a leisurely stroll through the woods. But the next, "A Hunter Waiting in Ambush," is agitated, with very fast triplets and rough chords. The music slows down in "Solitary Flowers," a serene and tender interlude. Schumann's juxtaposition of gentleness with terror continues throughout *Forest Scenes*: "Infamous Place," with words from a ghoulish poem by Hebbel, is followed by the vivacious "Friendly Landscape"; the peaceful "Shelter" by the shimmering "Prophet Bird"; and "Hunting Song," an assertive march, by a quiet "Farewell."

At the end of 1848 Schumann wrote *Pictures from the East* (op. 66), six "Impromptus for Piano Four-Hands." Inspired by a quasi-oriental poem by Rückert, they evoke imagery of the Arabian Nights. These and other later compositions for the piano differ from the music he had written for Clara before their marriage. They are in many ways more restrained, a difference that stems not from any lack of inventiveness but from the composer's deliberate effort to create a more refined style. "The musical content of my *earlier* piano compositions," Schumann wrote, "was damaged by my belief that they must be especially interesting for the performer and contain technically new difficulties."[83] *Forest Scenes*, *Pictures from the East*, and other late works may not tax the virtuoso as much as *Carnaval* and *Kreisleriana*, for example, but they are as original and imaginative. Some pianists even find them to be more subtle and intellectually challenging.

Economic worries again contributed to Schumann's creative pattern in

1849. *Album for the Young* had proved so successful that he now drove himself unmercifully to write shorter works that would sell readily, such as the religious cantata *Advent Song* (op. 71). In February he embarked on a spree of uninterrupted productivity: *Three Fantasy Pieces for Clarinet and Piano* (op. 73), *Adagio and Allegro in A-flat major for Horn and Piano* (op. 70), and *Concertpiece in F major for Four Horns and Orchestra* (op. 86). In March he wrote 14 *Ballads and Romances for Chorus* (opp. 67 and 75), 12 *Romances for Women's Voices* (opp. 69 and 91), and 10 *Songs for Vocal Quartet and Piano*, known as *Spanish Songs* (*Spanisches Liederspiel*, op. 74). Finally, in April and the first half of May, he produced 5 *Pieces for Violoncello and Piano* (op. 102), and *Song Album for the Young* (op. 79).

Schumann was experimenting with new combinations of sound (horn, clarinet, cello) that give a somber, dusky hue, and with novel blends of the human voice. His *Concertpiece for Horns* (op. 86), for example, shows his growing skill in orchestration, which he was acquiring gradually, laboriously, and without direct instruction. It opens with a blazing fanfare and carries the brass instruments to dizzying heights.

His vocal music was also making progress. Many of the *Romances for Women's Voices* are exquisite when well sung (which may not always have been the case when Schumann was conducting!), for example "Meerfey" (op. 69, no. 5), with its uncanny harmony. In the *Spanish Songs* Schumann tried to be a *caballero*, not easy for a German who had only minimal contact with a Latin culture. Yet the tunes are captivating, and the composer's enthusiasm contagious.

Soon Schumann was working on the *Requiem for Mignon* (op. 98b), based on Goethe's poems, and in July he completed three scenes for the *Faust* tragedy. After he played them for Clara on 14 July, she wrote, "I'm unable to find an expression for the delectable feelings that physically engulf me with this magnificent music."[84]

On 16 July their sixth child, Ferdinand, was born. After that, some of Schumann's compositions quite deliberately refer to marriage. In August, for example, he wrote *Four Songs for Soprano and Tenor* (op. 78), including a delightful waltz wherein husband and wife take turns articulating their excitement, and a most tender lullaby. Two weeks after the new baby's arrival Schumann also felt it urgent to obtain more income for his family. Accordingly, to Dr. Härtel in Leipzig he wrote:

> I yearn for a regular occupation. Although the recent years in which I could live exclusively as a composer are unforgettable, and in spite of my knowledge that such productive and happy times may not soon come again, I feel pressed to seek effective employment. My highest aspiration would be to help uphold the glory that has surrounded the [Gewandhaus] Institute for so long.[85]

Nothing positive came of this effort. The newly appointed Rietz did not vacate his post there as had been rumored, nor was Schumann offered another position he wanted, that of conductor at the Berlin Opera House. Although these rebuffs were demoralizing and prevented him from leaving Dresden, they at least allowed him to concentrate on creative work for the rest of the year. In September Schumann quickly composed more music for popular consumption, *Twelve Four-Hand Piano Pieces for Little and Big Children* (op. 85). These were announced by the publishers as his "Second Album." Full of drolleries—such as "Dancing Bear," and "At the Fountain"—the "Album" closes with one of his most sublime expressions of nocturnal quietude: "Evening Song."

Another important composition that month was *Introduction and Allegro for Piano and Orchestra* (op. 92), which opens with a melody similar to those we have learned to associate with Clara in the earlier piano music. In October he wrote the *Four Songs for Double Chorus* based on poems by Rückert, Zedlitz, and Goethe (op. 141), and in November, *Nightsong for Chorus and Orchestra*, based on words by, and dedicated to, Friedrich Hebbel (op. 108), and a second set of *Spanish Songs*, translated by Geibel, for solo voices and four-handed piano (op. 138). In December he completed *Three Hebrew Songs by Byron* with harp (or piano) accompaniment (op. 95), *Three Romances for Oboe and Piano* (op. 94), a Ballad (by Hebbel) to be spoken with piano accompaniment (op. 106), and the *New Year's Song* (Rückert) *for Chorus and Orchestra* (op. 144).

Schumann's popularity was on the upswing in 1849. Not only were his many compositions published almost immediately, but for the centennial celebration of Goethe's birth (28 August) the *Scenes from Faust* were chosen to be performed simultaneously in three places—Dresden, Weimar, and Leipzig—a singular honor. "If only I could have Faust's cloak and be everywhere to hear [the performances]," Schumann wrote in eager anticipation.[86] He was able to take part in the Dresden premiere, conducting the concluding scene ("Faust's Transfiguration"), and he enjoyed the account Hans von Bülow gave him of Liszt's fine performance in Weimar. As for Leipzig, Rietz's conducting there was said to have misfired, and the climactic final chorus of *Faust* was criticized as "dragging on too long."[87] Clara complained that she "couldn't understand" why her husband seemed "so indifferent" about this criticism,[88] but it was characteristic of him to swallow his pride, with rare exceptions refrain from outward displays of anger, and tell her that future generations would surely learn to appreciate his music.

There is something alarming about a highly creative person who reaches his peak—in Schumann's case more of a plateau—before middle age, and we cannot help being disturbed by his overwhelming compulsiveness, the driven quality of his death-fear, the agitation over every reminder of passing time. Also Schumann's seeming indifference, detachment, and suppression of feelings, punctuated by lapses of self-control and depressiveness, should give us concern. Perhaps we are witnessing the early signs of what psychoanalyst Elliot Jaques has identified as a special problem that besets men of genius who fear growing old. (Jaques called this "death and the midlife crisis."[89]) Other scholars have postulated a progressive mental impairment for Schumann, but his work habits remained so well organized and his output so prolific that any severe decay of his mind would have to be seriously questioned. Already as a youth, he had agonized over the possibility of one day being "abandoned" by his genius. Now, approaching the fifth decade of his life, he had already seen his best-loved composers die prematurely—Schubert, Schunke, Chopin, and Mendelssohn. (While in Dresden, Schumann also lost the last of his four siblings, another frightening reminder of mortality.) We can sympathize with him as he contemplated a new career, something few men of genius, especially during the romantic era, were able to do.

XIV.

Trouble on the Horizon, 1849–1852

ccording to Schumann's household book, he was in a comparatively good state of health in 1849. There had been only a few complaints of depression, clustered around his birthday: "stupid hypochondriacal brooding" (6 June); "the good Clara and my melancholia" (8 June). He had experienced four days of continuous "unwellness" in August, precipitated, interestingly enough, by his old anxiety about contracting an infectious disease: "rumors of cholera, and [my] sudden illness."[1] His medical expenses were decreasing. (Clara, though, had been "very unwell" with a bad cold.[2])

Then, in November 1849, Schumann received a letter offering what seemed, on the surface at least, a perfectly reasonable job. Ferdinand Hiller wanted to leave his position as music director in Düsseldorf for an analogous post in Cologne, and he suggested Schumann as his replacement. Hiller had lived and traveled widely throughout Europe and knew almost every major musician of his time. As we already know, he had taken a liking to Schumann—he had even asked him to be the godfather for his own son Robert—and he had greatly helped the Schumanns establish themselves in Dresden. No doubt Hiller was aware of Schumann's limitations as a conductor. He was certainly familiar with the character traits—social passivity, laconic speech, and nondirective manner—that might prove to be disadvantageous for a music director in a sizable community. Nevertheless, Hiller seems to have been sufficiently impressed with what Schumann had accomplished with the Dresden Choral Society to recommend him for Düsseldorf. It is also possible that Hiller, astute politician that he was, might not have wanted to be replaced by a superior conductor who could outshine him. Thus, Schumann, whose reputation depended more on his creativity than on his ability as a performer, probably seemed an ideal choice.

This would be a difficult proposition to refuse. Yet from the very beginning the idea of Düsseldorf aroused his suspicions. He knew that this town had come to be known as a hornet's nest for conductors, one reason perhaps for Hiller's wanting to go elsewhere. "Mendelssohn's opinion of the musicians there sounds bad enough in my memory," Schumann wrote to Hiller on 19 November 1849. "Rietz also mentioned at the time you left Dresden that he 'couldn't understand why you would take this position.'"[3] In the absence of a more desirable job offer, however, Schumann decided he could not afford to turn Hiller down. Thus with considerable bravado—and an obvious lack of modesty in regard to his own limitations as a conductor— he told Hiller that there were few "well-behaved orchestras" and that he, Schumann, knew "well enough how to deal with surly musicians, only not with rough or spiteful ones."[4]

With his customary concern for detail, Schumann presented Hiller with a long list of questions about the post:

1. Is it a city position? Who first of all belongs to the board of directors?
2. The salary is 750 thalers (not gulden)?
3. How strong is the chorus? How strong the orchestra?
4. Is life there as expensive as for instance here? What do you pay for your apartment?
5. Can one have a furnished apartment?
6. Ought some compensation for the move and the costly trip not be requested?
7. Could the contract not read that I can cancel were I offered another position?
8. Do the rehearsals go on all summer?
9. Would there be time in the winter for short vacations of 8–14 days?
10. Would it be possible to find a sphere of activities [*Wirkungskreis*] for my wife? You know her; she cannot be unoccupied.[5]

Despite his interest, Schumann did not really want to face the move. He guessed, correctly, that "the separation from our Saxon homeland will be very difficult for us."[6] He wrote a second letter to Hiller on 3 December, claiming "headaches" as the reason for his "delay in answering," and indicated that he did not want to decide about the post before Easter.[7] The hope that a different position would be offered was certainly still on his mind. Despite his many earlier rebuffs, Schumann was *still* hoping to be appointed as Gewandhaus director in Leipzig. He also was making discreet inquiries, through personal contacts like Dr. Carus, about the vacancy at the Royal Opera House created by Wagner's expulsion from Dresden (due to his revolutionary activities).

But Schumann was in a "stupid troubled [*trübselig*] mood" for quite another reason.[8] What seems to have been bothering him was a fantasy that by moving to Düsseldorf he would again become massively depressed, perhaps so mentally disturbed that hospitalization might be necessary. He articulated this fear in a roundabout way in another letter to Hiller:

> While rummaging through an old geography book for information about Düsseldorf I found, among other noteworthy items, three cloisters for nuns and one institution for the insane. The former doesn't bother me a bit, but reading about the latter was quite disagreeable.[9]

There can be no doubt that Schumann was apprehensive about another breakdown, and that he wanted Hiller to know it. He mentioned, for example, his unhappy experience in Maxen, where having to look at the insane asylum at Sonnenstein was "quite fatal for me and ruined my entire stay. . . . That's the way it might also be in Düsseldorf."

> I have to be very much on guard against any melancholic impressions of this sort. As you know, we musicians live on sunny heights and are cut deeply by the tragedies of reality, when these are presented naked to our eyes. At least that's how it goes in my lively imagination.[10]

Even on 31 March 1850, when Schumann sent an acceptance letter to Düsseldorf, Clara noted that he "still [was] very doubtful that he will go—he's always hoping to find a position closer by."[11] But Clara too was in a state of "fatal indecision," according to her diary. In her view, Dresden had come to be an artistic cul de sac. Schumann was composing many new works but finding it difficult to get them performed there. And of course she wanted to do more traveling and give more concerts. She thought the position would have many advantages, and although the salary offered, 700 thalers, was "not much," it would "surely [be] no mean source of secure income."[12] This was hardly a powerful incentive. In Weimar, a much smaller town than Düsseldorf, Liszt was being paid 1000 thalers plus 300 thalers for court concerts, whereas Wagner at the Dresden Opera had received 1500 thalers a year.

With her emphasis on the practical aspects of the position, Clara seems to have been denying Schumann's fear of madness. Her diary does not mention it, although Litzmann, reading between the lines, says, "One feels only too clearly the nervous hyper-irritability affecting them both." Clara herself was suffering from a depression of mood that carried over into her performance at concerts she and her husband had been giving. "I felt very unhappy," she said following a bad attack of stage fright—rare for her—during the Leipzig premiere of Schumann's *Introduction and Allegro for Piano and Orchestra* (op. 92), at the Gewandhaus on 14 February 1850. She felt "anger or rather despair" for letting herself "be mastered by fear to such an extent. I carry the guilt, I feel deeply aggrieved."[13]

Perhaps this feeling of despair, not to mention her absorption in her own career, blinded Clara somewhat to the realities of Schumann's behavior at this time. (In any case, she had lived with him now for nearly ten years, had learned to adjust to his eccentricities, and probably hoped, as he did, that he would never again have so severe a breakdown as he had had after moving to Dresden.) Schumann was now no longer holding back his criticism of Clara. For example, at a party he upbraided her for "rushing all the time" while playing duets with Moscheles. Clara responded by blaming Moscheles for "constantly making terrible ritardandos."[14]

Schumann knew that he was being rude and annoying—he commented on it in the household book—so we cannot assume that his behavior was simply the expression of a mental disorder that left him without insight. Much of Schumann's irritability at this time was actually the result of seemingly interminable delays before *Genoveva* could be produced. Dresden had not given him the courtesy of an opening there, so the premiere was scheduled for Leipzig, in February 1850. But before rehearsals could begin, Schumann's opera was postponed until June so that Meyerbeer's *La Prophète* could be produced first. Schumann was incensed. He took it not only as a personal insult but also as a refutation of his policy championing German opera, and he predicted (incorrectly, it turned out) that a later date so close to summer would draw only a very small audience for his own opera.

Clara took advantage of the delay by accepting concert engagements in northern Germany. Off they went in March to Bremen, Hamburg, and Berlin. There was trouble from the start. Arriving in Bremen, Schumann was asked by his old Heidelberg friend Theodor Töpken to take the initiative in patching up a quarrel with a certain Herr Eggers, a local impresario who had been impeding the performance of Schumann's music. Here was an opportunity for the future music director of Düsseldorf to exercise diplomatic finesse—but he adamantly refused to see Eggers and, according to Clara, "completely lost his temper" over the matter.[15]

In Hamburg he conducted the orchestra while his wife played his Piano Concerto. There was disappointingly little applause, for which Clara blamed

Schumann at forty, taken in
Hamburg, 1850.
(Daguerreotype, courtesy of
the Robert Schumann Haus.)

the audience. Schumann remained calm. Photographs taken at the time
show him in a thoughtful, serious mood. But his temper erupted again on
19 March, in a tavern, after he had proposed a birthday toast to Bach and
Jean Paul. A cellist, Carl Grädener, quipped that he would gladly salute
Bach but never Jean Paul. Schumann angrily "stood up, told the man he is
shameless, and walked out." [16] The next day he apologized profusely. Clara,
who described this incident, failed to mention how much alcohol had been
consumed. It seems that Schumann was not as withdrawn as he was during
their trip to Russia; and yet, when Johannes Brahms, then an unknown
sixteen-year-old Hamburg pianist, sent him some of his own compositions
for comment and criticism, Schumann did not look at them but simply
returned the package, unopened.

The tour seems to have been a shambles until Jenny Lind came to their
rescue for the second time. Schumann had suggested to the singer that the
three of them might spend a day together in Berlin. But she quickly decided
to come to Hamburg instead and immediately offered her services, thus
assuring Clara of a full house. Lind was an accomplished actress as well as a
consummate singer, and her renditions of Schumann's music gave enormous
satisfaction. In fact, Clara became quite enamored of Jenny Lind at this
point and commented that "never had I loved and revered a female creature

more than her." [17] It was a matter of artistic emulation. "We both [felt] sad," Schumann wrote after Lind's departure[18]—and not surprisingly, for with her help the concerts had brought them 800 thalers, the equivalent of more than one year's salary in Düsseldorf. "Never before have we made so lucrative a tour of Germany," Clara had to admit; "it's good that Robert's opera did not get performed." [19]

After that, Dresden seemed like the last place on earth that Clara wanted to live. "Under no circumstances will we stay here," she wrote. "We're terribly bored, everything seems so antiquated here. Not a single intelligent person can be seen on the street, they all look like Philistines!—Musicians one doesn't see at all." As soon as Schumann's first salary payment from Düsseldorf arrived, Clara stated with conviction that "he's got to have an orchestra under him once and for all." [20]

In April Schumann finally resigned himself to the move and began "organizing [his] many compositions." Some needed to be completed, and he was especially gratified when several of the *Faust Scenes* were finished in May. At the end of the month he even made plans to write another opera, *Romeo and Juliet*, but they never materialized. First he had to go to Leipzig again, for the *Genoveva* opening. In anticipation he felt "rather unwell." [21]

As was his custom, Schumann tried to delay his departure as long as possible, finally making it in time for the last round of rehearsals, beginning 22 May. Clara helped him coach the singers and chorus. They all did their best, and several members of the orchestra even paid the composer a personal tribute by serenading him on his fortieth birthday. Although Schumann reported "much pleasure" that day, he was "also [feeling] out of sorts and dejected," which suggests a conflicted emotional state. Clearly he was apprehensive about how *Genoveva* would be received. Some rehearsals, he felt, were "not too edifying," others quite frankly "misfired" (*verunglückt*). [22]

An impressive assemblage of out-of-town guests gathered for the opening performance on 25 June—Hiller, Liszt, Gade, and Spohr, among others. Schumann's widowed sister-in-law Pauline represented the family, and Kuntsch was there from Zwickau. The first two acts went surprisingly well, but the third act nearly collapsed when Golo forgot to bring an important letter from Siegfried on stage. "Both of the singers ran around the stage in consternation," wrote Clara, who also expressed dissatisfaction with the "shabbiness" of the production. Nevertheless, "the audience was very courteous and at the end called the singers and Robert back twice for applause." [23]

Schumann also conducted the second performance, which went much better and gave him "more pleasure than the first." [24] Clara was "ecstatic," but the tone in her diary seems foreboding:

Once again there is genuine German music which gladdens the heart. . . . This is truly genius, as heaven confers it only on a select few. May you, my beloved Robert, always perceive this as such and always be as happy within yourself as you deserve."[25]

The third performance (on 30 June), conducted by Rietz, was well received by the audience. But the newspapers were unenthusiastic, and one critic arrogantly scolded Schumann for his "musical transgressions," saying that *Genoveva* "makes a big mistake in almost never giving the vocal music its due. Everywhere the singers' voices are devoured by the instrumentation."[26] The opera was set aside after its debut—not an uncommon fate of operas premiered in Leipzig at that time—and has rarely been revived. (Twenty-five years later, Eduard Hanslick wrote, "Schumann's text is inadequate and without interest. . . . Unfortunately, his music is afflicted with the one incurable disease of being undramatic."[27] George Bernard Shaw, who heard a student performance of *Genoveva* in London, thought certain passages were "genuinely Wagnerian," but he dismissed the plot as "pure bosh."[28])

The Schumanns' leave-taking from their Dresden friends, in August, was cheerless and uncomfortable. Clara had become scornful to such a degree—"the people here are bloodless, with no enthusiasm for anything . . . like clods, showing no spark of life on their shriveled-up faces"[29]—that further social interaction must have been difficult. (It seems possible that her embittered attitude reflected, in part, resentment toward her father. Wieck had by this time pretty well lost interest in Clara's career, and he was actively promoting not only his other daughter, Marie, but also the singer Minna "Schulz-Wieck," whom he advertised as his daughter.)

As for Schumann, his gloomy irritability became worse, as usual, under the conditions of separation. He had been composing the beautiful but mournful *Lenau Songs* (op. 90), one of which, a lachrymose "Requiem," was to be performed for a private gathering at Professor Bendemann's house. Lenau had just died,* and Schumann, fearing he would be unable to enjoy the party, was reluctant to attend until his host urged him to. A few days later, at a public farewell party, Schumann is said to have behaved "in a most inconsiderate way" when some of his choral pieces were performed. He insisted that several be repeated, with himself conducting, "and then it went worse than before."[30]

---

*When Schumann started to write these songs, he thought the poet was already dead, and, strangely, he did die (in an asylum) by the time the songs were finished. Lenau (Franz Niembsch von Strehlenau) was the pessimistic Byronic type that Schumann so greatly admired. They had met in 1838, when both lived in Vienna.

The day of departure, 1 September 1850, was Marie Schumann's ninth birthday, but there was no time to celebrate it. The family boarded the train at 6 A.M. and traveled the entire day via Leipzig to Hanover, where they spent the night. The next day was again spent traveling. At 6 P.M. they arrived in Düsseldorf.

Düsseldorf, an attractive city on the east bank of the Rhine north of Cologne, had been a haven for painters and sculptors since the seventeenth century. One of Schumann's favorite poets, Heinrich Heine, was born there at the end of the eighteenth century; in the nineteenth century the city was vying for prestige as a musical center. Its population was 40,500 in 1850, when the Düsseldorf Music Society hired Schumann as music director. Ferdinand Hiller and other influential citizens welcomed him at the train station and escorted the Schumann family to their tastefully decorated rooms in the Breidenbach Hotel. (Only later did the composer discover, to his horror, that the hotel bill for one week was 55.5 thalers, more than the entire travel allowance he had been advanced by the Music Society.) In the evening, members of the Choral Society came to serenade him and Clara at the hotel. It was an exciting week, capped by their tenth wedding anniversary on 12 September 1850.

Finding a suitable residence for so large a family proved difficult, however. Clara was dismayed to discover that "all the houses are uncomfortable, with unpleasant large windows and completely flat brick walls." In addition, she reported, they were very disappointed not "to obtain lodgings amidst greenery and with a garden."[31] When their furniture arrived, they quickly rented a large apartment located on a busy and noisy intersection, Alleestrasse 782. Clara lamented that the windows were "so big it feels as if one is sitting right out on the street," and she grumbled about the cook who came to work for them but "prefers to have you wait on her. In short, everything conspired to put us in a bad mood."[32]

It was much more than the physical environment and the cook that displeased Clara. She found the people of Düsseldorf generally objectionable and wrote that "the lower class of people here are almost universally rude, insolent, and pretentious. . . . They consider themselves our equal [but] don't even say hello."[33]

Schumann—who actually found the new lodgings rather "pretty"— had other things to worry about. A new symptom had appeared on 14 September: "rheuma[tism] in the foot."[34] The cause is unknown, but it was only one of many such complaints he would have over the next few years, this time a soreness of his foot that lasted for a week. The move itself had been exhausting, and Schumann felt so out of sorts the first week that he excused himself from a party Hiller had arranged.

He did, however, go to the formal civic reception given in their honor. Again Clara complained: the mayor's speech was too long and afterward "there was bloody little food to eat." When Schumann's music was played, the conductor (soon to be Schumann's assistant) immediately rubbed her the wrong way—"Herr Tausch conducts fairly well, but I wish the man would just be personally more agreeable."*35

The informality of Düsseldorf's social life was an obstacle for the Schumanns, especially (for Clara) "the breezy, unconstrained conduct of the women, who at times surely transgress the barriers of femininity and decency." This part of Germany had been under French rule prior to its annexation in 1815 by Prussia, and the Napoleonic Code was relatively permissive in regard to sexual conduct. "Marital life around here," noted the astonished Clara, "is said to be more in the easy-going French style." She "liked the fact" that "people are always so gay when they get together here," but to be on the safe side she attached herself right away to the most conservative woman she could find, Frau Dr. Müller, a banker's daughter whose influential husband would soon be giving them medical advice.36

Schumann had been engaged as music director solely on Ferdinand Hiller's recommendation and was expected to maintain or even improve the standards set by his predecessors. The position would have been a challenge for even the best conductor. Many of the members of the orchestra and chorus were amateurs, and for the orchestra to give concerts at all it was necessary to augment the brass and woodwind sections with players from a military band.

At full strength, the Düsseldorf orchestra consisted of about forty members, less than half the size of a symphony orchestra today. There were twenty-seven strings, eight woodwinds, two to three horns, two each of trumpets and trombones, and a drummer (also from the military band). Many of these musicians had, in addition, to play in a smaller, thirty-two-member theater orchestra conducted by a Herr Kramer, which led to conflicts about when to schedule rehearsals. Crucial players were often absent, even during concerts.37 It has been said that this was one of the reasons why Schumann

---

*Clara may have been indulging in professional rivalry. Julius Tausch (1827–1895), a pianist, had studied briefly in Leipzig with Schumann, but seemed to prefer Mendelssohn, who had helped him obtain the post in Düsseldorf.

thickened the texture of many of his orchestral compositions, especially those written in Düsseldorf. By doubling the voices, he perhaps hoped to guarantee that in case a player was missing or had missed his cue, the main musical ideas could still be heard.* Surely, though, his depressiveness also affected his mode of musical expression.

The concerts were held in a smallish pavillion with a low roof, located in a public park on the outskirts of town. It was a much more informal atmosphere than what Schumann and his wife had become accustomed to at the Gewandhaus, or even in Dresden. During intermissions for example, twelve hundred or more people would "storm into the garden to devour masses of sandwiches, beverages, etc.," until a signal from the orchestra summoned them to return.[38] Anyone who has gone wine tasting along the Rhine can well imagine the commotion, and the levity, of these public events.

Schumann's programs were ambitious. He sought not only to present classics by Beethoven, Weber, Haydn, and other established composers, but also to initiate the Düsseldorf public to new compositions of his own, and to works by his friends Mendelssohn and Gade. He also introduced older, unfamiliar compositions, such as J. S. Bach's *St. John Passion* (presented on 13 April 1851 for the first time in Düsseldorf). To upgrade the orchestra and attempt to make these performances successful, Schumann brought in as his concertmaster a very capable violinist from Leipzig, Josef von Wasielewski. Wasielewski, who later would write the composer's first biography, appraised the music director as follows:

> Schumann had just as little positive talent for conducting as he did for teaching music. He lacked the requisite ingredients for both, first the capacity to establish a close rapport with others and to make his intentions clear and obvious, this because he either said nothing or spoke so softly that he would only rarely be understood. Second, he lacked the physical stamina and energy for a director's post; he was always very quickly exhausted and had to rest from time to time during rehearsals. Finally, he did not provide the breadth of vision and perspective that audiences need. On the other hand, in his favor was a highly significant and admirable artistic personality, which could impress with a posture both earnestly dignified and awe-inspiring. These qualities, plus the fact that his chorus and orchestra were well trained when he arrived, explain why the first half of his Düsseldorf tenure was accompanied by good and gratifying results.[39]

---

*Schumann's orchestral writing is often criticized for sounding muddy, and attempts to remedy this have been made by several major composers, including Gustav Mahler and Benjamin Britten.

The gala opening concert of the first season, on 24 October 1850, was a reasonable success. Important guests from neighboring cities were in attendance, and the orchestra was alert. They greeted Schumann with a trumpet fanfare, and launched into a Beethoven overture. Then Clara came on stage to perform Mendelssohn's G minor Piano Concerto. After Schumann led his own *Advent Song* (op. 71) for chorus and orchestra, she returned for a solo, Bach's A minor Prelude and Fugue. The concert ended with the premiere of *Comala* by Niels Gade, a dramatic poem for solo voices, chorus, and orchestra.

Ferdinand Hiller proposed a toast that evening in front of Düsseldorf's most distinguished citizens. But in doing so he created a small scandal by saluting Clara and not Robert. Schumann nearly "got up and left," wrote Clara. "It was most unpleasant for me, and totally upset both of us."[40] Three days later she sent Hiller a blistering letter in which she blamed the city administration for neglecting to pay her for participating in the concert. Clara had received only "a small basket of flowers" as compensation for the substantial help she provided before and during her husband's first concert. As her letter makes clear, she resented being viewed as Schumann's assistant, although that was the role his passivity often forced her into. "My playing is a separate matter on which they should not have counted when they hired my husband!"[41]

The second public event of the season was a "musical soirée" on 9 November, which featured "Clara Schumann, née Wieck" in every number of a very long program, starting with her husband's D minor Piano Trio (Wasielewski played the violin part). Hiller's *Impromptu* (op. 30, no. 2) closed the concert. The hall was "very full," commented Schumann, who on that very day had finished sketching the first movement of one of his greatest compositions, the Symphony in E-flat major (op. 97), later titled *Rhenish* Symphony.[42]

The strain on Schumann of having to be a conductor while also trying to preserve his integrity as a composer was soon evident. It took only a few rehearsals at the beginning of the first season in Düsseldorf before Clara noted his "highly nervous, irritable, excited mood."[43] This she attributed to "the incessant street noises, barrel-organs, screaming brats, wagons, etc.," which disturbed him as he worked on new compositions. Schumann too noted the "terrible street noises" in their neighborhood. But he added, perhaps somewhat more insightfully than Clara, that he had "house *anger*," and he soon began to think of moving.[44] They went on a Rhine tour at the end of September 1850, their first trip to this part of Europe together. It was a brief but enjoyable excursion, capped by a visit to the Cologne cathedral.[45]

Filled with these new impressions, and having moved to the Hofstube in a quieter neighborhood, Schumann soon experienced "urgent desires to compose" (*Compositionsgelüste*).[46] It took him less than a week to sketch what he first called simply a "concertpiece," one of his most daring and original works, the Concerto for Violoncello and Orchestra in A minor (op. 129). Despite the pressure of all sorts of social obligations,* he managed to complete the orchestration during the few days remaining before he had to conduct his above-mentioned inaugural concert with Clara as soloist, on 24 October.

There is something timeless and almost supernatural about the opening of Schumann's cello concerto. After four sparse measures of orchestral introduction, the solo voice sings, in high register, eight bars of a spellbinding theme, followed by twenty-one bars of declamation, one of the longest solo expositions on record. The music is both outgoing and contemplative. Florestanian energy triumphs in the superbly orchestrated symphonic interlude of his first movement, and in the tempestuous finale. The second movement is Eusebian poetry, eloquently articulated by a cello solo *within* the orchestra, playing a dialogue with the main soloist. (This innovation, a cellist in the orchestra accompanying the soloist, also appears in Clara Schumann's Piano Concerto (op. 7), which her husband helped orchestrate,[47] in the Violin Concerto in D minor, which Schumann later composed for Joseph Joachim, and in Brahms's Piano Concerto in B-flat major.)

Apparently confident that the move to Düsseldorf had not impaired his creative vitality, Schumann then started to compose another symphony. Five movements were sketched and orchestrated in a month (2 November to 9 December 1850). This work is now known as the *Rhenish* Symphony no. 3 in E-flat major (op. 97).† The jubilant opening theme, with its two-against-three rhythm, together with the structural integrity of this entire work, foreshadows Brahms's later symphonic music.[48] The second movement, a "Ländler," has some of the local color, the "folksy" quality that Schumann was then trying to inject into his writing. The third movement takes the listener to the banks of the Rhine with its sound of rippling waves and distant hunting horns. The majestic fourth movement was meant, according to the program notes of the first performance, to be "in the character of

---

*This was a very strenuous month, with numerous visitors, including the arrival in Düsseldorf of his new concertmaster, Wasielewski. Moreover, the first of four church concerts Schumann was contracted to conduct each year was scheduled for 13 October, in the midst of his work on the violoncello concerto. The strain took its toll; he complained of an "eye ailment" on 14 October.

†The title *Rhenish* was Wasielewski's idea.

a festive ceremony," [49] referring possibly to a processional that Schumann and Clara had recently witnessed near the Cologne cathedral. The spirited last movement of the *Rhenish* Symphony begins in the character of a march and leads back to some of the themes introduced in the first movement, thus producing symmetry and an effective closure.

With the completion of this outstanding orchestral work in December, Schumann experienced a surge of "joy" that continued for several weeks. [50] He felt generally well and complained little, if at all. Just before Christmas he conducted Handel's *Israel in Egypt*, an oratorio that inspired him to plan a similar composition of his own, based on the life of Luther. On 29 December he composed, at breakneck speed, his *Overture to "The Bride of Messina"* (op. 100).

As 1851 began, Schumann was euphorically making "plans for England." [51] He had just received an invitation from William Sterndale Bennett to visit London, and he hoped that he and Clara would be able to stay there for a while. But rehearsals and concerts in Düsseldorf came first. On 11 January Schumann conducted his fourth subscription concert, which included the first performance of his *New Year's Song* (op. 144). By the end of the month he was composing another overture, *Julius Caesar* (op. 128). On 6 February he conducted the first performance of his *Rhenish* Symphony, which was a resounding success. On 20 February he conducted another concert in Düsseldorf, five days later, his *Rhenish* Symphony in Cologne, and then a repeat performance of the symphony in Düsseldorf, on 13 March. These programs were very long, containing about twice as many works as we customarily hear performed today.

Not surprisingly, Schumann's enthusiasm for organizing and conducting symphony concerts faded fast under this enormous workload, especially after he began to realize that much of his effort was unappreciated. His eighth subscription concert, in March, had been marred when the audience refused to applaud the newly composed *Overture to "The Bride of Messina."* Schumann's plan was to write an entire opera based on this play by Schiller, but he lacked the time and energy to complete so major a project. The negative public response to his overture hurt him, but even more damaging was an uncomplimentary newspaper article, written, it was rumored, by a member of the Music Society.

Schumann's household book reports "loneliness—hesitations about remaining longer in Düsseldorf {17 March} . . . constant annoyances [3 April]." A letter to his friend Verhulst says that "for several days I've felt unwell, so that writing becomes an effort." [52] Another encroachment on Schumann's peace of mind at this time was Clara's discovery (26 March) that she was pregnant again. As usual he responded with malaise, as did she. This pregnancy was particularly ill timed, coming as it did when they were just getting their lives organized in the new environment. Also it meant that they had to postpone their plans for England once more.

Small wonder that at the completion of his first season as music director, Schumann felt enormously relieved, "joyful as he seldom is," according to Clara.[53] They were looking for a better place to live and during the summer moved into a new apartment on one of Düsseldorf's main streets, Königsallee 252, near the Benrather Bridge. Shortly thereafter, he took his pregnant wife on another tour along the Rhine River, this time up to Switzerland. He enjoyed reliving his youthful memories of Heidelberg, and Clara averred that it was "the best vacation ever."[54]

Schumann was trying to establish continuities, with Clara's help, not only between important experiences of the past and the present, but also between his role as a distinguished composer and an influential music director. The three concert overtures he wrote in 1851, for example, were frankly intended as showpieces for his orchestra.* That they were so poorly received was thus doubly disappointing. He also completed a considerable amount of nonorchestral music that first year in Düsseldorf. Schumann's interest in chamber music expressed itself with the unique *Fairy-Pictures for Viola and Piano* (op. 113), the two highly original *Sonatas for Violin and Piano* (opp. 105 and 121), and a beautiful *Trio for Violin, Cello, and Piano* (op. 110). He also produced new music for the piano, *Three Fantasy Pieces* (op. 111) for a soloist, and five four-handed pieces for children (included in op. 130). All in all, he wrote twenty-three songs in 1851, plus a number of longer choral works, including the delicately sentimental *Pilgrimage of a Rose* (op. 112) for solo voices, chorus, and piano. This fairy-tale oratorio was first tried out during a housewarming in Schumann's new apartment, and he later orchestrated it.

About one-third of Schumann's entire output of musical compositions stems from the few years he lived in Düsseldorf. This is extraordinary, considering his declining health and his many administrative and performing responsibilities there. When he wasn't composing new pieces he made piano reductions of older ones. One gets the impression that Schumann neglected some of his responsibilities as music director in favor of his creative work, and a letter he wrote to a friend in Zwickau tends to confirm that impression: "I am very satisfied with my present position, and since it does not demand too much of my physical strength (conducting can be quite stren-

---

* He finished his third, *Overture to Goethe's "Hermann und Dorothea"* (op. 136), in December.

uous) I cannot think of any I would like better."[55] Clara's diary, however, and the many letters exchanged with Hiller and other professional musicians, suggest that Schumann attended conscientiously to the many routines of concert administration, obtaining scores, getting parts copied, arranging and rearranging programs, negotiating with soloists, and interacting with members of the Music Society.

Still other competing obligations distracted Schumann from his creative work. For example, on 16 August 1851 he had to rush to Belgium to judge a competition of male choruses. This required twelve hours of almost constant listening to what Clara described as "such compositions! All the French choruses sang only the worst stuff." Immediately thereafter came a visit from Liszt and his mistress, Princess Carolyne Wittgenstein.[*] "All household orderliness is immediately disrupted," wrote Clara, "and one is put into a constant excitement. . . . We played a lot of music . . . [Liszt] as usual with a truely demonic bravura, really dominating the piano like a devil."[56]

In September came Schumann's first painful confrontation with members of the Music Society who were voicing dissatisfaction with his performances and the programs for his concerts. According to Wasielewski, Schumann's conducting was beginning to display "a certain indolence."[57] Morale was deteriorating in the orchestra and the chorus; attendance at concerts was slipping. Schumann quite frankly admitted that he did not feel well enough to continue doing all the many things that were required of him, and during a "stormy" conference he offered to give up his directorship of the chorus. This was not acceptable to the board of directors, however, and Schumann began to have "serious thoughts about the future."[58] Clara, six months pregnant at the time, sought to protect him by casting all the blame for his difficulties on the musicians and the audiences. "People here are often really so insolent, and we surely won't be staying here for long," she wrote. "People here have no respect either for art or for their conductor!"[59]

While some of this undoubtedly was true, Clara was unhelpful by denying Schumann's growing incapacity as music director. Having lived with him for more than a decade, she must have known that his frenetic overwork could have only one outcome: increasing physical exhaustion and depression. Yet instead of gently urging and helping him to step aside in favor of a more capable conductor, she blamed the Düsseldorfers and supported Schumann in his stubborn insistence on remaining on the podium. Perhaps Clara was afraid of his anger. Her own craving for the spotlight was also a factor. But in addition one suspects the unconscious influence of her father,

---

[*]Liszt was being recruited, unsuccessfully, as the new conductor in Cologne, Hiller having announced his resignation there to take on major responsibilities in Paris and London.

who had so often predicted a disastrous end to the marriage. In trying to free herself from pangs of guilt for having disobeyed Wieck, Clara may have had to delude herself into the belief that her husband was doing far better than he really was.

"Devoting one's strength to religious music remains the supreme goal of an artist" Schumann had written on 13 January 1851,[60] two days after conducting a difficult concert. A Lutheran, he had never been much of a churchgoer. But religious faith was part of Schumann's personal philosophy; his conscious identification with the Christian martyr Eusebius attests to that. Perhaps his return to the Catholic Rhineland provided the impetus for his irresistible wish now to compose music that would be "suitable for church as well as the concert hall."[61] A sense of approaching middle age may have contributed as well. "When we are young our roots go firmly into the earth, with all its joys and sorrows," wrote Schumann at age forty, "but as we grow older we also strive for the higher branches."[62]

What he had in mind was a gigantic oratorio based on the life of Martin Luther. It was to be a "dramatic" and "historically accurate" work about "Luther's relationship to music in general, his love for it as expressed in a hundred beautiful sayings,"[63] and featuring Luther's famous chorale "Eine Feste Burg" (which Mendelssohn had used in his *Reformation* Symphony). Who could be a more fitting inspirational hero for a Protestant composer in the Rhineland than the singer, translator, reformer, and theologian Martin Luther? For Schumann he was, above all, "a man of the people . . . a noble German struggling to make a powerful, national, popular statement."[64]

For more than two years Schumann tried to complete his Luther oratorio, but unsuccessfully. He corresponded at great length with Richard Pohl about a suitable libretto, but other projects kept interfering. Pohl, it seems, was so excited about the project that at one point he proposed a "Reformation Trilogy," almost as grandiose as Wagner's *Ring* cycle. It would have required three consecutive evenings to perform, and Schumann vetoed this extravagance. (He wanted *Luther* to last no longer than two and a half hours.) Schumann's relationship with Pohl was complicated. He yearned to have him close by—"Couldn't we live together for a while?" he wrote him in May 1851[65]—but when Pohl did come to Düsseldorf, he ran into exactly the same behavior as Hebbel had when he went to Dresden hoping to collaborate on *Genoveva*. Schumann sat immobile, saying not a word, waiting for his librettist to take the initiative and make all the suggestions, with which the composer, smiling sweetly, agreed—only to reject them later.

Pohl and Schumann did manage to work together on a choral ballad, *The Singer's Curse* (op. 139), but their personal contact soon deteriorated. A letter to Pohl at the end of 1852 shows the composer's ambivalence about *Luther*. His work on the oratorio had come to "rest, sadly," but he did not want to abandon the project, either. Health problems were to blame for his indecision, he said. "Almost half of this year I've been laid low, very sick because of a deep nervous depression [*Nervenverstimmung*]—the result perhaps of too much exhausting work."[66] (As late as 8 March 1853 Schumann was still dickering with Pohl about *Luther*, although he had by now found a new collaborator, his physician Dr. Hasenclever, to work with in the thankless task of "remodeling" poetry texts.[67])

The composition of religious music dominated much of Schumann's second year in Düsseldorf and was probably partly related to the considerable stress he was then experiencing. On 1 December 1851 Clara had given birth to another daughter, Eugenie.*

Soon Schumann was "extraordinarily busy again, composing a mass."[68] A formidable work for organ, orchestra, chorus, and solo voices, this Mass in C minor (op. 147) was designed to meet the spiritual needs of his new community in the Rhineland. Schumann used the liturgical Latin text, and in spite of the great haste with which he wrote the music (the sketches for this vast composition required only nine days), it is a work of stately beauty. He wanted his mass to be included in religious services in 1852 and went to considerable trouble to rehearse the "Kyrie" and the "Gloria" (although these sections were not performed for another year).

Again there were interruptions. Just as Schumann was beginning to orchestrate the mass, he had to leave, with Clara, for Leipzig. Performances of his *Pilgrimage of a Rose*, the *Rhenish* Symphony, and several new chamber music works were scheduled in what turned out to be an exhausting, nonstop round of social events. "We felt as though we were almost killed with music," wrote Clara. Liszt was there too, and as usual she derogated his "demonic noisemaking." By contrast, it was a pleasure to hear Schumann's music "sounding so differently than in Düsseldorf" when played by the excellent Gewandhaus orchestra.[69] This undoubtedly stirred up his regret at not having been appointed conductor there, and exacerbated his discomfort at having to return to the Rhineland. Especially painful for Schumann was his leavetaking from Dr. Reuter, his close friend and medical advisor in Leipzig. Reuter was not in good health when the two middle-aged *Davidsbündler* embraced for the last time on 22 March 1852, and he died the following year.

There was more commotion as soon as the Schumanns returned to Düsseldorf. The house they had been living in was sold, forcing them to move

---

*Eugenie, who lived until 1938, was Robert and Clara's last direct survivor. An unmarried piano teacher, she wrote memoirs about her famous parents and strove to protect their reputations.

quickly to a new location on the Herzogstrasse. It was far from the center of town and in an area noisy from new construction work. Robert began to have trouble sleeping, and he told Clara he was feeling depressed again and physically unwell. They consulted a doctor, Adolf Pfeffer, a general practitioner—we do not know how often—and for almost four weeks Schumann did no composing. Then, from 27 April to 8 May, he wrote another religious work, *Requiem* (op. 148).

It has been said that Schumann was obsessed with death and thinking about his own funeral while composing this work, which may well be, considering his depression and that composers often choose to memorialize death in this way.[70] The music certainly is very mournful in places, as befits a requiem. According to the Rehbergs' biography of Schumann, Clara later told Johannes Brahms that her husband, "like Mozart, thought he might be writing the Requiem for himself."[71]

A critical evaluation of Schumann's religious music would take us far afield at this point. Much of it has been neglected, and its reputation tarnished. As the pianist Harris Goldsmith points out in regard to so many of Schumann's later compositions, "One hears a lot of equivocation and fault-finding; with hindsight knowledge of his dismal end in an insane asylum it is all too easy to imagine in the music a diffuseness and ineptitude that isn't there."[72]

Treating a public figure, especially someone as unapproachable and disturbed as Schumann, could not have been a welcome responsibility for the doctors in Düsseldorf. But it was becoming increasingly obvious during his second season there that someone with medical authority would have to step in. Schumann was composing incessantly while also trying to discharge his obligations as a conductor, and Clara was doing nothing to get him to slow down. He had even been orchestrating other people's compositions, for example, part of a symphony by the minor composer Norbert Bergmüller. In December 1851 he completely reorchestrated his own D minor *Clara* Symphony in only seven days;* he planned to call it a "Symphonic Fantasy."[73]

---

* Thus his D minor Symphony exists in two versions. The one he wrote in 1851 and published as his Fourth Symphony (op. 120) is customarily heard today. The earlier version, composed in 1841, is lighter and more transparent in texture. Brahms liked it so well that he published it many years after Schumann's death, only to be severely reprimanded by Clara. She always insisted that the later, heavier, and more stately version was the better one. It is interesting to compare the two editions, for they demonstrate the changes in Schumann's orchestral technique over ten years.

In addition to the religious works already mentioned, Schumann also imposed two new literary chores on himself. He wanted to publish a large book of writings about music (the so-called "Poet's Garden," which he continued to work on almost to the day of his suicide attempt in 1854). Such a collection would require endless reading, and during the Easter holiday of 1852 he tackled one new play by Shakespeare each day, an exhausting task, needless to say. The second literary project he began at this time was a collected edition of his own early writings. In May and June 1852 Schumann was organizing all the old "*Davidsbündlerei*" and starting to negotiate with publishers about having them reprinted.[74]

This renewed compulsion toward verbal projects again suggests that musical activity was never enough to satisfy Schumann, and that he may have felt creatively unfulfilled unless he was doing something that could be clearly identified with his father and brothers. It seems he had to keep both motors running simultaneously, the literary as well as the musical, to stay in balance. His devotion to the job of music director is startling if one reviews the programs he tried to conduct in 1852. Some (by no means all) of the demanding works scheduled during the first five concerts were Handel's oratorio *Joshua*, Beethoven's *Eroica* Symphony, Schubert's big C major Symphony, and the premiere of Schumann's own *Pilgrimage of a Rose*.[75]

Schumann's sixth concert, on 4 March 1852, featured Clara as soloist again for the first time since Eugenie's birth. (She played Chopin's F minor Piano Concerto, and Schumann conducted, among other things, Beethoven's *Pastoral* Symphony.) The next day they had to leave for Leipzig and the many concerts and social activities to be held there.

While Schumann and Clara were gone from Düsseldorf, his assistant Julius Tausch led the seventh subscription concert (18 March). This alerted everyone to the marked discrepancies between the two conductors. Many people began to wonder why the younger and more energetic Tausch wasn't leading a greater number of performances so that Schumann's burden could be lightened. Consequently, arrangements were made for Tausch to rehearse the chorus and orchestra for the next concert a few weeks later, which was to feature Bach's *St. John Passion*. Schumann, however, wanted to conduct the concert himself. He did so and thought it went "fairly well."[76]

Two days later the composer began complaining of "terrible rheumatism," which evidently bothered him a great deal. (It was also the time when he began reading the Shakespeare plays, suggesting that he used the reading to distract himself from the pain.) He was "still unwell, but better" within a week and thereafter mentioned no further symptoms.

On 6 May Schumann conducted the ninth subscription concert. It featured his *Spring* Symphony (which was enthusiastically applauded) and other new compositions, and Clara played Beethoven's *Emperor* Concerto. A new student, Louise Japha, was taken on by both of them that month. On his forty-second birthday in June, Schumann reported "convulsive coughing."[77] This didn't last long; he was able to conduct Beethoven's Mass in C major two days later.

But one thing after another disturbed him during the next few weeks. Wasielewski had resigned to go to Cologne,* and the day after his departure, Schumann complained of a "terrible cold."[78] This was followed by some more "apartment annoyances," then "rheumatism" and insomnia.[79] Perhaps these symptoms were somewhat exaggerated so that Schumann could excuse himself from another long trip that would have followed on the heels of the trip to Leipzig. Liszt had invited Schumann to come to Weimar, where he was conducting the world premiere of *Manfred*, and although the composer surely hoped to attend, he did not want to travel again so soon. Besides, everyone knew that Liszt was championing the music of Richard Wagner. At the Weimar performance he even managed to sandwich Wagner's *Faust Overture* between the two halves of Schumann's *Manfred*. For the austere Schumann to sanction this with his presence might have been awkward. (It should be mentioned that not a single work by Wagner appeared on the Düsseldorf programs during Schumann's tenure there. "His music, when not staged, is shallow, often downright dilettantish, worthless and disgusting," Schumann wrote.[80])

Instead of making the long and exhausting trip to Weimar, Schumann and Clara took a ten-day vacation in the nearby Rhineland. He complained of the terribly hot weather, and one day, after a strenuous hike in the mountains near Bad Godesberg, he fainted. Although details of the incident were not recorded, the implications are serious. Unless of psychogenic origin, such a loss of consciousness usually connotes a physiological disturbance. Salt depletion and dehydration, a hypertensive crisis, or some transient interference with blood flow to the brain must be suspected. There is also the possibility that it might have been due to a discrete lesion, caused by a tumor, an aneurysm, a hemorrhage, or an infectious process encroaching directly on Schumann's brain. Clara used the term "nervous convulsion" (*nervöser Krampfanfall*) in telling Litzmann of his fainting spell, but she did

---

* Wasielewski had his own ambitions and ambivalence toward Schumann, whose orchestra he left (just as the going got rough in 1852) to become director of a male chorus in Bonn. He remained on cordial terms with the Schumanns and invited them to Bonn several times. Immediately after the composer's death, Wasielewski asked Clara for personal letters and documents so he could write a biography, but this shocked her and she did not comply. He also consulted Wieck, who had no such scruples. The first edition of Wasielewski's book appeared in 1857, only one year after Schumann died; Clara waged a life-long campaign to discredit it.

not describe a true epileptic seizure,* which would have been a highly dramatic event, impossible to ignore.[82]

Terribly worried about what had happened, Schumann and Clara decided to consult another physician upon returning to Düsseldorf. They chose Dr. Wolfgang Müller von Königswinter, a friend, influential member of the Music Society, and well-known poet. (The name "von Königswinter" refers to a town along the Rhine where he lived, and where a statue now stands in his memory.) Müller had corresponded with Schumann while the latter was still editor of the *New Journal for Music*.

Dr. Müller's position in regard to his patient has never been very clear, but it is known that he had decidedly mixed feelings about Schumann as a conductor, and about Clara as Schumann's wife. Dr. Müller regretted Hiller's departure from Düsseldorf. He did not approve of the Schumanns' insular lifestyle, which kept them out of circulation with the local people and thus reduced their "musical effectiveness." "Much of the blame," Müller had written in 1851, "lies with the wife, who protects her husband too anxiously, and in my opinion, takes away his masculine decisiveness."[83]

With the weight of his authority as a director of the Music Society, Müller told Schumann to do less conducting and to give Julius Tausch more responsibility. (Perhaps he favored Tausch as a conductor.) Tausch would be receiving 15 thalers quarterly, deducted from Schumann's salary, to compensate him for the additional work. Clara objected to this arrangement, but Dr. Müller tried to reassure her by saying that Schumann's illness was "only the result of too much exertion and will soon go away."[84] Arrangements were also made to excuse Schumann from having to conduct a choral festival that had been scheduled to take place in Düsseldorf in August.

With "Dr. Müller's consolation," as Schumann put it, he began a series of eighteen riverbath treatments on 8 July. This required him to go to the banks of the Rhine every day, disrobe in one of the bathing cabins, and plunge into the cold water. After the first bath Schumann already felt "somewhat better," and he reported steady improvement for the next eleven days. Then he suffered a setback—"still always very unwell"—on 20 July, the day Clara told him about "frightening hopes" of another pregnancy.[85]

It took a few more baths before Schumann again felt some "improvement," and after these treatments were finished, he seems to have been ready

---

* According to a letter Brahms sent to Clara when he later visited Schumann in the hospital at Endenich, *"Krampfanfall"* (convulsion) was a word the composer himself used when referring to severe anxiety attacks.[81] Such a letter cannot carry much weight, however. Not only did Schumann use medical terms loosely, but Brahms, himself no expert, may have wanted to keep the worst from Clara.

to dispense with Dr. Müller altogether. Against medical advice Schumann went to Tausch's first rehearsal on 30 July to hear the orchestra play his *Julius Caesar Overture* (op. 128). According to Clara, he suddenly "was seized with such composer's enthusiasm that he directed the overture himself," an experience that left him, as he himself said, "feeling sad." Afterward he would not socialize with the visitors who were arriving for the upcoming choral festival. The day of the concert (3 August), however, Schumann again asked Tausch to step aside, so that he could conduct his own overture. More tactless yet was his abrupt decision also to conduct a Beethoven overture that Tausch had rehearsed and was supposed to lead. It was a very long program, with Clara as soloist in the *Emperor* Concerto and several other works. Afterward Schumann's household book reports "sad weakening of my strengths. Very exhausted."[86]

Dr. Müller now recommended a much more drastic intervention. He told Schumann and Clara to go away for seabaths in a "cold-water establishment." After considerable resistance, they did go, with their daughter Marie, on 11 August, to a beach resort in Scheveningen, Holland. Here, during the first week of September, Clara had what might be considered a therapeutic abortion. ("I can only tell you the details orally," wrote Schumann to his Dutch friend Verhulst.[87]) It is not known whether Dr. Müller was aware of Clara's previous miscarriage while bathing in Norderney, nor whether a doctor in Scheveningen came to her assistance. All we have is eleven-year-old Marie Schumann's account of the event* (which terrified her) and Litzmann's comment that "Clara recovered quickly and stood at her post already after a few days with remarkable freshness and courage."[89]

After celebrating Clara's thirty-third birthday abroad, the Schumanns returned to Düsseldorf. Schumann had narrowly escaped another breakdown. But he continued to exhibit marked exhaustion, numerous vague physical complaints, and an inability to carry on in his job as music director. All that Dr. Müller could do now was palliate these symptoms with nonspecific remedies, and to recommend Schumann's retirement. This was the prelude to madness.

---

*"My mother suddenly became ill during the night. In the morning she lay in bed as if dead, and my father went around wringing his hands and crying loudly."[88]

XV.

Incipient Madness, 1852–1854

Upon returning from Holland in mid-September 1852, Schumann moved into yet another residence, the spacious townhouse at Bilkerstrasse 1032 (now no. 15), near the Rhine, which was to be the last place he and Clara would live together. A progressive emotional disengagement between them had already begun. Schumann, looking to the past, had found in the dead Elizabeth Kulmann another woman to idealize.

Kulmann (1808–1825), a minor poet of the nineteenth century, created a sensation with her voluminous writings in Russian, German, and Italian, and with her translations, which Goethe, Jean Paul, and other contemporaries commented on favorably. Schumann was smitten by her poems, in particular "Dreamview after My Death," which she wrote just before her tragic death at age seventeen. In the summer of 1851 Schumann had set eleven of Elizabeth Kulmann's poems to music (opp. 103 and 104). What impressed him especially, he said, was that "she created and wrote poems until the last minute before her death [and] left a heavenly vision behind." [1] Schumann may have projected on Elizabeth Kulmann some of the qualities he hoped for in himself. Her premature death may also have reminded him of his sister's. In his new home on the Bilkerstrasse, Schumann kept a portrait of Elizabeth Kulmann prominently displayed over his desk.

For Clara too the house on Bilkerstrasse provided greater autonomy. She had been looking to her own future for some time, planning programs for an eagerly anticipated concert tour of England, and collecting an increasingly larger coterie of piano students. "The greatest convenience," she observed, "is that I have my studio on the top floor, where Robert can't hear a thing. For the first time since our marriage we've found so happy a solution."[2] It took Clara a while to recover from the effects of the recently terminated pregnancy. The month of November was especially disagreeable. She and Schumann were not having sexual intercourse, and the household book describes how Clara was "always ailing" and that she had a "bad fainting attack" on 3 November. Whenever Clara "felt better," Schumann wrote, "so do I," suggesting that his own moods were strongly affected by hers, as well as by sexual frustration.[3]

It was in this setting that his madness gradually took on the shape and dimensions that finally expressed themselves when he became demonstrably psychotic a little more than a year later. Physical isolation undoubtedly contributed to this process. Tausch was conducting the concerts—a "time of resignation," noted Schumann.[4] Clara, busily working upstairs, was finding her way, as she said, "completely into my element again," while Schumann languished in what she called his "little cage" (Kästchen) on the ground floor.[5] He had seen Dr. Müller again and was imbibing a supposedly "curative" mineral water. Following an "attack of dizziness" in mid-October, Schumann had also begun taking what he called "health pills." (We don't know the ingredients, only the price: 1.11 thalers.) In addition, Schumann allowed himself to be bled by leeches in October, and reported that he felt well afterward.[6]

In November both the Vienna Academy of Music and the Music Institute of London honored him with memberships. This made Schumann feel proud but not secure. He had been working on a piano edition of *Scenes from Goethe's "Faust,"* and he was running out of money. On 12 November 1852 he wrote his publisher, Friedrich Whistling, asking for a payment before the end of the month and commenting, "For several weeks I've felt much better than during the summer months; but I have to guard myself against greater exertion, namely conducting, which really hurts me very much."[7]

Toward the end of the month Schumann also noted, without additional comment, that he was having "strange afflictions of hearing" (*merkwürdige Gehöraffectionen*).[8] Apparently he was hearing tonal sounds. (Recently, while in Leipzig, Schumann had startled his old friend and former *New Journal* correspondent Hieronymus Truhn by innocently asking, "Don't you also hear an A?"[9]) We can surmise that this was a different sort of problem from the "distortions" of hearing he had complained of earlier, in Dresden. Now, it seems, he no longer found the noises to be disagreeable or frightening— they were more like music inside his head. They had not yet, though, achieved the character of hallucinatory voices.

It should be emphasized that these "strange afflictions of hearing" usually occurred when Schumann was under severe emotional stress, so that it cannot be asserted that they were simply the result of physical irritation in his ear, brain, or auditory nerves. (Stress can, however, influence the way someone perceives an organically induced sensory disturbance.) As mentioned earlier, Schumann had been relieved of his responsibilities as music director, but only temporarily. His auditory problem in November 1852 coincided with his worry that he might soon have to start conducting again.

Julius Tausch had led the summer concerts and was now beginning to take over the winter season, which posed a threat to Schumann's prestige and income. Tausch's opening concert (28 October) featured Clara as soloist in a Henselt piano concerto and a Beethoven sonata. The second concert (18 November, three days before Schumann heard his strange tones) featured a work for which Schumann felt nostalgia: the E minor Violin Concerto by Mendelssohn. It was performed by Ruppert Becker (1830–1904), a young violinist who had just arrived to replace Wasielewski as concertmaster.

Becker was the son of one of Schumann's old friends, Ernst Adolph Becker, and the composer regretted not being able to conduct the concert. "Schumann is not yet completely restored [*hergestellt*]," wrote the young Becker to his father on 7 November. "Therefore he doesn't conduct yet. . . . To play with [Clara] is naturally unthinkable, since he can't listen to any music yet." [10]

In December Schumann did begin to conduct again, but not yet full time.* He also attended a chamber music recital by Ruppert Becker and wrote his father afterward:

> I listened to your Ruppert really properly for the first time, since unwellness had held us from making music with him earlier. . . . I'm really happy that your son has turned into such an exceptional artist; his intonation is really as clean as one hears it only from the greatest masters. [11]

It was, in fact, while sitting with his new concertmaster in a tavern one evening that Schumann again confided that he heard the tone A. Later, as

---

*It was the third subscription concert, on 2 December. Tausch conducted the first half, then turned the baton over to Schumann, who led his own recently completed *Ballad "Of the Page and the King's Daughter"* (op. 140), for solo voices, chorus, and orchestra. An anonymous admirer presented him with a laurel wreath.

we already know, he talked with young Becker about hallucinating entire compositions.

Becker was surely in a difficult position, having to serve both as concertmaster for two competing conductors and as Schumann's confidante. There had been agitation again for Schumann's dismissal after the December concert. It was said that he seemed remote and withdrawn, beating time so sluggishly that the musicians had difficulty following.* Another "stormy conference" was held with the Music Society on 11 December to discuss Schumann's tenure, and three days later he received what he called an "impudent letter" from three of the officials, asking that he resign.[13] Schumann seems to have taken it calmly, but Clara was very agitated over the letter.

At the same time, the formation of an "Anti-music Society" was announced, dedicated to fight against "bad and badly performed music."[14] An unkind joke, this open criticism was leveled not only against the inclusion of amateurs in the concerts, but also against Schumann's conducting and programming (no Mozart, no French music, too many works by him and his friends, and so on.) Ready to quit immediately, he wrote (17 December) to his friend Carl Van Bruyck, "I would like to move to Vienna if an effective circle of activity could somehow be found there for a conductor."[15] It took every bit of diplomacy the Düsseldorfers could muster to get the winter season under way again. They sent a high-ranking member of the Music Society, Dr. Richard Hasenclever, to Bilkerstrasse, hoping he would soothe Robert and Clara. Finally, Schumann accepted a letter of apology from the chorus. Tausch tactfully added his own name and let it be known that he wanted to do some traveling. Thus on 30 December 1852 Schumann returned to the podium to conduct, among other things, Beethoven's Seventh Symphony—a favorite work, for which as a young composer he had written piano variations—and Niels Gade's *Spring Fantasy*, with Clara as solo pianist.

The Lower Rhine Music Festival, a major cultural event held in Düsseldorf in 1853, seemed to spark, for the last time, Schumann's more extroverted inclinations. It was to open on 15 May with his newly reorchestrated Symphony in D minor (op. 120) and to close on 17 May with his *Festival*

---

*Much has been written about Schumann's often lethargic sense of time, which is known from his metronome markings. It was even assumed once that his metronome must have been at fault! Gerd Nauhaus has checked it and says, correctly, that "the change in Schumann's subjective feeling for time was a manifestation which one often observes among melancholic and depressed patients."[12]

Overture and Chorus on the "Rhine Wine Song" (op. 123). Clara would play Schumann's Piano Concerto, and there would be fifteen other difficult works, including Handel's *Messiah* and Beethoven's Choral Symphony and Violin Concerto. Two soloists had been invited: the stunning soprano Clara Novello, in whom Schumann had once been romantically interested, and the spellbinding violinist Joseph Joachim. Here was an occasion for Schumann to pull himself together and demonstrate his capabilities to the world.

His mood had started to improve in January. (There had been a brief emergency around Christmas, when Clara worried that she might have become pregnant again after having had intercourse only once, their first sexual experience in over a month. "Clara's apprehension destroyed, and her joy," reports the household book tersely on Christmas Eve.[16]) Schumann was working assiduously on piano accompaniments for the solo violin sonatas and partitas of J. S. Bach, an activity that had several motivations, as usual. First was his need to get his mind in order. Another had to do with his wish to make Bach's music more accessible to the public, and thereby possibly to earn money. Finally there was Schumann's new friendship with the violinist Becker, who frequently came to the house to try out these new arrangements. *

Planning conferences for the music festival got underway in mid-January.[17] Clara in the meantime was busily arranging concerts for herself in Bonn. Hoping to shield Schumann from the knowledge that she was actively trying to supplement their meager income, she asked Wasielewski not to tell Schumann that she had asked him to arrange a soirée for her in Bonn.[18] Clara feared Schumann would criticize her for wanting to play in Bonn, so she made it appear as if the invitation had come from Wasielewski. Of course Schumann would have to go along.

He conducted Haydn's *Seasons* in Düsseldorf on 17 February and read one book after another (including Shakespeare's *Taming of the Shrew* and Harriet Beecher Stowe's *Uncle Tom's Cabin*) before leaving. Three days after returning from Bonn, he began a new composition, the *Ballade for Male Chorus, Solo Voices, and Orchestra* (op. 143). Dr. Hasenclever had helped arrange the text. Schumann quickly finished it, which left him time to give music lessons to his daughter Marie in March.[19]

April saw the beginning of an activity that occupied Schumann off and on for most of the rest of the year: holding séances. He found "table moving" to be a "wonderful" and "astonishing" pastime, and even wrote an essay about it.[20] Schumann's enthusiasm for table moving led him to conduct

---

*That year Schumann also wrote piano accompaniments for the Bach Violoncello Suites (in March 1853) and finished another set of contrapuntal studies, *Seven Pieces in Fughetta Form* (op. 126).

séances for his friends, his children, and out-of-town visitors, including the musicians who were beginning to arrive for the festival in May. "One is surrounded with miracles," he wrote to Ferdinand Hiller, who would be one of the conductors. "When you get here maybe you will take part as well." One time Schumann asked the table to beat out the opening of Beethoven's Fifth Symphony. "It hesitated longer than usual before answering," but finally complied![21]

None of the musicians who participated in these "magnetic experiments," as Schumann called them, seemed to find anything unusual about his craze for table moving, nor did Clara. "Robert is quite enchanted with these marvelous powers and has fallen thoroughly in love with the little table and promised him [sic] a new dress (i.e., a new tablecloth)."[22] She actually seemed pleased to observe that her often morose husband would become more "jovial [and] quite pleasantly excited" when he played the mysterious game. Both Wasielewski and Litzmann later insisted that "table moving" was a symptom of the composer's incipient madness. That may be so, but it should also be pointed out that interest in mediums was then rather fashionable. Books by the French mesmerist Leon Ravail (better known by his *nom de plume* Allan Kardek) had begun to circulate widely after the 1848 revolution, and Schumann could well have been exposed to this literature, which recommended the sort of mystical "experiments" he was making.

Holding séances may also have helped Schumann temporarily stave off psychosis. As in his earlier experiences with magnets, the wearing of amulets, and hypnosis, it delighted him to engage in magical thinking; it was a refuge from the painful reality of his frustrations and anger. Psychic practices of the sort he engaged in in 1853 also seemed to give Schumann an illusion of having contact with great composers (Beethoven, for example).

In mid-May Joseph Joachim arrived in Düsseldorf to perform the Beethoven Violin Concerto, with Schumann conducting. Called "Pepi" by his friends, Joachim (1831–1907) was the seventh of eight children born to a Jewish couple in the tiny Hungarian village Köpcsény. Like Schumann, he had as a baby fallen in love with the female voice (his sister's, according to his biographer, Andreas Moser) and soon became attracted to musical instruments. His father took him for lessons to the best violinist in Budapest, Stanislaus Serwaczyński. Joachim gave his first recital in public at age eight. The next year he was sent off to Vienna, for instruction with Joseph Böhm, a distinguished violinist who more or less adopted him.*[23]

Perhaps as a result of this premature separation from his home and

---

*Such treatment of musical prodigies is by no means uncommon. The eleven-year old pianist Arthur Rubinstein, for example, was taken in 1898 from Lodz, to be supervised in Berlin, by none other than Joseph Joachim, then a distinguished professor of music.

parents, Joachim had lifelong difficulties in establishing intimate relationships. His personal motto was "Free but lonesome" (*Frei aber einsam*). At the time of his participation in the Düsseldorf festival, he was leading a solitary existence in Hanover, as concertmaster of the court orchestra. (He had recently left Weimar, where he had played under Liszt.) As his biographer Andreas Moser puts it, Joachim "felt so orphaned and alone the first years in Hanover that he was in danger of becoming a hypochondriac. . . . A veritable Hamlet mood descended over him."[24] In this mood he had started to compose, and he wanted Schumann to take an interest in him. (Just before Schumann's birthday in 1853, Joachim sent him the score for the *Overture to "Hamlet"* he had just finished. Schumann was delighted. "While reading the score," he wrote Joachim, "I felt as if there is a scene illuminated on every page, with Ophelia and Hamlet stepping out in the flesh."[25]

As Joachim was playing the Beethoven concerto with Schumann on 17 May, an extraordinary rapport seemed to spring up between them. It was felt by the orchestra, which responded beautifully, and the audience, which, Schumann said, expressed "tremendous enthusiasm."[26] According to Clara,

> With the Beethoven concerto, Joachim won victory over us all—he played with a perfection and deep poetry, so much soul in every tiny tone, a real ideal, such violin playing as I've never heard. . . . And how perfectly the genial work was accompanied! It was as if a religious devotion reigned over the entire orchestra.[27]

Thus was established the first of two passionate friendships with young men—later called "demons"—who accompanied Schumann into the labyrinth of his mental decline and hospitalization.

After his forty-third birthday, Schumann sent Joachim a critique of his *Hamlet Overture* and requested permission to conduct the work in Düsseldorf later that year.[28] Joachim complied instantly, and he then asked whether Schumann would compose a violin concerto for him.

It may be recalled how early in his career Schumann had relied on the figure of a great violinist, Paganini, to inspire him. This had resulted mostly in music for the piano, however. Lately, with his concertmasters Wasielewski and Becker in mind, he had again been writing violin music. But, despite his success with a concerto for the piano and one for the violoncello, he had never attempted a violin concerto. Joachim's highly flattering request now provided the incentive to do so.

May Beethoven's example incite you, wondrous guardian of the richest trea-
sures, to draw a work out of your deep quarry, and bring into the light something for us poor violinists, who can elevate our instrument only through
chamber music.[29]

Schumann had the usual interruptions before he went to work on the
concerto. The music festival in May had drained him physically. (Hiller, by
previous arrangement, shared much of the conducting, and Tausch also
helped.) Yet instead of being able to rest, Schumann agonized in June over
another possible pregnancy of Clara's (a false alarm). During the month of
July he again settled into a heavy literary program: in preparation for his
"Poet's Garden" anthology, he reread all the books by Jean Paul that had
interested him as a teenager. Then came another series of concerts in Bonn,
which Clara and Wasielewski had arranged. One of these would include, on
29 July, a performance of Schumann's ballad for chorus and orchestra, *The
King's Son* (op. 116), shortly to be published.

Dutifully the composer made the trip south. He was very tired and the
next day complained of a "severe attack of rheuma[tism]"—the household
book says "unfit for anything."[30] That surely was a worrisome situation; the
Schumanns had to get back to Düsseldorf, and he was in such pain that he
could barely move.

Much has been made, retrospectively, of this brief and not unusual episode. Dr. Domenicus Kalt, a physician recommended by friends in Bonn,
came to the hotel and, according to Clara, spoke with Schumann about
"sciatica" (*Hexenschuss*), a painful condition of the sciatic nerve.[31] The composer's reaction to what this doctor told him is difficult to ascertain. "*Sehr
gescheut*" is his comment in the household book, which can be translated as
"very frightened," or as slang for "very intelligent."[32] That same evening
the Schumanns returned to Düsseldorf on a steamboat, arriving at 10 o'clock,
and he was well enough to enjoy "moving tables with guests" the next day.*
Two nights later he read, for a group of ladies, the dreary poems he had
written in Moscow about the saga of the great bell that fell out of its socket
in the Kremlin (see pp. 187–188). For Clara he made a piano reduction of
two string quartets, then in only five days composed an *Overture to Faust*,
culminating ten years of intermittent labor on the *Scenes* for Goethe's play.
On 20 August he wrote a "Birthday Song for Clara," in preparation for a

---

*Dr. Kalt received only 1.15 thalers for his visit, so evidently it was a very brief consulta-
tion.[33] But many years later, long after Schumann's death, rumors began to circulate that on
his way out of the Golden Star Hotel, Dr. Kalt, who had just called on a patient whose
identity he was unaware of, told a bystander that the man was incurably ill due to "softening
of the brain."[34] This dubious information has been cited by several clinicians to support their
assumption that Schumann may have had one or more "strokes."[35]

surprise party on 13 September. The last week of August he composed for her the *Introduction and Allegro in D minor for Piano and Orchestra* (op. 134).

On 28 August Joseph Joachim appeared on their doorstep with his violin. Schumann was "enchanted" by everything he played for them, and the next forty-eight hours were an almost nonstop orgy of chamber music, at the end of which the household book reports "strange weakness of the speech organ."[36] Unfortunately we have no description of his speech disturbance from others, including Joachim. But a significant loss of control must have taken place, for Schumann's handwriting that day seems more jagged and even less legible than usual—although not in his musical manuscripts. Some psychiatrists—Philippe André, for example[37]—have gone so far as to say that Schumann had dysarthria, that is, trouble articulating the syllables of words. That would suggest a neurological problem rather than an emotionally induced weakness.

The speech disturbance was very transient, however, and whatever caused it was not serious enough to interfere with Schumann's ability to continue with his plans for Clara's birthday. Without her knowledge he had ordered a new piano from the Klems factory in Düsseldorf. This was a major expense, 204 thalers, and Clara afterward thought he had been much too generous. The instrument was to be embellished with flowers. Schumann purchased other presents as well,* and he invited a group of friends, arranging for Clara to be out of the house so they could surprise her by singing his "Birthday Song." (Schumann also wrote the text for this new composition, a poem that refers to the presents he had given her, thirteen years earlier, for their wedding. All of this makes it unlikely that he was having memory problems or difficulty organizing his thoughts, as one would expect had there been a serious neurological impairment.) Clara, who suspected nothing, was "completely overwhelmed" by Schumann's gift of the new piano. "Am I not the happiest wife on earth?" she asked.[38]

Schumann's mind continued to race. Coincident with the making of birthday plans for his wife, he had been composing music for Joseph Joachim. In only six days he wrote the Fantasy in C major (op. 131) for violin and piano. (He also orchestrated the piece.) It was dedicated and presented to Joachim during his next visit to Düsseldorf, on 23 September.† The Fantasy is one of Schumann's most successful compositions, written in his best ro-

---

*His usual birthday presents for Clara were bottles of cologne, items of clothing like scarves or aprons, fruit—especially melons—champagne, and a birthday cake. He also would regularly supplement her household allowance with a generous gift of cash on such occasions, so that it would be difficult to say that his gift of a piano in 1853 was *excessively* generous (that is, a possible sign of poor judgment).

†By then, Schumann had also composed his charming *Children's Ball* (op. 130), six easy dances for piano, four-handed.

Schumann's handwritten score (including piano reduction) of the slow movement of his violin concerto, composed for Joachim in 1852. (Original in the Universitätsbibliothek, Freie Universität, West Berlin.)

mantic style, fluctuating between rhythmic excitement and a darkly mysterious moodiness. Joachim was very pleased with the composition, often performed it, and helped make it popular.

Schumann was less fortunate with his *Concerto for Violin and Orchestra in D minor*, which remains to this day a controversial work. He composed it in less than a fortnight, and expected that Joachim would make technical improvements and edit the manuscript. But the violinist, preoccupied with his own work in Hanover, did not even have the time to practice the solo part properly before playing it for Schumann and Clara during their visit there in January 1854, just before the composer's suicide attempt. This rehearsal-performance was unsatisfactory, and after Schumann's hospitalization, Joachim offered to play it for him in Endenich.[39]

The hospital concert never took place, but on 15 September 1855, ten months before Schumann's death, Joachim performed the concerto for Clara, to commemorate the anniversary of her marriage. She never liked the work, claiming that it had a "defect" and "showed definite traces of [Schumann's] last illness." She even asked Joachim to recompose the work and "make a really magnificent last movement for me," which he refused to do. Eugenie Schumann, the last surviving witness, stated that in the 1880s, when an edition of Schumann's as-yet-unpublished music was under discussion, Clara decreed, "the concerto should never be brought into the open," and said that she wanted the manuscript to be destroyed.[40]

After Joachim's death in 1907, however, his son Johannes sold the manuscript to the Prussian State Library in Berlin, on the condition that only in 1956—one hundred years after Schumann's death—could it be published. Thus the violin concerto lingered in obscurity. Only a handful of people even knew of its existence. One of them was Jelly d'Aranyi, a violinist and distant relative of Joachim living in England. She, like Joachim himself, believed in spiritualism; d'Aranyi even claimed that since 1933 Schumann had been giving her telepathic instruction on how to perform his violin concerto![41] Additional pressure to have the manuscript released came from within Germany, where violinists were being forced to play the music of non-Jewish composers only. Thus in August 1936 Joachim's son reversed his position on the one-hundred-year clause.[42] Hoping that Schumann's "lost" concerto would now get world-wide attention, the publishers offered it to Yehudi Menuhin.* He responded enthusiastically and declared that here was the "historically missing link" between the Beethoven and the Brahms violin concertos.[44]

> The concerto is a treasure, and I am completely enchanted! It is real Schumann, romantic and fresh and so logically interconnected in every impulse. Thoroughly mentally healthy throughout. . . . Except for a small section in the first movement everything is playable and sounds beautiful. Evidently Joachim has changed nothing.
>
> Perhaps one was startled at the time by the audacious harmonies which today's ears do not find at all surprising.
>
> I hope there were better reasons than that for putting Schumann into an insane asylum![45]

The concerto begins in a grandly Handelian style, very formal and in the classical tradition, which soon gives way to Schumann's innate romanticism. His second subject is a passionate melody that soars over the orchestra and contains thematic material which is further developed throughout the rest of the concerto. His slow movement is so transcendently beautiful and original in design that one must seriously question the idea that the composer's creative abilities had suffered as a result of his difficult years in Düsseldorf. (The main theme, spun out soulfully by the solo violin, anticipates the one Schumann hallucinated just before his suicide attempt.) The

---

* Although Menuhin gave the first performance in the United States and made a recording, he was not allowed to play the Schumann concerto in Germany until after the war, with Benjamin Britten as his accompanist. The Berlin premiere had been given by Georg Kulenkampff, and it was blown out of all proportion by Nazi propaganda: "by permission of the Führer . . . Robert Schumann has entered Valhalla."[43]

Finale, a vigorous polonaise, was obviously intended for Joachim, of whom Schumann said (on 26 October 1853), "one just can't love him enough."[46] The correct tempo is often debated among violinists and conductors. (Schumann indicates "lively, but not fast." Perhaps he wanted the finale to sound improvised, like his *Fantasy* for the violin. But his metronome mark, 63 to the beat, seems generally too slow.)

The name Brahms evokes the image of a gruff and paunchy middle-aged man with a gray beard. But that was not how he looked on 30 September 1853 when he arrived in Düsseldorf. Just turned twenty, Johannes Brahms, according to his biographer Max Kalbeck, was "a vigorous youth who still seemed almost like a child. With his blond hair, his high voice, and his big blue eyes he came upon Schumann like an apparition from another world, sent down to resurrect and soothe his repressed, hopeless, and despairing self."[47] Clara compared him to a heavenly messenger who had been "deliberately sent by God."[48] Schumann, responding as he had on earlier occasions to Götte, Bennett, Schunke, and other attractive young men, called Brahms "a genius," "the true Apostle . . . he could capsize the world in a few days," "a young blood," "the young eagle," and finally a "demon."[49]

Brahms shared with Schumann a deep love of the romantic tradition. He identified so closely with its spirit that he even adopted the name "Johannes Kreisler junior," a figure straight out of Schumann's own Hoffmannesque past. Brahms had recently left home for the first time, to go on a concert tour with Eduard Remenyi, a violinist of Hungarian extraction, who introduced him to Joachim and Liszt and then abandoned him. Brahms then stayed in Hanover with his lonely friend Joachim, who told him to give regards to the Schumanns on his way home to Hamburg.

It was an explosive combination of personalities. Brahms, like Schumann, had a complicated family background. His mother, a tiny, crippled woman, was seventeen years older than his handsome father, an itinerant musician. Brahms's older sister was an invalid, his younger brother, a ne'er-do-well. Johannes had turned to the piano at an early age, and when he was ten he had performed with such brilliance that a talent scout offered him a tour of the United States. Instead, Brahms began studying with his teacher's teacher, Eduard Marxsen, a distinguished musician who interested him in composing. When only a teenager, Brahms had to earn money, which he did by singing and playing the piano in various taverns.*

---

*It is not entirely clear whether some of these were frequented by prostitutes, but an early exposure to prostitution has often been blamed for Brahms's ambivalence toward women and

Both Schumann and his wife were immediately taken by the young stranger from Hamburg. Clara reported that Brahms "played his own sonatas, scherzos, etc. for us, all full of superabundant fantasy, most intimate feelings and mastery of form. Robert thinks there is nothing he can tell him about what to delete or to add. It is really touching to see this person at the piano with his interesting, youthful face which is completely transformed as he plays, his beautiful hands which achieve victory over the greatest difficulties with the greatest ease."[51]

Brahms appealed strongly to Clara Schumann at what was a critical moment both in her marriage and in her career. Not only was her husband visibly failing, but she was pregnant again ("Clara's certainty," says the household book on 3 October 1853, just three days after Brahms's arrival in Düsseldorf[52]). This necessitated, again, the postponement of plans for concerts in England. "My last good years go by, as well as my strength," wrote the probably angry Clara, "reason enough to feel depressed."[53] Brahms's physical androgyny—"the delicate maidenlike profile of an exceptionally beautiful man," as Kalbeck calls it[54]—may have made him an exciting but safe object of desire for both Schumann *and* his wife, who would certainly not be able to continue having intercourse much longer. Also, Brahms's personality—Joachim described him as "having two natures, one childishly genial . . . the other like a demon, lying in wait"[55]—was sufficiently like Schumann's to make him seem like a younger version of Clara's husband. (The fact that she was fourteen years older than Brahms might have contributed to their mutual attraction, since Brahms had observed a similar age difference between his own parents.)

Thus the ambitious young Brahms, away from home for the first time and wanting desperately to be loved and accepted, found himself pulled in two directions. Schumann, a famous composer he respected, drew him into his circle of loyal disciples, while Clara, a beautiful pianist, embraced him as a free spirit and fellow virtuoso. What had been intended as only a brief visit stretched into a month, during which Brahms was the Schumanns' daily guest. He often had his meals with the family and was accepted as a sort of older brother by the children.*

Was Brahms ever sexually intimate with Clara Schumann? The question titillates, but it is ultimately unanswerable. Much of the relevant correspondence has been destroyed, at her request. Only two letters survive that shed any light on the matter. Both were written while Schumann was hospital-

---

his unwillingness to marry. What probably lay behind this was the composer's abiding attachment to his adoring mother, as well as his later, complicated, relationship with Clara Schumann.[50]

* The parallel with Schumann's own arrival in Leipzig and involvement with the Wieck family when he was Brahms's age may also have been a factor in their rapport at this critical moment.

ized; if Brahms and Clara ever did have a sexual liaison, it was probably during this difficult stretch of time.*

The first letter was written to Joachim on 19 June 1854, when Brahms was living with Clara in Düsseldorf:

> I think . . . I am in love with her. Often I have to hold myself back forcibly from just simply putting my arm around her and—: I don't know, it seems so natural to me, as though she wouldn't mind it at all.[57]

The other suggestive letter was written on 17 May 1855 by Clara to her friend Bertha Voigt, who wanted to visit. Brahms and Clara were still living under the same roof and Clara did not know where Bertha and her husband could stay.[58] One wants to know why Clara could not have asked Brahms to move to a hotel for a few nights, or insisted that he room with his good friend Albert Dietrich.

Before we leave this subject, the rumor that Brahms may have fathered Clara's last child deserves comment. It was circulated by Alfred Schumann, a grandson, in the form of a booklet called *Johannes Brahms, The Father of Felix Schumann*,[59] copies of which are now hard to find. Those that Clara's daughters did not immediately buy were later confiscated by the Nazis, because, according to Professor Max Flesch-Thebesius of the Schumann Society of Frankfurt/Main, they were considered "sufficiently damaging to German honor to warrant being burned."[60] One copy, however, does survive in Zwickau. It is a nasty pamphlet, filled with maudlin poetry and mediocre drawings. Alfred Schumann made no effort to explain how Brahms could have seduced Clara (or vice versa) that first week of his visit to Düsseldorf. Also, since Schumann's household book shows that he and Clara had intercourse seven times during the preceding month, it seems extremely unlikely that the "young demon," no matter how importunate, could have fathered their last child.

Besides, it was Schumann and Brahms, rather than Clara and Brahms, who were more involved with each other at the beginning. Hardly a week had passed before Schumann was writing ecstatically to Joachim about "the young eagle . . . the true Apostle."[61] Schumann was in the process of putting together an idolatrous essay about Brahms, which was published later that month in the *New Journal for Music*. He had written nothing for his old newspaper for years, so this article, "New Paths" (*Neue Bahnen*), created a sensation. Schumann called the hitherto unknown composer "a man of des-

---

* After Schumann's death, their relationship cooled noticeably. Brahms was briefly involved with another woman, Agathe von Siebold, who would have liked to marry him, but Clara disapproved. Clara Schumann gradually became more like a second mother to Brahms, and after that none of his fleeting romances with other women even went as far as an engagement.[56] He died on 3 April 1897, less than a year after Clara.

tiny," the "most significant talent" of the day. Genuinely impressed with Brahms's versatility—his music at age twenty was far more mature and technically proficient than Schumann's at a comparable age—the older composer correctly predicted that Brahms would one day excel as a symphonist. He envisioned Brahms "lowering his magic wand over the mighty and massed combination of chorus and orchestra," and described other sexually suggestive images, for example Brahms as "a surging stream, uniting everything into a single waterfall, with peaceful rainbows hovering over this cascade, and butterflies and nightingales delighting on its banks."[62]

This sounds like the young Schumann again, now speaking in a slightly out-of-fashion romantic style. He even seemed to be mobilizing another army of *Davidsbündler*. "New Paths" lists twelve composers Schumann considered suitable to walk in his apostle's company. Included were Joachim and Gade. Excluded were Berlioz, Wagner, and Liszt. A few days later Schumann sent a copy of "New Paths" to Brahms's father, saying, "You can look forward with confidence to the future of this darling of the muses and always count on my most intimate involvement with his success."[63]

Brahms thanked Schumann profusely; "You've made me terribly happy," he wrote. But he questioned whether it was justifiable for the older composer to "raise expectations, about what I can do, to such an extraordinary pitch."[64] Brahms was a severe self-critic, and he later destroyed some of the youthful compositions Schumann had admired so much.* As for other reactions to "New Paths," Joachim complimented Schumann on his "prose poem,"[66] while Hans von Bülow, first a harsh critic but later a solid supporter of Brahms, wrote Lizst sarcastically, "It doesn't trouble my sleep in the least, Mozart-Brahms or Schumann-Brahms. Fifteen years ago Schumann said exactly the same thing about the 'genius' of William Sterndale Bennett."[67]

An early sign of Brahms's ambivalence toward Schumann (as well as Joachim) was the way he reacted when the older composer invited him to join in writing a sonata honoring the violinist. It was to be based on the tone sequence FAE, symbolizing the first letters of Joachim's personal motto, "Frei Aber Einsam." Schumann asked his young disciple Albert Dietrich to write the first movement, which he did, using the FAE theme throughout. Schumann himself composed the second movement, a lovely Intermezzo that also embroiders these three notes. Brahms contributed the third movement, a Scherzo, but he made no mention at all of Joachim's motto.† Schumann also wrote a wild Finale for the FAE Sonata. He later composed a first

---

* Luckily for Brahms, who was promised "50 goldpieces" for them,[65] his most important early compositions were published in Leipzig, on Schumann's recommendation.

† This movement, today occasionally performed as an encore piece, may actually have been written earlier; it bears an uncanny resemblance to the Scherzo of Schumann's Piano Trio in F major (op. 80).

and third movement, as well, to make this his own *Third Sonata for Violin and Piano*.

It is interesting to note that Clara was excluded from writing the sonata. She wanted to be better known as a composer in her own right and could easily have contributed at least one movement in Joachim's honor. But Schumann seems no longer to have wanted a woman in his *Davidsbund*. He did not mention her in the article about Brahms either.

These were symptoms of his increasing hostility toward Clara, undoubtedly related to his despair over their unwanted pregnancy and the onset of his psychosis. Sometimes Schumann's criticism of his wife was vicious. For example, it is reported that on one occasion in Düsseldorf, he objected to Clara's playing of his piano quintet and told Julius Tausch, "You play it, a man understands that better."[68] At the end of his tenure as music director, Schumann even had the gall to dismiss Clara as his associate at choir rehearsals—poor judgment, considering how essential she was to his work as a conductor. This was a man's job, he told Tausch, who was only too pleased to take over.

Most disastrous for Schumann's well-being was his loss of prestige as a conductor and his virtual abandonment, in November 1853, of all further responsibilities as Düsseldorf's music director. Schumann's household book gives an organized, sequential account of these sad events. We also have the complete story from Niecks, later a member of the orchestra, who had direct access to many of the local musicians and the civic bureaucracy in Düsseldorf.

Apparently Schumann had of late been behaving most undiplomatically toward the city officials. According to Niecks, "He could not brook contradiction, even in trifling matters of opinion; he even took offense if, when he asked a question, the answer was not to his taste. In such cases he usually rose and walked away without saying a word. . . . His wife and friends always urged the chairman of the committee to agree to his wishes so that everything disagreeable might be kept out of his way."[69] Often there were last-minute rearrangements of the program, with Schumann stepping in to conduct works he had not rehearsed or did not know well enough.

> Once at a mass he went on conducting after the movement was finished and the priest had begun to intone. At a choir practice the sopranos were singing several high A's and the effect was such that it aroused laughter; the sopranos stopped singing and the other parts gradually followed suit until Tausch was left playing the pianoforte alone. Schumann noticed nothing and went on beat-

ing time, and Tausch, thinking it was no use going on by himself, stopped too. Schumann beckoned to him to come, and Tausch expected a reproof for having broken off. But no—Schumann showed him a passage in the score and said, "Look, this bar is beautiful."[70]

An astute observation by Joseph Joachim gives a clue to why Schumann was so out of touch with his surroundings: "He is constantly so filled up with music that I really can't blame the man for preferring not to be disturbed by the sounds of the outer world."[71] Schumann's perception of external reality was evidently being drowned by his musical imagination, a flood of irresistible inner voices. Maintaining contact with the environment was becoming increasingly difficult. For example, during another trip to Bonn, on 13 November 1853, the composer arose suddenly while Clara was rehearsing, said he was unwell, and insisted that they go home.[72]

In trying to placate these eccentricities, Dr. Julius Illing, an attorney and the chairman of the Music Society in Düsseldorf, called a planning conference to announce that henceforth the chorus would no longer appear in public unless conducted by Tausch. Schumann strode out of the room without saying a word, leaving the committee to debate how best to resolve this delicate situation. Finally it was decided to send Dr. Illing and another board member to Schumann's house to try to effect a compromise. Their strategy was to offer him the "larger" works on the program if he would allow Tausch to conduct the "shorter" ones. It was an inartistic solution; works of music simply cannot be divided up on the basis of size. For example, the committee wanted Mendelssohn's *First Walpurgisnight* to be considered a "short" work. It had been scheduled for the opening concert, on 27 October, and, since a chorus is required, Tausch would have to be in charge. Schumann adamantly refused to comply with this arrangement. Angry at these "shameless people,"[73] he decided to reorganize the opening concert according to his own wishes.

This was a concert for which Joachim had been engaged as soloist, and the young violinist had been in and out of the house on Bilkerstrasse several times during the preceding weeks. The commotion must have been terrible—Brahms's visit, committee meetings, and a séance (which, according to the household book "did not succeed"[74]). That Schumann could do any serious work under these conditions is astonishing, but he not only finished orchestrating his Violin Concerto in October but also wrote the F A E Sonata for Joachim and a highly original set of pieces for clarinet, viola and piano, called *Fairy-Tales* (op. 132). This almost futuristic music, with its dark melodies, nervous rhythms, and subtly contrapuntal texture, demonstrates not only the soundness of Schumann's composing, even on the brink of psychosis, but also the amazing way in which he was incorporating Brahms's

Johannes Brahms at twenty,
when he first met Schumann.
(Sketch by Jean-Joseph
Laurens, 1853.)

genius into his own musical style. This is apparent, for example, in his *Songs of Early Morning* (op. 133), written in October 1853, and inspired not only by Brahms's youthful compositions for the piano but also by Hölderlin's "Hyperion," which Schumann had recently read.

That month Schumann had another visitor, the painter Jean-Joseph Laurens, who sketched several portraits of him, as well as of Brahms. Thus we know approximately what these two composers looked like shortly before the concert with Joachim. Brahms had the delicate, "maidenlike" appearance described earlier. Schumann looked gloomy, with a slack face and somewhat drooping eyes. The painter pointed this out to Clara, mentioning that Schumann's pupils seemed enlarged, and she acknowledged that her husband was unwell.

Since pupils enlarge in response to internal states of arousal such as fear and curiosity, Schumann's most likely were enlarged as a result of Brahms's visit and all the stress he was experiencing at the time. However, if structural changes were taking place in Schumann's brain, they too could have influenced his eyes, as well as the appearance of his face. Inequality of the pupils and absence of responsiveness to darkness, the so-called Argyll Robertson phenomenon, is found in a little over half the patients who have brain syphilis. Their pupils are characteristically small. As far as can be seen, Laurens's portrait of Schumann does not show unequal pupils; they do not even seem unduly dilated, and certainly not contracted.

Schumann's last concert in Düsseldorf brought out all the worst in him. Joachim was to perform the Beethoven concerto and Schumann's *Fantasy*. Joachim's own composition, the *Hamlet Overture*, which Schumann liked so much, was also on the program. But Schumann simply wasn't up to the demands of Joachim's difficult overture. Niecks mentions that one of Schumann's "humorous and pathetic predicaments" was that he would "let his baton fall" while conducting. One day at a rehearsal he went up to a member of the orchestra and, "showing him a baton with a string attached to it and to his wrist, said with childlike simplicity and a pleased expression of face and voice, 'Look, now it can't fall again!'"*[75]

Schumann's humiliation at the concert was described by Joachim, who tried to be sympathetic.

> Just before the rehearsal Schumann chatted with me about Hamlet and spoke about a certain horn passage in the Overture. . . . "This has to sound really magical; I look forward to it with special pleasure!" he said. After letting the piece be played through from beginning to end—piles of notes fell on the floor of course—he came up to me, full of disappointment, to say, "Strange, how wrong one can be, the horn solo was completely inaudible. Well then, let's just try it once more." I intervened by saying that what happened is really quite understandable, because the horn player never actually came in with his solo . . . whereupon Schumann simply told him to pay closer attention and avoid miscounting in the preceding rest. The obvious solution would have been to give cues to the musicians for their entrances. But that he did not do. The second run-through produced exactly the same results, so the orchestra started to grumble and requested that I conduct the piece myself. When I finally did so, with Schumann's approval, everything was suddenly in perfect order, and the horn solo had its desired effect. But now the members of the orchestra, and several gentlemen of the committee, pleaded with me to lead the Overture at the concert as well. I had great difficulty to make it clear to these people that this might make so honored an artist and human being as Schumann feel insulted, and that I would under no circumstances want to make myself guilty of doing such a thing. Incidentally, at the evening performance the piece went just as well under Schumann's direction as one could possibly expect, considering the modest abilities of the Düsseldorf orchestra at the time.[76]

---

* All of this could be interpreted as evidence of disease. Weakness, a neurological disturbance, faulty position sense, or diminished motor control, might have caused Schumann to drop his baton. (Of course, some poor conductors drop theirs when they become overly excited.) The suspicion that he may have had an organic psychosis is further strengthened by Nieck's observation of Schumann's "childlike simplicity" in the face of so humiliating a situation in front of the orchestra, as well as other signs of grossly impaired judgment, to be mentioned shortly.

After this concert the Music Society finally decided, unanimously, to put Tausch officially in charge of the orchestra. The question was how to present this unpleasant news to the Schumanns. On 7 November Herr Illing once again went to their house, accompanied this time by another attorney. The composer was not available, so they told Clara that henceforth Schumann would be allowed to conduct nothing but his own music. "Impertinent effronteries" (*Unverschämtheiten*), wrote Schumann, seemingly unaware that his inadequacies had brought this about. Unfortunately, Clara also took that position and, in backing him, probably made the situation even worse. She believed that the plan to have Tausch do more conducting was "an infamous intrigue and an insult," and without consulting her husband she told the gentlemen that their demand would force him to resign his position as music director. "Oh, these are vile people," she wrote, enraged. "Vulgarity is in charge here."[77]

The next day, 8 November 1853, Clara left for Cologne, to play Beethoven's *Emperor* Concerto and some of her husband's works there. In her absence Schumann "vacillated between Berlin and Vienna" and then "decided for Vienna."[78] But these were delusional fantasies. Neither of these places had anything to offer him and his "decision" to go to Vienna was meaningless. Another indication of his faulty judgment was the stiff, legalistic letter he wrote that week "To The Honorable Board of Directors of the General Music Society," reminding them that "a contract exists . . . beginning 1 April [1850] which year after year ends on 1 October in such a way that at least three months' advance notice must be given for either party to cancel it by that date." Denying any personal responsibility for the predicament he was in, he blamed the board for "hindering me from exercising the official duties that I have . . . always fulfilled conscientiously." Insofar as Schumann accused the city officials of "having completely forgotten that the contract also places certain obligations on them," this could be called a defensive, if not paranoid, letter. Of course they hadn't forgotten their obligations, as indicated by their extreme caution in seeking legal advice before taking this final step. Yet Schumann implied that by asking Tausch to conduct, the board had committed a breach of contract. He asserted his "moral obligation under no circumstances to do any directing or collaborating as long as the contract is not upheld, which means I alone exercise the power of director." Finally he threatened "in any event to make use of my existing right to give notice at the proper time, namely from 1 October 1854 on."[79]

Schumann's threat was exactly what the Music Society wanted. Their official answer (dated 14 November 1853) made obeisances to Schumann's "genius" and his "highly esteemed and honored spouse," but did nothing to retract the unacceptable conditions that would have left him director in name only.[80] As for the "awkward matter of being called on to debate contractual terms," there really was nothing left to discuss, since Schumann had already by then refused to appear for a concert on 10 November, thus in effect breaking the contract unilaterally. He had sent Tausch a note warning, "If you conduct today and as long as we are here, at the rehearsals and concerts, I cannot regard you as well disposed." According to Niecks, "The orchestra assembled at 6 P.M. to rehearse, and by 6:15 Dr. Schumann had not come. The committee then asked Tausch to proceed and the performance satisfied the public."[81]

Schumann continued to fume at the "miserable people here" and to complain about the city administrators' "rascally tricks." On 19 November he mailed them one more distinctly paranoid letter—he called it an "ultimatum"—recounting how they "dealt behind [his] back with someone [Tausch] who ten years ago was my student," and referring impotently to "an open breach of contract."[82] Two days later, he sent a very peculiar letter to Joachim ("Dear Comrade of the War"), which shows evidence of psychosis. He had aimed "a 20-pound explosive into the enemy camp," he wrote, only to discover that "another comrade of the war was secretly employed by the foul enemy to blow me up with an underground mine." (Perhaps the alleged traitor was Dr. Hasenclever, who in the past had voted for Schumann at committee meetings but now was taking sides against him.) The letter also discloses that Schumann had a delusion that Joachim was going to get married: "I will compose a Wedding Symphony for you, with a violin solo."[83]

After considerable debate about what to do next, Schumann and his pregnant wife left on 24 November for a month of concerts in Holland, some of which he would conduct. On the day of departure, she had a "bad accident" (although not another miscarriage), while he complained of the auditory disturbance that would soon escalate into psychotic hallucinations.[84] Schumann had also been focusing hypochondriacally on his "illness due to a cold" and he was concerned that two of his children had measles.[85] Away from Germany he seems to have kept his psychosis under control. "My dear wife was ill occasionally, but not at the piano," Schumann wrote Joachim (on 11 December, from Utrecht). "The Dutch audiences are most enthusiastic. . . . In the major cities I found my compositions prepared for performance, so that all I had to do was stand up and conduct them."[86] His diary mentions sexual intercourse frequently and comments on the joy of eating and drinking plentifully. Clara was able to gain access to royalty, with the usual complication—they were treated as lackeys. Once after she performed for a "noisy assemblage of people," their royal host turned to

Schumann and asked, "Are you musical too . . . what instrument do you play?"[87] This time he responded not with indignation, but with apathy—smiling, nodding agreeably, and saying nothing.

On 22 December 1853 the Schumanns returned to Düsseldorf. He was exhausted and demoralized. Clara managed to cheer him up a little, with a Christmas present of a new portrait of her (painted by Carl Sohn). It shows a lovely, sensitive, but pensively sad woman dressed in black—which she wore for the rest of her life.

After the New Year, Schumann started to catalogue all his musical compositions with the thought that a complete edition might one day be published. * The musicologist Siegfried Kross finds Schumann's editing remarkably "accurate and precise."[88] There is no evidence of any disturbance in sequencing or handwriting. Every item is neat, orderly, relevant, and legible, just the opposite of what might be expected in a case of organic brain disease. This is true also of Schumann's "Poet's Garden," the anthology of quotations about music that he worked on almost uninterruptedly beginning in January 1854, although in that task Clara and a professional copyist assisted him.

And yet Düsseldorf's music director, now unemployed but still on salary, was becoming increasingly eccentric. Karl Schorn, a member of the Music Society, recalled him as so "monosyllabic and sparing of words that any conversation was possible only when his wife, who was always at his side, would intervene. . . . His outward appearance gave more the impression of a pedagogue or evangelical minister than that of an unconventional genius."[89]

"Where is Johannes? Is he with you?" asked Schumann of Joachim in a letter on 6 January 1854. "Does he fly high—or only among flowers? Does he not yet sound any drums and trumpets?"[90] It was a momentary spurt of euphoria, stimulated by the thought that Brahms might be composing a symphony. Schumann himself had composed nothing since the beginning of November, when he wrote *Romances for the Violoncello.* (They were not published, though, and Clara later destroyed them in the belief—which she held also for his violin concerto—that the music associated with Schumann's madness ought never to be performed.)

On 18 January the Schumanns set out for Hanover, intending to see Brahms and Joachim there and to give a few more concerts. How this trip ended we already know. It was to be their last journey together.

---

* Schumann had recently finished editing all of his newspaper articles, in preparation for the *Collected Writings About Music and Musicians,* due to appear in May 1854.

XVI.
Endenich, 1854–1856

Schumann's first—and undoubtedly frightening—contact with institutional psychiatry had been during his adolescence, when he visited the Caruses in Colditz and observed the inmates there. German medicine in the romantic era had reverted to a kind of medieval approach, which emphasized mystical speculation about the "soul" and punishment rather than treatment of the mentally ill.[1] A more enlightened approach, in particular the reforms in patient care that the great French psychiatrist Philippe Pinel (1745–1826) had inaugurated, were slow to penetrate the feudalistic German states. During the early part of the century, psychotic people roamed the streets as beggars, were flogged in poorhouses, or were imprisoned in huge stone fortresses.

But the twelve years Schumann spent in Leipzig had exposed him to a more humane and modern tradition. In that city, Johann Christian Heinroth (1773–1843), a disciple of Pinel, had become Germany's first professor of psychiatry, and the homeopathic physicians who treated Schumann had impressed him with their medical approach to mental illness. In Dresden Schumann had learned about the use of hypnosis and hydrotherapy. Thus it is not surprising that after losing control of his mind in January 1854 the composer asked for psychiatric care and cooperated with the doctors who agreed to take care of him. He hoped a brief hospitalization would help him regain his health and resume the career that had been so immensely productive.

Schumann's leap into the Rhine had been suicidal, to be sure. But it could also have been a cry for help. He wanted to leave his wife, fearing that he might do her some harm, but she, in her advanced state of pregnancy, had continued to cling to him. By suddenly taking the matter into his own hands and making a public spectacle of their problems, he had forced the doctors to separate them. Thus Schumann placed himself, Clara, and some of their closest friends under medical authority for an indefinite period. On a deeper level, his self-immersion in the "majestic Father Rhine . . . a German god,"[2] as he described this body of water in his adolescence, may also have symbolized rebirth and the wish for magical reunion with an all-powerful parent. (After Schumann's death Clara discovered a suicide note he had left for her. "Dear Clara," it said, "I will throw my wedding ring into the Rhine. Do the same and both rings will then be united."[3])

The doctors who cared for Schumann in the hospital belonged to a new wave in German psychiatry, the so-called organicist school, which looked for physical causes of mental disease, preferred pharmacological interventions, and looked askance at the older moralistic and soul-searching practices of their "psychicist" colleagues. Thus it is difficult to assess whether they understood Schumann's various and conflicted motives.

Franz Richarz (1812–1887) had studied medicine in Bonn, where psychiatry was taught by Friedrich Nasse (1773–1851), an influential "organicist" who knew Goethe personally and believed that all mental disease stems basically from a disturbance of the heart and blood circulation.[4] Nasse treated patients liberally with medication (drugs and herbs) and physical methods (baths, immersion in mineral springs, climate cures), and only rarely by hypnosis.[5]

Profoundly impressed by Nasse's personality and teaching, young Richarz decided to devote his life to psychiatry, and after completing medical school he apprenticed himself to Dr. Maximillian Jacobi, director of the Rhineland's largest asylum for the mentally ill, in Siegburg. It was a discouraging experience. Jacobi had relatively little faith in medical treatment. He claimed that 80 percent of the patients who recovered from mental diseases did so because of the "hygienic, disciplinary, and moral" policies enforced in his asylum.[6]

After eight years of work there as Jacobi's assistant, Dr. Richarz was ready to open his own, much smaller, mental hospital. He purchased an attractive seven-acre private estate, in Endenich, near Bonn, and remodeled the main building, a two-story structure, to accommodate a maximum of

Dr. Franz Richarz,
psychiatrist in charge of the
hospital at Endenich, where
Schumann spent the end of his
life. (Artist unknown.)

fourteen psychiatric patients.* It was the Rhineland's first private mental hospital.[7] On the ground floor were Richarz's examining rooms and the living quarters for his nurse. Patients lived upstairs; Schumann's bedroom faced southeast, with a view of the mountains along the Rhine.[8] In a nearby sitting room stood the piano he occasionally played—the same instrument Franz Liszt had used to dedicate the Beethoven Memorial at Bonn in 1843.

In larger, state-supported institutions, patients were customarily segregated those who seemed treatable were placed in separate buildings from those who seemed incurable and needed mainly custodial care. Richarz wanted to abolish this distinction.[9] What is incurable today, he believed, might with the progress of science be curable tomorrow. He abhorred the overcrowded conditions of most public institutions and justified the existence of a smaller hospital by saying that no more than fifty patients could be prop-

---

*Endenich is within walking distance of the center of Bonn. The estate that Dr. Richarz purchased had belonged to a prominent family named Kaufmann, and during the Napoleonic upheaval, when Bonn University was closed, the estate became a sort of campus for law students. As the city of Bonn expanded, it incorporated the outlying Endenich within its city limits. Partly damaged by bombing during the second world war, the hospital has been rebuilt and can be seen today at Sebastianstrasse 182.

erly supervised by the doctor in charge. One of the few advantages of a larger asylum was that it could supply a much greater amount of autopsy material, and Dr. Richarz somewhat sarcastically suggested that by working in a bigger hospital an ambitious psychiatrist could further his academic career. Organicists, including Richarz, believed that brain dissection could establish the causes of mental disease, and autopsy reports were often published as contributions to science.

Finally, Dr. Richarz believed that small private hospitals made access to a patient's family easier. By reducing the distance between the asylum and the community, he hoped to facilitate the rehabilitation and early discharge of his patients. In that respect he was well ahead of his time. All in all, he was probably one of the most experienced and competent psychiatrists to be found in the Rhineland at that time.

Regrettably, by the time Schumann was admitted to Endenich, Dr. Richarz could no longer live up to his own high ideals. Within a decade of its opening, his hospital had expanded quickly. Two additional buildings were opened to accommodate the mushrooming population of patients, which finally exceeded sixty. No longer could Richarz supervise everyone.[10] Almost from the beginning, he had to employ other physicians, for example, Dr. Peters, whom he put in charge of Schumann. (Often these assistants would leave the staff after a while to open competing private asylums.) The hospital's nursing staff remained minimal, so that Richarz often had to delegate the daily care of patients to untrained lay personnel from the neighborhood, who did not always act in the patients' best interests. Some of the local innkeepers in today's Endenich recall the asylum very well (it had continued to function until 1925). One recalled his grandfather's tales about the wintry days when attendants, with their patients, would spend a considerable amount of time in the tavern. By getting them intoxicated, said the innkeeper, the attendants would feel they were helping not only the patients but also the doctors, who could then justify recommending a longer hospital stay.

Community care in the sense that Dr. Richarz had originally proposed it was out of the question for Schumann, who was far from home and completely isolated from his family. Only a few friends, including Brahms and Joachim, ever visited him. Probably an even greater obstacle for Dr. Richarz in treating patients was his progressive deafness, which led to his early retirement.* Schumann, when he talked at all, spoke softly. Even after the composer recovered from the acute phase of his psychosis, Dr. Peters, ac-

---

*In 1872 his nephew, Dr. Bernard Oebeke—who had been his assistant since 1859—took charge of the Endenich asylum, and Richarz stayed on only as a consultant.

cording to a visitor in August 1854, complained about his silence, "which makes it difficult if not impossible to explore his inner life." [11]

It therefore seems unlikely that the doctors in Endenich understood very much of what was troubling Schumann. They had no access to information about his personal history, his emotional conflicts, or his previous breakdowns, as we do today. When he was admitted to the hospital, only Dr. Hasenclever was on hand to convey facts about the patient, and these were mainly about his recent suicide attempt. Clara, who could have provided a great deal of relevant information about her husband's personality, including what constituted his "normal" behavior, remained uninvolved in his treatment. Not until June 1855, fifteen months after his admission, did she venture to speak with Dr. Richarz (and then not at the hospital but in Brühl, 23 kilometers away). Even then Clara undoubtedly had difficulties disclosing to the doctor some of the more important aspects of the case. She probably felt guilty, as the close relatives of a suicidal patient often do, about having allowed the situation to get so out of control. Brahms, writing to Clara on 29 January 1855, said that he too was withholding information from Dr. Richarz, presumably at her request, specifically about Schumann's "premonitions of death." Brahms urged Clara to "write the doctors and tell them that [Schumann] has often before talked about such things." [12]

If Dr. Richarz had maintained a daily record of Schumann's hospital care, it would have helped immensely to explain what happened in Endenich. Such a document has never been found, however. Dr. Richarz did maintain files at Endenich, and the "loss" of Schumann's case record has been a cause for speculation. Some people think he destroyed it to keep the unhappy facts from Clara. But that seems unlikely, since she was given a copy of the autopsy report, which was probably more frightening. Richarz passed on to Wasielewski some carefully edited and gruesome extracts from this post-mortem examination, suggesting that he was trying to present a certain picture of Schumann as having had an irreversible and advanced form of brain disease. (Richarz later published a somewhat milder diagnosis, as will be discussed shortly.) Perhaps he was concerned about the effect the release of Schumann's detailed hospital records might have on Clara's reputation, or that of other well-known musicians like Brahms and Joachim, who had benefited from Schumann's support.

There is, of course, the possibility that Dr. Richarz's medical records perished after the hospital was closed in 1925. This seems unlikely, however, for other case histories of famous men treated in Endenich at the time have survived. A reasonable speculation is that because Schumann's record would have revealed the terrible details of an unsuccessful hospital treatment, Dr. Richarz suppressed all of it except the autopsy report.

Not until 1871, a year before his retirement, and only very cautiously in a professional journal, did Richarz disclose that there had been an epidemic of suicides by self-starvation in Endenich.[13] As we shall see, Robert Schumann was probably one of its victims. Wanting to protect his hospital's good reputation and to continue to draw patients away from competing institutions, Dr. Richarz may have asked his nephew to conceal or destroy any case records that might be used as potential evidence of malpractice. He later wrote enthusiastically about his experimental treatments of self-starvation.

Schumann seems to have enjoyed being cared for by men. He liked having Herr Bremer and another attendant in his bedroom before being transferred to Endenich. Upon his arrival there on 4 March 1854, Dr. Richarz received Schumann "in a very kindhearted way and gave him an attendant all his own, whom he liked immediately."[14] It was a regression, perhaps, to the agonizing weeks after his first breakdown, at age twenty-three, when Carl Günther was his roommate.

Clara, after more than thirteen years of living with Schumann, missed him a great deal at the beginning, especially during the night. On 8 March, she reported in her diary, "I cannot sleep at all or just lie in a kind of half-sleep, during which nothing but horrifying images hover about me—I constantly see and hear him."[15] Two days later, she sent an anguished appeal for news to Wasielewski, in Bonn:

> Oh what agony it is for me! My heart breaks completely when I don't even know how he lives, what he does, whether he still hears the voices. . . . How does he sleep, what does he do during the day, and does he ask for me or not?[16]

On 13 March, she sent her mother to Endenich, only to learn that "Robert's condition was much the same; he mostly lies on the bed, but goes walking twice a day and when not too fearful converses with the doctors in a friendly way."[17]

A week later Dr. Peters notified her that Schumann was "generally better," but that "the anxieties [*Beängstigungen*] recur frequently as yet, so that he paces restlessly back and forth in his room and now and again gets down on his knees and wrings his hands."[18]

At the end of the month Johannes Brahms, who had gone to Cologne for a performance of Beethoven's Ninth Symphony—which he had never heard before—stopped in Endenich. (He was accompanied by Wasielewski and another musician, the cellist Christian Reimers.) Dr. Richarz did not allow them to see Schumann, but he told them that his patient was sleeping a great deal. When he awakened he usually talked about Düsseldorf, about the mountains he had climbed and the flowers he had picked there, but not about his wife.[19] This news distressed Clara. "If he thinks about flowers," she wondered, "why doesn't he think of me, why does he never ask about me, why doesn't he request news about me?" She was beginning to realize, painfully, that her husband was withdrawing from her. "Has he closed off his longing [for me] within himself? then how terrible[!] what must he be suffering?"[20]

Clara made repeated, agitated complaints about not getting information about her husband, even though she was hearing about him nearly every day. No one was able to tell her what she wanted to hear, however: that he was thinking of her and still in love with her. Another letter from Dr. Peters (1 April 1854) diplomatically avoids this issue but sounds reassuring:

> I am happy to be able to inform you that your husband's better state of health and calm behavior has been maintained since Monday [27 March]. He still wants to rest a great deal, and except for the time he satisfies his wish to go walking, most of the day is spent dozing on the sofa, or preferably on his bed. Anxiety attacks have not been noted at all during this period, nor have the earlier auditory hallucinations reappeared. Altogether he has been gentle, friendly, easy-going, but brief in conversations.[21]

We must remember that by now Schumann had been hospitalized for nearly a month, and he was undoubtedly sedated, which would account for his desire to sleep. Dr. Richarz's favorite remedies for emotional excitement were chloral hydrate, chloroform, and morphine (by injection). Chloral hydrate is still occasionally used as a sedative-hypnotic today, but not chloroform, which is a dangerously toxic chemical that can produce liver or kidney damage. Morphine, one of the most powerful and highly addicting analgesics, was used liberally by nineteenth-century psychiatrists. An opiate, morphine, is not a very desirable treatment for patients like Schumann, who have depressive tendencies. (His son Ferdinand later became addicted to it.)

The 1 April letter from Dr. Peters (probably dictated by Dr. Richarz) is the only existing document from Endenich that alludes to violence on the composer's part. An attendant apparently felt threatened in Schumann's presence, but it seems probable that upon being admitted to the hospital Schumann was in a state of extreme agitation, which might have escalated into aggressive behavior if he had been interfered with (a scenario that he feared when Clara came too close to him). Peters reported:

> He was not violent toward his attendant, as surely happened at the beginning [*Gewalttätig gegen seinen Wärter, wie dies in der ersten Zeit wohl vorgekommen, ist er nicht gewesen*]; on the contrary he showed himself kindly disposed toward him,

expressed his regret that earlier he had made so much trouble for him, and yesterday, while asking him about the date, made a joke referring to the first of April. On his walks he often looks for violets. His appearance is better, appetite and sleep are very good.[22]

If physical violence did occur, or if Schumann's attendant did feel threatened, then an order to restrain the patient was undoubtedly given to the staff. Strait jackets, handcuffs, and other apparatus used in the larger asylums were kept to a minimum at Endenich, since Dr. Richarz had observed, quite rightly, that physical restraint can worsen or prolong a psychotic excitement. "Medical" techniques, however—bleeding, cupping, blistering, chemical ulcers (produced with antimony ointment), and other painful and sometimes injurious remedies—were much in vogue, and they were widely used in private as well as in public hospitals.[23] Schumann probably did not escape at least some of this "treatment," or the inevitable water cures—hot, cold, and lukewarm baths. We know from his earlier illnesses (but did Richarz?) that they had little if any lasting benefit.

Schumann seems to have made a remarkably rapid recovery in Endenich. His fearfulness and agitation subsided, he welcomed attention, went walking, ate, slept, and looked better, all within the first month of his hospitalization. This is not unusual for an illness of sudden onset, especially when there have been environmental stresses from which the patient can be quickly removed. It is paradoxical but nevertheless true that psychoses that are acute, chaotic, and disorganizing often will heal more easily and with less damage to the personality than those that begin insidiously, are unrelated to outer stress, and have only a few noticeable symptoms.

Schumann's verbal inaccessibility and his persistent inner voices continued to worry the psychiatrists, however. In late April Clara wrote, "I obtained very bad news [that] my poor Robert has been suffering again from uninterrupted auditory disturbances and a deep turning into himself."[24] These symptoms made it difficult for the hospital staff to predict what he might be thinking or planning to do, and in view of the abruptness and dangerousness of his recent suicide attempt, they had to exercise utmost caution and never leave him alone.

This probably bothered Schumann, who valued his privacy. It also brought with it the threat of prolonged custodial care, a very expensive proposition in a private hospital. The costs at Endenich were estimated to run between 45 and 60 thalers per month, the equivalent of Schumann's entire salary as music director, and there was no way to know how long he would need to be confined. With his contract due to run out in September, financial difficulty had to be anticipated. Clara discussed this problem with Hiller, who advised her to go to Cologne where she could earn more than in Düsseldorf.

But she decided not to move, for she expected her husband to be back before fall and wanted him to "find everything the way he had left it."[25]

Fortunately, Paul Mendelssohn, Felix's brother, immediately offered assistance. On 18 March he sent Clara a check for 400 thalers, enough to pay for more than six months of hospital care. After much pondering, she nearly sent the money back, but she finally conceded that since it might take "3 to 4 months" before Schumann could go on a "recovery trip" with her—traveling seems never to have been far from Clara's mind—it would be compatible with her "honor" to accept Mendelssohn's help.[26]

Yet after only two months, Clara again worried about money: "My primary effort must now be to earn whatever Robert's illness costs."[27] She was eager to get on with her concerts and regretted being pregnant.

Meanwhile, Clara was developing a growing attachment to "the good Brahms." Her diary mentions "his facial expressions, his telling eyes" and the appealing way he moved his body at the piano. At first she tried to explain away her interest in the young man by referring to "the way he [Brahms] mourns with me for the Beloved."[28] But as time passed, she acknowledged a feeling of attraction, couched delicately in terms of the romance that had sprung up among all three musicians before Schumann was hospitalized. On 27 May 1854, after strolling with Brahms through a park where she and Robert used to walk, Clara wrote, "It is with Brahms that I prefer to talk about Robert, first because Robert loves him more than anyone, and then because with all his youthfulness he has such a soothingly tender feeling for me! The whole man is such a remarkable phenomenon, partly advanced far beyond his years, and partly always so childlike in his reactions."[29] Clara's "most painful" suspicions that Schumann was falling out of love with her probably fed her romantic feelings for Brahms.

As we have already learned from his correspondence with Joachim, Brahms too felt sexually stimulated in Clara's presence. For the moment, though, their mutual attraction would have to be suppressed. On 6 June 1854, three months after Schumann's admission to Endenich (and two days before his forty-fourth birthday) Clara received news from the doctor suggesting that the end of the ordeal might be in sight.

> Robert has been quiet, without any auditory hallucinations, without fears, is not talking in a confused way, and has asked certain questions which show that he is beginning to recall the past.[30]

Five days later, Felix Schumann was born. Clara postponed the christening, hoping that her husband would be able to attend. (Eventually Brahms stood in for him as Felix's godfather.) But there was encouraging news from Endenich. In July, Mathilde Hartmann, a soprano from Düsseldorf and a friend of the family, was allowed to observe Schumann, but not to speak with him. She found him "looking very well . . . walking firmly and fairly fast, inspecting the flowerbeds with his lorgnette, talking and greeting in a friendly manner."[31] By this time the mayor of Düsseldorf, Ludwig Hammers, had decreed that Schumann's salary should be paid until the end of the year, to allow ample time for his treatment and rehabilitation without burdening Clara too much financially.

In August, Clara received further information from Julius Grimm, who had been permitted to observe Schumann for a considerable length of time:

> Herr Schumann had just returned from a walk, accompanied by his attendant whom he seems to like and with whom he spoke many times in a friendly way. As I entered, Dr. Peters approached him from the courtyard and led him to the window behind which I was concealed. Herr Schumann had visited the Bonn cemetery. . . . To Dr. Peters's questions about how he was feeling, where he had been, what he had seen, he responded with very clear, friendly answers. He talked spontaneously about the burial places of Niehbur and Schiller's son. Herr Schumann's speech wasn't in the least confused, and the sound of his voice was rather soft, as usual. He laughed somewhat more loudly only when his attendant made a joke, but this subsided quickly. When not talking, he always held a white handkerchief to his lips. I could detect no derangement in his eyes—his gaze was always openly directed toward Dr. Peters, and as friendly, gentle, and mild as when I had seen it earlier, during our last meeting in Hanover. Incidentally, Herr Schumann looks well and strong—only he's put on some weight I think. . . . As you know, he hasn't had any auditory hallucinations or become excited for a long time.[32]

Grimm's informative and presumably objective letter about Schumann during the sixth month of his confinement sounds encouraging. Nevertheless, it mentions behavior that the doctors felt was sufficiently psychopathological to justify keeping him in the hospital longer. For example, he was wearing dark clothing and a vest even though the weather was quite hot. He had a strange way of reminiscing, which Grimm found difficult to follow.

> Herr Schumann told Dr. Peters that the town which he sees is not Bonn—whereupon Dr. P. says "How so? Aren't those the towers of the Bonn Cathedral?"—Schumann: "Exactly; I know very well that the Beethoven Monument is next to the Bonn Cathedral."[33]

Dr. Peters was probably intent on demonstrating for young Grimm that his patient was mentally confused. Schumann seemed to be trying to deny where he was. Perhaps it was wishful thinking, based on his desire to be somewhere other than in a hospital. Or he might truly have been disoriented. Litzmann, in his biography of Clara, adds in a footnote that the doctors considered Schumann "very absent-minded; after one hour he doesn't know any more what he did before."[34]

Schumann had not done any composing at Endenich, but he was starting to collect some song texts and appeared to be writing something, which Dr. Richarz considered "unreadable, I can only decipher that it is about music." At one point the composer is supposed to have written "Robert Schumann, honorary member of heaven."[35] These observations would suggest delusional thinking, the false belief perhaps that he was already dead, or a grandiose fantasy about elevation to heaven. Dr. Richarz probably did not know that Schumann had often written notes to himself that were barely legible, or that in his early diaries he had practiced writing signatures of great men like Napoleon. Nor might he have appreciated Schumann's habitual oddities, his way of stringing bits and pieces of memory together, or his perpetual interest in mystical and magical thinking. But the heavenly discourse Schumann was engaging in, mostly with himself, would have reminded the psychiatrist of his patient's recent psychotic episode, in which delusions and hallucinations about the supernatural played so prominent a role. Thus Dr. Richarz had to be cautious and could not recommend an early discharge.

Richarz mentioned another disturbing item to Grimm, who in turn conveyed it to Clara: "Last night [Schumann] was drinking wine. But before finishing the last drops, he suddenly paused and said there is poison in the wine—thereupon he poured the rest on the floor."[36] Such behavior would ordinarily be called paranoid. But in Schumann's case, we must remember that alcohol affected him adversely, and that a fear of being poisoned had obsessed him on and off for over twenty years. His loss of social inhibitions was of course alarming, and indicates that there was still a risk of impulsive, possibly dangerous behavior.

Nevertheless, Dr. Richarz gave a cautiously optimistic prognosis, as befitted a conscientious hospital director responsible for a difficult and famous patient whose course of treatment was being closely watched by friends, family, and the world at large. "[Richarz] hopes confidently for a return to health [*Genesung*]," said Grimm. "But he cannot say when; obviously the recovery is going ahead slowly."[37]

Schumann resumed communication with Clara the day after her birthday (13 September), which was also their wedding anniversary. He had already sent her some flowers, in July, "the first sign of love from him," as she said.[38] But his first letter was undoubtedly stimulated by one she had sent him on their anniversary. The coherence and neatness of what he wrote is remarkable. Every sentence is logical and meaningful, and the penmanship seems, if anything, *more* legible than before his psychosis. (Perhaps Schumann was being watched, or helped, while writing to his wife; he may also have been sedated.)

He began by thanking her for remembering to write to him on their wedding anniversary, and for sending her and the children's love. "Greet and kiss the little ones," he wrote. "Oh if I could see and talk to all of you sometime; but the distance is just too great."[39]

He followed with a flood of questions. How was Clara getting along, did she still "play as magnificently as usual," had Marie and Elise been making "progress," did they still sing, did Clara still have the Klemms piano he had given her the previous year? He asked about his manuscripts, about some recent compositions (the *Requiem* and *The Singer's Curse*), about his "autograph collection of Goethe, Jean Paul, Mozart, Beethoven, Weber," and about his own correspondence and publications. Schumann seemed to be exercising his memory, perhaps to show the doctors as well as himself that his mind was working again.

> Is it a dream that last winter we were in Holland, and that you were received so brilliantly everywhere, namely in Rotterdam, and that they gave us a torchlight procession, and how magnificently you played the E-flat major Concerto and the Sonatas in C major and F minor by Beethoven, Chopin's Etudes, Mendelssohn's Songs Without Words, and also my new Concertpiece in D?

The letter also shows an interest in the present and the future:

> Could you perhaps send me something interesting, maybe the poems by Scherenberg, some early volumes of my newspaper, and the Musical Rules for the Home and for Life. Then I need note paper very badly, since I sometimes want to write down some music.

Schumann described his life in the asylum as "very simple," but he "always enjoys the beautiful view of Bonn, when I go there," and he saw and remembered "Godesberg, where, as you will also remember, I had attacks of seizures [*Krampfanfälle*] while working . . . in the strongest heat of the sun." This brought him closer to the subject of his psychosis, and he asked Clara whether she too could recall "a theme in E-flat major, which I once heard during the night and wrote variations for; could you send them, and maybe also include something from your own compositions?"

With considerable objectivity, Schumann remarked that his letter was full of "so many questions and requests"; he wanted to "come to you and speak with you about them at length." As if wanting to protect his wife from any further unpleasantness, he added, "If you would like to put a veil over this or that which I've asked you about, then do so." ("Putting a veil [*Schleier*]" over something was one of Schumann's favorite expressions, a typically romantic idiom that alludes to mystery and obscurity. In the context of this first letter to his wife, the phrase may also be interpreted to connote mourning, as well as chastity, which his hospitalization made necessary.)

Four days later, Schumann wrote again, to thank Clara for "such good news" about their newborn son, and to praise her choice of the "dearest name," Felix, a tribute to Mendelssohn. Again he asked her to send him "one thing or the other."[40] This second letter also contained innumerable questions—about her, about Joachim and Brahms—as well as reminiscences and comments about the children, friends and relatives, trips, the Music Festival, his music, his letters from Vienna. In addition, he reported, "I am now much stronger and look much younger than in Düsseldorf. . . . My life is not as agitated as before. How completely different it used to be."

There can be no doubt that Schumann was trying to establish contact with his wife. Why then was no reconciliation with Clara and the children attempted at this point? The usual explanation, supported by documents, is that Dr. Richarz did not encourage Clara to see her husband. Family therapy, as we know it today, was unheard of at the time, and the doctors may not have known how to deal with Schumann's latent hostility toward, and fear of, his wife. They may have thought he might become excited again and suffer a setback.*

Most likely the psychiatrists had noticed Clara's mixed feelings. Despite her many requests for news, she never really pressed the matter of visiting her husband. Instead she sent her mother to Endenich and repeatedly asked Brahms, Joachim, and other mutual friends to go there. In one of his letters, Brahms wrote that Schumann had asked fearfully if Clara might have died, since he hadn't heard from her for so long.[42] In fact, the doctors had withheld Clara's letters.

Nonetheless, at times it seemed that Clara was deliberately avoiding a visit to Endenich. In July 1854, when Schumann's recovery seemed to be imminent, she traveled all the way to Berlin without making the short detour to Bonn. In August and September 1854, Clara went on a vacation to Ostend in Belgium, but she did not stop in Endenich on either leg of the journey. In October she began giving concerts and traveled widely, to Hamburg, to Holland (with Brahms), to Berlin once more, and to other cities—again without going to Endenich. She did not visit Schumann for Christmas

---

* We know that patients much sicker than Schumann were discharged from Endenich if family circumstances permitted it. Alfred Rethels, for example, was allowed to go home to his mother shortly before he died.[41]

or the New Year (1854–1855). In April 1855, she went to Cologne with Brahms, but did not continue 25 kilometers farther south to Bonn. (She sent Brahms there in her place.) That summer she also spent five days walking along the Rhine with Brahms, when their romance was blossoming, but she did not stop in Endenich.

It has also been suggested that Dr. Richarz kept Clara from visiting Schumann in 1854 because of the assumption that it might upset *her* too much. But then how do we explain that he allowed her to see him in 1856, when self-starvation had turned her husband into a living skeleton? Clara was an assertive woman; she had defied her own father to marry Schumann. Therefore the argument that she now wanted to be with her husband but was thwarted by his doctors is not convincing. After 1854 Clara was paying for Schumann's hospitalization, so had she wanted to see him she could have insisted.

Thus we must assume that there were several reasons for Schumann's nonrehabilitation. Clara probably felt guilty and shameful because what had been a private problem was now out in the open. It was one thing to have a husband who was moody, inept as an administrator, and awkward or embarrassed in social situations; she could always make excuses. But the realization that he had actually become dangerously psychotic was more difficult for her to integrate into her concept of a loving husband. Even his suicide attempt, which newspapers around the world had commented on, was something Clara had to deny. Finally, to have Schumann residing in a mental institution was worse than anything her father had ever predicted, even though he had foreseen, correctly, that she would eventually have to support herself and her children.

After what happened in Düsseldorf, Schumann's chances of finding work again—had he been released from Endenich—probably would have been very limited. His experience and ability as a teacher were meager, and as a conductor he had failed. Surely Wasielewski, who lived in Bonn, told Richarz that no city in Germany would want to have Schumann as a music director. Neither would Schumann play the piano. Richarz did invite him several times to his home, to perform on the instrument there.[43] The results, as we can imagine, were far from satisfactory. Schumann had not been a virtuoso for many years. He might have continued to do some music criticism, but it is doubtful that he would have earned an income from such an occupation.

That left musical composition. But Schumann's output while a patient in Endenich was trifling. He wrote piano accompaniments for the Paganini Caprices, hoping that Joachim and Brahms would play them.[44] He also started, but did not finish, a piano reduction of Joachim's *"Heinrich" Overture*.[45]

Exactly when we do not know, but sometime during his interminable hospitalization, Schumann harmonized an old chorale melody. (This tune, which dates back to 1569, had already been used three times by Johann Sebastian Bach.) Schumann's handwriting on the manuscript is impressively neat; no tremor, elision, or other signs of organicity can be detected. But shattering in their psychological implication are the words of the hymn he chose to harmonize. They suggest strongly that Schumann had resigned himself to the only course left open to him: death.

Wenn mein Stündlein vorhanden ist	*When my final hour arrives*
Aus dieser Welt zu scheiden,	*To depart from this earth,*
So hilf Du mir, Herr Jesu Christ,	*I beg Thee Lord Jesus Christ*
In meinem letzten Leiden.	*To help me in my last suffering.*
Herr, meine Seel' an meinem End'	*Lord, my soul at the end*
Befehl ich Dir in Deine Händ',	*I commit into Thy hands.*
Du wirst sie wohl bewahren.	*Thou knowest well how to protect it.*

Without the physical presence of Clara, their children, and their closest friends to sustain his creativity, the composer turned inward, using the remaining power of his imagination to construct a fantasized social environment. Clara's letters, and the reminders she sent of their life together, helped to give shape to this mental microcosm. "After many sleepless nights my fantasies were very confused," he wrote her; "now I can see you again in the noble and earnest strokes of your pen." His thoughts embraced Clara's mother and stepfather, her women friends, his own relatives, even "Florestan and Eusebius."[46]

The imaginary community he created and regularly conversed with in Endenich was also populated by unfriendly, critical, and hostile figures. His correspondence never mentions this, but Dr. Richarz reported that Schumann's "hallucinations dealt frequently with issues of the artistic value of his own work. He would grow indignant. The voices apparently criticized his capabilities as a musician."[47]

To defend himself against what his doctor called "a feeling that his own work as an artist was being treated disdainfully,"[48] Schumann leaned heavily on contact with Brahms, the only meaningful link remaining to Clara and the world of reality. No letter fails to mention this angelic demon. Schumann expressed delight after learning from Clara that Brahms had "moved his residence completely to Düsseldorf." He was "surprised" to find out that "Brahms is driven to do counterpoint exercises." He told Clara that he could visualize "the portrait of Brahms by Laurens, but not my own." (By focusing his attention on a healthy, virile, young man, Schumann probably was able to protect what was left of his own fading, deteriorating self-image.) "Does the picture [of Brahms] still hang in my study?" he asked. "He is one of the most beautiful and genial youths."[49]

After nearly nine months of hospitalization, in November 1854, Schumann finally addressed Brahms directly. "Dear One! If I could only come to you, to see and hear you again." He praised him lavishly for composing a set of "magnificent variations": "How singularly well-rounded the whole work is, how one recognizes you, in the richest, most fantastic radiance."[50]

This warm, affectionate, but rather short letter was inspired by the receipt of an important new composition by Brahms, a set of *Variations for the Piano, on a theme by Robert Schumann, dedicated to Clara Schumann* (op. 9). The work symbolizes effectively and in musical language Brahms's special position as a mediator between Clara and her alienated husband. He took a melody of Schumann's that Clara herself had once written variations for, composed strikingly original variations—some in the manner of Schumann himself, others in his own inimitable style—and dedicated them all to the woman they both loved. Schumann of course was deeply moved.* He even wrote a brief musical analysis of the new work:

> Here and there the theme bobs up, and very mysteriously, then more passionately and intimately, only to disappear again completely. And how magnificent is the end of the fourteenth [variation], so artfully developed in the canonic second, the fifteenth in G-sharp major with the genial second part, and the last.

Eighteen days later (15 December 1854), Schumann renewed his request, somewhat more energetically, to see Brahms. Brahms also wanted to see Schumann. He was remarkably in tune with both Schumann and Clara and, sensing the danger of their prolonged separation, he offered to serve as a go-between. "I wish the doctor would employ me as an attendant or male nurse over Christmas," he wrote Clara on 15 December 1854. "If that were possible, I could write to you about him every day, and I could talk to him about you all day long."[52] Joachim too was becoming concerned. Over Christmas he went to Endenich again to try to cheer Schumann up, but he came away feeling dissatisfied with the hospital. "I can't accept the doctor's

---

*He may even have been "gravely shaken" by Brahms's new composition, as Karl Geiringer suggests.[51] In drafting a reply to the young composer, Schumann enumerated past performances of his own *Genoveva, Manfred Overture*, and other works, and he doodled numbers that suggest future dates—1860, 1870, and so on—giving the impression that he was contemplating the future and could now no longer deny that Brahms's career was ascending while his own had declined.

words as those of an oracle," he wrote Clara in March 1855, and he suggested using electro-stimulation—"galvanizing"—to jolt Schumann out of his depression.[53]

Brahms went to Endenich on 11 January, played for him, and apparently aroused Clara's fantasies about a possible reunion. But she had already gone on a concert tour, and in Holland received a letter in which Schumann expressed a premonition of his death: "My Clara, I feel as if something terrible stands before me. Will I not see you and the children again, what agony!"[54]

Brahms told Schumann that he would help with the business of getting his latest works corrected for publication. That seems to have stimulated one last, daring effort on Schumann's part to fight off his engulfing psychosis. In March he wrote some letters to his publishers and answered theirs. He wrote to Brahms:

> I want to get out of here! Since 4 March, for more than a year, it's been exactly the same lifestyle, and the same view of Bonn. Where else can I go! Think about it! Benrat is too close, but Deutz [across the Rhine from Cologne] might do, or maybe Mühlheim [along the Moselle].[55]

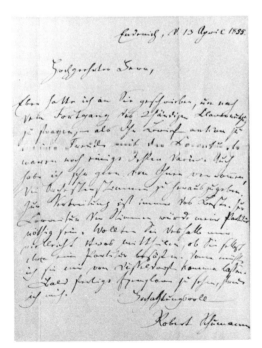

Letter written by Schumann during his hospitalization at Endenich, dated 13 April 1855. (Original in Robert Schumann Haus, Zwickau.)

He requested more music paper, more newspapers, more of his manuscripts and letters, more poems by the tragic Elizabeth Kulmann, and "an atlas"[56] with which to plan his escape. When Brahms went to Endenich again in April, Schumann repeated these demands to him verbally, and the doctors, alarmed by his "increasingly pathological activity,"[57] warned Clara accordingly and restricted their correspondence.

One final letter did get through from Schumann to his wife. It was intended to arrive for Brahms's birthday, 7 May 1855. (As a present, Schumann had given him his manuscript score for the *Overture to "The Bride of Messina."*)

> Dear Clara! On 1 May I sent you a spring message; but the following days were very restless; you will learn more about it from my letter which you will receive the day after tomorrow. There is a shadow in it; but what else it contains will make you, my darling, happy. . . . I have included a drawing of Felix Mendelssohn, so you can put it into the Album. A priceless memento!
> Farewell, you dear one!
> Your Robert[58]

This was the last Clara ever heard from her husband directly. But indirectly she found out much more, such as from Elisabeth ("Bettina") von Arnim, a prominent poetess and social figure, to whom Schumann had dedicated his *Songs of Early Morning* (op. 133). Frau von Arnim went to Endenich in May 1855 and "demanded" to see Schumann. She reacted very negatively to his confinement, calling Dr. Richarz "a hypochondriac" who "regards Schumann as a symptom of illness, rather than understanding his noble mind."

> After coming through a dreary courtyard into a dreary house without any signs of life [she wrote to Clara], we entered an empty room. . . . After an hour had gone by [Schumann] arrived—I ran to him—his face aglow with pleasure at seeing us. . . . He told me, in words which could only be articulated with effort, that it has gotten to be difficult for him to speak, and now that he hasn't spoken with anyone for over a year this ailment has gotten even worse. He conversed about everything of interest that he had encountered in life, about Vienna, about Petersburg and London, about Sicily, about works by Brahms . . . in short he talked uninterruptedly about all the things that had ever pleasurably excited him.[59]

Much has been made of Schumann's speech disorder, a presumptive sign of organic disease. He had often spoken inaudibly—or even been mute—long before entering the asylum. Yet, Frau von Arnim, as well as other visitors, found that he could also speak quite normally (or what they thought was "normal" for him.) Her description of his speech pattern suggests that

Schumann may have manifested a rush of uninhibited verbal associations, which psychiatrists term "flight of ideas." In telling Clara about it, she used the term "nervous attack," adding that "his astonishing illness . . . would have come to an end more quickly if only one had understood him better or at least just used intuition to find out what was affecting him internally."[60]

This letter from the older and influential Frau von Arnim discomposed Clara, who immediately dispatched Joachim to Endenich. His report sounds fairly reassuring (undoubtedly for Clara's benefit):

> I saw the dear Master early this morning and he was cheerful and obviously pleased by my visit and conversation. We laughed, often really heartily—and he is happy that I will be coming back with Johannes to play him the Paganini Etudes, which are now completed except for four.[61]

Frau von Arnim's pointed suggestion that one ought to try bringing Schumann back into the "circle of his family again" led Clara, for the first time, to request a conference with Dr. Richarz. She claimed he gave her hope of "recovery." On 26 July 1855 she told Joachim of the supposedly "cheerful news from the doctor . God willing Robert and I will be visiting you [this winter]."[62]

Schumann apparently had a major setback after that. He was restricted and probably sedated when Wasielewski visited the hospital later that summer. Not permitted to interact with the composer, Wasielewski had to observe him "through an opening in the door." Schumann was sitting at the piano and improvising. "To see this noble and good man with his mental and physical power fully broken down was heart-rending," he wrote. "His playing was intolerable."[63] Joachim remained more optimistic, however. "Schumann is better," he wrote Clara on 3 January 1856.[64] He also raised funds for further hospitalization from musicians who were still concerned about Schumann's future.

Schumann declined pitiably during his third year of hospitalization, and he was abjectly psychotic when Brahms visited him in April 1856.

> We sat down, it became increasingly painful for me, his eyes were moist, he spoke continuously, but I understood nothing. . . . Often he just blabbered, sort of bababa—dadada. While questioning him at length I understood the names Marie, Julie, Berlin, Vienna, England, not much more. . . . Richarz says that Schumann's brain is decidedly exhausted (no softening of the brain). . . . He will remain, at best, in this significantly apathetic state; in one or two months only supportive care will probably be necessary.[65]

In his regressed condition, Schumann refused to eat. This negativistic behavior was potentially suicidal, and Dr. Richarz, in an article describing his management of such cases, told how the problem was probably handled.

First his staff used tact and persuasion. If this method proved ineffective, they inserted a gastric tube through the patient's nose or mouth (rectal tubes were also used, but only for intractable cases, after 1862). The doctors experimented with various infusions, including wine, milk, meat extracts, and saltwater.[66] With what, or how often, Schumann was tube-fed we do not know. Clara knew only that "for weeks now he's taken nothing but a little wine and jellied consommé.[67]

She by now had returned full-time to her concert career and was playing in England, where Schumann had often dreamed of going. Notified that his feet were getting swollen, a sign of starvation edema, and that he was confined in bed, she decided to interrupt her tour. But still Clara could not face going to Endenich. First she planned to take a vacation with Brahms. But when he reneged, there was no longer any way for her to avoid making the trip. Thus on 14 July 1856, almost two and a half years after Schumann had been admitted to the hospital, she went there for the first time. But still she did not visit her husband. Dr. Richarz, she said, told her that "he can't promise another year of life" for him, and would not allow her to see him.[68]

Nine days later Clara went to Endenich once more, this time accompanied by Brahms. She entered the building where Schumann was confined, but only Brahms went into his room. Then they left. Four days after that they returned. This time Clara was able to look at her husband.

> He smiled at me and embraced me with great effort, because he could no longer control his limbs. Never will I forget it. For all the world's treasures I wouldn't exchange this embrace. My Robert, that's how we have to meet again. With what effort I had to search for your beloved expressions. What a picture of pain![69]

It seemed to Clara that Schumann was "always talking a lot with his spirits. He would become restless if one stayed with him too long. One can barely understand him any more. Just once I heard him say 'my,' surely he wanted to say 'Clara,' because he looked at me in a friendly way; then again 'I know'—'you' probably." When, the next day, she went to see him again, "his limbs twitched constantly, his speech was often very violent." Brahms thought Schumann had had some kind of an "attack which the doctors believed would soon be followed by death (I don't know the name, a lung-seizure?)"[70]

Nevertheless, Clara tried to feed the emaciated patient, apparently with some success. "He accepted [wine and jellied consommé], with the happiest expression and truly in haste. He gulped the wine from my fingers—ah, he knew that it was me."[71]

These observations suggest that the muscles of Schumann's mouth and throat, which are especially vulnerable to neurological disease, were *not* paralyzed. He seems to have taken food when Clara offered it, and he swallowed it without gagging or vomiting, all suggesting that his terminal self-starvation was probably voluntary. The fact that he ate so impulsively, after a prolonged period of starvation, may have contributed to his death.*

Schumann died at 4 P.M. the next day, 29 July 1856. He was alone. Clara had gone with Brahms to pick up Joachim at the train depot.

> I saw him only half an hour later. . . . I stood by his corpse, my ardently beloved husband, and was quiet; all my thoughts went up to God with thanks that he is finally free. And as I knelt at his bed . . . it seemed as if a magnificent spirit was hovering over me—ah, if only he had taken me along.[73]

---

*Sudden feeding of patients who have lost a great deal of weight as a result of chronic starvation is known to induce neurocirculatory collapse, a physiological shock so severe that many cannot survive.[72]

XVII.

The Problem of Diagnosis

wenty-four hours after Clara's farewell, Dr. Richarz performed an autopsy on Schumann's body with Dr. Peters's help. This report, dated 30 July 1856, has never been published, but an abridged summary of it was given the following year to Josef von Wasielewski for his biography of the composer.

The original document[1] is difficult if not impossible to interpret in the context of any known disease process. It contains many random, loosely organized observations presented in a style that typified nineteenth-century pathology.* "One must assume," writes one of today's leading East German neuropathologists, Professor W. Jänisch of Halle University, who has reviewed Dr. Richarz's report, "that the autopsy surgeons were not trained pathologists and were oriented exclusively toward the central nervous system."[2] And according to Professor Nathan Malamud of the University of

---

*Rudolf Virchow (1821–1902), a German physician, anthropologist, and politician, finally put this field on a scientific footing with his important discoveries in cellular pathology, published in 1858.

California in San Francisco, "There are many vague and contradictory statements, and no one today would accept these findings as being reliable."[3]

To begin with, Dr. Richarz's autopsy suggests that there may have been abnormalities of Schumann's skull. "The cranial vault [is] very thick and firm, with little interstitial substance, much thicker and tighter at the occiput than the anterior part. All bony protruberances, points, sutures, and ridges, and the base of both middle cranial fossae [are] exceptionally notable and sharp." But such findings are really quite common; they occur as often among people who have never had any serious problems as they do among psychiatric patients, and without miscroscopic study we can attach no diagnostic significance to them. Furthermore, while the description of Schumann's skull is quite detailed, Richarz gave no objective measurements, so that it is impossible to say how thick the bones actually were. (An examination of the exhumed skull in 1885 by Professor Schaaffhausen, a medical anthropologist, disclosed no bony abnormalities.[4])

The autopsy report goes on at considerable length about the meninges, a layer of firm and soft tissues containing a liquid that cushions the brain within the skull. It states that the firm dura mater is "moderately thin [and] very tightly adherent to the skull wall"—again an observation of dubious significance—and that the softer pia-arachnoid tissues are "very congested . . . colored brown . . . engorged with blood." In addition, there were other signs of "blood-extravasation" and "blood-congestion" throughout the brain.

This may have nothing to do with any pathology of the brain itself. Congestion of the meninges is normally the result of death itself, when blood circulation stops. Dr. Richarz reported no frank hemorrhages or other changes that would suggest primary cardiovascular disease. As for the meninges adhering to the brain substance and leaving "cavities shaped like grains of sand" when they were removed, Dr. Malamud commented, "Could the surgeons have been referring to the normal Pacchionian granulations which are sometimes seen with advancing age? If so, that would not be significant."[5] Dr. Jänisch thinks it likely that the finding is a post-mortem artifact, and points out that "such artifacts often appear, especially when the surgeon is not very experienced or if he is somewhat impatient."[6]

If we assume, however, that there actually were adhesions between Schumann's brain and the meninges, this would indicate the presence of an infectious process, perhaps a previous meningitis, or scarring from a subarachnoid hemorrhage due to an old head injury. We know that Schumann contracted malaria in his twenties, which might have led to meningitis with subsequent thickening. Perhaps he also had a head injury in his youth, when after heavy drinking he sometimes passed out and had to be carried home. The resulting scars would have been a problem, however, only if in the course of time they had interfered with the flow of cerebrospinal fluid through the meninges and around the brain. That would have produced blockage and swelling (hydrocephalus), leading to destruction of brain substance. No such findings are present in the autopsy report.

A very important point involves the question of how much Schumann's brain weighed at the time of the autopsy. If it weighed less than a normal brain, this would support Dr. Richarz's visual impression of "considerable atrophy of the brain substance," which he conveyed to Wasielewski (who, not being medically trained, accepted it at face value along with all the other findings). The "46 *Unzen und 120 Gran (preussisches Medizinalgewicht)*" recorded by Dr. Richarz converts to 1337.52 grams in today's system of measurement.* Although that weight could be interpreted to be somewhat on the low side—Dr. Richarz thought it was below normal—Schumann's brain weight actually falls well within the standard deviation from average brain weight for normal men between forty-one and fifty years of age, which is 1360 grams.[7]

Schumann was forty six years old when he began starving himself, and his brain at autopsy may have been on the light side. To conclude from this that it had begun to shrink or atrophy, we would need to know what the weight was before he died.† We would also expect an abnormal enlargement of the ventricles inside the brain if the brain substance had begun to contract, as Dr. Richarz's report suggests. Yet he mentioned no such enlargement of the ventricles.

The report does have something to say, though, about the surface of the brain: its convolutions were "numerous and narrow." This is a very confusing observation. "Numerous" gyri would imply a condition of *microgyria*, a developmental brain defect associated with mental deficiency, which was obviously impossible for a man like Schumann. "Narrow" convolutions would imply brain atrophy, a moot point. Microscopic study might give us a clue. But Richarz said only that he saw "nucleated and non-nucleated cells," which is most unclear, since all brain cells contain nuclei. (Microscopy was exceedingly primitive in 1856. Among other shortcomings, tissues were sectioned with a knife, stains were either unavailable or not very good, lenses were of poor quality, and illumination was usually inadequate.[8]) It is impossible to tell from his report whether Richarz was observing neurons or glial cells. If

---

* 1 Unze = 28.92 grams; 1 Gran = 0.06 grams.
† It was thought at one time that men of genius had unusually heavy brains, and the Russian writer Turgenev was supposed to have had a heavy one. No studies to date, however, have shown a correlation between weight of the brain and unusual mental abilities.

there had been an infectious process, such as syphilis, inflammatory cells, plasma cells, and lymphocytes would be expected. But no inflammatory cells are mentioned.

Richarz described Schumann's pituitary gland as "underdeveloped [and] surrounded by yellowish, gelatinous material." Without microscopic examination, that is meaningless. In the rare instance of a pituitary apoplexy caused by circulatory disturbance to this vital gland, there would have been a history of a sudden and massive collapse quickly leading to death. Schumann's medical history contains no such event, however. Had his alcoholism produced the kinds of lesions, called Wernicke's or Korsakoff's encephalopathy, seen in some chronic alcoholics, the autopsy findings would have had to report some very specific pathological changes in the region of the third ventricle. These were not reported, but of course they might have been overlooked by the surgeons.

The incompleteness of the autopsy—nothing is said about liver, kidneys, gastrointestinal tract, genitalia, adrenal glands, thyroid, and so on—suggests either that Dr. Richarz did not examine these organs, or that he found nothing unusual to report. He did describe Schumann's heart as "big, flaccid, thin-walled, in all chambers symmetrically too large," which suggests that he thought there was heart disease. (It should be remembered that Richarz's teacher Nasse attributed many severe psychiatric illnesses to the heart.) If Schumann had had syphilis affecting the valves or the aorta, that might have caused cardiac enlargement. Other long-standing circulatory disorders—caused by, say, rheumatic fever, high blood pressure, or arteriosclerosis—could also have led to findings of the sort Richarz reported. But his description is much too vague to permit a diagnosis.

"Infiltration of the lungs, in the upper lobes serous, in the lower ones bloody," was Dr. Richarz's concluding statement. With this he was referring to a terminal phenomenon, of no diagnostic value. The only other pertinent remark would be "severe emaciation of the entire body, as well as great atrophy of fatty and muscular tissue." These pathological findings most likely reflect the hunger strike Schumann had been on for probably about two months, leading to the starvation, weight loss, edema, and severe physical weakness and wasting that Clara observed when she last saw him.

The first recorded psychiatric diagnosis of Schumann appears in Dr. Richarz's autopsy report: "incomplete general paralysis," a highly controversial term at the time (and for that reason probably not disclosed to Wasielewski). This disease concept had recently come from France, where it was customarily applied to patients whose mental, emotional, and behavioral problems were thought to be the product of a diffuse, nonlocalizable brain disturbance. Psychiatrists wanted to distinguish these patients from "completely" paralyzed patients, who had strokes, tumors, syphilitic lesions, or other discrete and localizable pathology of the brain. (Into this latter group Richarz placed, for example, Alfred Rethels, whom he had discharged from Endenich in 1854 as "incurable," with the diagnosis "Dementia, Paralysis-General."[9])

In 1873, partly in response to Clara Schumann's criticism of Wasielewski's biography, Richarz made his diagnosis public and tried to explain in some detail what he meant by it. Schumann's "abnormality" had a hereditary component, which Richarz attributed to his mother. His depressiveness was similar to the "spontaneous melancholic moods" seen in "almost all great artists" including "Mozart and Goethe" (neither of whom Richarz had ever examined). As for Schumann's "last, ruinous illness" (*letzte verderbliche Krankheit*)—the phase Richarz had observed in Endenich—he thought this was "a slow, but irreversible and progressive deterioration [*Verfall*] in organization and strength of the entire nervous system."

Richarz described the cause of this "deterioration" as "overexertion" (*Überanstrengung*). According to his theory, the composer's "immoderate mental, especially artistic, productivity" had "exhausted the substance of psychically active central components of the nervous system."[10]

It was not unusual in the nineteenth century for a psychiatrist to formulate his diagnosis in this manner. The French had suggested that "*la paralysie générale incomplète*" was the result of "moral" excesses such as alcoholism, "violent passions," or sexual overindulgence.[11] A few experts speculated about inflammatory processes. German psychiatrists like Dr. Richarz tended to believe that the brain decomposed because of interference with its blood supply. Of special interest in this respect is that his autopsy report refers to a textbook on brain diseases written in 1852 by Joseph Guislain (1797–1860), a Belgian psychiatrist whose influence extended to West Germany. Under the heading "Softening of the Brain" Guislain described what Dr. Richarz thought was wrong with Schumann. By the time Richarz published his explanation of the diagnosis in 1873, he would also have seen the excellent description of incomplete general paralysis in Wilhelm Griesinger's textbook of psychiatry, which became influential in Germany.[12]

Already at that time a few psychiatrists were speculating about a possible connection between this disease and syphilis. Richarz evidently was not one of them.* He emphatically made the point that Schumann did *not*

---

*Not until 1913, when the causal syphilitic spirochete was demonstrated in the brains of certain patients with *general paralysis*, could it be said with confidence that some of the patients who were previously diagnosed as having *incomplete general paralysis* may also have had syphilis.[13]

manifest any exaltation of mood or other mental changes commonly observed among patients with a full-blown organic dementia due to syphilis. "His self-awareness was beclouded, distorted, but not destroyed," he wrote; "he was not alienated from himself, not transformed. Until the thread of life was ripped, depression [*die Schwermuth*] . . . remained true to him."[14]

By the end of the nineteenth century, two developments had conspired to overthrow Dr. Richarz's "exhaustion" theory about Schumann. First was the publication of Litzmann's biography of Clara, which stated that the composer had been a "sick man" almost all his life and that his illness had "manifested itself to varying degrees and in changing forms, with long intervals of quiescence but gruesome regularity, and always in overexcitement."[15] Second were advances in psychiatry that recognized illnesses of this type to be disturbances in the *function* rather than the structure of the brain.

A leading figure in German psychiatry at this time was Paul Möbius, M.D. (1853–1907). After listening to Schumann's music, he came to the conclusion that this must have been "a very nervous man"; he also characterized the composer as extraordinarily "passive" and "feminine."[16] It was Möbius's belief that Schumann had been "mentally ill since his youth" and that the correct diagnosis was dementia praecox (called schizophrenia since 1911). This form of disease is characterized by mental disorganization, usually beginning in adolescence, and accompanied by disturbing delusions, hallucinations, odd mannerisms, and social eccentricity. Möbius believed that Schumann's first schizophrenic episode occurred when, at age twenty-three, he became confused, fearful, and depressed, and lost control over his behavior. Although these symptoms subsided gradually, "he was never the same again." Recurrent schizophrenic episodes occurred at ages thirty-two, thirty-four, thirty-seven, and forty-two, according to Möbius: "Then at the beginning of the year 1854 came the catastrophe that turned the sick man into a ruin. In 1855 his condition improved once more, but it was a brief deception. Soon there was another collapse, followed in 1856 by his death."[17]

Paul Möbius enjoyed taking extreme positions in debates about clinical issues, and his monograph on Schumann was but one of several so-called pathographies that tried to prove that genius and madness had something in common, namely, a process of "degeneration," rooted supposedly in the individual's racial and genetic background.[18] According to Möbius, Schumann's psychosis was to be regarded as the "opposite or reverse side" of his creativity. "We see here an excellent example of how great talent is paid for by illness."[19]

Less than a year after the Möbius monograph was published, another distinguished psychiatrist, Professor Hans Gruhle of Heidelberg University, took issue and in an open letter to Möbius argued for "a cyclothymic form of manic-depressive madness," a diagnosis that refers to patients who suffer from abnormal fluctuations in their emotions, but do not deteriorate mentally.

> We think of their great irritability, of their capacity to register and react to the most delicate stimuli, of the associated tendency to be mistrustful, of their trend toward savoring every sensation to its utmost, of their power to experience supreme jubilation and deepest pain, their tendency to cry, of their often precipitously changing moods, and their preference for judging everything according to whether it pleases or displeases them.[20]

It was Gruhle's belief, shared by many of his colleagues, that such highly emotional behavior is typically feminine, and that it plays an important role in artistic creativity. He took Möbius to task for suggesting that Schumann had had a "sudden mental breakdown," or that his "mental functions [were] gradually extinguished." On the contrary, according to Gruhle (who had no more information to base his opinions on than did Möbius), the composer displayed "an overwhelming abundance of creative power" and "a rich mental life" until age forty. Thereafter, he fell victim either to a progressive "paralysis" as Dr. Richarz had described it, or to "some other severe organic brain disease, perhaps syphilis."

Möbius countered immediately, pointing out that in clinical practice it is often very difficult to make a clear-cut distinction between schizophrenia and manic-depressive disease. Both conditions belong to the category of "endogenous" psychoses resulting from internal predispositions and malfunctions of the brain, rather than to the "exogenous" ones that are produced when poisons, bacteria, gunshots, or other invaders from the outside damage this organ.[21]

Such debates among the experts are of course commonplace in medical science, where progress often depends as much on inductive reasoning as on deductive logic. Even today there are often disagreements among physicians attempting to make an accurate diagnosis when the exact causes of a patient's illness are not known. Both schizophrenia and manic-depressive psychosis (now called bipolar affective disorder) are conditions of unknown etiology. Moreover, they share certain symptoms, including disturbances in mood and even auditory hallucinations, so that in any single instance of psychotic breakdown it may be very difficult to distinguish between the two disorders. Only by studying a patient's family background, the course of the illness, and the responses to specific antipsychotic medication (not available in Schumann's day) can one gain certainty about the diagnosis. Thus the Möbius–Gruhle debate over schizophrenia versus affective disorder continued.[22]

In addition to these two diagnoses, the possibility of tuberculosis has been discussed in the psychiatric literature on Schumann.[23] He probably became infected through close contact with his brother Julius and with Ludwig Schunke, who both died as a result of this disease. Tuberculosis was also a frequent killer of patients whose health deteriorated during lengthy hospitalization in overcrowded institutions. Another important diagnosis, syphilis, was favored by Slater and Meyer.[24] One must always keep this possibility in mind when examining a nineteenth-century figure who was sexually promiscuous, had a long history of physical and psychological problems, and went mad in his forties.

A very thorough (but chronologically confusing) summary of Schumann's various possible diagnoses was published in 1959 by Hans Martin Sutermeister, M.D. He believed that the composer "aged prematurely," beginning at thirty-five, and developed an "involutional depression" in his forties. High blood pressure, heart disease, and the "overwork" mentioned by Dr. Richarz may have contributed to this process. Sutermeister also suggested that Clara's "maternal vitality" had put Schumann on the defensive and gradually brought about a kind of "psychic castration" that made him helpless in the face of Brahms's affection for her. During his hospitalization, Schumann experienced a "flight into illness," but no mental decay. It was a way of trying to deal with his "inescapable life situation."[25]

Scientific advances over the past two decades have led to important new developments in psychiatry. From discoveries in molecular biology, for example, has come knowledge about the sequential arrangement of amino acids in the chromosomes of the cells. Thus our understanding of the genetic transmission of character traits and illness predispositions has been dramatically enhanced. From neurobiology we have learned that chemical transmitters can speed up or slow down the flow of signals from one nerve cell to another, and that endorphins, opium-like chemicals secreted by the brain, are capable of sedating the central nervous system, thus reducing pain and modulating the range and expression of human emotion. Newer techniques of visualizing the brain have demonstrated atrophy in a substantial number of chronically schizophrenic patients, and electrophysiologic study has shown abnormalities of neurotransmission associated with affective disorder.[26] Thus many of the time-honored conceptual dichotomies found useful by practicing clinicians are disappearing. Rigid distinctions can no longer be made between organic and psychogenic disease processes, or between endogenous and exogenous mental disorder.

These changes are reflected in a new "systems" approach to psychiatric diagnosis. Today each patient's clinical condition is described on five separate but interrelated levels: the major mental disorder; the patient's personality and any significant disturbances in its development; physical disorders that are relevant to an understanding of the illness; contributing psychosocial stress factors; the highest level of adaptive functioning recently achieved.[27] Below is a multidimensional diagnosis of Robert Schumann.

I MENTAL DISORDER

The most comprehensive diagnosis for Schumann's psychiatric illness would be a *major affective disorder*.[28] He suffered from severe, recurring depressive episodes. The symptoms consisted of feelings of extreme sadness and irritability. Often he was sleepless, agitated, and hopeless. Guilt and self-accusatory ideas accompanied many of these depressive episodes, occasionally leading to self-destructive behavior. Thoughts about death, and a wish to die, were prominent. When depressed, Schumann felt sluggish, behaved in a lethargic manner, had difficulty concentrating, and spoke of pessimistic delusions and hallucinations. Imaginary voices would accuse him of crimes and tell him that his work was insufficient or worthless. These delusions and hallucinations were congruent with his depressed mood.

Schumann also had mood swings in the opposite direction, toward mania, which makes this a "bipolar" type of affective disorder. These episodes of manic excitement often resulted in creative overactivity. He would write or compose incessantly, sometimes for several days consecutively, sleeping very little and aware that his mind was racing. Music presented itself to his conscious mind with tremendous speed and intensity. But there would soon be another letdown in mood, with pathological sadness and physical exhaustion.

Schumann's pattern of extreme mood fluctuation seems to have had hereditary as well as environmental determinants. Both his mother and father were occasionally severely depressed. Two previous suicides are known in the family. Among Schumann's children, every one of the sons had serious health problems, suggesting a possible sex-linked predisposition. Emil died in infancy. Ludwig failed to develop normally, was hospitalized (at Colditz) in his twenties, and died at age fifty-one after many years of invalidism. Ferdinand became a morphine addict in his thirties after participating briefly in the Franco-Prussian war; he died at forty-one. Felix (the last child, whom Schumann never met) died at twenty-four of tuberculosis. The daughters

The Schumann children,
about 1855, from left:
Ludwig, Marie (holding Felix
on her lap), Elise, Ferdinand,
Eugenie (Julie is absent).

did somewhat better. Three of them lived long, healthy, and productive lives. Marie and Eugenie both became piano teachers, like their mother, but did not marry or distinguish themselves as performers. Elise married, had children, and lived part of her life in the United States. Julie, having married, died tragically young, at twenty-seven, of tuberculosis.

As has been emphasized earlier in this book, Schumann's affective disorder took shape within the context of the romantic era. Emotional exuberance, moodiness, heightened creativity, and suicidal despair were fashionable if not actively cultivated attributes. Some atypical features also characterize his illness. (This is often the case with patients who are unusually gifted and intelligent.) For example, an obsessive-compulsive quality of worry and "nervousness" seems to have been part of some of Schumann's depressive episodes, while a bizarre, schizophrenic-like quality accompanied some of his manic episodes, especially the one leading up to his hospitalization. (The term "schizo-affective" disorder might be applicable here.[29])

II PERSONALITY DISORDER

It is difficult to define the personality disorder of a genius like Schumann according to concepts that have been developed for ordinary, more "normal," patients. He had what seems to have been a severely divided self, with conflicts centering around dependency versus independence, attachment versus separation, and femininity versus masculinity. His anxiety increased not only when he was alone, but also whenever he sought to establish a relationship. Hence his social behavior fluctuated between isolation and intimacy. Love and hate felt simultaneously toward the same person added to his disturbance. Today we would call this a "narcissistic" or "borderline" personality disorder.[30]

Schumann made an effort to meliorate his disorder through his creativity. Florestan and Eusebius were temporary, poetic solutions. So was his music, which brought about some inner harmony. But these artistic devices were insufficient. In his youth Schumann often manifested a "histrionic" overdisplay of emotion. After his marriage, he became more restrained, orderly, and "obsessive-compulsive." As depressive episodes and other health problems gradually weakened him, a pompous, suspicious, and even "paranoid" personality style became more manifest.

III PHYSICAL DISORDERS

Schumann's health was significantly undermined by numerous physical disorders. Acute alcohol intoxication was a frequent problem throughout his late teens and early twenties, and it temporarily disabled him later on as well. In his twenties Schumann had contracted malaria, which lead to considerable weight loss and may have produced a mild meningitis. Signs of cardio-vascular disease (an "apoplectic constitution") were noted by his physicians in Leipzig. On his way to Russia he developed anal problems (presumably hemorrhoids). In Dresden he was treated for recurring aches and pains ("rheumatism"), which may have had an organic basis although Schumann regularly attributed them to his "hypochondria." Severe fatigue, occasional fainting spells, transient attacks of dizziness, and rare auditory disturbances also suggest one or more physical disorders. Migraine attacks, labyrinthitis, and other possibilities have been mentioned earlier, as was tuberculosis.

Whether Schumann had generalized arteriosclerosis or syphilis will continue to remain a matter of speculation. (Dr. Richarz's autopsy report cannot be relied upon to make a diagnosis.) However, there is no evidence that Schumann became demented, except possibly at the very end of his hospitalization. (Richarz specifically emphasized *depression* and not *dementia* as the terminal state.) Schumann's final delirium and twitching (convulsions?) were most likely the agonies of a nutritionally depleted, metabolically deranged, hopelessly suicidal, and possibly overmedicated patient.

IV PSYCHOSOCIAL STRESS FACTORS

External sources of stress have been identified in each decade of Schumann's life. During childhood, the Napoleonic invasion of his community, and his mother's illness, disrupted the family and occasioned a prolonged separation from home. In adolescence his sister became psychotic and committed suicide and his father died, events that evoked grief and spurred Schumann's creativity. His twenties were years of repeated stress: the failure of his career as a pianist, his new career as a writer and newspaper editor, the troubled relationship with Wieck and Clara, the engagement to Ernestine von Fricken, and the attachment to Schunke ending in his death. Schumann's marriage—at age thirty—brought financial problems, the demands of his many children, and the conflicts between his own artistic aspirations, which required a stable and sedentary life, and his wife's career as a virtuoso pianist, which involved a great deal of travel. One of the most severe and lingering stresses throughout Schumann's adult life was Clara's loyalty to her father, a man who had become his loathsome and bitter enemy.

The loss of Felix Mendelssohn, who had served as both model and rival, was particularly traumatic. Accession to the Düsseldorf music directorship, a post Mendelssohn had once held and given up, proved to be Schumann's undoing. He lost confidence, popularity, prestige, and then the job itself. Finally there was the stress of Brahms's unexpected visit to Düsseldorf, which excited Schumann enormously and probably made him feel that he had nothing more to contribute to music or to Clara's happiness.

Prolonged isolation at Endenich was Schumann's nemesis. It destroyed what was left of his marriage, made it impossible for him to return to his former status as a writer or musician, and confirmed his deepest dread and suspicions about being mad. Dr. Richarz's asylum, tragically, turned out to be the antithesis of everything Schumann had hoped for when he asked to be hospitalized. The doctors were unable to cure his mental illness, preserve his marriage, or restore his creativity. He could never be discharged.

V HIGHEST LEVEL OF ADAPTATION
RECENTLY ACHIEVED

After reaching a plateau in Dresden, Schumann's career had taken a progressively downhill turn. Many of his artistic goals had already been achieved. He had expressed himself in letters, poetry, plays, novels, newspaper articles, diaries, piano pieces, songs, symphonies, chamber music, oratorios, and operatic work. He had experimented with a wide variety of styles (improvisation, free-associative, declamatory, didactic, realistic, surrealistic, orderly, disorderly, fashionable, unfashionable). Yet Schumann's impact on the public had not been as great as he had wished, and he felt an urgent need to do more. As a critic himself, he probably was dissatisfied with his success, and he hoped, with Clara's help, to launch a new career as music director in Düsseldorf. Temperamentally unsuited for such a position, and handicapped by recurring illness, he failed miserably in this last chosen assignment. But before slipping into psychosis, Schumann had recognized the genius of Brahms and predicted a "new path" to the future of music. Thus he not only acknowledged his own capitulation as an artist, but also consolidated his unique historical position.

Schumann was a dreamer, a romantic tone-poet and writer whose inner voices were those of childhood, of wonder, of love, of turmoil, even of madness. Essentially a self-trained musician, he had used his prodigious talents to compose in great haste and voluminously, sometimes outstripping his resources. Fearing death, he immortalized himself through creative achievement, and he brought an end to his life through suicide.

Notes

KEY TO ABBREVIATIONS

I   Robert Schumann, *Jugendbriefe*, 2d ed., edited by C. Schumann
            (Leipzig: Breitkopf & Härtel, 1886).

II   Robert Schumann, *Briefe, Neue Folge*, 2d ed., edited by G. Jansen
            (Leipzig: Breitkopf & Härtel, 1904)

CS–JB   Clara Schumann and Johannes Brahms, *Briefe aus den Jahren 1853–
            1896*, edited by B. Litzmann, 3 vols. (Leipzig: Breitkopf & Härtel,
            1927).

GS   Robert Schumann, *Gesammelte Schriften über Musik und Musiker*, 2 vols.
            (Leipzig: Breitkopf & Härtel, 1883).

HHB   Robert Schumann, *Haushaltbücher 1837–1856*, edited by G. Nau-
            haus, 2 vols. (Leipzig: VEB Deutscher Verlag für Musik, 1982).

Litz.   Berthold Litzmann, *Clara Schumann, Ein Künstlerleben*, 7th ed., 3
            vols. (Leipzig: Breitkopf & Härtel, 1925).

RSH-Z   Archives of the Robert Schumann Haus, Zwickau.

TB   Robert Schumann, *Tagebücher 1827–1838*, edited by G. Eismann (Leipzig: VEB Deutscher Verlag für Musik, 1971).

I. CRISIS

1. Maps, paintings, and photographs showing the location of the old pontoon-bridge and the streets of Düsseldorf in relation to Schumann's house at Bilkerstrasse 15 (still standing) were obtained from the *Stadtgeschichtliches Museum,* Düsseldorf. Also see Kast (1981), pp. 40, 54–55, 158. The description of the composer's appearance is based on a sketch by Laurens; see Eismann (1964), p. 155. Reconstruction of Schumann's suicide attempt is from the diary of Ruppert Becker, concertmaster of the Düsseldorf Orchestra, available in the Robert Schumann House, Zwickau. See also II, p. 534.

2. II, pp. 391–392.

3. Ibid., pp. 389–390.

4. Ibid., pp. 379–380. For a discussion of the "messianic" implications of this meeting, see Kross (1981a).

5. Schumann's travel diary (unpublished), RSH-Z. Also see Litz., Vol. 2, p. 291.

6. Schumann's travel diary.

7. Ibid.

8. Litz., Vol. 2, p. 295.

9. Cited in Eismann (1956), Vol. 1, p. 186.

10. II, p. 392.

11. Personal communication from W. Boetticher.

12. Unpublished letter, Robert Schumann House, Bonn.

13. Unpublished letter, Heinrich Heine Institute, Düsseldorf.

14. Unpublished letter, Stadtarchiv, Bonn. For an abridged version, see Kast (1981), p. 157.

15. HHB, 10 February 1854, p. 648.

16. Litz., Vol. 2, p. 296.

17. HHB, 11 Feb. 1854, p. 648.

18. Litz., Vol. 2, p. 296.

19. Ibid.

20. For quotations from Becker's diary, see II, pp. 533–534.

21. HHB, p. 648. (Part of this entry is barely legible; Litz., Vol. 2, p. 14, reads the word *mitgenommen* as *musiziert,* i.e., "made music.")

22. *Allgemeine Deutsche Biographie,* Vol. 10, pp. 736–737, and Neuss (1965), pp. 113–117.

23. All Clara's diary writings in this and the next four paragraphs are from Litz., Vol. 2, pp. 297–298.

24. Cited in II, pp. 533–534.
25. Litz., Vol. 2, p. 298.
26. Cited in II, pp. 533–534.
27. Clara's account in this and the following paragraphs from Litz., Vol. 1, pp. 299–301.
28. Earle (1853), pp. 64–66.
29. Litz., Vol. 2, p. 302.
30. Kalbeck (1921), Vol. 1, p. 163.
31. Litz., Vol. 2, p. 303.

II.   A VULNERABLE PERSONALITY

1. Rehberg and Rehberg (1969), p. 18.
2. For data about the family, see Martin Kreisig's "Biographische Angaben zum Stammbaum Robert Schumann" (1930), RSH-Z. Rehberg and Rehberg (1969), p. 9, describe the effect of Grandmother Böhme's illness.
3. For Goethe's opinions about *Sturm und Drang*, see Ruf (1856).
4. C. Richter (1826).
5. Ibid.
6. Ibid.
7. Pickering (1974).
8. The books by August Schumann mentioned here are available in the library of the British Museum in London.
9. C. Richter (1826).
10. E. Schumann (1931), p. 17. (See also a poem written by Schumann's maternal grandmother, in Friedrich Schumann's "Stammbuch," RSH-Z.)
11. Wasielewski (1906), pp. 6–7.
12. Brion (1956), p. 27.
13. Data about Schumann's hometown are from the RSH-Z.
14. Niecks (1925), pp. 16–17. Some of these descriptions can also be found in R. Taylor (1982), pp. 22–23.
15. Quotations are from Schumann's autobiography, RSH-Z. Only part of this document has been published, by Schoppe and Nauhaus (1973). The pertinent passage is on p. 43.
16. Ibid.
17. E. Schumann (1931), p. 20.
18. Stern (1977). For a discussion of musical development in early childhood, see Ostwald (1973a).
19. E. Schumann (1931), p. 20.
20. For information about Zwickau's music life, see Schoppe (1980).

21. Schumann's statements about Kuntsch and his own composing are found in his autobiography; see Eismann (1956), Vol. 1, pp. 12, 17. The quotation about "models" is from Wörner (1949), p. 28.

22. See Rehberg and Rehberg (1969), p. 19, Schauffler (1945), p. 13, and Dahms (1925), p. 19.

23. Cited in Shitomirski (1961), p. 37.

24. Schumann autobiography, RSH-Z.

25. Schumann's childhood friend is mentioned by Rehberg and Rehberg (1969), p. 19, and Niecks (1925), p. 28. Dahms (1925), p. 18, gives his name, and Wörner (1949), p. 27, gives his hometown.

26. I, p. 136.

27. II, pp. 350–351.

28. Cited in Eismann (1956), Vol. 1, p. 14.

29. Ibid.

30. Ibid., p. 18.

31. The collection can be seen at the RSH-Z.

32. Cited in Schoppe and Nauhaus (1973), pp. 43–44.

33. Ibid.

34. Niederland (1958).

35. Schoppe and Nauhaus (1973), p. 44.

36. See C. Richter (1826).

37. Rehberg and Rehberg (1969), p. 16.

38. Jansen (1904).

39. Sutermeister (1959), p. 1177.

40. E. Schumann (1931), p. 60.

41. Dr. G. F. Schumann's suicide is recorded in Kreisig (1930).

42. Freud (1917); Pollock (1978).

43. TB, pp. 23, 236.

44. Ibid., pp. 22–23.

45. Ibid., p. 21.

46. Wasielewski (1906), p. 19.

47. Eismann (1956), Vol. 1, p. 15.

48. I, pp. 1, 2.

49. Ibid.

50. TB, p. 28.

51. I, p. 18.

52. Eismann (1956), Vol. 1, pp. 15–16.

53. Ibid.

54. Ibid., p. 19.

55. Ibid., p. 22.

56. TB, p. 30.
57. About the nineteenth-century preoccupation with double personalities, see Ellenberger (1970), pp. 145, 162–163.
58. TB, p. 82.
59. Richter (1804).
60. Fragments from Schumann's unfinished novel are in his diary; see TB, pp. 99–102.
61. TB, p. 97.
62. Ibid., p. 24.
63. I, p. 11.
64. TB, pp. 23–24.
65. Ibid., p. 20.
66. I, p. 7.
67. TB, p. 192.
68. Ibid., p. 25.
69. Ibid.
70. Ibid.
71. Ibid., p. 89.
72. Ibid., pp. 94, 109, 112, 117, 175.
73. Ibid., p. 94. *Heilig* ("holy") has the same root as *heilend* ("healing").
74. Bräuer (1976).
75. Adelmann (1854). See also *Biographisches Lexicon Hervorrangenden Aerzte* (1929), Vol. 1.
76. TB, p. 54; I, p. 6.
77. Earle (1853), p. 141. I am grateful to the present medical director, Dr. K. Weisske, for a tour of the hospital and castle.
78. Mora (1980), pp. 57–58.
79. I, p. 128.
80. Litz., Vol. 1, p. 13.
81. TB, pp. 54, 111, 170.
82. Eismann (1956), pp. 11–12.
83. I, p. 137.
84. Ibid., pp. 20–21.

III.   CHALLENGES AND OPPORTUNITIES

1. I, p. 13.
2. Trip with Rosen described in TB, pp. 55–57, 60–66.

3. For description of Heine, see Schumann's letter to Dr. Kurrer (6 September 1828) in Schneider (1974), p. 109; also Schnapp (1924), p. 16.

4. TB, pp. 64–65.

5. Schneider (1974), p. 105

6. I, pp. 22–23.

7. Ibid.

8. Eismann (1956), Vol. 1, p. 28.

9. Ibid., p. 43.

10. I, pp. 25–26.

11. Ibid., p. 25.

12. TB, p. 83.

13. For a description of the diagnosis "dissociative disorder," see American Psychiatric Association (1980), p. 253.

14. II, pp. 3–5.

15. TB, p. 495. For a description of the apartment, see Niecks (1925), p. 59.

16. TB, p. 86.

17. Ibid., pp. 84–85.

18. Ibid., pp. 82, 93.

19. Ibid., pp. 92–93.

20. I, pp. 35–36.

21. Unpublished essay, RSH-Z.

22. Ibid.

23. TB, p. 97.

24. Ibid.

25. Ibid., p. 195.

26. Ibid., p. 112.

27. Ibid., p. 127.

28. Ibid., p. 157.

29. Ibid., p. 152.

30. Eismann (1956), Vol. 1, p. 44.

31. TB, p. 174.

32. Ibid., pp. 168, 183, 184.

33. Schafer (1975).

34. TB, p. 151. According to G. Eismann, editor of the diaries, Schumann is referring here either to *Studies of Emotional States and Mood Disorders* by Michael von Lenhossek, published in 1805, or to the same author's *Lectures on Human Emotional States, for Physicians and Educators*, published in 1806.

35. TB, pp. 94, 184, 186.

36. I, p. 37.

37. TB, pp. 134–140.

38. Ibid.
39. Kubie (1973).
40. TB, p. 154.
41. Ibid., p. 177.
42. Ibid., p. 178.
43. Ibid., pp. 131–132.
44. Ibid., p. 452.
45. Ibid., p. 180.
46. Schneider (1974), p. 73.
47. See *Sechs frühe Lieder* (op. posth.), Universal Edition, Vienna, 1933.
48. Eismann (1956), Vol. 1, pp. 38–41.
49. I, pp. 27–29.
50. For details of Wieck's career, see Joss (1902).
51. Ibid., p. 14.
52. Litz., Vol. 1, pp. 1–2.
53. Dahms (1925), p. 36.
54. Eismann (1956), Vol. 1, p. 44.
55. Litz., Vol. 1, p. 207.
56. About Emilie Reichold, see TB, pp. 109, 110, 152, 156, 168.
57. Ibid., p. 170.
58. Eismann (1956), Vol. 1, pp. 43–45.
59. TB, p. 96.
60. Ibid., p. 214.
61. Eismann (1956), Vol. 1, p. 69.

IV. METAMORPHOSIS

1. I, pp. 32, 39.
2. Schneider (1974), p. 113.
3. Ibid.
4. Thibaut (1825).
5. Schneider (1974), p. 119.
6. Ibid.
7. Ibid.
8. TB, pp. 187–189, 192.
9. Ibid., pp. 49–50.
10. I, p. 47.
11. Wörner (1949), p. 37.
12. I, pp. 62, 63.

13. TB, pp. 199–203.
14. Schneider (1974), p. 116.
15. TB, pp. 204–206.
16. Ibid., p. 201.
17. I, pp. 67–71.
18. TB, pp. 246–247. Quotes about the baths and the widow are from I, p. 72.
19. TB, p. 248.
20. I, p. 71.
21. Ibid., pp. 73, 72.
22. Schneider (1974), p. 122.
23. Ibid.; TB, pp. 256–257.
24. TB, pp. 252, 257, 261, 262.
25. Ibid., p. 265.
26. Ibid., pp. 266, 275.
27. I, p. 76.
28. TB, pp. 267–268, 270, 276, 277.
29. Ibid., p. 277.
30. I, pp. 87, 91.
31. Ibid., p. 91.
32. See, for example, Rosen's letter dated 16 October 1828, in Boetticher (1979), pp. 156–158.
33. I, p. 92.
34. Eismann (1956), Vol. 1, p. 55.
35. Ibid.
36. These and the following excerpts from Schumann's letter to Wieck can be found in I, pp. 78–85.
37. Ibid.
38. Available in the Stadtarchiv, Bonn.
39. Köhler (1975).
40. TB, pp. 225, 227, 233, 295.
41. Sams (1972).
42. I, pp. 99–100.
43. TB, pp. 210–212.
44. I, pp. 64–65.
45. Wasielewski (1906), pp. 56–57.
46. TB, p. 212.
47. Ibid., pp. 215–224.
48. Ibid., p. 213.
49. Ibid., pp. 215–217, 224.

50. Ibid., p. 222.
51. Ibid., p. 226.
52. Niecks (1925), p. 87.
53. TB, pp. 226, 231.
54. Ibid., p. 234.
55. Ibid., p. 235.
56. Ibid., p. 236.
57. Ibid., pp. 242–243.
58. I, pp. 96–97.
59. Kross (1978), p. 28.

V.   A NEW BEGINNING

1. I, p. 106.
2. Ibid.
3. Walker (1972), p. 6.
4. I, p. 110.
5. See TB, pp. 160, 174, 181.
6. Ibid., pp. 280, 283.
7. Ibid., p. 282.
8. I, p. 114.
9. Ibid., p. 116.
10. E. Schumann (1931), p. 108.
11. I, pp. 116–119.
12. Ibid., p. 118.
13. Ibid.
14. Kross (1982), p. 28.
15. I, p. 119. Emphasis in the original.
16. Eismann (1956), Vol. 1, pp. 62–63.
17. Excerpts from Wieck's letter to Frau Schumann in this paragraph and the next can be found in ibid., pp. 63–65.
18. Ibid., p. 65. Emphasis in the original.
19. II, pp. 25–26.
20. Ibid.
21. I, pp. 120–124.
22. II, pp. 26–27.
23. I, p. 124.
24. TB, p. 295.

25. Ibid., pp. 296, 297.

26. Ibid., p. 321.

27. Ibid., p. 298.

28. I, p. 125.

29. Ibid., p. 126.

30. Ibid., p. 127.

31. Ibid.

32. E. Schumann (1931), p. 126.

33. Eismann (1956), Vol. 1, p. 77.

34. I, p. 128.

35. Ibid., p. 130.

36. Ibid., p. 128.

37. Ibid., p. 130.

38. Litz., Vol. I, pp. 25–26.

39. I, p. 131.

40. Eismann (1954), Vol. 1, pp. 67–68.

41. I, p. 134.

42. Ibid., p. 133.

43. Ibid., pp. 134–135.

44. Ibid., pp. 133, 134.

45. Ibid., p. 136.

46. Ibid., pp. 134, 135.

47. Unpublished letter dated 10 November 1830, RSH-Z.

48. E. Schumann (1931), p. 123.

49. I, p. 144.

50. Sachs (1980), pp. 783–784.

51. I, pp. 143, 138.

52. Boetticher (1942).

53. TB, p. 364.

54. Reich (1983), p. 8.

55. TB, p. 364.

56. Released in 1983 by Warner-Columbia. Clara is played by Nastassia Kinski.

57. Nagera (1969).

58. I, p. 143.

59. Ibid., p. 142.

60. TB, pp. 330–333, 339, 342, 344, 349, 350, 355, 360, 372, 374, 386, 387.

61. Ibid., p. 330.

62. Ibid., p. 336.

63. Personal communication.

64. TB, p. 343.
65. Ibid., pp. 330–331.
66. Ibid., p. 332.
67. Ibid.
68. Ibid., p. 334.
69. Ibid., pp. 336–337.
70. Ibid., p. 336.
71. Unpublished letter, RSH-Z. Emphasis in the original.
72. TB, pp. 338–339.
73. Ibid., pp. 342, 371.
74. Litz., Vol. 1, p. 154.
75. TB, p. 341.
76. Ibid., p. 339.
77. Ibid., p. 342.
78. Ibid., pp. 343, 344.
79. Ibid., p. 344.
80. Ibid.
81. Ibid., p. 339.

VI. CUMULATIVE STRESSES

1. TB, p. 346.
2. Ibid., p. 349.
3. Eismann (1956), Vol. 1, p. 74.
4. TB, p. 358.
5. Schneider (1974), pp. 85–86.
6. Eismann (1956), Vol. 1, p. 74.
7. Pleasants (1965), p. 17n.
8. *Allgemeine Musikalische Zeitung*, 7 December 1831.
9. I, p. 162.
10. TB, p. 344.
11. *Allgemeine Musikalische Zeitung*, 7 December 1831.
12. I, pp. 148–150.
13. Ibid.
14. Ibid., pp. 151–153.
15. Unpublished letter dated 9 October 1831, RSH-Z.
16. TB, p. 354.
17. Ibid., p. 362.

18. I, p. 149.
19. Ibid., p. 151.
20. TB, pp. 333–334.
21. I, p. 157.
22. TB, pp. 371, 372.
23. Ibid.
24. Eismann (1956), Vol. 1, p. 78.
25. I, p. 160.
26. Ibid.
27. TB, p. 378.
28. Litz., Vol. 1, pp. 28–37.
29. TB, p. 217.
30. I, pp. 164–165. Emphasis added.
31. TB, p. 386.
32. Petzholdtz (1956).
33. Henry Pleasants, who is currently working on Wieck's essays published under the title *Clavier und Gesang*, has kindly furnished me with the translation quoted here.
34. I, p. 295.
35. Ibid., pp. 168–169.
36. TB, p. 379.
37. Ibid., p. 381.
38. Ibid., p. 383.
39. Ibid., p. 384.
40. Ibid., pp. 386, 394, 389, 393, 396, 397.
41. Rothe (1970). Emphasis added.
42. Ibid.
43. TB, pp. 394, 397.
44. Ibid., pp. 383–385, 393, 395, 405.
45. Ibid., p. 400.
46. See Köhler (1976a) for a more detailed discussion of the *Intermezzi* (op. 4).
47. TB, p. 412.
48. Ibid., pp. 404, 406.
49. Ibid., p. 354.
50. Ibid., p. 406.
51. I, p. 182.
52. TB, p. 410.
53. I, p. 184.
54. TB, p. 411.

55. I, pp. 188–190.
56. Hovorka and Kronfeld (1909), pp. 217, 246, 282, 285.
57. I, pp. 188–190.
58. Ibid.
59. Morris et al. (1979), pp. 81–82.
60. I, p. 188; II, p. 40. Emphasis added.
61. Schauffler (1945), p. 44.
62. Sams (1971).
63. Henson and Urich (1978).
64. Carerj (1979).
65. Hochberg et al. (1983).
66. Jansen (1883), p. 74.
67. I, p. 194.
68. Ibid.
69. TB, p. 415.
70. I, pp. 192–193.
71. The instrument can be seen in the RSH-Z.
72. Eismann (1956), Vol. 1, p. 78.
73. Litz., Vol. 1, p. 54.
74. I, p. 200.
75. Ibid., p. 196.
76. Ibid., p. 198.
77. Ibid., p. 210.
78. TB, p. 417.
79. Litz., Vol. 1, p. 55.
80. I, pp. 199–200.
81. Wasielewski (1906), p. 106.
82. I, pp. 204–205.
83. Walker (1972), p. 14.
84. I, pp. 210–211.
85. Haehl (1922). See Vol. 1, pp. 415–418, for more about Dr. Hartmann.
86. I, p. 214.
87. Ibid.

VII.   BREAKDOWN AND AFTERMATH

1. I, pp. 226–227.
2. Ibid.

3. Ibid., p. 209.

4. Ibid., p. 221.

5. TB, p. 419.

6. Ibid.

7. Litz., Vol. 1, pp. 83–85.

8. Ibid.

9. Wasielewski (1906), p. 110.

10. See American Psychiatric Association (1980), pp. 230–231, for a description of panic disorders. For a summary of recent research into this problem, see Shader et al. (1982).

11. TB, p. 419.

12. Ibid.

13. I, pp. 227–228.

14. Rehberg and Rehberg (1969), p. 147.

15. Letter dated 27 November 1833, RSH-Z.

16. Schunke (1966), pp. 105–106.

17. Ibid., p. 106.

18. Warrack (1968).

19. Jansen (1883), p. 57.

20. Ibid., p. 128.

21. Litz., Vol. 1, p. 85.

22. Jansen (1883), p. 60.

23. I, pp. 229, 228.

24. Rehberg and Rehberg (1969), pp. 149–150.

25. I, pp. 232–233.

26. Jansen (1883), pp. 53–54.

27. Kross (1981), pp. 429–432.

28. Eismann (1956), Vol. 1, pp. 87–88.

29. Plantinga (1972), p. 168.

30. Eismann (1956), Vol. 1, p. 87.

31. II, pp. 77–79.

32. Eismann (1956), Vol. 1, p. 87.

33. Ibid., p. 94.

34. Ibid., Vol. 2, pp. 28–29.

35. Ibid., p. 141.

36. Ibid., pp. 66–67.

37. I, p. 239.

38. Ibid., p. 242.

39. Ibid., pp. 240, 238.

40. Ibid., p. 243.
41. Ibid., p. 211.
42. Ibid., p. 243.
43. Ibid., p. 278.
44. Solomon (1978).
45. Solomon (1981), p. 153.
46. TB, p. 420.
47. Eismann (1956), Vol. 1, pp. 95–96.
48. TB, p. 420.
49. I, pp. 251–255.
50. Ibid., p. 254.
51. Ibid., p. 257.
52. Ibid.
53. TB, p. 420.
54. I, pp. 258–265.
55. Ibid., p. 261.
56. Ibid., pp. 260–261.
57. Ibid.
58. Joss (1902), pp. 46–55.
59. TB, p. 420.
60. Kross (1981), p. 427.
61. GS, pp. iii–iv.
62. Erler (1887), p. 118.
63. Ibid., p. 57.
64. Michalowski (1980), p. 295.
65. Wasielewski (1869), p. 118n.
66. Litz., Vol. 1, p. 74.
67. TB, p. 421.

VIII.   THE ROAD TO MATURITY

1. Kupferberg (1972).
2. Marek (1972), p. 165.
3. GS, Vol. 1, p. 113.
4. R. Schumann (1948).
5. II, pp. 71–72.
6. Litz., Vol. 2, p. 82.
7. R. Schumann (1948), p. 71.

8. GS, Vol. 1, p. 113.
9. Litz., Vol. 2, p. 86.
10. R. Schumann (1948), p. 22.
11. Wasielewski (1906), p. 156.
12. Ibid., p. 157.
13. R. Schumann (1948), p. 68.
14. Ibid., p. 64.
15. Ibid.
16. Wagner (1894), Vol. 3, p. 117.
17. Marek (1972), p. 187.
18. Robert and Clara Schumann's marriage diary, 1840, unpublished, RSH-Z.
19. Walker (1972), p. 434.
20. R. Schumann (1948), pp. 51–52, 74.
21. Ibid., p. 64.
22. Marek (1972), p. 258.
23. Litz., Vol. 1, p. 86.
24. Schumann, R. (1965), p. 21. Emphasis in the original.
25. II, pp. 65–66.
26. Litz., Vol. 1, p. 86.
27. Ibid., p. 101.
28. II, p. 73.
29. Ibid.
30. Litz., Vol. 1, p. 97.
31. Ibid., p. 98.
32. Ibid.
33. II, pp. 67–68.
34. GS, Vol. 1, pp. 255–261.
35. Litz., Vol. 1, p. 110.
36. Ibid., pp. 110–111.
37. TB, p. 422.
38. Joss (1902), pp. 47–54.
39. II, p. 85.
40. Litz., Vol. 1, p. 113.
41. GS, Vol. 1, pp. 286–288.
42. Bennett (1907), pp. 54, 60. Emphasis in the original.
43. Hofmann (1979), pp. 26–27.
44. Litz., Vol. 1, p. 109.
45. Rosen (1980), p. 314.
46. Köhler (1976a), p. 81.

47. Solomon (1972), p. 50.
48. Litz., Vol. 1, p. 186.
49. Ibid.
50. Erler (1887), Vol. 1, p. 101.
51. I, p. 278.
52. Ibid., p. 302.
53. Ibid., p. 303.
54. Köhler (1976b), p. 43.
55. Litz., Vol. 1, p. 351.
56. II, pp. 75–76.
57. Ibid., p. 150.
58. Reich (1983).
59. Perényi (1974), p. 186.
60. Litz., Vol. 1, pp. 118–119.
61. Ibid., p. 119.
62. Ibid., p. 120.
63. Ibid., p. 123.
64. Ibid., pp. 123–125.
65. Ibid., p. 126.
66. II, pp. 98–99.
67. Litz., Vol. 1, pp. 126–127.
68. Ibid., pp. 127–128.
69. Ibid., pp. 127–128, 129.
70. Ibid.
71. Ibid., pp. 132–133.
72. Ibid., p. 133.
73. I, p. 172.

IX.   SYMBOLIC UNION WITH CLARA

1. GS, Vol. 2, pp. 8–22.
2. Ibid., pp. 48–56.
3. Ibid., p. 52.
4. Abraham (1980).
5. Litz., Vol. 1, p. 154.
6. Ibid., p. 156.
7. Ibid., p. 143.
8. Ibid., pp. 140–141.

9. Ibid., p. 159.
10. Ibid., p. 141.
11. Ibid., p. 165.
12. Ibid., p. 147.
13. Ibid., p. 149.
14. Ibid., pp. 151, 153.
15. Ibid., p. 170.
16. Boetticher (1962), p. 47.
17. Litz., Vol. 1, p. 162.
18. Köhler (1979), p. 42.
19. I, p. 298.
20. Litz., Vol. 1, p. 160.
21. Ibid., p. 163.
22. Ibid., pp. 163–164.
23. Ibid., p. 164.
24. Ibid., p. 166.
25. Ibid.
26. Ibid., p. 167.
27. Ibid.
28. Ibid., p. 175.
29. Ibid., p. 187.
30. Ibid.
31. Ibid., p. 187n.
32. Ibid., p. 193.
33. Ibid., p. 192.
34. Ibid.
35. II, pp. 113–115.
36. Litz., Vol. 1, p. 181.
37. Ibid., p. 178.
38. Boetticher (1962).
39. Litz., Vol. 1, p. 178.
40. Ibid.
41. Erler (1887), Vol. 1, p. 206.
42. Köhler (1977a), p. 79n15.
43. Litz., Vol. 1, pp. 182, 193.
44. Ibid., p. 186.
45. Ibid., p. 194.
46. Ibid., pp. 193–194.
47. Ibid., p. 206.

48. Ibid., p. 207.
49. Ibid., p. 206.
50. Ibid., p. 222.
51. Ibid., p. 224.
52. See Hoffmann (1969), Vol. 2.
53. Litz., Vol. 1, p. 199.
54. HHB, Vol. 1, p. 42.
55. Litz., Vol. 1, p. 212.
56. Ibid., p. 215.
57. Ibid., p. 217.
58. E. Schumann (1931), p. 261.
59. Litz., Vol. 1, p. 216.
60. Ibid., p. 218.
61. II, p. 134.
62. Wasielewski (1869), p. 332.
63. II, pp. 138–140.
64. Litz., Vol. 1, p. 240.
65. II, pp. 138–140.
66. Schenk (1956), p. 13.
67. Ibid.
68. GS, Vol. 2, p. 143.
69. Litz., Vol. 1, p. 247.
70. Ibid., p. 251.
71. Ibid.
72. Ibid., p. 252.
73. II, p. 144.
74. Litz., Vol. 1, p. 255.
75. Ibid., p. 307.
76. II, p. 424.
77. GS, Vol. 2, p. 141.
78. Solomon (1981), p. 137.
79. Litz., Vol. 1, p. 259.
80. Köhler (1977b), pp. 33–34.
81. Ibid., p. 33.
82. II, pp. 148–151.
83. I, p. 298.
84. Ibid., p. 297.
85. Litz., Vol. 1, p. 297.
86. Köhler (1977c), p. 44.

87. Litz., Vol. 1, p. 283.
88. Ibid., p. 288.
89. Ibid., p. 291.
90. Ibid., p. 311.
91. Ibid., p. 309.
92. I, p. 301.
93. Köhler (1978), p. 25.
94. I, p. 301.
95. HHB, p. 63.
96. Litz., Vol. 1, pp. 313–314.
97. Boetticher (1962).

X.   DELAYS BEFORE MARRIAGE

1. Litz., Vol. 1, p. 312.
2. Ibid., p. 340.
3. Ibid., p. 349.
4. Ibid., pp. 321–322.
5. Ibid., p. 343.
6. Ibid., p. 364.
7. Ibid., p. 371.
8. Unpublished court records, RSH-Z.
9. Ibid.
10. Ibid.
11. Litz., Vol. 1, p. 362.
12. Eismann (1956), Vol. 1, p. 120.
13. Litz., Vol. 1, p. 388.
14. Ibid., p. 327.
15. HHB, pp. 150, 106.
16. Ibid., p. 700n129.
17. Unpublished court records, RSH-Z.
18. II, pp. 115–117.
19. HHB, pp. 110, 150.
20. Schumann's Poetry Book, RSH-Z.
21. Critchley and Henson (1977), p. 411.
22. Litz., Vol. 1, p. 408.
23. Ibid., p. 410.
24. II, p. 158.

25. Sams (1969).
26. E. Grieg, cited in Komar (1971), pp. 118–122.
27. Litz., Vol. 1, p. 407.
28. Ibid., p. 421.
29. Hallmark (1976), p. 120.
30. Liszt's letter to Schumann, cited by Perényi (1974), p. 135.
31. GS, Vol. 2, pp. 159, 160.
32. Ibid., p. 160.
33. Litz., Vol. 1, p. 413.
34. Ibid., p. 414.
35. Ibid., p. 412.
36. Ibid., pp. 417–418.
37. Ibid., p. 421.
38. Ibid., p. 413.
39. GS, Vol. 2, pp. 158, 165.
40. Eismann (1956), Vol. 1, p. 128.
41. Litz., Vol. 1, p. 421.
42. Quotation from the court transcript, RSH-Z.
43. HHB, p. 155.

XI. HARMONY AND DISCORD

1. HHB, pp. 150, 155.
2. Litz., Vol. 1, p. 426.
3. Ibid., p. 430.
4. Ibid., p. 429.
5. Frisch (1978). The figures cited pertain to England. No comparable statistics about men on the continent are available.
6. HHB, p. 274.
7. Marriage diary, as cited in E. Schumann (1931), p. 294.
8. See Taylor (1953), pp. 196, 198.
9. E. Schumann (1931), p. 279.
10. Ibid., p. 282.
11. HHB, p. 164.
12. E. Schumann (1931), pp. 277, 281, 284.
13. Ibid., p. 284.
14. Ibid., p. 289.
15. Ibid., p. 288.

16. HHB, pp. 174–175.
17. Marriage diary, as cited in Litz., Vol. 2, p. 15.
18. E. Schumann (1931), p. 290.
19. Ibid., p. 291.
20. Ibid., p. 246.
21. Ibid., p. 296.
22. HHB, p. 173.
23. For a fuller discussion, see Epstein (1979), pp. 153, 157.
24. Marriage diary; see E. Schumann (1931), pp. 292–293.
25. HHB, p. 178.
26. E. Schumann (1931), p. 293.
27. Litz., Vol. 2, p. 30.
28. Ibid., p. 32.
29. E. Schumann (1931), p. 304.
30. HHB, pp. 190–193.
31. E. Schumann (1931), p. 306.
32. HHB, p. 193.
33. Litz., Vol. 2, p. 33.
34. E. Schumann (1931), p. 308.
35. HHB, pp. 196, 197, 198.
36. Ibid., p. 198.
37. E. Schumann (1931), p. 314.
38. Ibid., pp. 315–316.
39. Litz., Vol. 2, p. 37.
40. HHB, p. 209.
41. Ibid., pp. 210, 212, 213.
42. Ibid., p. 211.
43. Litz., Vol. 2, p. 52.
44. HHB, p. 217.
45. E. Schumann (1931), pp. 329–330.
46. HHB, pp. 223–224.
47. Ibid., pp. 226–228.
48. Ibid., p. 232.
49. Marriage diary (unpublished segments), RSH-Z.
50. Marriage diary, as cited in E. Schumann (1931), pp. 286–287.
51. Marriage diary, RSH-Z.
52. E. Schumann (1931), p. 299.
53. Forner (1983), p. 83.
54. H. J. Rothe (1970).

55. Ibid.
56. HHB, pp. 103, 117, 139.
57. H. J. Rothe (1970).
58. Litz., Vol. 2, p. 40.
59. Ibid., p. 41.
60. Ibid., p. 43.
61. Ibid., p. 50.
62. HHB, pp. 210–211.
63. Ibid., p. 212.
64. E. Schumann (1931), pp. 318–319.
65. Ibid., pp. 335–336.
66. HHB, p. 233.
67. Ibid., pp. 237, 238.
68. II, pp. 228–230.
69. HHB, p. 239.
70. II, p. 229.
71. HHB, p. 223.
72. Rehberg and Rehberg (1969), p. 685.
73. II, p. 228.
74. Litz., Vol. 2, p. 56.
75. Dohm (1974).
76. HHB, p. 248.
77. HHB, p. 727n365.
78. Ibid., p. 253.
79. Niecks (1925), p. 210.
80. Litz., Vol. 2, pp. 57–58.
81. Eismann (1956), Vol. 1, p. 136.
82. HHB, p. 268.
83. Shitomirski (1961), p. 28.
84. Litz., Vol. 2, pp. 64–65.
85. Travel diary, 29 February 1844, RSH-Z.
86. I, pp. 288–289.
87. Ibid.
88. Shitomirski (1961), pp. 33–34.
89. Litz., Vol. 2, pp. 73–74.
90. Clara Schumann's diary, 15 April 1844, RSH-Z.
91. Eismann (1956), Vol. 1, pp. 140–142.
92. II, pp. 241–242.
93. Eismann (1956), Vol. 1, p. 144.

94. Litz., Vol. 2, p. 75.
95. II, pp. 240–242. See also Schneider (1974), p. 146.

XII.   ENGULFING DEPRESSION

1. Hamerow (1958).
2. Becker (1978), pp. 28–29.
3. HHB, pp. 369–370.
4. Ibid., p. 371.
5. Litz., Vol. 1, p. 76.
6. HHB, p. 373.
7. Nauhaus (1981), p. 16.
8. Tischner (1937), Vol. 3, p. 425.
9. Müller (1902), pp. 68–72.
10. HHB, p. 373.
11. Litz., Vol. 2, p. 76.
12. Ibid.
13. Ibid.
14. Ibid.
15. HHB, p. 365.
16. II, p. 228.
17. Litz., Vol. 2, p. 77.
18. Moser (1908), Vol. 1, p. 72.
19. HHB, p. 245.
20. Ibid., p. 376.
21. Ibid.
22. Ibid., p. 377.
23. II, p. 249.
24. HHB, p. 404.
25. Ibid., p. 378.
26. Ibid., p. 377.
27. Wasielewski (1906), pp. 351–353. (Helbig's original letter is in the RSH-Z.)
28. Ibid.
29. Ibid.
30. Ibid.
31. Schaaffhausen (1885).
32. HHB, pp. 383–384, 387.
33. Ibid., pp. 391, 392.

34. Ibid., p. 396.
35. Schumann's travel diary, unpublished, RSH-Z.
36. HHB, p. 397.
37. II, pp. 440–441.
38. HHB, p. 382.
39. Peterson (1982).
40. Linder (1959), p. 120.
41. Ibid., pp. 118, 116.

XIII. PLATEAU

1. HHB.
2. GS, Vol. 2, pp. 362–374.
3. II, p. 249.
4. HHB, pp. 408–410.
5. II, p. 300.
6. Litz., Vol. 1, p. 160.
7. Laux (1956), p. 35.
8. Ibid., p. 34.
9. Litz., Vol. 2, p. 104.
10. HHB, pp. 411–412.
11. Ibid., p. 413.
12. Ibid., p. 414.
13. Ibid., pp. 414, 415.
14. Litz., Vol. 2, p. 126.
15. HHB, p. 415.
16. Ibid., p. 416.
17. Ibid., p. 273.
18. Ibid., p. 279.
19. Ibid., p. 277.
20. Ibid., p. 287.
21. Ibid., pp. 279–280.
22. Ibid., p. 731n397.
23. Ibid., p. 281.
24. Earle (1853), p. 132–133.
25. Nauhaus (1978a).
26. HHB, p. 288.
27. Schneider (1974), p. 150.

28. HHB, pp. 290–291.

29. Ibid., pp. 330, 331.

30. Litz., Vol. 2, p. 97.

31. Ibid., pp. 143, 144.

32. HHB, p. 339.

33. Litz., Vol. 2, pp. 144–145.

34. Ibid., p. 145.

35. Ibid., p. 146.

36. Ibid., p. 147.

37. Ibid., p. 146.

38. Ibid., p. 153.

39. Ibid., pp. 155–156.

40. Ibid., p. 157.

41. Ibid., pp. 160–161.

42. HHB, p. 449.

43. Ibid., p. 739n456.

44. Ibid., p. 769n658.

45. Ibid., p. 440.

46. Billington (n.d.).

47. Ibid.

48. Litz., Vol. 2, p. 164.

49. Ibid., p. 169.

50. Franken (1979), pp. 186–190.

51. Litz., Vol. 2, p. 171.

52. Ibid., p. 172.

53. HHB, p. 449.

54. Unpublished letter from Carl Schumann, RSH-Z.

55. Unpublished letter from Rosalie Schumann, RSH-Z.

56. HHB, pp. 455–456.

57. II, pp. 284–285.

58. Ibid.

59. HHB, p. 761n613.

60. Niecks (1925), pp. 290–291.

61. Litz., Vol. 2, p. 186.

62. Ibid.

63. Ibid., p. 187.

64. Ibid., p. 188.

65. Ibid.

66. Ibid., p. 190.

67. Ibid., p. 191.
68. HHB, p. 491.
69. Litz., Vol. 2, p. 191.
70. II, pp. 302–303.
71. Perényi (1974), p. 158.
72. II, p. 283.
73. Litz., Vol. 2, p. 121.
74. HHB, p. 462.
75. Litz., Vol. 2, pp. 121–122.
76. Eismann (1956), Vol. 1, pp. 133–134.
77. II, pp. 290–291.
78. HHB, p. 674.
79. GS, pp. 366–374. Ludwig (1976) has written an interesting essay about the rules.
80. HHB, p. 466.
81. Byron (1951), pp. 113–156.
82. II, p. 294.
83. Kreisig (1925). Emphasis added.
84. Litz., Vol. 2, p. 194.
85. II, pp. 307–309.
86. Ibid., p. 463.
87. Eismann (1956), Vol. 1, p. 162.
88. Litz., Vol. 2, p. 195.
89. Jaques (1965).

XIV. TROUBLE ON THE HORIZON

1. HHB, p. 499.
2. Ibid., pp. 507–509.
3. II, pp. 318–319.
4. Ibid., pp. 322–323.
5. Ibid., pp. 318–319.
6. Ibid., p. 319.
7. Ibid., pp. 322–323.
8. HHB, p. 510.
9. II, pp. 322–323.
10. Ibid.
11. Litz., Vol. 2, p. 213.

12. Ibid., pp. 201–202.
13. Ibid., p. 203.
14. Ibid.
15. Litz., Vol. 2, p. 205.
16. Ibid., p. 207.
17. Ibid., p. 209.
18. HHB, p. 522.
19. Litz., Vol. 2, p. 213.
20. Ibid.
21. HHB, pp. 523–526.
22. Ibid., pp. 529–530.
23. Litz., Vol. 2, p. 217.
24. HHB, p. 530.
25. Litz., Vol. 2, pp. 217–218.
26. Eismann (1956), Vol. 1, p. 168.
27. Ibid., p. 165.
28. Shaw (1978), p. 199.
29. Litz., Vol. 2, p. 219.
30. HHB, p. 786n770.
31. Litz., Vol. 2, p. 223.
32. Ibid., p. 226.
33. Ibid., p. 227.
34. HHB, p. 537.
35. Litz., Vol. 2, pp. 225–228.
36. Ibid., p. 228.
37. Kast (1981), p. 11.
38. Ibid., p. 9.
39. Wasielewski (1906), pp. 448–449.
40. Litz., Vol. 2, p. 229.
41. Sietz (1958), pp. 85–86.
42. HHB, p. 544.
43. Litz., Vol. 2, p. 227.
44. HHB, p. 539. Emphasis added.
45. Litz., Vol. 2, p. 227.
46. HHB, p. 541.
47. I am grateful to Nancy Reich for calling this to my attention.
48. Epstein (1979), pp. 148–157.
49. Kast (1981), p. 71.
50. HHB, p. 547.

51. Ibid., p. 549.
52. II, p. 338.
53. Litz., Vol. 2, p. 239.
54. Ibid., p. 261.
55. II, pp. 345–346.
56. Litz., Vol. 2, pp. 262, 263.
57. Wasielewski (1906), p. 449.
58. HHB, p. 571.
59. Litz., Vol. 2, p. 240.
60. II, p. 235.
61. Ibid., pp. 336–337.
62. Ibid, p. 235.
63. Ibid., pp. 336–337.
64. Siegmund-Schultze (1956).
65. II, pp. 342–343.
66. Ibid., p. 364.
67. Ibid., p. 369.
68. Litz., Vol. 2, p. 266.
69. Ibid., p. 268.
70. Pollock (1975).
71. Rehberg and Rehberg (1969), p. 690.
72. Goldsmith (1971).
73. HHB, pp. 578–579, 580.
74. Ibid., pp. 594–595.
75. Kast (1981), p. 180.
76. HHB, p. 590.
77. Ibid., p. 595.
78. Ibid., p. 596.
79. Litz., Vol. 2, p. 270.
80. II, pp. 372–373.
81. CS–JB, Vol 1, p. 67.
82. Litz., Vol. 2, p. 270.
83. Kast (1981), p. 96.
84. Litz., Vol. 2, p. 270.
85. HHB, pp. 597, 598.
86. Ibid., pp. 600, 601.
87. Jansen (1886), p. 304.
88. Kast (1981), p. 119.
89. Litz., Vol. 2, p. 271.

XV.   INCIPIENT MADNESS

1. Schneider (1974), p. 54.
2. Litz., Vol. 2, p. 272.
3. HHB, p. 607.
4. Ibid., p. 606.
5. Litz., Vol. 2, p. 273.
6. HHB, p. 605.
7. Kast (1981), p. 91.
8. HHB, p. 608.
9. Wasielewski (1906), p. 487.
10. Kast (1981), p. 119.
11. II, pp. 361–362.
12. Nauhaus (1980).
13. HHB, p. 610.
14. Kast (1981), p. 29.
15. II, p. 363.
16. HHB, p. 612.
17. Ibid., p. 614.
18. Berenbruch and Hellberg (1981), p. 5.
19. HHB, pp. 618–620.
20. Ibid., p. 623. The essay has been lost.
21. II, pp. 370–371.
22. Litz., Vol. 2, pp. 253–254.
23. Moser (1908), Vol. 1, pp. 5, 26.
24. Ibid., p. 145.
25. II, pp. 373–374.
26. HHB, p. 625.
27. Litz., Vol. 2, p. 278.
28. II, pp. 373–374.
29. Moser (1908), Vol. 1, pp. 154–155.
30. HHB, p. 631.
31. Litz., Vol. 2, p. 275.
32. HHB, p. 631.
33. Ibid., p. 634.
34. Rehberg and Rehberg (1969), p. 692.
35. Slater (1972), p. 410.
36. HHB, p. 634.
37. André (1982), p. 20.

38. Litz., Vol. 2, p. 277.

39. Moser (1908), Vol. 1, p. 213.

40. E. Schumann, "Über das letzte Werk Ihres Vaters Robert Schumann," privately published letter, Ascona, Switzerland, 1937.

41. Macleod (1969), pp. 186–203. See also Johannes Joachim, unpublished letter (7 January 1938) to Eugenie Schumann; original in the City Archives of Bonn.

42. Johannes Joachim, unpublished letter (3 August 1936); original in the Library of the Free University of Berlin (Dahlem).

43. Newspaper article about "Walhalla," dated 1 September 1938, in the Düsseldorf City Archives.

44. Magidoff (1973), p. 182.

45. Unpublished letter from Yehudi Menuhin, 18 April 1937; original in the City Archives of Bonn.

46. Moser (1908), Vol. 1, p. 181n.

47. Kalbeck (1921), Vol. 1, p. 115.

48. Litz., Vol. 2, p. 281.

49. HHB, p. 637; II, pp, 379–380; GS, Vol. 2, p. 375; II, pp. 380–381, 391–392.

50. Hitschmann (1956).

51. Litz., Vol. 2, p. 281.

52. HHB, p. 637.

53. Litz., Vol. 2, p. 279.

54. Schneider (1974), p. 118. This refers to the famous sketch of Brahms made by the painter Laurens when he visited the Schumanns in 1853. (See p. 268.)

55. Joachim and Moser (1911), Vol. 1, p. 303.

56. Ostwald (1983).

57. Holde (1959), p. 314.

58. Unpublished letter from Clara to Bertha Voigt (17 May 1855), in the Heinrich Heine Institute, Düsseldorf.

59. The author is Titus Frazeni, a pseudonym.

60. Personal communication from Professor Flesch-Thebesius.

61. II, pp. 379–380.

62. GS, Vol. 2, pp. 374–375.

63. Kalbeck (1921), Vol. 1, p. 133.

64. Ibid., p. 134.

65. Stephenson (1973), p. 50.

66. Joachim and Moser (1911), Vol. 1, p. 87.

67. Kalbeck (1921), Vol. 1, p. 128.

68. Niecks (1925), p. 270.

69. Ibid.

70. Ibid., p. 276.
71. Joachim and Moser (1911), Vol. 1, p. 74.
72. Berenbruch and Hellberg (1981), p. 7; HHB, p. 641.
73. HHB, p. 639.
74. Ibid.
75. Niecks (1925), p. 294.
76. Moser (1908), Vol. 1, pp. 382–383.
77. Litz., Vol. 2, p. 245.
78. HHB, p. 641.
79. Litz., Vol. 2, pp. 248–249.
80. Ibid., pp. 250–251.
81. Niecks (1925), p. 279.
82. HHB, p. 810n924A.
83. Joachim and Moser (1911), Vol. 1, pp. 105–106.
84. Schumann's travel diary (RSH-Z) provides information about the stress of his departure on 24 November 1853.
85. HHB, pp. 641–642.
86. Joachim and Moser (1911), Vol. 1, p. 127.
87. Litz., Vol. 2, p. 286.
88. Kross (1978), p. 49.
89. Schröter (1956).
90. Joachim and Moser (1911), Vol. 1, p. 139.

XVI. ENDENICH

1. Ackerknecht (1968), p. 60.
2. Cited in Berenbruch and Hellberg (1981), p. 3.
3. Litz., Vol. 2, p. 401.
4. *Biographisches Lexicon* (1929), Vol. 4.
5. Altmaier (1977).
6. Earle (1853), pp. 58–59.
7. Jetter (1966), Vol. 1, p. 227.
8. Schumann's rooms in Endenich are described by Kross (1956).
9. Richarz (1844).
10. Kellner (1929).
11. Litz., Vol. 2, pp. 327–328.
12. CS–JB, Vol. 1, p. 25.
13. Oebeke and Richarz (1871), pp. 202–215. (Dr. Richarz's personal comments are on pp. 211–215.)

14. Clara Schumann, cited in Litz., Vol. 2, p. 304.
15. Ibid., p. 305.
16. Berenbruch and Hellberg (1981), p. 10.
17. Litz., Vol. 1, p. 307.
18. Ibid., p. 309.
19. Brahms (1983), pp. 24–25.
20. Litz., Vol. 2, p. 311.
21. Berenbruch and Hellberg (1981), p. 10.
22. Ibid.
23. For a discussion of psychiatric treatment in German hospitals at Schumann's time, see Albers (1855), Earle (1853), and Leubuscher (1852).
24. Litz., Vol. 2, p. 314.
25. Ibid., p. 307.
26. Ibid., p. 308.
27. Ibid., p. 315.
28. Ibid., p. 311.
29. Ibid., pp. 317–318.
30. Ibid., p. 319.
31. Brahms (1908), Vol. 1, pp. 50–51.
32. Cited in Litz., Vol. 2, p. 327.
33. Cited in ibid., p. 328.
34. Ibid., p. 329.
35. Ibid., p. 328.
36. Ibid.
37. Ibid., p. 329.
38. Ibid., p. 322.
39. Schumann's letter can be found in II, pp. 397–398.
40. Ibid., pp. 398–399.
41. Schemuth (1975).
42. Brahms (1908), Vol. 1, pp. 59–60.
43. Kast (1981), p. 161.
44. Joachim and Moser (1911), Vol. 1, p. 287.
45. Ibid., p. 364.
46. II, pp. 399–400.
47. Richarz (1873).
48. Ibid.
49. II, pp. 398, 400.
50. Schumann's letter to Brahms can be found in ibid., p. 402.
51. Geiringer (1939).

52. CS–JB.
53. Joachim and Moser (1911), Vol. 1, pp. 270, 337.
54. Litz., Vol. 2, p. 364.
55. II, p. 406.
56. Ibid., p. 408.
57. Payk (1977), p. 158.
58. Litz., Vol. 2, p. 374.
59. Ibid., pp. 375–376.
60. Ibid., p. 376.
61. Joachim and Moser, Vol. 1, p. 287.
62. Ibid., p. 290.
63. Wasielewski (1906), p. 497.
64. Joachim and Moser, Vol. 1, p. 303.
65. Brahms (1908), Vol. 1, p. 130.
66. Oebeke and Richarz (1871).
67. Litz., Vol. 2, p. 415.
68. Ibid., p. 413.
69. Ibid., p. 414.
70. See Hans Schneider, Catalogue #241, p. 11, Tutzing: Musikantiquariat Hans Schneider.
71. Litz., Vol. 2, p. 415.
72. Keys et al. (1950), pp. 399, 560, 633.
73. Litz., Vol. 2, p. 415.

XVII.   THE PROBLEM OF DIAGNOSIS

1. RSH-Z. I am grateful to James Ellison, M.D., for his help in translating this document.
2. Autopsy evaluation report by Dr. Jänisch, RSH-Z.
3. Personal communication from Dr. Malamud.
4. Schaaffhausen (1885).
5. Personal communication from Dr. Malamud.
6. Autopsy evaluation report by Dr. Jänisch, RSH-Z.
7. Greenfield (1963).
8. Personal communication from William B. Ober, M.D., Director of Laboratories, Hackensack Hospital, Hackensack, N.J.
9. Schemuth (1975).
10. Richarz (1873).

11. Meyer (1959).

12. Griesinger (1861).

13. Rosen (1968), pp. 247–258.

14. Richarz (1873).

15. Litz., Vol. 2, p. 138.

16. Möbius (1906), pp. 1, 14.

17. Ibid., pp. 42–43.

18. See Schiller (1982).

19. Möbius (1906), p. 1.

20. Gruhle (1906), pp. 809, 806, 810.

21. Möbius (1907).

22. Nussbaum (1923); Linder (1959); Payk (1977); Haesler (1982).

23. MacMaster (1928).

24. Slater and Meyer (1959). Contrary to popular opinion, brain disease was a rare complication of syphilis, as shown in the Oslo study of 1,404 untreated cases. Only 3 percent of the males developed general paresis, while 3.6 percent had diffuse meningo-vascular syphilis (Clark and Danbolt, 1964).

25. H. Sutermeister (1959), p. 1180.

26. Davis and Maas (1983).

27. American Psychiatric Association (1980).

28. Ibid., pp. 206–224.

29. Ibid., p. 202.

30. Stone (1980); Kernberg (1975).

Bibliography

Abraham, G., ed. 1952. *Schumann: A Symposium*. London: Oxford University Press.

———. 1980. "Robert Schumann." In *The New Grove Dictionary of Music and Musicians*, edited by S. Sadie. Vol. 16. London: Macmillan.

Ackerknecht, Erwin H. 1968. *A Short History of Psychiatry*. 2d ed. New York: Hafner.

Adelmann, G. 1854. *Ernst August Carus, Eine Biographische Skizze*. Dorpat: H. Laakmann.

Albers, J. F. H. 1855. *Memoranda der Psychiatrie*. Weimar: Landes-Industrie-Comptoirs.

Altmaier, G. 1977. "Versuch zu einem systematischen Entwurf der Anthropologie bei Friedrich Nasse." Dissertation, University of Heidelberg.

American Psychiatric Association. 1980. *Diagnostic and Statistical Manual of Mental Disorders*. 3d ed. Washington, D.C.

André, Philippe. 1982. *Schumann—Les Chants de l'ombre*. Paris: J. C. Lattès.

Barkan, Hans, ed. and trans. 1957. *Johannes Brahms and Theodor Billroth: Letters from a Musical Friendship*. Norman: University of Oklahoma Press.

Becker, George. 1978. *The Mad Genius Controversy: A Study in the Sociology of Deviance*. Beverly Hills, Calif.: Sage Publications.

Bennett, J. R. Sterndale. 1907. *The Life of William Sterndale Bennett*. Cambridge: Cambridge University Press.

Berenbruch, B., and H. Hellberg. 1981. *Robert Schumann und Bonn*. Bonn: Zimnoch & Sons.

Billington, Stephen. N.d. "Robert Schumann's *Genoveva*: A Source Study with a Critical Edition." Ph.D. dissertation, New York University.

Biographisches Lexicon der Hervorragenden Ärzte aller Zeiten und Völker. 1929–1934. 2d ed. Edited by F. Hübotter. 5 vols. Berlin: Urban & Schwarzenberg.

Bleuler, E. 1911. "Dementia Praecox oder die Gruppe der Schizophrenien." In *Handbuch der Psychiatrie*, edited by G. Aschaffenburg. Leipzig: Deuticke.

Boetticher, W. 1942. *Robert Schumann in Seinen Schriften und Briefen*. Berlin: Hahnefeld.

———. 1962. "Neue Materialien zu Robert Schumanns Wiener Bekanntenkreis." In *Festschrift Erich Schenk*. Graz.

———, ed. 1979. *Briefe und Gedichte aus dem Album Robert und Clara Schumanns*. Leipzig: VEB Deutscher Verlag für Musik.

Brahms, J. 1908, *Johannes Brahms im Briefwechsel mit Joseph Joachim*. Edited by A. Moser. 2 vols. Berlin: Deutsche Brahms-Gesellschaft.

———. 1983. *Briefe*. Edited by M. Hansen. Leipzig: Reclam.

Bräuer, A. P. 1976. "Ludwig Schumann und Colditz." *Der Rundblick* 23: 128–129.

Brion, Marcel. 1956. *Schumann and the Romantic Age*. Translated by G. Sainsbury. London: Collins.

Byron [George Gordon, Lord Byron]. 1951. *Selected Poetry and Letters*. Edited by E. E. Bostetter. New York: Holt, Rinehart and Winston.

Carerj, Leonardo. 1979. "La mano invalida di Robert Schumann." *Nuova Rivista Musicale Italiana* 13: 609–619.

Carus, Carl G. 1852. *Über Geistes-Epidemien der Menschheit*. Leipzig: Goedsche.

———. 1853. *Symbolik der menschlichen Gestalt—Ein Handbuch zur Menschenkentniss*. Leipzig: Brockhaus.

Chissell, Joan. 1948. *Schumann*. Master Musicians Series. London: Dent.

Clark, E. G., and N. Danbolt. 1964. "The Oslo Study of the Natural Course of Untreated Syphilis." *Medical Clinics of North America* 48, 3:613–623.

Cooper, F. 1972. "Operatic and Dramatic Music." In *Robert Schumann—The Man and His Music*, edited by A. Walker. London: Barrie & Jenkins.

Critchley, Macdonald, and R. A. Henson, eds. 1977. *Music and the Brain: Studies in the Neurology of Music*. London: Heinemann.

Dahms, Walter. 1925. *Schumann*. Stuttgart: Deutsche Verlags-Anstalt.

Davis, J. M., and W. Maas, eds. 1983. *The Affective Disorders*. Washington, D.C.: American Psychiatric Press.

Dohm, J. 1974. "Das Paradies und die Peri." Program Booklet. Cologne: EMI Electrola Recording.

Earle, Pliny. 1853. *Institutions for the Insane in Prussia, Austria, and Germany*. Utica: New York State.

Edler, Arnfried. 1982. *Robert Schumann und Seine Zeit*. Düsseldorf: Laaber-Verlag.

Eismann, G. 1956. *Robert Schumann, Ein Quellenwerk über Sein Leben und Schaffen*. 2 vols. Leipzig: Breitkopf und Härtel Musikverlag.

———. 1964. *Robert Schumann, A Biography in Word and Picture*. Leipzig: VEB Edition.

Ellenberger, Henri F. 1970. *The Discovery of the Unconscious: the History and Evolution of Dynamic Psychiatry*. New York: Basic Books.

Epstein, D. 1979. *Beyond Orpheus—Studies in Musical Structure*. Cambridge, Mass.: MIT Press.

Erler, Hermann. 1887. *Robert Schumanns Leben. Aus seinen Briefen geschildert*. Berlin: Ries & Erler.

Forner, Johannes, ed. 1983. *Die Gewandhauskonzerte zu Leipzig 1781–1981*. Leipzig: VEB Deutscher Verlag für Musik.

Franken, F. H. 1979. *Krankheit und Tod grosser Komponisten*. Cologne: Witzstrock.

Freud, Sigmund. 1917. "Mourning and Melancholia." In Strachey, J., ed. *Standard Edition of the Complete Psychological Works of Sigmund Freud*. London: Hogarth Press, 1973, Volume 14, pp. 243–258.

Friedreich, J. B. 1852. *System der Gerichtlichen Psychologie*. Regensburg: Joseph Manz.

Frisch, Rose E. 1978. "Population, Food Intake, and Fertility." *Science* 199: 22–30.

Gal, Hans. 1963. *Johannes Brahms, His Work and Personality*. New York: Knopf.

Garrison, F. H. 1934. "The Medical History of Robert Schumann and His Family." *Bulletin of the New York Academy of Medicine* 10 (September): 373–388.

Geiringer, Karl. 1939. "New Light on Schumann's Last Years." *The Listener*. (Reprinted in Felix Aprahamian, ed., *Essays on Music*. London: Cassell, 1967, pp. 228–231.)

———. 1947. *Brahms, His Life and Work*. 2d ed., translated by H. B. Weiner and B. Miall. New York: Oxford University Press.

Girard, Patrick. 1980. "Historical Foundations of Anti-Semitism." In *Survivors, Victims, and Perpetrators—Essays on the Nazi Holocaust*, edited by Joel E. Dimsdale. Washington, D.C.: Hemisphere.

Goldsmith, H. 1971. "Schumann's later music." Commentary on record jacket. RCA Vics-1621.

Greenfield, J. G. 1963. *Neuropathology*. 2d ed. Baltimore: Williams & Wilkins.

Griesinger, W. 1861. *Die Pathologie und Therapie der psychischen Krankheiten*. 2d ed. Stuttgart: Krabbe.

Grieve, M. 1931. *A Modern Herbal*. Vol. 1. New York: Harcourt, Brace.

Gruhle, H. 1906. "Brief über Robert Schumann's Krankheit an P. J. Möbius." *Zentralblatt für Nervenheilkunde* 29: 805–810.

Gumpert, Martin. 1945. *Hahnemann: The Adventurous Career of a Medical Rebel*. Translated by C. W. Sykes. New York: Fisher.

Haehl, R. 1922. *Samuel Hahnemann—Sein Leben und Schaffen*. Leipzig: Schwabe.

Haesler, L. 1982. "Sprachvertonung in Robert Schumanns Liederzyklus 'Dichterliebe' (1840): Ein Beitrag zur Psychoanalyse der musikalischen Kreativität." *Psyche* 36: 908–950.

Hallmark, Rufus. 1976. *The Genesis of Schumann's Dichterliebe: A Source Study.* Ann Arbor, Mich.: University Microfilm International Research Press.

Hamerow, Theodore S. 1958. *Restoration, Revolution, Reaction—Economics and Politics in Germany, 1815–1871.* Princeton, N.J.: Princeton University Press.

Henson, R. A., and H. Urich. 1978. "Schumann's Hand Injury." *British Medical Journal* 1: 900–903.

Historische Commission bei der Königlichen Akademie der Wissenschaften. 1875–1912. *Allgemeine Deutsche Biographie.* 56 vols. Munich.

Hitschmann, E. 1956. "Johannes Brahms and Women." In *Great Men—Psychoanalytic Studies by E. Hitschmann.* New York: International Universities Press.

Hochberg, F. H., R. D. Leffert, M. D. Heller, and L. Merriman. 1983. "Hand Difficulties Among Musicians." *Journal of the American Medical Association* 249: 1869–1872.

Hoffmann, E. T. A. 1969. *Selected Writings.* Translated by L. J. Kent and E. C. Knight. Chicago: University of Chicago Press.

Hofmann, Kurt. 1979. *Die Erstdrucke der Werke von Robert Schumann.* Tutzing: Hans Schneider.

Hofstadter, D. R. 1981. "Metamagical Themas, the Music of Frederic Chopin, Startling Aural Patterns That Also Startle the Eye." *Scientific American* 246: 16–28.

Holde, Artur. 1959. "Suppressed Passages in the Brahms–Joachim Correspondence Published for the First Time." *Musical Quarterly* 45: 312 324.

Hovorka, Oskar von, and A. Kronfeld. 1909. *Vergleichende Volksmedizin.* Vol. 2. Stuttgart: Strecker & Schroder.

Jansen, F. Gustav. 1883. *Die Davidsbündler: Aus Robert Schumanns Sturm und Drangperiode.* Leipzig: Breitkopf & Härtel.

————. 1886. *Robert Schumanns Briefe: Neue Folge.* Leipzig: Breitkopf & Härtel.

Jaques, E. 1965. "Death and the Mid-life Crisis." *International Journal of Psychoanalysis* 46: 502–514.

Jetter, Dieter. 1966. *Geschichte des Hospitals.* 2 vols. Wiesbaden: Franz Steiner.

Joachim, J., and A. Moser. 1911. *Briefe von und an Joseph Joachim.* 2 vols. Berlin: J. Bard.

Joss, V. 1902. *Der Musikpädagoge Friedrich Wieck und seine Familie, mit besonderer Berücksichtigung seines Schwiegersohnes, Robert Schumann.* Dresden: Oscar Damm.

Juda, A. 1953. *Höchstbegabung: Ihre Erbverhältnisse sowie ihre Beziehungen zu psychischen Anomalien.* Munich: Urban & Schwarzenberg.

Kalbeck, Max. 1921. *Johannes Brahms.* Vol. 1. 4th ed. Berlin: Deutsche Brahms-Gesellschaft.

Kast, P., ed. 1981. *Schumanns rheinische Jahre.* Düsseldorf: Droste Verlag.

Kellner, A. W. 1929. "Zur Geschichte der Privatanstalt Bonn-Endenich." *Psychia-trische-Neurologische Wochenschrift* 22: 274–278.

Kernberg., Otto F. 1975. *Borderline Conditions and Pathological Narcissism.* New York: Jason Aronson.

Kerner, D. *Krankheiten Grosser Musiker.* 1973. Vol. 2. 3d ed. Stuttgart: Schattauer Verlag.

Keys, A., J. Brožek, A. Henschel, O. Michelsen, and H. L. Taylor. 1950. *The Biology of Human Starvation.* Vol. 1. Minneapolis: University of Minnesota Press.

Köhler, H. J. 1974. Concluding remarks for *Schumann's Album for the Young, opus 68.* Leipzig: Edition Peters.

———. 1975. Concluding remarks for *Robert Schumann's Papillons, opus 2.* Leipzig: Edition Peters.

———. 1976a. Concluding remarks for *Schumann's Two Piano Sonatas, opus 11 and opus 22.* Leipzig: Edition Peters.

———. 1976b. Concluding remarks for *Schumann's C major Fantasy, opus 17.* Leipzig: Edition Peters.

———. 1977a. Concluding remarks for *Schumann's Novelletten, opus 21.* Leipzig: Edition Peters.

———. 1977b. Concluding remarks for *Schumann's Faschingsschwank aus Wien, opus 26.* Leipzig: Edition Peters.

———. 1977c. Concluding remarks for *Schumann's Humoreske, opus 20.* Leipzig: Edition Peters.

———. 1978. Concluding remarks for *Schumann's Nachtstücke, opus 23.* Leipzig: Edition Peters.

———. 1979. Concluding remarks for *Schumann's Fantasiestücke, opus 12.* Leipzig: Edition Peters.

Komar, A., ed. 1971. *Robert Schumann, Dichterliebe.* New York: Norton.

Kötz, H. 1933. *Der Einfluss Jean Pauls auf Robert Schumann.* Weimar: n.p.

Kraepelin, Emil. 1962. *One Hundred Years of Psychiatry.* Translated from German by Wade Baskin. New York: New York Philosophical Press.

Kreisig, M. 1925. "Einige unbekannte Worte Robert Schumanns über die Art seines Schaffens." *Zeitschrift für Musik* 92: 165–166.

———. 1930. "Biographische Angaben zum Stammbaum Robert Schumann." Pamphlet at Robert Schumann Haus, Zwickau.

Kross, S. 1956. "Schumanns Sterbehaus in Endenich und die Bonner Schumann Tradition." *Bonner Geschichtsblätter* 10: 180–185.

———. 1978. "Die Schumann-Autographen der Universitätsbibliothek Bonn." *Beiträge zur Rheinischen Musikgeschichte* 116: 9–19.

———. 1981a. "Brahms und Schumann." *Brahms-Studien* 44: 7–44.

———. 1981b. "Aus der Frühgeschichte von Robert Schumanns Neue Zeitschrift für Musik." *Die Musikforschung* 34: 423–445.

————, ed. 1982. *Briefe und Notizen Robert und Clara Schumanns.* 2d ed. Bonn: Bouvier Verlag.

Kubie, Lawrence S. 1973. "The Drive to Become Both Sexes." *Psychoanalytic Quarterly* 43: 349–426.

Kupferberg, Herbert. 1972. *The Mendelssohns—Three Generations of Genius.* New York: Charles Scribner.

Lange-Eichbaum, W. 1961. *Genie, Irrsinn und Ruhm: eine Pathographie des Genies.* Edited by W. Kurth. Munich: E. Reinhardt.

Laux, Karl. 1956. "'Dresden ist doch gar zu schön'—Schumann in der sächsischen Hauptstadt—Eine Ehrenrettung." In *Robert Schumann, Aus Anlass Seines 100. Todestages*, edited by H. J. Moser and E. Rebling. Leipzig: Breitkopf & Härtel.

————. 1964. *The Dresden Staatskapelle.* Leipzig: VEB Edition.

Leeser, O. 1933. *Lehrbuch der Homöopathie, Spezieller Teil: Arzneimittellehre.* Stuttgart-Leipzig: Hippokrates Verlag.

Leubuscher, R. 1852. *Über die Entstehung der Sinnestäuschung.* Berlin: Dummler.

Linder, M. 1959. "Die Psychose von Robert Schumann und ihr Einfluss auf seine musikalische Komposition." *Schweizer Archiv Neurologie* 83: 83–129.

Litzmann, Berthold. 1925. *Clara Schumann, Ein Künstlerleben.* 7th ed. 3 vols. Leipzig: Breitkopf & Härtel.

Ludwig, J. 1976, *Schumann-Tage des Bezirkes Karl-Marx-Stadt.* Zwickau: City of Zwickau.

Macleod, J. 1969. *The Sisters d'Aranyi.* London: Allen & Unwin.

MacMaster, Henry. 1928. *La Folie de Robert Schumann.* Paris: n.p.

Magidoff, Robert. 1973. *Yehudi Menuhin—The Story of the Man and the Musician.* 2d ed. London: Robert Hall.

Marek, George R. 1972. *Gentle Genius—The Story of Felix Mendelssohn.* New York: Funk & Wagnalls.

Marmor, Judd. 1983. "Systems Thinking in Psychiatry: Some Theoretical and Clinical Implications." *American Journal of Psychiatry* 140: 833–838.

Masterson, J. F., Jr. 1967. *The Psychiatric Dilemma of Adolescence.* Boston: Little, Brown.

Meyer, A. 1959. A Note on the Concept of Dementia Paralytica at the Time of Robert Schumann's Death in 1856. *Journal of Mental Science* 105: 116–123.

Michalowski, K. 1980. "Frederic Chopin." In *The New Grove Dictionary of Music and Musicians*, edited by S. Sadie. Vol. 4. London: Macmillan.

Möbius, Paul J. 1906. *Über Robert Schumanns Krankheit.* Halle: Marchold.

————. 1907. *Über Scheffels Krankheit, Kritische Bemerkungen über Pathographie.* Halle: Marchold.

Mora, George. 1980. "Historical and Theoretical Trends in Psychiatry." In *Comprehensive Textbook of Psychiatry III*, edited by H. I. Kaplan, A. M. Freedman, and B. J. Sadock. Vol. 1. Baltimore: Williams & Wilkins.

Morris, D., P. Collett, P. Marsh, and M. O'Shaunessy. 1979. *Gestures*. New York: Stein and Day.

Moser, A. 1908. *Joseph Joachim, Ein Lebensbild*. 2 vols. Berlin: Deutsche Brahms-Gesellschaft.

Müller, C. 1902. *Charakteristic der wichtigsten homöopathischen Heilmittel*. 4th ed. Leipzig: Taschner.

Nagera, H. 1969. "The Imaginary Companion: Its Significance for Ego Development and Conflict Solution." *Psychoanalytic Study of the Child* 24: 165–196.

Nauhaus, G. 1975. *Robert Schumanns Genoveva*. Zwickau: Robert Schumann Haus.

———. 1978a. "Robert and Clara Schumann in Norderney." *Kurzeitschrift des Nordseeheilbades Norderney* 20: 39–45.

———. 1978b. "Die Bedeutung der Metronombezeichnungen Robert Schumanns für die Interpretation seiner Werke." *Wissenschaftliche Arbeitstagung zu Fragen der Schumann Forschung* 3: 34–38.

———. 1980. "Die Interpretation: Sind Robert Schumanns Metronomangabungen richtig." *Musik und Gesellschaft* 30: 228.

———. 1981. *Robert Schumanns Scenen aus Goethes "Faust."* Zwickau: Kulturhaus.

Neuss, R. 1965. *Festschrift "100 Jahre Verein der Ärzte Düsseldorf."* Düsseldorf: Heinrich-Heine-Institut.

Niecks, Frederick. 1925. *Robert Schumann*. New York: E. P. Dutton.

Niederland, William G. 1958. "Early Auditory Experiences, Beating Fantasies, and Primal Scenes." *Psychoanalytic Study of the Child* 13: 471–504.

Nussbaum, F. 1923. "Der Streit um Schumanns Krankheit." Dissertation, Cologne University.

Oebeke, B., and F. Richarz. 1871. "Über die Behandlung der Nahrungsverweigerung der Irren ohne gewaltsame Fütterung." *Allgemeine Zeitschrift für Psychiatrie* 27: 202–215.

Ostwald, Peter F. 1973a. *The Semiotics of Human Sound*. The Hague: Mouton.

———. 1973b. "Musical Behavior in Early Childhood." *Developmental Medicine and Child Neurology* 15: 367–375.

———. 1981. "Baby Cries." *Infant Mental Health Journal* 2: 108–117.

———. 1984. "Johannes Brahms—Frei aber (nicht immer) froh." *Proceedings of the 3rd International Gewandhaus Symposium* (Johannes Brahms Festival). Leipzig: DDR.

Payk, T. R. 1977. "Robert Schumann as Patient in Bonn-Endenich." *Confinia Psychiat* 20: 153–161.

Perényi, Eleanor. 1974. *Liszt—The Artist as Romantic Hero*. Boston: Little, Brown.

Peterson, J. D. 1982. "Schumann's Fugues on B-A-C-H, a Secret Tribute." *The Diapason* 5: 12–13.

Petzholdtz, R. 1956. *Robert Schumann, Sein Leben in Bildern*. Leipzig: n.p.

Pickering, Sir George. 1974. *Creative Malady*. London: Oxford University Press.

Plantinga, Leon B. 1967. *Schumann as Critic*. New Haven, Conn.: Yale University Press.

―――. 1972. "Schumann and the Neue Zeitschrift für Musik." In *Robert Schumann, The Man and His Music*, edited by Alan Walker. London: Barrie and Jenkins.

Pleasants, Henry, ed. and trans. 1965 *The Musical World of Robert Schumann—A Selection of His Own Writings*. London: Victor Gollancz.

Pollock, George H. 1975. "Mourning and memorialization through music." *Annual of Psychoanalysis* 3: 423–436.

―――. 1978. "On siblings, childhood sibling loss, and creativity," *Annual of Psychoanalysis* 6: 443–481.

Rehberg, Paula, and Walter Rehberg. 1969. *Robert Schumann, Sein Leben und Sein Werk*. 2d ed. Zürich: Artemis Verlag.

Reich, N. B. 1983. "Clara Schumann." Unpublished paper presented at Stanford University.

Richarz, Franz. 1844. *Über öffentliche Irrenpflege und die Notwendigkeit ihrer Verbesserung*. Bonn: n.p.

―――. 1873. "Über Robert Schumanns Krankheit." *Signale für die Musikalische Welt* 40: 625–629.

Richter, C. E. 1826. *Biographie von August Schumann*. Zwickau: Gebrüder Schumann.

Richter, Jean Paul. 1804. *Flegeljahre*. Tübingen: n.p.

Rosen, Charles. 1980. *Sonata Forms*. New York: Norton.

Rosen, G. 1968. *Madness and Society*. Chicago: University of Chicago Press.

Rothe, A. [1895] 1976. *Geschichte der Psychiatrie in Russland, Leipzig und Wien*. Translated as *Psychiatry in Russia and Spain*. New York: Arno Press.

Rothe, Hans-Joachim. 1970. "Neue Dokumente zur Schumann-Forschung aus dem Leipziger Stadtarchiv." In *Bericht über den Internationalen Musikwissenschaftlichen Kongress Leipzig, 1966*. Leipzig: n.p.

Ruf, Sebastian. 1856. *Die Delirien, die Visionen und Halluzinationen des Tag-und-Nachtlebens, und die phantastischen Zustände*. Innsbruck: Wagner.

Runyan, William McK. 1982. *Life Histories and Psychobiography—Explorations in Theory and Method*. New York: Oxford University Press.

Sachs, Joel. 1980. "Johann Nepomuk Hummel." In *The New Grove Dictionary of Music and Musicians*, edited by S. Sadie. Vol. 8. London: Macmillan.

Sammons, Jeffrey L. 1979. *Heinrich Heine—A Modern Biography*. Princeton, N.J.: Princeton University Press.

Sams, Eric. 1969. *The Songs of Robert Schumann*. New York: Norton.

―――. 1971. "Schumann's Hand Injury." *Musical Times* 112: 1156–1159.

―――. 1972. "Schumann and the Tonal Analogue." In *Robert Schumann—The Man and His Music*, edited by Alan Walker. London: Barrie & Jenkins.

Schaaffhausen, Hermann. 1885. "Einige Relequien berühmter Männer." *Correspon-*

denz-Blatt der Deutschen Gesellschaft für Anthropologie, Ethnologie, und Urgeschichte 16: 147–149.

Schafer, R. Murray. 1975. *E. T. A. Hoffmann and Music.* Toronto: University of Toronto Press.

Schauffler, Robert H. 1945. *Florestan: The Life and Work of Robert Schumann.* New York: Henry Holt.

Schemuth, U. 1975. *Die Krankheit Alfred Rethels.* Düsseldorf: Triltsch.

Schenk, Erich. 1956. "Der Aufenthalt Robert Schumanns in Wien 1838/39." In *Robert Schumann, Aus Anlass Seines 100. Todestages*, edited by H. J. Moser and E. Rebling. Leipzig: Breitkopf & Härtel.

Schiller, F. 1982. *A Möbius Strip: Fin-de-Siecle Neuropsychiatry and Paul Möbius.* Berkeley: University of California Press.

Schilling, J. A. 1863. *Psychiatrische Briefe, oder die Irren, das Irresein und das Irrenhaus.* Augsburg: Schlosser Verlag.

Schnapp, F. 1924. *Heinrich Heine und Robert Schumann.* Hamburg: n.p.

Schneider, Hans. 1974. *Robert Schumann: Manuskripte, Briefe, Schumanniana.* Katalog Nr. 188. Tutzing: Musikantiquariat Hans Schneider.

Schoppe, M. 1980. "Zwickau." In *The New Grove Dictionary of Music and Musicians*, edited by S. Sadie. Vol. 20. London: Macmillan.

Schoppe, Martin, and Gerd Nauhaus. 1973. *Das Robert Schumann Haus in Zwickau.* Zwickau: Robert Schumann Haus.

Schröter, M. M. 1956. "Das Dunkel kam wieder: Erinnerungen an Schumanns letzte Lebenszeit." *Musica* 10: 466–469.

Schumann, Clara, and Johannes Brahms. 1927. *Briefe aus den Jahren 1853–1896.* Edited by B. Litzmann. 3 vols. Leipzig: Breitkopf & Härtel.

Schumann, Eugenie. 1925. *Erinnerungen.* Stuttgart: Engelhorns.

———. 1931. *Robert Schumann, Ein Lebensbild Meines Vaters.* Leipzig: Koehler & Amelana.

Schumann, Robert. 1883. *Gesammelte Schriften über Musik und Musiker.* 2 vols. Leipzig: Breitkopf & Härtel.

———. 1886. *Jugendbriefe.* 2d ed. Edited by C. Schumann. Leipzig: Breitkopf & Härtel.

———. 1904. *Briefe, Neue Folge.* 2d ed. Edited by G. Jansen. Leipzig: Breitkopf & Härtel.

———. 1948. *Erinnerungen an Felix Mendelssohn Bartholdy.* Edited by Georg Eismann. Zwickau: Predella Verlag.

———. 1965. *Gesammelte Schriften über Musik und Musiker—Eine Auswahl.* Edited by H. Schulze. Wiesbaden: VMA-Verlag.

———. 1971. *Tagebücher 1827–1838.* Edited by G. Eismann. Leipzig: VEB Deutscher Verlag für Musik.

———. 1982. *Haushaltbücher 1837–1856.* Edited by G. Nauhaus. 2 vols. Leipzig: VEB Deutscher Verlag für Musik.

Schunke, Michael. 1966. "Ludwig Schunke (1810–1834) und Seine Familie." In *Sammelbände der Robert-Schumann-Gesellschaft*. Vol. 2. Leipzig: VEB Deutscher Verlag für Musik, pp. 99–110.

Shader, R. I., M. Goodman, and J. Gever. 1982. "Panic Disorders: Current Perspectives." *Journal of Clinical Psychopharmacology* 2: 2–10.

Shaw, G. B. 1978. *The Great Composers: Reviews and Bombardments*. Edited by L. Crompton. Berkeley: University of California Press.

Shitomirski, Daniel W. 1961. "Schumann in Russland." In *Sammelbände der Robert-Schumann-Gesellschaft*. Vol. 1. Leipzig: VEB Deutscher Verlag für Musik.

Siegmund-Schultze, W. 1956. "Schumann und das Oratorium." In *Robert Schumann, Aus Anlass Seines 100. Todestages*, edited by H. J. Moser and E. Rebling. Leipzig: Breitkopf & Härtel.

Sietz, R. 1958. *Aus Ferdinand Hillers Briefwechsel (1826–1861)*. Festgabe zum 7. Kongress der Internationalen Gesellschaft für Musikwissenschaft, Cologne.

Slater, E. 1972. "Schumann's illness." In *Robert Schumann—The Man and His Music*, edited by A. Walker. London: Barrie & Jenkins.

Slater, Eliot, and Alfred Meyer. 1959. "Contributions to a Pathography of the Musicians: 1. Robert Schumann." *Confinia Psychiatrica* 2: 65–94.

Solomon, M. 1978. *Beethoven*. New York: Schirmers.

———. 1981. "Franz Schubert's *My Dream*." *American Imago* 38: 137–154.

Solomon, Yonty. 1972. "Solo Piano Music—I. The Sonatas and the Fantasie." In *Robert Schumann—The Man and His Music*, edited by A. Walker. London: Barrie & Jenkins.

Stephenson, K. 1969. *Clara Schumann 1818–1896*. Bonn: Internationes.

———, ed. 1973. *Johannes Brahms in Seiner Familie—Der Briefwechsel*. Hamburg: Hauswedell.

Stern, Daniel. 1977. *The First Relationship—Mother and Infant*. Cambridge, Mass.: Harvard University Press.

Stone, M. H. 1980. *The Borderline Syndromes—Constitution, Personality, and Adaptation*. New York: McGraw-Hill.

Sutermeister, Hans M. 1959. "Das Rätsel um R. Schumanns Krankheit." *Schweizerische Rundschau* 48: 1177–1185.

Sutermeister, Peter. 1959. *Robert Schumann: sein Leben nach Briefen, Tagebüchern und Erinnerungen*. 2d ed. Zürich: Ex-libris.

Taylor, G. R. 1953. *Sex in History*. London: Thames & Hudson.

Taylor, R. 1982. *Robert Schumann: His Life and Work*. New York: Universe.

Thibaut, A. F. J. 1825. *Über Reinheit der Tonkunst*. Heidelberg: n.p.

Tischner, R. 1937. *Geschichte der Homöopathie*. Leipzig: Schwabe.

Tovey, Donald F. 1935. *Essays in Musical Analysis*. London: Oxford University Press.

Wagner, R. 1894. *Prose Works*. Translated by W. A. Ellis. 6 vols. London: Routledge and Kegan Paul.

Walker, Alan, ed. 1972. *Robert Schumann—The Man and His Music*. London: Barrie & Jenkins.

———. 1979. "Schumann, Liszt, and the C major Fantasie opus 17: A Declining Relationship." *Music and Letters* 9.

Walsh, Stephen. 1971. *The Lieder of Schumann*. New York: Praeger.

Warrack, John. 1968. *Carl Maria von Weber*. Cambridge: Cambridge University Press.

Wasielewski, J. W. 1869. *Robert Schumann, Eine Biographie*. 2d ed. Dresden: Randolf Kuntze.

———. 1906. *Robert Schumann, Eine Biographie*. 4th ed. Leipzig: Breitkopf & Härtel.

Wörner, Karl H. 1949. *Robert Schumann*. Zürich: Atlantis Verlag.

Index of Musical Works

This is not an index of *all* Schumann's compositions; it contains only those compositions mentioned in the text.

Index